Great is Thy Faithfulness?

# Great is Thy Faithfulness?
*Reading Lamentations as Sacred Scripture*

*Edited by*
ROBIN A. PARRY *and* HEATH A. THOMAS

◆PICKWICK *Publications* · Eugene, Oregon

GREAT IS THY FAITHFULNESS?
Reading Lamentations as Sacred Scripture

Copyright © 2011 Wipf and Stock Publishers. All rights reserved. Except for brief quotations in critical publications or reviews, no part of this book may be reproduced in any manner without prior written permission from the publisher. Write: Permissions, Wipf and Stock Publishers, 199 W. 8th Ave., Suite 3, Eugene, OR 97401.

The translation of Lamentations Rabbah was reproduced by kind permission of the copyright holder, Jacob Neusner (© 2008 Jacob Neusner).

The translation of Targum Lamentations was reproduced by kind permission of the copyright holder, Christian M. M. Brady (© 2010 Christian M. M. Brady)

Pickwick Publications
An Imprint of Wipf and Stock Publishers
199 W. 8th Ave., Suite 3
Eugene, OR 97401

www.wipfandstock.com

ISBN 13: 978-1-61097-453-0

## *Cataloging-in-Publication data:*

Great is thy faithfulness? : reading Lamentations as sacred scripture / edited by Robin A. Parry and Heath A. Thomas.

xii + 296 p. ; 23 cm. Includes bibliographical references and indexes.

ISBN 13: 978-1-61097-453-0

1. Bible. O.T. Lamentations—Criticism, interpretation, etc. 2. Bible. O.T. Lamentations—Criticism, interpretation, etc.—Christian. 3. Bible. O.T. Lamentations—Criticism, interpretation, etc.—Jewish. 4. Bible. O.T. Lamentations—Criticism, interpretation, etc.—Feminist criticism. 5. Bible. O.T. Lamentations. Greek—Versions—Septuagint. I. Parry, Robin A. II. Thomas, Heath A. III. Title.

BS1535.2 G20 2011

Manufactured in the U.S.A.

*Robin dedicates this book to
Carol,
Hannah,
and
Jessica*

*Heath dedicates this book to
Jill,
Harrison,
Isabelle,
Simon,
and
Sophia*

# Contents

*Acknowledgments / ix*

*List of Contributors / xi*

*Introduction*—Robin A. Parry and Heath A. Thomas / xi

1   Holy Scripture and Hermeneutics: Lamentations in Critical and Theological Reflection—*Heath A. Thomas* / 1

2   Outrageous Demonstrations of Grace: The Theology of Lamentations —*Paul R. House* / 26

## ❦ Soundings in Jewish Reception History

A   Lamentations in Isaiah 40–55—*Lena-Sofia Tiemeyer* / 55

B   The Character and Significance of LXX Lamentations —*Kevin J. Youngblood* / 64

C   Targum Lamentations—*Christian M. M. Brady* / 70

D   Lamentations Rabbati—*Jacob Neusner* / 77

E   Introduction to Rashi's Commentary on Lamentations —*Mayer I. Gruber* / 83

F   Lamentations in Jewish Liturgy—*Elsie R. Stern* / 88

G   Lamentations in Modern Jewish Thought—*Zachary Braiterman* / 92

## ❦ Soundings in Messianic Jewish Reception History

H   Holocaust Theology in the Light of Yeshua? Messianic Jewish Reception of Eikah—*Richard Harvey* / 101

## ❦ Soundings in Christian Reception History

I   Lamentations in the Patristic Period—*Heath A. Thomas* / 113

J   Christian Interpretation of Lamentations in the Middle Ages —*David S. Hogg* / 120

Contents

    K    John Calvin's Interpretation of Lamentations—*Pete Wilcox* / 125

    L    Lamentations for the Lord: Great and Holy Friday in the Greek Orthodox Church—*Eugenia Scarvelis Constantinou* / 131

    M    Lamentations and Christian Worship
        —*Andrew Cameron-Mowat SJ* / 139

### 🔥 Soundings in Artistic and Contemporary Reception

    N    Musical Responses to Lamentations—*F. Jane Schopf* / 147

    O    Lamentations in Rembrandt van Rijn: "Jeremiah Lamenting the Destruction of Jerusalem"—*Heath A. Thomas* / 154

    P    Psychological Approaches to Lamentations—*Paul M. Joyce* / 161

    Q    Feminist Interpretation(s) of Lamentations—*Heath A. Thomas* / 166

3    Wrestling with Lamentations in Christian Worship—*Robin A. Parry* / 175

4    Confession and Complaint: Christian Pastoral Reflections on Lamentations—*Ian Stackhouse* / 198

Appendix 1: A Translation of LXX Lamentations—*Kevin J. Youngblood* / 211

Appendix 2: A Translation of Targum Lamentations
—*Christian M. M. Brady* / 228

Appendix 3: Lamentations Rabbati on Lamentations 3:1–21
—*Jacob Neusner* / 248

Appendix 4: Rashi on Lamentations 3:1–21 / 264

Appendix 5: Calvin on Lamentations 3:1–23 / 267

*Index of Scripture* / 279

*Index of Names* / 287

*Index of Subjects* / 291

## Acknowledgments

THIS BOOK HAS BEEN a labor of love over the past few years, and the authors are indebted to many kind folks, far and wide, who helped make the vision a reality. In particular, we would like to thank Jacob Neusner for his permission to include his previously published material on Lamentations Rabbah in this volume, as well as Christian Brady for permission to use his translation of the Targum Lamentations. We are very grateful to Luke Wisley, who deserves an award for his painstaking work culling the essays and preparing the indices. Heath would like to thank his students who provided helpful interaction with various parts of the volume over the past few years and to express his gratitude for the administration at Southeastern Seminary, who kindly afforded a flexible teaching load to help accommodate the publication of this volume. The folks at Wipf and Stock Publishers have been a joy to work with during this process. Patrick Harrison deserves recognition for his close attention and care in the editing process. Finally, the authors are grateful to God for the grace to bring this task to completion. May His Name be ever blessed.

# Contributors

CHRISTIAN M. M. BRADY is Dean of Schreyer Honors College, The Pennsylvania State University and author of *The Rabbinic Targum of Lamentations: Vindicating God* (Brill, 2003).

ZACHARY BRAITERMAN is Associate Professor of Religion, Syracuse University. He is author of *(God) After Auschwitz: Tradition and Change in Post-Holocaust Jewish Thought* (Princeton University Press, 1998) and *The Shape of Revelation: Aesthetics and Modern Jewish Thought* (Stanford University Press, 2007).

ANDREW CAMERON-MOWAT SJ is Lecturer in Liturgy at Heythrop College, University of London. He has authored various articles on liturgy, including in Dwight Vogel, ed., *Primary Sources of Liturgical Theology* (Liturgical Press, 2000), the *New SCM Dictionary of Liturgy and Worship* (SCM, 2002), the *New Catholic Encyclopedia* (Gale, 2002), and the English translation of the 1st Lateran Council in Decrees of the Ecumenical Councils (Georgetown University Press, 1990).

EUGENIA SCARVELIS CONSTANTINOU is Postdoctoral Teaching Fellow in Theology and Religious Studies, University of San Diego. She received her PhD from Université Laval, Quebec City, Canada, in 2008, writing her doctoral dissertation on "Andrew of Caesarea and the Apocalypse in the Ancient Church of the East."

MAYER I. GRUBER is Professor in the Department of Bible, Archaeology, and Ancient Near East at Ben Gurion University of the Negev, Israel. He is the author of, among other things, *Rashi's Commentary on the Psalms* (Jewish Publication Society, 2004).

RICHARD HARVEY teaches Hebrew Bible and Jewish Studies at allnations College in Ware, UK. He is author of *Mapping Messianic Jewish Theology* (Paternoster, 2009) and is currently writing a Messianic Jewish systematic theology (Cascade, forthcoming).

DAVID S. HOGG is Associate Dean of Academic Affairs and Associate Professor of Divinity at Beeson Divinity School, Samford University. He is author of *Anselm of Canterbury: The Beauty of Theology* (Ashgate, 2004).

PAUL R. HOUSE is Associate Dean and Professor of Divinity at Beeson Divinity School, Samford University, Birmingham, Alabama. He is author of, among other things, the Word Biblical Commentary on Lamentations (Thomas Nelson, 2004).

PAUL M. JOYCE is University Lecturer in Theology at St Peter's College, University of Oxford, and is author of *Ezekiel: A Commentary* (T. & T. Clark, 2007) and is co-authoring

*Contributors*

the Blackwell Bible Commentary on *Lamentations through the Centuries* with Diana Lipton.

JACOB NEUSNER is Distinguished Service Professor of the History and Theology of Judaism at Bard College, Annandale-on-Hudson, New York. He has written and edited many books on Judaism.

ROBIN A. PARRY is an editor at Wipf and Stock Publishers and author of *Old Testament Story and Christian Ethics: The Rape of Dinah as a Case Study* (Paternoster, 2004), *Worshipping Trinity* (Paternoster, 2005), *The Evangelical Universalist* (Cascade, 2006) and The Two Horizons commentary on *Lamentations* (Eerdmans, 2010).

FIONA JANE SCHOPF is Programme Director of Opera Studies at Rose Bruford College in Kent, England. She is author, among other things, of *Musical Gender Constructs in the Operas of Richard Wagner* (University of Birmingham, 1999).

IAN STACKHOUSE is Senior Pastor of Guildford Baptist Church (Millmead) UK. He is author of *The Gospel-Driven Church: Retrieving Classical Ministries for Contemporary Revivalism* (Paternoster, 2004) and *The Day is Yours: Slow Spirituality in a Fast-Moving World* (Paternoster, 2008).

ELSIE R. STERN is Associate Professor of Bible at the Reconstructionist Rabbinical College. She is author of *From Rebuke to Consolation: Exegesis and Theology in the Liturgical Anthology of the Ninth of Ab Season* (Brown Judaic Studies, 2005).

HEATH A. THOMAS is Assistant Professor of Old Testament and Hebrew at Southeastern Baptist Theological Seminary (USA) and Fellow in Old Testament Studies at The Paideia Centre for Public Theology (Canada). He is currently writing a commentary on Habakkuk (Eerdmans) and a theological introduction to the Minor Prophets (IVP Academic). His book on Lamentations—*Poetry and Theology in Lamentations*—is forthcoming from Sheffield Phoenix Press.

LENA-SOFIA TIEMEYER is Lecturer in Old Testament/Hebrew Bible at the University of Aberdeen, Scotland. She is author of *Priestly Rites and Prophetic Rage: Post-Exilic Prophetic Critique of the Priesthood* (Mohr Siebeck, 2006) and *For the Comfort of Zion: The Geographical and Theological Location of Isaiah 40–55* (Brill, 2011).

PETE WILCOX is Canon Chancellor at Lichfield Cathedral and a Calvin specialist. His books include *Walking the Walk: The Rise of King David for Today* (Paternoster, 2009) and *Talking the Talk: The Fall of King David for Today* (Lutterworth Press, 2011).

KEVIN J. YOUNGBLOOD is Associate Professor of Religion at Harding University. His PhD was on translation technique in the Greek Lamentations (Southern Baptist Theological Seminary, 2004). Currently he is working on the Lamentations commentary for the SBL Commentary on the Septuagint (Society of Biblical Literature).

# Introduction

ROBIN A. PARRY AND HEATH A. THOMAS

LAMENTATIONS HAS NEVER HAD a place of honor at the table of Christian spirituality. It is not one of those texts that everyone wants to converse with—a John's Gospel, an Exodus, an Isaiah, a Romans. It is one of those texts people feel uncomfortable around, not quite sure what to do with. Indeed, were it left to us, it may well not have had a place at the table *at all*. Rather, like the desolate character of Lady Jerusalem sitting alone as people pass by on the other side of the road (Lam 1), the book of Lamentations itself has been passed by, ignored by the other guests. After all, who wants to be a companion to someone as miserable as Lady Jerusalem? Who would want such a depressing text getting an invite to the meal? Knowing your luck you'll end up sitting next to her! So the church has often discretely "looked away" so as not to catch Lady Jerusalem's eye and get dragged into an awkward conversation. We spend our time mingling with the "fun" guests, like Genesis or John or Paul, or the "interestingly dressed" guests, like Daniel and Revelation. We often turn away from that text sitting alone in the corner weeping, the book of Lamentations.

The book that you are now reading was written for the Christian church and was born out of the conviction that God is in the business of inviting unexpected and discomforting guests to banquets—the poor, the lame, the outcasts. The guests at the table of Christian spirituality are there at *God's* invitation and his purposes are not necessarily aimed at maximizing warm and fuzzy feelings for Christians.

Lamentations is such a guest as it sits in the church's Bible. It is part of the collection of texts that Christians have always accepted as Holy Scripture. That fact constitutes its invitation to the banquet. You or I may not have chosen to issue that invitation but there is nothing that we can do to revoke it. The only question concerns *our behavior* at the meal: do we ignore the Scripture seated beside us or do we engage it in conversation? If the church is to seek to receive its Scripture *as Scripture* then it needs to find ways of welcoming and comforting this desolate, broken hearted guest. And in so doing the church may find itself learning fresh—sometimes disturbing—ways of being with God in the world.

The seed idea for this project was sown during conversations between the editors several years ago in Worcester, UK, and in Philadelphia and San Diego, USA. We were interested in the question of how the book of Lamentations could function as sacred

*Introduction*

Scripture for the church. How could it engage Christian readers afresh as they sought to walk in the ways of the LORD? We were both working on the book of Lamentations at the time—Heath was doing his PhD on it and Robin was writing a commentary for The Two Horizons series (Eerdmans)—and we had become convinced that it was a neglected resource for the life of the church. The idea was to provide a book that served as a resource and stimulus to challenge this state of affairs. In the original designs, the current editors as well as Paul House (author of the Word Biblical Commentary on Lamentations) were to develop the book. But as things progressed, the editorial makeup shifted and Paul provided the thorough chapter on Lamentations within its own horizons. Still the focus of the volume remained constant.

However, it was not long before we felt the need to give attention to the reception history of the book. The book's reception in history could give insight into, and possible ideas for, modern appropriation. First, we discovered that no contemporary *Christian* attempt to engage with Lamentations as Scripture could afford to ignore the rich history of *Jewish* reception of the text. Here one finds a fertile cultivation of this challenging book, whose produce has impacted Jewish spirituality and worship through the centuries. We came to realize that the book of Lamentations was written *by* Jews, *for* Jews, and has been in continuous use within Jewish communities from the days in which it was written and compiled until today. Lamentations has had a place of honor at the table of Jewish spirituality and our conviction is that the followers of Jesus have much to learn from a community that has allowed this book to function as Scripture. So we have included the book's reception in Jewish textual and worship tradition as well as reflection on Lamentations after the Shoah. These are powerful testimonies of the persistent voice of Lamentations in Jewish memory.

Second, and in spite of our opening comments, we discovered that there have been some *Christian* engagements with this text and we felt the need to sample some of these. However limited, Lamentations is a book that has fed the Christian soul and we wanted to shed a little light on some of that heritage. As such the editors have included samplings on Lamentations' reception drawn from all three major strands of Christianity: Catholic, Orthodox, and Protestant. These essays explore Lamentations in the Patristic and Medieval periods, the book's use (direct or indirect) in the Christian worship of Holy Week, and Calvin's reading of Lamentations. We also felt it appropriate to include a chapter on Messianic Jewish reception of this little book. Messianic Jews tend to have been located outside the mainstream discussion in both the Jewish and the Christian circles. We wanted to give them a place at the table.

Finally, the book of Lamentations has had a cultural impact, not least in music and the arts, and the way in which it has been interpreted has itself been impacted by certain cultural shifts, such as the rise of psychological and of feminist analysis. Christians, we believe, need to be open to learn from any insights that can enable this part of the Bible to be opened afresh and to function as sacred Scripture—to play its role in shaping the community of faith. This openness includes an openness to learn from voices with which we may not always agree. So the reception studies aim to scratch the surface of some potentially helpful ways of looking at Lamentations.

Now some readers will not be terribly interested in a "Christian" appropriation of Lamentations. Still, these readers we hope will discover here a bevy of resources that they may find illuminating or interesting in terms of Lamentations' use in Jewish and Christian practice as well as modern appropriation of the book. Indeed the reception history essays that are provided here offer snapshots of this biblical book through the ages that one would be hard pressed to find in one volume. And the appendices are especially useful for anyone interested in Lamentations research.

Nonetheless, this is only the tip of the iceberg. One could easily have expanded the list of studies to include, say, Thomas Aquinas's commentary on Lamentations, Saint John of the Cross' use of Lamentations in his reflections on the "dark night of the soul," Peter Martyr Vermigli's commentary on Lamentations, Marc Chagall's various workings of Lamentations (e.g., his painting "Jeremiah's Lamentations" (1956) from his prophets series or his "Lamentations of Jeremiah" (1958) from his Bible etchings), Leonard Bernstein's Symphony No. 1 (the "Jeremiah" Symphony) composed in 1942, and the impact of Lamentations on various poets, past and present. Our goal was not to be exhaustive but to take important samplings from across Jewish and Christian history. For a more expansive reception history, the editors await the research of Paul Joyce and Diana Lipton in their monograph *Lamentations through the Centuries*, to be published in the Blackwell Bible Commentary Series.

We are indebted to all the authors of the reception studies for their enlightening input. Of course, not all of these authors will agree with the editors' general outlook in the volume—that Lamentations is a word for the Christian church. Nonetheless, Lamentations is a work, all agree, that needs to be heard widely. We especially express gratitude to the Jewish authors in this volume, who willingly gave their time and expertise to write for a project primarily intended to enable the Christian *ekklesia* to better appreciate and appropriate the book of Lamentations.

The main chapters of the book fall into two sections. The first (chapters 1 and 2) address issues in hermeneutics and in reading the text in its canonical context. Heath Thomas considers what it might mean to read Lamentations as "Holy Scripture." The matter is by no means simple as prior theological commitments as well as methodological questions very much shape how this activity works. He argues that any contemporary Christian attempt to receive the text as a good word from God must give due consideration to historical, literary, and cultural aspects of the text as well as to its canonical context and theological relationship with Christ. Application needs to be grounded in a careful attention to the text itself. Short-circuiting the process and leaping directly to "what the passage means to me/us" runs the great danger of careless and sloppy misappropriation of the text.

Paul House's essay provides a very well informed overview of recent scholarship on Lamentations tracking trends in interpretation over the past sixty years. To model a way forward in theological hermeneutics he offers a study of "the book's characterization of Jerusalem in light of Lamentations' historical, canonical, and discrete-book settings," taking into account the book's genre and rhetorical progression/plot. *En route* he engages a wide range of recent interpreters—sometimes affirming their insights, sometimes dis-

*Introduction*

puting their claims—and in conclusion he draws out several theological contributions that he believes Lamentations offers the church.

The second section (chapters 3 and 4)—deliberately located after the reception studies—is focused on *application*. How can this ancient text engage the church afresh today? In chapter 3 Robin Parry argues that Christian worship needs to be reconfigured to accommodate the kind of pain expressed in Lamentations. He explores the ways in which historic Jewish and Christian use of this text in worship can offer insights for contemporary practice.

Finally, no reflections on the function of Lamentations as Scripture would be complete without some *pastoral* input. In chapter 4, Ian Stackhouse—a British pastor-theologian in the Baptist tradition—argues that Lamentations confronts our church cultures at two critical points: first, it speaks sin's name and calls us to acknowledge our own culpability; second, it legitimizes brutally honest complaint to (and about) God. These two aspects of the book's challenge must be held in tension or pastoral dangers arise. But if they are held in tension in our communal life then, like the wings of a bird, they can work together to help carry the church forward.

The present volume sets out to be a stimulus to further reflection and changing praxis. It offers neither the "first word" nor the "last word" on anything but rather an intermediate challenge to the church to catch the eye of the guest sitting alone in the corner of the table and to invite her to join the main conversation. It is a risky thing to do because it will change the dynamics of that conversation, sometimes in uncomfortable ways, but if the canon of Scripture means anything to the church—and it does—then anything less would be to miss out on the unexpected riches this awkward guest can bestow upon her conversation partners.

# 1

## Holy Scripture and Hermeneutics

*Lamentations in Critical and Theological Reflection*

Heath A. Thomas

### INTRODUCTION

Lamentations remains a difficult book to appropriate as Holy Scripture, with its strident protestation against God (Lam 2:20), presentation of divine violence (Lam 1:15; 2:1–10; 3:1–17), as well as vivid images of cannibalism and rape (Lam 1:10; 4:10). How can *this* book be in any way holy? This is a delicate question, to say the least, with responses varying from an outright rejection of the text to its full-orbed embrace. The purpose of this chapter is to lay out the parameters of what it has meant, as well as what it might mean, to identify Lamentations as Holy Scripture.

To do so adequately, it is necessary to explore how the text of Lamentations has been read. So the first half of this chapter will explore how Lamentations has been read in the academy. Academic reading practices of the Bible have been influential in recent times, as Kugel's *How to Read the Bible* demonstrates.[1] An effect of critical readings, however, has been a fragmentation of focus, so that the Bible may be seen in various ways, such as a cultural artifact, literature, history, or even a political tool. The variety arises in part from particular interests in these different critical approaches that act as "lenses" that shape interpretative practice.

One should note that these approaches do not inevitably eventuate into appropriating Lamentations as a word from God. In my view, it is necessary to become cognizant of the literary, political, historical, and cultural aspects of Lamentations (or the Bible for that matter), and this is valuable in its own right, but still there remains another move to be made to begin to understand the book as Holy Scripture. So after the survey of academic approaches, it will be appropriate to press further to see exactly how Lamentations as "Holy Scripture" has been understood, with particular emphasis given to the hermeneutical "stance" of the question: "How have (and can) people interpret Lamentations as a sacred text?" This query necessitates deeper reflection regarding the need for an inter-

---

1. Kugel, *How to Read the Bible*.

preter to embody or adopt certain religious or theological viewpoints (be they Jewish or Christian) in order to coherently construe the text of Lamentations.

## HERMENEUTICAL "LENSES" IN LAMENTATIONS RESEARCH

How does one read Lamentations? This may seem, at first, a rather innocuous query, with a rather simple answer—"in many ways!" In the academy especially, Lamentations has been read as: history, political propaganda, quality literature, a cultural artifact, or even a tool of social oppression that needs to be jettisoned. This list is not exhaustive, but accounts for some major reading practices.[2] Three major interpretative "lenses" however, have focused reading Lamentations particularly in the past century: history, literature, and culture.

### *Lamentations and History*

One may read the Lamentations as history, or at least as a window through which one may view history, and then focus upon its particular facets such as religion, social structure, or politics, and so on. Reading the Bible as history has a rather distinguished pedigree, especially in the last 300 or so years. But the difficulty in this enterprise, of course, is how one conceives of, and then presents, the very concept of history and its relationship to the Bible![3] Frei's *The Eclipse of Biblical Narrative* exhibits the force that this reading practice exerted in the modern era (as well as its drawbacks).[4]

Even before the eighteenth century, historical reading certainly was advocated. For early Christian hermeneutics, a tension existed between those who emphasized reading the Bible historically—with a focus upon real "flesh-and-blood" events through the course of time (the Antiochene School)—and those who stressed symbolic and allegorical readings (the Alexandrian School), which moved beyond a purely historical accent.[5] The Reformation is well known for refocusing interpretation upon literal and historical realities of the Bible, so as to see in what historical timeframe the texts spoke and why,

---

2. For other approaches, see Gillingham, *One Bible, Many Voices*; Thiselton, *New Horizons in Hermeneutics*.

3. Halpern, *The First Historians*, xix–xxxiv, 3–32. For a recent discussion: Bakker, *History as a Theological Issue*. Traditional reading of the Bible as a historical text generally views the Bible as though it gives primarily a consequential narrative about events that have occurred, are occurring, or will occur, in history. On this view, the Bible gives historical information that is relatively clear; there is one universal history and the Bible gives clear information about these events. On the other hand, there has been a tendency since the seventeenth century, stemming from the Reformation, to see the Bible's presentation of history not as something to be accepted, but rather as a problem in need of a solution, specifically in terms of historical reconstruction of the Bible or revision of its perspective(s) of historical events; in short, the problem for some is that the Bible does not offer objective facts of history (e.g., Davies, *In Search of "Ancient Israel"*; Whitelam, *The Invention of Ancient Israel*). Finally there are re-appropriations of traditional categories of understanding of "history," in which ways of understanding it prior to seventeenth century changes might be re-appraised critically. For further discussion, see Wright, *The New Testament and the People of God*; Bartholomew, Evans, Healy, and Rae, eds., *"Behind" the Text*; and especially Clark, *History, Theory, Text*.

4. Frei, *The Eclipse of Biblical Narrative*.

5. Jeanrond, *Theological Hermeneutics*, 19–22.

and what information might be gained from this.⁶ Although it has a rich history of its own, reading the Bible as history remains a complicated enterprise indeed.

In Lamentations study, this focus upon history surfaces in two primary ways. On the one hand, there has been a concerted effort to read Lamentations alongside the book of Jeremiah, and through Jeremiah's voice, as the liturgical text of the exilic period in Judah. As a historical text, it speaks of the people's experience of pain concerning the destruction of Judah and Jerusalem in 587 BCE. This view is supported by ancient versions, especially the old Greek version of Lamentations (LXX), which evinces a prologue to the text that explicitly conjoins Lamentations, Jeremiah, and the aftermath of exile, whilst something similar appears in the prologue to the Aramaic version of Lamentations (Targum).⁷ The Greek tradition in particular reads the whole of Lamentations filtered through the historical framework of the trauma of Judahite exile as seen through the eyes of Jeremiah the prophet. Notably, however, the MT and Qumran Lamentations do not evince the prologue apparent in the LXX Lam and Targ Lam, leaving this explicit linkage somewhat looser than in these traditions. This point is significant if one holds the MT as being close to the original Hebrew parent text, as it reveals something of theological interpretation going on in the versions, especially in regard to the LXX Lam.

However, recent work understands Lamentations' historical context(s) differently. Historical research in this vein ascertains disparate views of God as well as different genres, perspectives, and the like in Lamentations and then charts deviation upon a historical trajectory. In this way, theological variance is seen to be embedded within different historical strata of the text. Through rational assessment, the historian traces textual discrepancies and then maps out theological development along with the growth of the text.⁸ For this methodology, historical reconstruction is the clue for theological interpretation. Gottwald and Albrektson, for instance, attempt to understand Lamentations in light of either theological traditions in dialogue in its poetry (Albrektson) or a particular theological tradition attempting to cope with the hard reality of Jerusalem's destruction (Gottwald).⁹ Both monographs centre upon the presence and nature of hope in Lamentations, and how it arises theologically in the text. Gottwald looks at this question from the perspective of both the history of Jerusalem and the presence of the Deuteronomic tradition in Judah at the time of Jerusalem's destruction. Albrektson, like Gottwald, also seeks to understand the theological issues in Lamentations by locating them within the history of Jerusalem. However, Albrektson sees within Lamentations another purported tradition (Zion theology) being set in critical dialogue with Deuteronomic theology.

Other historical approaches generally argue that the book's five chapters (or portions therein) are written at different times and therefore reflect different views of the

---

6. For a discussion of pre-modern and reformation historical readings, see Thiselton, *New Horizons*, 142–203.

7. See the articles by Youngblood and Brady in this volume, respectively.

8. For a discussion on how historical critical research treats theology, see Brueggemann, *Theology of the Old Testament*, 9–42.

9. Albrektson, *Studies in the Text and Theology*; Gottwald, *Studies in the Book of Lamentations*. See Paul House's chapter in the present volume.

disaster of exile. Often, this means that Lamentations 1, 2, and 4 are of a piece, whilst Lamentations 5 and 3 represent later texts, reflecting somewhat different theological views. Brandscheidt advocates this view, and she does so by exploring what she understands to be the redactional history of the book.[10] Westermann somewhat differently focuses instead upon on the development of the theology of the Lamentations by observing early oral formulation and later written redaction.[11] Perhaps the most recent and well argued approach in this vein is that of Middlemas.

Middlemas thinks that Lamentations embodies two divergent historical voices in the text: the first perspective embodied by Lamentations 1, 2, 4, and 5, and the other exemplified in the later addition of Lamentations 3.[12] These two perspectives represent two historical communities, in fact. The former (Lamentations 1, 2, 4, and 5) represents the native Judahite voice that survives in the region of Yehud between 587 BCE to roughly 515 BCE. The latter group, whose views are embodied in Lamentations 3, most likely represent a Babylonian exilic (*Golah*) perspective distinct from the Judahite one. In this configuration, the former voice represents the Judahite populace embroiled in desperation, anger, and a tendency to strike out against God in protest over the destruction of Jerusalem and serial trauma of the exiles of 597, 587 (especially), and 582 BCE. The latter perspective, exemplified in the third chapter, presents a theodicy, affirms God's control, the people's sin(s), and the necessity of penitence and patience in the light of God's discipline. The third chapter, in this view, is a piece of theological correction that disciplines the (chronologically) earlier four chapters. As Middlemas avers, the "man" of Lam 3:1, 39 is a "mask for the *Golah* interpreters who struggled to explain the downfall of Jerusalem and to encourage ongoing belief in [the LORD]."[13]

And yet Joyce notes that Lamentations, at least as represented in the MT text tradition, sits looser to history than has been previously admitted.[14] Lamentations contains no explicit references to Babylon, Nebuchadnezzar, or specific leaders of Judah at the time of Jerusalem's fall. The outcome is that Lamentations may be viewed as a liturgical text that is designed to exceed the confines of a strict exilic setting. Further, Provan has noted the lack of specificity as to time, location of writing, and individual enemies and the like makes it difficult to date the book with any kind of certainty.[15]

One notes a diversity of opinion on how to relate Lamentations to history. When focusing upon the particular period in which the text was created, following the lead of LXX Lam, for instance, one reads the book as historically situated in the exile stemming from the mouth of the prophet Jeremiah. Incidentally, this is the common approach of pre-modern interpreters such as Rashi, the church fathers, Aquinas, and Calvin.[16] The

---

10. Brandscheidt, *Gotteszorn und Menschenleid*; Brandscheidt, *Das Buch der Klagelieder*.

11. Westermann, *Die Klagelieder*.

12. Middlemas, *The Troubles of Templeless Judah*, 177–84; Middlemas, "Did Second Isaiah write Lamentations III?"; Middlemas, *The Templeless Age*, 44–51.

13. Middlemas, "Did Second Isaiah write Lamentations III?" 524.

14. Joyce, "Sitting Loose to History," 246–62.

15. Provan, *Lamentations*, 7–19.

16. Note studies included in this volume by Gruber, Thomas ("Lamentations in the Patristic Period"), and Wilcox.

works of Albrektson, Gottwald, Westermann, Brandscheidt, and Middlemas move beyond this view, however, noting shifts and changes in the fabric of the text and situating these along a historical timeline in order to reflect upon the people(s) to whom the text points as well as their varying theological views. But undoubtedly, this focus upon history shapes the interpretative practice of reading the book.

### *Lamentations and Literature*

Beyond historical approaches, appreciating the Bible as profound literature has gained currency since Robert Alter's groundbreaking trilogy on biblical narrative, poetry, and literature.[17] His work may be considered a changing of the tides in biblical study, as more attention was paid to issues like characterization, plot, sequencing, poetics, and repetitive structures, and how these elements were employed in unique ways compared to other canons of world literature.

Recent research has paid greater attention to Lamentations as literature. With an emphasis upon literary theory and understanding the aesthetic quality of its poetry, explorations into the use of metaphor,[18] voicing techniques,[19] poetic structure,[20] repetition,[21] and parallelism[22] are now common. Greater sensitivity to the literary quality of Lamentations has led Renkema to note the unique ways in which it hangs together as a book rather than sits disparately into discreet chapters. This discovery leads House, for one, to read the text *and* its theology synthetically rather than as divergent theologies (Lam 3 versus Lam 1, 2, 4, and 5) as do Westermann, Brandscheidt, and Middlemas.[23]

It is appropriate as well to give attention to recent studies that have understood Lamentations' structure through the lens of literary theory. For Kaiser, Longman, and Dillard, Lamentations curiously fits what is known as a "tragic structure" in literary theory. Identified as Freytag's Pyramid for the theorist who originated it,[24] the tragic structure illustrates how plot develops within a five-act tragedy. Freytag concluded that five-act tragedies contain three essential elements: rising action, climax, and falling action. The climax represents the most significant point or turning point in the action of the work. The rising action remains developmental and secondary to the climax. The

---

17. Alter, *The Art of Biblical Narrative*; Alter, *The Art of Biblical Poetry*; Alter, *The World of Biblical Literature*. For an earlier work exploring the literary merits of the Bible, Auerbach's analysis stands as a classic: Auerbach, *Mimesis*.

18. Heim, "The Personification of Jerusalem"; Labahn, "Fire from Above."

19. Lanahan, "The Speaking Voice in the Book of Lamentations"; Gwaltney, Jr., "The Biblical Book of Lamentations," 206.

20. Johnson, "Form and Message in Lamentations"; Renkema, *Lamentations*; Dobbs-Allsopp, "Lamentations as a Lyric Sequence"; Dobbs-Allsopp, *Lamentations*, 20–23.

21. Thomas, "The Liturgical Function of Lamentations."

22. Kaiser, "Reconsidering Parallelism."

23. Renkema, *Lamentations*; Garrett and House, *Song of Songs/Lamentations*, 278–329.

24. Holman and Harmon, *A Handbook to Literature*, 153–54, 207–8; Freytag, *Technique of the Drama*.

# GREAT IS THY FAITHFULNESS?

falling action represents the shift in perspective which comes after the climax, sometimes accompanied by catastrophe or restored order.[25]

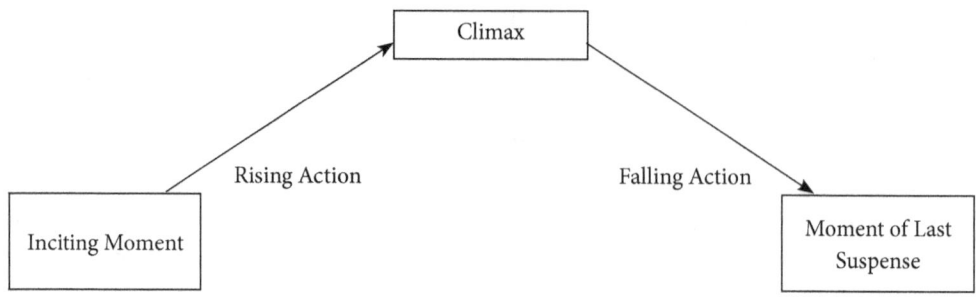

Nägelsbach originally suggested Lamentations evinces a structure quite similar to that of Freytag's Pyramid, though without explicitly noting the connection: crescendo (chapters 1–2), climax (chapter 3), and decrescendo (chapters 4–5).[26] For him, Lamentations 3 is central both stylistically and theologically when one recognizes its literary structure, and this chapter gives hope to God's people after the events of 587 BCE.[27] Kaiser, Longman, and Dillard follow this basic structure[28]:

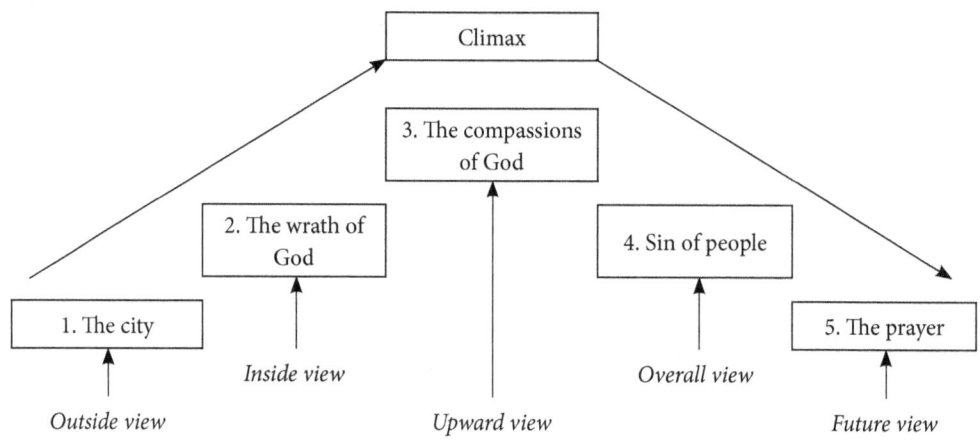

---

25. Diagram adapted from Holman and Harmon, *Handbook*, 85.

26. Chapter 3 serves as the climax, or "Spitze," of the poem: "Dadurch ist die Hervorhebung des Mittelgliedes und im Zusammenhang damit ein Hinauf- und Herabsteigen, ein crescendo und decrescendo mit deutlich markierter Spitze möglich gemacht." See Nägelsbach, *Die Klagelieder*, vi, vii.

27. Nägelsbach, *Die Klagelieder*, vii–viii.

28. Kaiser, *Grief and Pain in the Plan of God*, 22; Longman and Dillard, *An Introduction to the Old Testament*, 349.

Whilst interesting, the difficulties associated with the tragic structure ultimately undermine its value. It is anachronistic to place a nineteenth-century CE literary structure over a sixth-century BCE text. One must query as to what textual clues drive the reader to conclude that Lam 1 and 2 represent something analogous to "crescendo" or "ascent" and further, what clues drive one to surmise that Lam 4 or 5 display "decrescendo," falling action, or resolution as the tragic framework suggests. The argument offered by Kaiser—that the pain of the poems decreases with the shift away from first to third person speech—is hardly satisfying. The level of pain brought to the fore in Lam 1 and 2 is redressed once again in the final chapters; and with the unsure conclusion of Lam 5:22, it is not certain that resolution has been achieved when the reader reaches the final verse.[29]

The tragic structure also fails in light of the logic of Lam 3. Though prominent theologically, hope that marks the central section of Lam 3 may not serve as the kind of climax or change in perspective that Kaiser desires. It is appropriate to highlight Dobbs-Allsopp's opinion on the chapter. Far from offering a climactic point to the book, he believes that chapter 3 offers a complicated vision of God, where Yhwh's justice is "localized, countered, questioned, and generally complicated in important ways."[30] The return to lament after Lam 3:18–39 mitigates their role as the theological "core" of the book.[31] The preponderance of the alphabetic form in chapter 3 prevents the reader from remaining at the central, hopeful, portion of the chapter. Seen in this light, the acrostic serves to move the reader up to, but *then beyond*, the supposed climactic section of hope. The return to lament in Lam 3:56–66 reveals that the central parenetic, hopeful section (Lam 3:19–39) did not ameliorate the pain in the poem.

Finally, one must question the use of narrative structure for understanding a non-narrative text like Lamentations. The idea of reading Lamentations with a five-act tragedy assumes that the two in some way parallel one another as narrative modes of discourse: as the five-act tragedy tells its story in a certain manner, so then does Lamentations. This assumption is misleading. Lamentations does not "tell a story" in the same manner of tragedy or many other modes of narrative discourse. One of the key features in tragedy is the character development of the protagonist for his/her great fall. Though there are speaking voices in the poetry of Lamentations, they are *personae*, but not characters. The personae primarily tell their experiences through the language and imagery in the poetry rather than plot or character development, as in narrative. Interpreting Lamentations through a narrative structure moves beyond what the poetry offers. Hillers summarizes, "Neither narrative nor logical sequence is a dominant feature in contributing to the structure of Lamentations."[32]

---

29. See the explanation of Goldman, "Lamentations," 102.
30. Dobbs-Allsopp, *Lamentations*, 48.
31. See Villanueva, *The "Uncertainty of a Hearing."*
32. Hillers, "Lamentations, Book of," 137.

## GREAT IS THY FAITHFULNESS?

### *Lamentations and Culture*

But beyond reading Lamentations as literature, one may assess the Bible's value as a piece of culture in the history of humanity. This is the perspective of Northrop Frye, who argued that the value of the Bible lay in the way that it persists as a founding piece of culture for all Western literature.[33] Here one may wish to explore how the Bible, or its central themes, or metaphors, or values, appear in, or impact, culture.[34] One notes such a move in the Blackwell Bible Commentary, whose Lamentations volume is being cowritten by Paul Joyce and Diana Lipton. Moreover, as Linafelt has shown, Lamentations in particular has had an impact upon Jewish culture in its "afterlife."[35] As a piece of culture, then, Lamentations may be explored as a source of inspiration and reflection in the history of the world, and in this volume its importance is explored in the studies on Post-Holocaust interpretation of Lamentations, Rembrandt, psychology, music, as well as Jewish and Christian worship, but its force is felt in all of the reception studies. Each of these contributes to understanding the lasting impact and value of Lamentations in culture.

But this view may be taken further to suggest, as Bloom does, that the Bible remains *nothing more than* a piece of culture whose impact is no more significant than any other piece of culture, whether Freud or Shakespeare or the like.[36] An implication arising from this perspective is that Lamentations may be recognized as a degrading, improper, or oppressive artifact, which the present culture must in turn *resist*.

For instance, in a far-ranging article, Hugh Pyper avers that Lamentations reflects melancholia and ultimately presents "monstrous" views that ought to be avoided. Working from Freud's article "The Ego and the Id,"[37] Pyper notes that melancholia can be represented as a "revolt against the loved one which becomes an ambivalence turned on the self. Bereavement almost invariably evokes anger, but if I am angry at the beloved who has died, what a despicable person I am."[38] Inevitably, Pyper believes, the poet of Lamentations may have mitigated this anger by directing it against the victim,[39] in this case, personified Zion. He deduces that Lamentations justifies God at the expense of the degraded and raped woman, Zion herself (as well as her children, the inhabitants of Jerusalem). Moreover, he believes the poet fashions Zion as a lascivious woman through her admissions of sin, fashioning herself into an adulterous and abandoning mother.[40] Thus the poet uses Zion's admissions of sin to justify God (the Father) and degrade the

---

33. Frye, *The Great Code*.

34. This is how *Wirkungsgeschichte* ("impact history") is described by John F. A. Sawyer in his discussion on the aims of the Blackwell Bible Commentary in: "The Place of Reception-History in a Post-modern Bible Commentary."

35. Linafelt, *Surviving Lamentations*. Note as well Lee and Mandolfo, eds., *Lamentations in Ancient and Contemporary Cultural Contexts*.

36. Bloom, *Ruin the Sacred Truths*.

37. Freud, "The Ego and the Id." See Pyper, "Reading Lamentations," esp. 57.

38. Ibid., 57.

39. Ibid., 56.

40. Ibid., 63–65.

mother (Jerusalem). In Pyper's reading, Lamentations offers a case of theodicy at the expense of the feminine. Seen in this way, the modern reader sees that God's justice constructed in Lamentations actually takes on a "monstrous" aspect, God is confirmed at the expense of a degraded and raped woman. This is not a view to be embraced.

Some feminist criticism particularly evinces a similar impulse and reads against the grain of the text of Lamentations so as to expose areas where it is seen to be oppressive, unjust, or immoral.[41] In postcolonial readings, deconstruction, and reading the Bible from the perspective of the "margins" one may anticipate similar interpretative moves for Lamentations research in the future. In these present and future receptions of Lamentations, the book may not be embraced as a source of inspiration, hope, or beautiful literature, but an oppressive text that needs to be exposed as such by the present culture, with the tyrannical aspects then either revised or expunged.[42]

## EXPLORING LAMENTATIONS AS "HOLY SCRIPTURE"

It is hoped that the discussion above has revealed that particular hermeneutical emphases focus outcomes like lenses focus one's sight. Each of the lenses identified, however, does not necessarily clarify the issue of Lamentations as *sacred* text. Whilst each approach remains illuminating in its own right, to understand Lamentations as Holy Scripture one must press further to query how one might receive this book recognizing its reality as a word from God—a divine self-disclosure of God and his dealings with the world.

In this section, such a view will be contrasted against two others. Crucial to this discussion is how one understands the claim (if any) the Bible has on one's life in regards to its status as divine revelation. The first view approaches the question of Holy Scripture in terms of general historical description. Here, one may describe the general impulse by people groups to identify Lamentations as sacred text, exploring the ways that these peoples have done that. Obviously, reading Lamentations in terms of history, literature, or culture as described in the previous section may ground this approach. But what is interesting is that such an approach does not really bind one to the claims of the text, and the interpreter may stand at a rather safe distance from it via the mediating tool of historical, literary, or cultural description. Probing a bit more deeply, however, one may begin by assessing Lamentations as Holy Scripture employing the historical, literary, or socio-cultural tools identified above, but then move further to actually respond to, and evaluate, the text critically in terms of any modern appropriation. In so doing, the interpreter necessarily becomes involved with the claims of the text, and may either embrace or reject (some or all) of them. We saw some indication of this in the reading of Pyper.

In lieu of these two views, I will conclude by exploring how one might embrace Lamentations as Holy Scripture, as a word from God that makes a claim on one's life in the present context. In effect, this is how both Jews and Christians read the text, as well as Messianic Jews, as Harvey reveals. I will make brief mention of Jewish appropriation of

---

41. See "Feminist Interpretation(s) and Lamentations" in this volume.
42. See especially Castelli, Moore, et al., eds., *The Postmodern Bible*.

Lamentations as divine disclosure, but will focus upon a Christian appropriation of the book as Holy Scripture.

### *Lamentations as "Holy Scripture" and General Historical Description*

Lamentations may be understood as "Holy Scripture" when set within a category of many sacred texts in the world. In this way, it is sacred insofar as being reflective of particular religious traditions in history that viewed the text as sacred. The question of whether it is *actually* divine revelation is circumscribed to another field of enquiry, namely dogmatics. What is necessary, then, in this understanding, is assessing how the text originated, how it came to be understood as holy, and then how it has been received. This is an especially common way to understand Lamentations in the academy. For instance, ancient Judahites, Jews, and Christians have all embraced the poems as sacred text given by God. In recognition of this fact, one may explore the theology of the book, its poetry, style, and historical Judahite context, or alternatively its impact in later Jewish or Christian traditions.[43]

The reception studies that follow chapter 2 of this book are based generally around this approach to understanding Lamentations as Holy Scripture, which indicates the importance of this kind of work to meet the aims of this volume. Now whilst many contributors represent different streams of Jewish and Christian tradition, one should note that it is not necessary to subscribe to particular theological views in order to expound upon the work of those who do, so that the category of Lamentations as "Holy Scripture" remains *historical* and *descriptive*. In other words, it is possible for scholars to simply *describe* what, say, ancient Judahites, Rashi, or Calvin, or the like thought without then having to *adopt* those theological views themselves to actually understand ancient Judahites, Rashi, or Calvin. But it is important to note the converse remains logical as well: it is not necessary to *exclude* certain theological views in order to make these assessments either.

This last point runs counter to Barr's proposal for proper biblical enquiry. In his view, the interpreter must "suspend traditional theological convictions" in order to norm potential problems of traditional (theological) readings of the Bible.[44] Note Barr's language: "Biblical scholars, therefore, whatever their allegiance in these matters, work usefully in so far as they ask the question: granted that I believe this or that to be in accord with my theological tradition, to be relevant today, to be socially and ethically desirable, my duty to the church or community is to put into brackets, into parenthesis, these my own convictions and to ask whether the Bible supports them. If it does, then one can continue as one has been; if not, then a process of theological change may begin."[45] The rationale behind this lay in his view that scientific and critical enquiry rests on a clearer standard of "scientific objectivity" than does theology, or more specifically, critical en-

---

43. James Barr, for instance, advocates this kind of historical approach to religion in terms of biblical theology: *The Concept of Biblical Theology*, 209–21.

44. The quotation above derives from an account of Barr in Topping, *Revelation, Scripture and Church*, 158–59. See also Barr, *The Scope and Authority of the Bible*, 28.

45. Barr, *The Concept of Biblical Theology*, 208.

quiry exhibits a "creative prejudice" against predetermined theological commitments.[46] The objective stance of critical interpretation serves to norm the subjective infelicities of theological foundations.[47]

Now this logic at first blush appears reasonable. Advocacy of a "theological" point of view may be seen to be problematic in that it depends upon a number of religious (pre-)commitments that impact outcomes and skew results. However, it should be noted that pre-commitments are not *necessarily* detrimental to the outcomes of historical or descriptive enquiry. Pre-commitments are a part of any biblical or theological construction, as Eichrodt saw nearly a century ago, and so are tacit to the discipline.[48] The question is which kind of pre-commitments stand as viable and which sit out of bounds.

For Barr, faith commitments should stand by the wayside while more-or-less objective historical approaches governed by reason pave the way to truth. This premise appears reasonable, but it elides a fundamental question: what if certain pre-commitments that scientific study of the Bible "bracket out" are precisely the ones advocated and necessitated by the text? That is, certain theological pre-commitments illumine rather than occlude the text for its proper understanding? Barr does not give due account of this possibility.

In contradistinction to Barr's position, it does not follow that all "faith commitments" must somehow be corrected, or that they necessarily warp biblical texts. Nor does it follow that these commitments determine the outcomes of interpretation in advance, or, put another way, that the hermeneutical circle is vicious in this regard. Barr omits the possibility that some theological faith-commitments, excluded in biblical studies in his approach, are precisely the kinds of exclusions that need to be corrected by the text. Moreover, to my mind, the actual process of excluding theological commitments (or any other set of commitments for that matter) at the outset of interpretation is, on the one hand, philosophically unrealistic and, on the other, practically undesirable, following the hermeneutical logic of Paul Ricoeur and Hans-Georg Gadamer.[49]

Now Barr's approach, one must admit, does not do away with pre-commitments or even "faith commitments"[50] but rather shifts the calculus of traditioning community

---

46. Barr, *Holy Scripture*, 113.

47. See Barr, *The Concept of Biblical Theology*, 196–208. For Barr's helpful and thoughtful response to objectivity, historicism, and faith commitments, see especially Barr, *The Concept of Biblical Theology*, 189–208; Barr, *Holy Scripture*, 105–126.

48. Eichrodt, "Hat die alttestamentliche Theologie noch selbständige Bedeutung innerhalb der alttestamentlichen Wissenschaft?" esp. 85–90. Eichrodt provides two major areas where the biblical theologian, for instance, is necessarily and subjectively *invested* in the process of analysis of the history of the Old Testament. First, the variety of criteria offered for the principle of selection by which the historian orders the quantitative data. Second, what concept of purpose the historian believes to be at work in the historical development that he or she constructs. Eichrodt rightly understood that naïve constructions of objectivity or 'faithless' notions of historical development remain problematic methodologically. Instead, Eichrodt argues that for an assessment of Old Testament and biblical theology, the historian (both in the micro and macro perspectives) must be thoroughly reflective about both oneself and the material one assesses.

49. Ricoeur, *Interpretation Theory*; Ricoeur, *Essays on Biblical Interpretation*; Gadamer, *Truth and Method*.

50. As he takes pains to point out. Particularly, faith-commitments are fine as long as they are suspended in the process of biblical studies and then reappear in dogmatics (Barr, *Holy Scripture*, 105–26).

from the church or synagogue to another one—specifically a modernistic Enlightenment traditioning community.[51] His "creative prejudice" (his term) that employs a critical, rationalistic, and non-sectarian hermeneutic stance ultimately gains the upper hand in relation to theological commitments, though without proper rationale as to its warrant.[52] But why should theological pre-commitments need to be corrected (at best) or (at worst) discounted *a priori* from the process of interpretation? In my view, there is no compelling reason to suppose these pre-commitments necessarily occlude the biblical text, and so there is no need to exclude them *toute courte*.[53] Rather historical description of Lamentations as sacred text does indeed have an analytical element to it, but it is possible to do this analysis working from theological pre-commitments (or not, as the case may be).

### *Lamentations as "Holy Scripture" Critically Evaluated*

Beyond this conception of Lamentations as Holy Scripture, one may recognize the historical fact that some have envisioned it as sacred text, but then make the further point that just because some have treated it this way in the past, it must be further evaluated to assess its impact in the present world. In other words, there are both historical-descriptive as well as evaluative aspects to this understanding of the Bible as "Holy Scripture." For some, modern appropriation of the text may be problematic either because there is no need to claim this text as revelatory in any way or that the revelatory nature of the text as a word of God must be recast.

Dawkins, though not a biblical scholar at all, recognizes that the Bible is sacred Scripture for many people, but further evaluates this claim as ludicrous. The Bible is not "holy" but rather "common" and, at points, dangerous: it was created by humans rather than God, and its violent views (especially in texts like Lamentations) must go the way of the dodo, like any naïve views of life. Otherwise, human progress is stunted in terms of diminished views of self, recurrent expressions of violence in the name of God, and obfuscation of scientific knowledge. For Dawkins, then, Lamentations as "Holy Scripture" would stand as a designation that remains only provisional but then changes in light of new and emancipated human understanding. The violent side of the Bible (like in

---

51. For a useful summary of modernistic assumptions which ground the tradition of Enlightenment rationality: see Foster, ed., *The Anti-Aesthetic*, xxiv.

52. There must be, in fact, possible philosophical warrants for Barr's approach, though he does not explore these adequately. But such attempts are being made to establish warrant: see Gordon, "A Warranted Version of Historical Biblical Criticism?"

53. This discussion impinges upon what is viable work in the academy. It is reasonable to argue that in the present context a plurality of methods is and should be legitimate. However, this plurality should make room for properly warranted faith-committed claims and approaches to the Bible (rather than naïve fideism) which should not be excluded though they may not fit the regnant paradigms (epistemological, rational, historical, or otherwise). To deny this eventuates into authoritarianism and imperialism, which remain oppressive, as recent feminist, womanist, and post-colonial critiques have demonstrated aptly. See: Castelli, Moore, et al., eds., *The Postmodern Bible*.

Lamentations) exemplifies antediluvian sentiments that must be overcome in light of modern knowledge.[54]

In some feminist criticism in particular, one notes a similar evaluative impulse working alongside description. Guest and Seidman, for instance, represent a kind of feminist analysis that assess the meaning of Lamentations as a sacred text, but then resist it explicitly, leading Seidman to want to burn the text for its oppressive nature and driving Guest to explicitly denounce its violent tendencies.[55] In both these cases Lamentations is assessed as Holy Scripture only to evaluate it as potentially destructive for culture. It is violent and oppressive. What is denied is a sense of the Bible as "word" of God that makes a claim on the life of the interpreter. Neither Guest nor Seidman make any claim about the revelatory status of the text, but implied in their works is a general devaluation of this kind of view.

Not all espousing this general descriptive/evaluative approach, however, will claim Lamentations needs to be abandoned, resisted, or disavowed as inherently destructive. For instance, O'Connor rehabilitates Lamentations as Holy Scripture in her conception of "witness" through the voice of Daughter Zion in the book. She does not jettison Lamentations, but in her assessment of the book's import for modern religious life, she believes it should be read critically and with fidelity, whose currency might appear only and through a reading that accounts for divine abuse as well as the feminine voice in the book.[56] Likewise, in her evaluation of Lamentations' potential as Holy Scripture, Mandolfo can state, "My hope [in *Daughter Zion Talks Back to the Prophets*] is to contribute to the dethroning of biblical authority as it is now construed . . . I want to resound the 'words' of God, rather than the 'Word' . . . Biblical authority, rather, should inhere in the recognition that biblical discourse is a projection of a never-ending cosmic dialogue (which Bakhtin called 'Great Time'), 'in which no meaning dies' and new meanings are ever born."[57]

Lamentations as "Holy Scripture" in Mandolfo's conception cannot be conceived as a final word from God. Rather, its role as sacred text is found in "its ability to mirror the diversity and complexity of human existence. It brings together in one book voices with, at the most extreme, diametrically opposed worldviews."[58] As such, both Mandolfo and O'Connor reconfigure the notion of Lamentations as "Holy Scripture" in their evaluation of its claim upon the life of the interpreter. And finally, even in Pyper's view, Lamentations should not be jettisoned but rather understood as Holy Scripture and only appropriated in the way that it prevents a shameful deity (inherently abusive) and by implicating shames humanity for similar practices. He concludes, "Reading Lamentations is in that sense deeply shaming, and in that very fact, potentially salutary."[59] In these three

---

54. Dawkins, *The God Delusion*, 31–38, 237–50.

55. See "Feminist Interpretation(s) and Lamentations" in this volume, as well as: Guest, "Hiding Behind the Naked Women in Lamentations"; Seidman, "Burning the Book of Lamentations."

56. O'Connor, "Lamentations," 187–91; O'Connor, *Lamentations and the Tears of the World*, 123.

57. Mandolfo, *Daughter Zion Talks Back to the Prophets*, 5–6.

58. Ibid., 128.

59. Pyper, "Reading Lamentations," 68.

views, Lamentations is "Holy Scripture" but only in a circumscribed sense—it is revelation (a word from God) insofar as the text is evaluated continuously by modern cultural paradigms, and its value for religious culture in particular is measured in light of current reality. Differently to Dawkins, Guest, and Seidman, the text is not abandoned outright, but neither is it fully embraced.

### Embracing Lamentations as "Holy Scripture"

But finally it is possible to understand Lamentations as Holy Scripture in the sense so denigrated by Dawkins—as fundamentally a word from God speaking in the present context. This approach will have historical, literary, cultural, *and* synthetic components—but it will work these out from a hermeneutical stance that is critically-reflected and theologically-grounded.[60] The point is that Lamentations as Holy Scripture conceived of in this manner anticipates that God not only spoke in these words in the past but also speaks today in and through the text—and it is a good word. Attention to historical, literary, or other qualities will be necessary and fruitful, but only insofar as these elements are recognized as elements that comprise divine disclosure to his people. As such, the text, especially in Christian understanding, will make a claim as unique discourse (word of God) that obligates its hearers into worshipful response. In this view, one cannot evade the real possibility that the voice of God addresses the interpreter (by the power of the Holy Spirit) through the text even as one addresses the text through critical faculties.[61]

The kind of thing envisioned here finds resource in Brevard Childs and his understanding of biblical theology. With Childs, this idea of the Bible as "Holy Scripture" depends upon a commitment to reflect upon the Old and New Testaments, grounded upon the notion that these are Christian Scripture that witness to, and are, the revelation of God.[62] As such, there is an obligatory facet inherent in them in that God, through the Scriptures, calls upon humanity to respond to him.[63] The reception of Lamentations as sacred text is done within a hermeneutics of faith, where the text is embraced as the very word of God, who is both the source of life and goodness in the created world. As such, whilst it is possible for one to describe this view without adopting it *per se*, it is another

---

60. Similar to the discussion of Bartholomew in his understanding of biblical theology: "Biblical Theology," 86. See also Williamson, *Catholic Principles for Interpreting Scripture*, 103–4. I do not for one moment assume that the kind of approach advocated here is the *only* kind of that can be employed; I fully agree with Barr that in the present context, a plurality of methods are legitimate (see n. 53, above).

61. Childs, *Biblical Theology of the Old and New Testaments*, 86–87. Recent, fuller explications of the role of the Holy Spirit in the process of interpretation is Treier, *Virtue and the Voice of God*, 125–27, 187–206; Fowl, *Engaging Scripture*, 97–127.

62. Childs, *Biblical Theology*, 55–94. For a fuller discussion on his concept of revelation, see Childs, *Biblical Theology*, 379–83; Childs, *Old Testament Theology in a Canonical Context*, 20–27.

63. Note that I employ the term "respond" here rather than "obey." Scriptures may demand obedience through teaching, but also invite delight, joy, or worship, amongst other responses including confession, question, reflection, and prayer. Reducing the role of the Scriptures to only one category fundamentally devalues its richness and density. See Thiselton, *The Hermeneutics of Doctrine*, 518; Ricoeur, *Essays on Biblical Interpretation*, 73–95; Tyndale, *Doctrinal Treatises*, 8–29. I am indebted to Thiselton's discussion for Tyndale's insights.

thing for one to actually embrace this view of Lamentations so that it makes a claim on his or her life.

For a Jewish appropriation of Lamentations as Holy Scripture, one may note how the text is received in tradition and figured as part of a larger engagement with God, as the articles in this volume by Neusner, Stern, Braiterman, and Gruber reveal. It is best for me, as a Christian, to let those voices speak fully and for themselves in that regard. But it is relatively clear to me that in Jewish understanding, Lamentations may be conceived as something to be embraced—not in a naïve manner as a monolithic "solution" to pain and suffering, nor in order to silence the strident protests within the book—but rather as a reflection of God's disclosure of himself to be received by his people and his world. In the Jewish tradition, clearly, reception of Lamentations encounters heated exchange and even anger and protestation, but never is it done outside of a perspective that sits before the Lord and addresses him, as the insights from Blumenthal's protest theology reveal and Braiterman's explorations in Post-Holocaust theology in general confirm.[64]

A Christian embrace of Lamentations as Holy Scripture must have a similar spirit to the Jewish impulse, to hear Lamentations as God's word, engaging him and his voice through this text and its interaction within the revelation of the two testaments. But, as this construal intimates, the shape of the Christian embrace will be necessarily different to the mainstream Jewish one, as it will be informed by *two* testaments that centre upon Jesus. However, I submit that it will not retreat from, or preempt, Lamentations' distinctive voice by escaping to the (perhaps) more familiar confines of the New Testament. Rather, reading Lamentations as Holy Scripture will embrace *this* text as God's word to be negotiated and engaged in its own horizons as well as within larger horizons of the canon, Christ, and the church.

Now it may be argued that such an approach could coerce a monolithic appropriation of Lamentations, a view that demands the interpreter to recognize his or her sin, confess, and admit that God is right in his judgment. As such, the violence present in the book is justified without question, and so the intricate way that the poetry voices lament, even against God, aborts before it grows to vibrant life (e.g., Lam 2:20–22). For this kind of critique, one need only note the careful discussions of Berlin, Dobbs-Allsopp, or especially Linafelt and Mandolfo.[65] Each of these in turn helpfully surface the virtue of voicing pain in Lamentations, and further explore how one might appropriate this insight in modern culture. House's contribution in this volume accents the justification of God and even his "outrageous demonstrations of grace" in and through Lamentations, which may be seen by these interpreters as problematic. But despite their line of critique, a close read of the distinctive contribution of Lamentations will take account of its emphasis upon prayer and protest, human finitude and the necessity of divine response, *as well as* the issue of human sin and its devastating effects in the world.[66] So it is not necessary to see

---

64. Blumenthal, *Facing the Abusing God*; Braiterman, *(God) After Auschwitz*, esp. 161–78, and in this volume.

65. Berlin, *Lamentations*, 67–77; Dobbs-Allsopp, *Lamentations*, 27–48, 67–74, 98–104; Linafelt, *Surviving Lamentations*; Mandolfo, *Daughter Zion Talks Back to the Prophets*, 79–102.

66. Thomas, "The Liturgical Function of Lamentations"; Thomas, "Lamentations and the Trustworthiness of God"; Garrett and House, *Song/Lamentations*, 327–29.

in general Christian embrace of Lamentations as Holy Scripture an obligatory *silencing* of certain tendencies present in the book, whether (to use Braiterman's language picked up by Dobbs-Allsopp) *theodic* or *antitheodic*: implicitly justifying God's activity or questioning the same.[67]

To my mind, a Christian embrace of Lamentations ought to reflect deeply upon the text within its own horizons. When done, one notes that the textual strategy of Lamentations demands the book remain "open" to multiple actualizations because it is, by design, an "open" text rather than a "closed" one. I have argued elsewhere that Lamentations meets the requirements of an "open" textuality, where the text is conceived, at the moment of its generation, to elicit multiple (though not innumerable) possible responses from its receiver(s). Such a text is designated by Umberto Eco as "open." "Closed" texts are those that are designed to elicit one and only one response from its receiver. Too often, Lamentations tacitly has been conceived as being a "closed" text, with emphasis falling upon Lam 3, and a word of hope in tragedy as well as instruction to the suffering: confess sin and trust God. The problem with this view is that the voices of protest and petition in other portions of the text largely are eclipsed (e.g., Lam 1:20–22; 2:20–22; Lam 3:59–66; Lam 5:1). Likewise, more recent contributions have tended to drive a wedge between the book's presentation of prayer and pain (Lam 1, 2, 4, and 5) and its presentation of instruction (confess sin and trust in God) and hope through Lam 3, functionally treating Lamentations as being "closed," but from the other perspective. Reifying either presentation at the expense of the other grossly under-reads the book, because both should be seen to be operating symphonically within Lamentations as an "open" text. One telling indication of this lay in the repetition of formulaic prayer in Lamentations. Formulaic divine address, along with the variety of petitions arising out of it, reveal the multiple ways for worshippers to actualize the text, revealing its "openness": to confess sin (Lam 1:11c, 20a), to request for relief from enemies (Lam 1:9c; 3:59), to complain about disgrace (Lam 5:1), and even to protest against God's actions (Lam 2:20).[68]

But beyond allowing the discreet voice of this text its say, a Christian embrace of Lamentations as Holy Scripture must also learn to frame the word that God speaks through the broader horizons of Christian Scripture and Christ himself. Thus, one should note a historical dimension in its configuration, as this word from God was spoken in particular contexts and received by the community/ies of faith in succeeding generations. One may see this in, for instance, the interaction between Isaiah and Lamentations, but also between Lamentations and Jeremiah, which is well-trod ground.[69] But this can be taken further to relate biblical themes that appear in Lamentations which are picked up in New Testament texts as well: "no comfort" (Lam 1:2, etc.) which is then perhaps employed in 2 Cor 1:3–4, "Blessed be the God and Father of our Lord Jesus Christ, the

---

67. Braiterman, *(God) After Auschwitz*; Dobbs-Allsopp, *Lamentations*.

68. Thomas, "The Liturgical Function of Lamentations"; Thomas, "Aesthetic Theory of Umberto Eco and Lamentations Interpretation." For a fuller discussion of "open" versus "closed" textual strategies, see Eco, *The Role of the Reader*, 3–40, 47–56, 175–99.

69. See the articles by Sophia-Tiemeyer and Youngblood in this volume.

Father of mercies and God of all comfort, who comforts us in all our afflictions so that we may be able to comfort those who are in any affliction, with the comfort with which we ourselves are comforted by God."[70] The comfort of the Spirit then speaks to the situation described in Lamentations, and for a purpose beyond individual suffering. This kind of theological reflection will be more difficult due to the relative absence of Lamentations' quotation in the New Testament. But as Parry shows, such theological reflection between the testaments will prove creative, imaginative, and enriching.[71]

But to nuance the matter, embracing Lamentations as Holy Scripture may also invite theological interpretation by setting this text within the larger creation-fall-redemption history as presented in both testaments. As O'Donovan argues: "A Christian response to historicism will be to wish to make precisely the opposite point: when history is made the categorical matrix for all meaning and value, it cannot be taken seriously *as history*. A story has to be a story about something . . . The story of what has happened in God's good providence to the good world which God made is 'history' in the fullest sense."[72] So to understand Lamentations as "Holy Scripture" in this sense, one must observe how this thread is situated within the tapestry of God's story that gives a basis for the meaning of history itself, and further, how the interpreter may fit into that story.

In light of Christ, the clue to creation and the hinge of history in biblical understanding, how might Lamentations be embraced as Holy Scripture, *historically*? I submit one way to do this is to understand Lamentations as a "kingdom text." This would establish a kind of analogical relationship between the liminality of the prayers of Lamentations and the liminality of the kingdom of God—a relationship that will drive the interpreter towards the text of Lamentations and more deeply into one's identity in God's kingdom.[73] That is to say, this approach may provide both information about God's dealings in history and a means for the interpreter to "perform" the text in light of this theological disclosure.[74] Now this will be out of bounds for one who does not embrace this vision of reality but for a Christian understanding of Lamentations as sacred text, it remains crucial. Ultimately, in the grand movement of the biblical drama, death and hell are defeated, and suffering will also be swallowed up in the end because of the work of Christ and the movement of his kingdom (Rev 21). It is important to remember that God's kingdom was always assumed to be real in the Scriptures: *that God would really reign on the earth justly, righteously, and eternally.* And it is in the Christ-event that the real and present suffering of the world is embodied as well as (finally) overcome by God's real and present

---

70. See also Tremper Longman's association of Lamentations and the New Testament via the theme of the divine warrior: Longman, *Jeremiah, Lamentations*, 336–41. To see other ways Lamentations is received in the New Testament, see Beale and Carson, eds., *Commentary on the New Testament Use of the Old*.

71. Parry, "Prolegomena to Christian Theological Interpretation of Lamentations." For a helpful discussion on the role of imagination in theological interpretation, see Chapman, "Imaginative Readings of Scripture and Theological Interpretation."

72. O'Donovan, *Resurrection and Moral Order*, 60, 53–75. O'Donovan, for one, does not abandon the results of traditional historical-criticism, but like Childs, sees these as only initial steps along a larger course of God's revelation, which can be seen in and through the final shape of the Scriptures.

73. On analogical imagination, see Chapman, "Imaginative Readings," 434–36.

74. Young, *The Art of Performance*; Treier, *Virtue and the Voice of God*, 148–62.

reign. But the Christ-event remains a prolepsis—an occurrence that has taken place that reveals (and anticipates) the reality of a future completed event. In this way, for example, those who are "in Christ," to use the Pauline language, are freed from death and sin by faith in Jesus. However, all Christians still face sin or the outcomes of sin, and they die in their physical body; death is defeated by Christ, but the Christian fully experiences this reality only at the culmination of the kingdom. It is only after Jesus makes "all things new" that death will ultimately be defeated and sin will no longer be present in this world (Rom 6:8; 1 Pet 1). God's kingdom is established now because of the Christ-event but will be consummated by Christ at the end of all things.[75] What is interesting is the kingdom of God that Christ has inaugurated *now* through his life, death, burial, resurrection, and ascension is not fully consummated . . . until *then*, in the future. What about meantime? What of the period between "then"—vindication—and "now"—present suffering? The kingdom of God, thus, contains a liminality to it that awaits the final inbreaking of God, much like the liminality reflected in Holy Week.[76]

This liminal tension between hope anticipated "now" but realized "not yet" is manifest in Lamentations as well. The prayers in Lamentations are grounded on the (tacit) view that God is indeed a trustworthy Lord, but they contain pleas, perhaps even demands, that his goodness, trustworthiness, and mercy be made real in the present world. Renkema understands the liminality of Lamentations to be the very heart of its message: "Cast out from peace is my soul, I am forced to forget the good [Lam 3:17] until he looks down and sees, YHWH from the heavens [Lam 3:50]."[77] In this one sees that the prayers of Lamentations are designed to move God to respond to the petitioners. Miller says that this reveals biblical prayer to be, at least in part, a persuasive action. He says, "[The] fundamental ground of prayer, that is, the responsiveness of God to the cry of human need, is lifted up. All the description of the plight of the afflicted, wherever it occurs in prayer, assumes God's care and compassion, especially for those in distress."[78] Prayer, especially of the kind found in Lamentations, finds hope in what God has done and what he will do, and awaits God's good response.

Similarly, despite glimmers of God's in-breaking kingdom in the world today, humanity lives in brokenness and has cause to lament before him. But there is also reason and cause to hope, just as Lamentations hopes for response from God. But in both, hope is liminal and awaits God's final consummation of his creation. In Lamentations, to use the analogy, paradise (pain removed) is anticipated, but not gained. That is not to imply, as I have argued, that there is no hope. Rather, hope is always peeking around the corner, anticipated in the work of God. This is the case as well in perhaps the most overt positive expression in the corpus: "Your iniquity/punishment, Dear Zion, is complete. He will not add to your exile" (Lam 4:22a). In this vision, exile is finished, and presumably, the enemies of Zion will get their just desserts! The hope for this reality is touched upon, but

---

75. For a helpful discussion on the kingdom of God, see Wright, *Who Was Jesus?*, 97–103. For a review of scholarly views on the kingdom of God, see Viviano, *The Kingdom of God in History*.

76. See Lewis, *Between Cross and Resurrection*.

77. Renkema, *Lamentations*, 337.

78. Miller, "Prayer as Persuasion," 359.

never consummated as the very next verse in the book is Lam 5:1, by all counts a plea to God about the *ongoing* distress.

When one thinks theologically about Lamentations through analogical imagination, it opens up a number of horizons for the Christian. First, as House notes, the reality that God deals with sin in judgment, but that judgment always breaks into new life in salvation. This is part and parcel of the way God engages the broken world in which we live, and aims to heal it through his kingdom and Christ. Lamentations reflects this notion of judgment in a particular time in history. As such, it highlights sin, confession, and suffering, and *may* lead present day Christians to "perform" the text along those lines. However, as Lamentations also opens up the horizon of prayer, it anticipates God's ultimate response to pain, suffering, and death. Through the kingdom of God, it is clear that God's response to death is life and restoration through Jesus, but Lamentations provides a focus upon the "not yet" dimension to the reign of God in Christ. As such, Lamentations opens a horizon of appeal, where Christians might pray in effect, "come quickly Lord Jesus" (Rev 22:20); Christians might request God to break in and ease pain and suffering (as in Lam 1:20–22; 2:20–22; 3:55–66; 5). This too, is a viable performance of the text. Multiple horizons open up when reflecting theologically upon the text.

So it is apparent that a Christian understanding will not use the whole narrative-historical arc of the Scriptures, creation (Gen 1–2) to New Creation (Rev 21), as a means to "explain away" the particulars, namely the prayers and tears of Lamentations. It is one thing to recognize that God has given a narrative that is world-encompassing, with a beginning and an (eschatological) end. It is quite another to use that grand narrative to squash or silence particular voices in parts of that narrative, such as Lamentations, where the immediacy of the present realities of life, death, and survival are foregrounded so explicitly. Any propensity to run too quickly to "the end of the story" would preclude the necessary and urgent presence of the expression of pain in the text at hand.

But this is precisely what Lamentations does not do. Rather, it gives not a theological treatise but a series of poems to deal with the realities of death, life, and survival. It takes the real experience of life, death, and survival and refuses to shy away from these very real experiences: whether dealing with sin, suffering, or anger towards God. These realities comprise part of the human condition, and the book of Lamentations does not give a "cheap" or "easy" reflection to any of them. Rather, like the life, death, burial, resurrection, and ascension of Christ, Lamentations provides a stern view of the brokenness of present reality while anticipating a time when brokenness (ultimately) will be eradicated by the goodness of God in the culmination of his kingdom. Lamentations, then, serves to affirm the trustworthiness of God but appeals to him to be just that—faithful, true, merciful, and trustworthy, as his kingdom really is: "Your kingdom come, Your will be done, on earth as it is in heaven" (Matt 6:10). The hope is found in the centrality of Jesus, whose death and resurrection provides the model for this new and anticipated life. But with Lamentations, the accent falls on the threshold of this new life.

Finally, it is in place to mention address the apparent dissonance between the concept of Lamentations as God's word in the discussion above and the reality that in the book God never speaks, but rather voices speak *about* God—how, then, can I identify this book as "*God's* word" (the voice of God) when it evidently uses human words and human voice(s) to speak *to* and *about* God? What could God be saying (or is he speaking at all)? Whilst it is incontestable that God does not address anyone directly in Lamentations, when one receives the book as Holy Scripture, one must say that God certainly provides the framework for divine address through the text itself. God speaks insofar as he gives a means for his people to address him. House's view in this volume looks at the issue of God's address by focusing upon the issues of sin and confession in Lamentations (especially in chapter 3) set in dialogue with the larger canon: God speaks a word that calls for confession in light of judgment.

In both House's and my view, understanding Lamentations as Scripture revolves around a claim about divine revelation—Lamentations is not merely human words, but God's word in human words (Holy Scripture). House views the revelation of God in Lamentations to be about his grace in the face human sin. But it seems to me, in light of the multiplicity of *kinds* of prayer (protest, confession, plea), it is more coherent with the text to let these petitions shape the substance of the voice of God through Lamentations: God's call for his people to confess is one note sounded, but not the *only* one. The words about God, given by God through the (ancient) community, provide for the reader (both ancient and modern) a vehicle designed for address and anticipatory encounter with the Lord: confession, appeal, protest, and questioning. In the case of the prayers of Lamentations flagged above, their rhetoric depends upon the logic of such an anticipated encounter.[79] This holds true as well when one reads Lamentations as a "kingdom text" outlined above.

The precise shape of this encounter may vary: communal and liturgical, or personal and private.[80] However shaped and actualized, the logic of Lamentations in general depends upon this anticipated response from God. God has given a book created for encounter with him. One might call Lamentations, then, an "encounter mechanism" and this is indeed a gift. Theologically, it implicitly underscores the notion of a God reaching out to humanity, providing the means for his people to petition, confront, and even protest him. So Lamentations *is* about what people thought about God in the past, but it is also about how God speaks about viable ways of interacting with him. To reduce Lamentations to only human words, without recognizing this divine dimension, elides the gift of Lamentations as Holy Scripture.

As might be intimated in this discussion, one who does not embrace Lamentations as divine discourse which centre upon God in Christ may not find these comments persuasive or helpful. But that is precisely what identifies this approach as distinctively *Christian* in its orientation—reflecting upon the two testaments and their witness to God in Christ. As such, an embrace of Lamentations as Holy Scripture does, in fact demand that one sit within the community of faith to be identified with this reading practice. However, such a practice does not slight other approaches, but would urge them to press further to the substance of the text—God in Christ—without demanding they do so.

79. Miller, "Prayer as Persuasion."

80. For some possibilities of actualization of lament prayer in Christian life, see Brown and Miller, eds., *Lament*.

## CONCLUSION

This chapter has explored what it has meant, and what it might mean, to read Lamentations as Holy Scripture. I hope to have demonstrated that this is not a simple endeavor, as methodological foci as well as theological commitments do in fact impinge upon reading this text as sacred. Lamentations may be resisted or embraced as *holy* insofar as the interpreter believes the text to be a word from God which is rather good for one's health. Reponses have varied. Future work that embraces Lamentations as a word from God must work through the historical, literary, and cultural facets of the text, but also must press further to the text's relationship(s) between the larger canon, Christ, and the church.

## BIBLIOGRAPHY

Albrektson, Bertil. *Studies in the Text and Theology of the Book of Lamentations: With a Critical Edition of the Peshitta Text.* Studia Theologica Lundensia, 21. Lund: Gleerup, 1963.
Alter, Robert. *The Art of Biblical Narrative.* New York: Basic, 1981.
———. *The Art of Biblical Poetry.* New York: Basic, 1985.
———. *The World of Biblical Literature.* New York: Basic, 1992.
Auerbach, Erich. *Mimesis: The Representation of Reality in Western Literature.* Translated by Willard R. Trask. Princeton, NJ: Princeton University Press, 1953.
Bakker, Nico T. *History as a Theological Issue.* Theological Seminar Series, 2. Leiden: Deo, 2000.
Barr, James. *The Concept of Biblical Theology: An Old Testament Perspective.* London: SCM, 1999.
———. *Holy Scripture: Canon, Authority, Criticism.* Oxford: Oxford University Press, 1983.
———. *The Scope and Authority of the Bible.* Philadelphia: Westminster, 1980.
Bartholomew, Craig. "Biblical Theology." In *Dictionary for Theological Interpretation of the Bible*, edited by Kevin Vanhoozer, Daniel Treier, N.T. Wright, and Craig Bartholomew, 84–90. Grand Rapids: Baker Academic, 2005.
Bartholomew, Craig, C. Stephen Evans, Mary Healy, and Murray Rae, eds. *"Behind" the Text: History and Biblical Interpretation.* Scripture and Hermeneutics Series, 4. Carlisle, UK: Paternoster, 2003.
Beale, Gregory K., and Donald A. Carson, eds. *Commentary on the New Testament Use of the Old.* Grand Rapids: Baker, 2007.
Berlin, Adele. *Lamentations.* Old Testament Library. Louisville: Westminster John Knox, 2002.
Bloom, Harold. *Ruin the Sacred Truths: Poetry and Belief from the Bible to the Present.* Cambridge: Harvard University Press, 1991.
Blumenthal, David R. *Facing the Abusing God: A Theology of Protest.* Louisville: Westminster John Knox, 1993.
Braiterman, Zachary. *(God) After Auschwitz: Tradition and Change in Post-Holocaust Jewish Thought.* Princeton: Princeton University Press, 1998.
Brandscheidt, Renate. *Gotteszorn und Menschenleid: Die Gerichtsklage des leidenden Gerechten in Klgl 3.* Trier Theologica Studien, 41. Trier, Germany: Paulinus, 1983.
———. *Das Buch der Klagelieder.* Geistliche Schriftlesung, 10. Düsseldorf: Patmos, 1988.
Brown, Sally A., and Patrick D. Miller, eds. *Lament: Reclaiming Practices in Pulpit, Pew and Public Square.* Louisville: Westminster John Knox, 2007.
Brueggemann, Walter. *Theology of the Old Testament: Testimony, Dispute, Advocacy.* Philadelphia: Fortress, 1997.
Castelli, Elizabeth A., Stephen D. Moore, et al., eds. *The Postmodern Bible: The Bible and Culture Collective.* New Haven: Yale University Press, 1995.
Chapman, Stephen. "Imaginative Readings of Scripture and Theological Interpretation." In *Out of Egypt: Biblical Theology and Biblical Interpretation*, edited by Craig Bartholomew, Mary Healy, Karl Möller and Robin Parry, 409–47. Scripture and Hermeneutics Series, 5. Milton Keynes, UK: Paternoster, 2004.
Childs, Brevard. *Biblical Theology of the Old and New Testaments: Theological Reflection on the Christian Bible.* Minneapolis: Fortress, 1993.
———. *Old Testament Theology in a Canonical Context.* Philadelphia: Fortress, 1986.
Clark, Elizabeth A. *History, Theory, Text: Historians and the Linguistic Turn.* Cambridge: Harvard University Press, 2004.
Davies, Philip R. *In Search of "Ancient Israel."* JSOT Supplement, 148. Sheffield: JSOT, 1992.
Dawkins, Richard. *The God Delusion.* Boston: Houghton Mifflin, 2006.
Dobbs-Allsopp, F. W. *Lamentations.* Interpretation. Louisville: John Knox, 2002.
———. "Lamentations as a Lyric Sequence." (Unpublished manuscript.)
Eco, Umberto. *The Role of the Reader: Explorations in the Semiotics of Texts.* Bloomington, IN: Indiana University Press, 1984.
Eichrodt, Walther. "Hat die alttestamentliche Theologie noch selbständige Bedeutung innerhalb der alttestamentlichen Wissenschaft?" *Zeitschrift für alttestamentliche Wissenschaft* 47 (1929) 83–91.
Foster, Hal, ed. *The Anti-Aesthetic: Essays on Postmodern Culture.* New York: New, 2002.
Fowl, Stephen E. *Engaging Scripture.* Challenges in Contemporary Theology. Oxford: Blackwell, 1998.

Frei, Hans W. *The Eclipse of Biblical Narrative: A Study in Eighteenth and Nineteenth Century Hermeneutics.* New Haven: Yale University Press, 1974.

Freud, Sigmund. "The Ego and the Id." In *On Metapsychology: The Theory of Psychoanalysis*, 350–408. Penguin Freud Library, 11. Harmondsworth, UK: Penguin, 1991.

Freytag, Gustav. *Technique of the Drama: An Exposition of Dramatic Composition and Art.* Translated by Elias J. Macewan. Honolulu: University Press of the Pacific, 2004.

Frye, Northrop. *The Great Code: The Bible and Literature.* Toronto: Academic, 1982.

Gadamer, Hand-Georg. *Truth and Method.* 2nd ed. Translated by Joel Weinsheimer and Donald G. Marshall. New York: Continuum, 2002.

Garrett, Duane and Paul R. House. *Song of Songs/Lamentations.* Word Biblical Commentary. Nashville: Thomas Nelson, 2005.

Gillingham, Susan E. *One Bible, Many Voices: Different Approaches to Biblical Studies.* London: SPCK, 1998.

Goldman, S. "Lamentations." In *The Five Megilloth: With Hebrew Text, English Translation, and Commentary*, edited by A. Cohen, 66–102. London: Soncino, 1970.

Gordon, Robert P. "A Warranted Version of Historical Biblical Criticism? A Response to Alvin Plantinga." In *"Behind" the Text: History and Biblical Interpretation*, edited by Craig G. Bartholomew, C. Stephen Evans, et al., 79–91. Scripture and Hermeneutics Series, 4. Milton Keynes, UK: Paternoster, 2003.

Gottwald, Norman K. *Studies in the Book of Lamentations.* 2nd ed. Studies in Biblical Theology, 14. London: SCM, 1962.

Gwaltney Jr., W. C. "The Biblical Book of Lamentations in the Context of Ancient Near Eastern Literature." In *Scripture in Context II: More Essays on the Comparative Method*, edited by William W. Hallo, James C. Moyer, and Leo G. Perdue, 191–212. Winona Lake, IN: Eisenbrauns, 1983.

Guest, Deryn. "Hiding Behind the Naked Women in Lamentations: A Recriminative Response." *Biblical Interpretation* 7 (1999) 413–48.

Halpern, Baruch. *The First Historians: The Hebrew Bible and History.* University Park, PA: Pennsylvania State University Press, 1996.

Heim, Knut. "The Personification of Jerusalem and the Drama of Her Bereavement in the Book of Lamentations." In *Zion, the City of Our God*, edited by Richard S. Hess and Gordon J. Wenham, 129–69. Grand Rapids: Eerdmans, 1999.

Hillers, Delbert. "Lamentations, Book of." In *Anchor Bible Dictionary*, Vol. IV, edited by David Noel Freedman, 137–41. New York: Doubleday, 1992.

Holman, Hugh, and William Harmon. *A Handbook to Literature.* 6th ed. New York: Macmillan, 1992.

Jeanrond, Werner. *Theological Hermeneutics: Development and Significance.* London: SCM, 1994.

Johnson, Bo. "Form and Message in Lamentations." *Zeitschrift für alttestamentliche Wissenschaft* 97 (1985) 58–73.

Joyce, Paul M. "Sitting Loose to History: Reading the Book of Lamentations without Primary Reference to Its Original Historical Setting." In *In Search of True Wisdom: Essays in Old Testament Interpretation in Honour of Ronald E. Clements*, edited by Edward Ball, 246–62. JSOTSupp, 300. Sheffield: JSOT, 1999.

Kaiser, Barbara. "Reconsidering Parallelism: A Study of the Structure of Lamentations 1, 2, and 4." Ph.D. diss., University of Chicago, 1983.

Kaiser, Walter C. *Grief and Pain in the Plan of God: Christian Assurance and the Message of Lamentations.* Fearne, UK: Christian Focus, 2004.

Kugel, James L. *How to Read the Bible: A Guide to Scripture, Then and Now.* New York: Free, 2007.

Labahn, Antje. "Fire from Above: Metaphors and Images of God's Actions in Lamentations 2:1–9." *Journal for the Study of the Old Testament* 31 (2006) 239–56.

Lanahan, William. "The Speaking Voice in the Book of Lamentations." *Journal of Biblical Literature* 93 (1974) 41–49.

Lee, Nancy C. and Carleen Mandolfo, eds. *Lamentations in Ancient and Contemporary Cultural Contexts.* SBL Symposium Series. Atlanta: Society of Biblical Literature, 2008.

Lewis, Alan E. *Between Cross and Resurrection: A Theology of Holy Saturday.* Grand Rapids: Eerdmans, 2001.

Linafelt, Tod. *Surviving Lamentations: Catastrophe, Lament, and Protest in the Afterlife of a Biblical Book.* Chicago: University of Chicago Press, 2000.

Longman III, Tremper. *Jeremiah, Lamentations*. New International Biblical Commentary. Peabody, MA: Hendrickson, 2008.

Longman III, Tremper and Raymond B. Dillard. *An Introduction to the Old Testament*. 2nd ed. Grand Rapids: Zondervan, 2006.

Mandolfo, Carleen. *Daughter Zion Talks Back to the Prophets: A Dialogic Theology of the Book of Lamentations*. Semeia Studies. Atlanta: Society of Biblical Literature, 2007.

Middlemas, Jill. "Did Second Isaiah write Lamentations III?" *Vetus Testamentum* 56 (2006) 505–25.

———. *The Templeless Age: An Introduction to the History, Literature, and Theology of the "Exile."* Louisville: Westminster John Knox, 2007.

———. *The Troubles of Templeless Judah*. Oxford Theological Monographs. Oxford: Oxford University Press, 2005.

Miller, Patrick D. "Prayer as Persuasion: The Rhetoric and Intention of Prayer." *Word and World* 13 (1993) 356–62.

Nägelsbach, Eduard. *Die Klagelieder*. Theologisch-homiletisches Bibelwerk. Die heilige Schrift. Alten Testament, 15. Leipzig: Belhagen und Klasing, 1868.

O'Connor, Kathleen. "Lamentations." In *The Women's Bible Commentary*. Expanded Edition, edited by C. A. Newsom and Sharon Ringe, 187–91. Louisville: Westminster John Knox, 1998.

———. *Lamentations and the Tears of the World*. Maryknoll, NY: Orbis, 2002.

O'Donovan, Oliver. *Resurrection and Moral Order: An Outline for Evangelical Ethics*. 2nd ed. Leicester, UK: Apollos, 1994.

Parry, Robin A. "Prolegomena to Christian Theological Interpretation of Lamentations." In *Canon and Biblical Interpretation*, edited by Craig Bartholomew, Scott Hahn, Christopher Seitz, and Al Wolters, 393–418. Scripture and Hermeneutics Series, 7. Milton Keynes, UK: Paternoster/ Grand Rapids: Zondervan, 2006.

Provan, Iain. *Lamentations*. New Century Bible Commentary. Grand Rapids: Eerdmans, 1991.

Pyper, Hugh S. "Reading Lamentations." *Journal for the Study of the Old Testament* 95 (2001) 55–69.

Renkema, Johan. *Lamentations*. Historical Commentary on the Old Testament. Leuven: Peeters, 1998.

Ricoeur, Paul. *Essays on Biblical Interpretation*. Edited with introduction by Lewis S. Mudge. Philadelphia: Fortress, 1980.

———. *Interpretation Theory: Discourse and the Surplus of Meaning*. Forth Worth: TCU, 1976.

Sawyer, John F. A. "The Place of Reception-History in a Post-modern Bible Commentary." Paper given at the SBL North American Congress, Nashville, Tennessee, USA, 2000.

Seidman, Naomi. "Burning the Book of Lamentations." In *Out of the Garden: Women Writers on the Bible*, edited by Christina Büchmann and Celina Spiegel, 278–88. New York: Fawcett Columbine, 1995.

Thiselton, Anthony C. *New Horizons in Hermeneutics*. Grand Rapids: Zondervan, 1992.

———. *The Hermeneutics of Doctrine*. Grand Rapids: Eerdmans, 2007.

Thomas, Heath Aaron. "Lamentations and the Trustworthiness of God." *Miqra* 7 (2008) 6–11.

———. "The Liturgical Function of Lamentations." In *Thinking Toward New Horizons: Collected Communications to the XIXth Congress of the International Organization for the Study of the Old Testament, Ljubljana 2007*, edited by Matthias Augustin and Hermann Michael Niemann, 137–47. Beiträge zur Erforschung des alten Testaments und des antiken Judentums. 55. Frankfurt: Lang, 2008.

———. "Aesthetic Theory of Umberto Eco and Lamentations Interpretation." Paper given at the SBL International Congress, Edinburgh, UK, 3 June 2006.

Topping, Richard R. *Revelation, Scripture and Church: Theological Hermeneutic Thought of James Barr, Paul Ricoeur, and Hans Frei*. Ashgate New Critical Thinking on Religion Theology and Biblical Studies Series. Aldershot, UK: Ashgate, 2007.

Treier, Daniel J. *Virtue and the Voice of God: Toward Theology as Wisdom*. Grand Rapids: Eerdmans, 2006.

Tyndale, William. *Doctrinal Treatises and Introduction to Different Portions of the Holy Scripture*. Parker Society, edited by Henry Walter. Cambridge: Cambridge University Press, 1948.

Villanueva, Federico. *The "Uncertainty of a Hearing": A Study of the Sudden Change of Mood in the Psalms of Lament*. Supplements to Vetus Testamentum, 121. Leiden: Brill, 2008.

Viviano, Benedict T. *The Kingdom of God in History*. Eugene, OR: Wipf & Stock, 2002.

Westermann, Claus. *Die Klagelieder: Forschungsgeschichte und Auslegung*. Neukirchen: Neukirchener, 1990. [= *Lamentations: Issues and Interpretation*. Edinburgh: T. & T. Clark, 1994.]

Whitelam, Keith W. *The Invention of Ancient Israel: The Silencing of Palestinian History*. London: Routledge, 1996.

Williamson, Peter. *Catholic Principles for Interpreting Scripture: A Study of the Pontifical Biblical Commission's The Interpretation of the Bible in the Church*. Subsidia Biblica, 22. Rome: Pontifical Biblical Institute, 2001.

Wright, N. T. *The New Testament and the People of God*. Christian Origins and the Question of God, 1. Minneapolis: Fortress, 1992.

———. *Who Was Jesus?* Grand Rapids: Eerdmans, 1993.

Young, Frances M. *The Art of Performance: Towards a Theology of Holy Scripture* (London: DLT, 1990).

# 2

# Outrageous Demonstrations of Grace

*The Theology of Lamentations*

PAUL R. HOUSE

## INTRODUCTION

IN THE PAST TWENTY years a number of commentaries, articles, and monographs that address directly or touch on Lamentations' theology have appeared. Some of these were prompted by the normal and good activity of the publication of scholarly materials, such as the completion of commentary series. But others were at least in part a response to catastrophic international events that have led biblical scholars to attempt to link lament and today's world more closely than in the past.

This interest in Lamentations' theology is a welcome development even though there are many elements of it that reveal as much about current frustration with world events and a fascination with certain types of literary theory than a realistic reading of the book in canonical context. This chapter will examine some of these recent approaches in light of their predecessors, will then offer a literary-theological analysis of Lamentations, and finally will summarize selected key parts of the book's theology. At its core Lamentations' theology depends on the expectation of outrageous acts of grace on YHWH's part. Though this thesis runs counter to recent trends I will seek to demonstrate its coherence based on historical, canonical, and literary grounds.

## RECENT TRENDS IN THE STUDY OF THE THEOLOGY OF LAMENTATIONS[1]

It is never easy to divide the history of the study of a biblical book into appropriate categories and time frames. Nonetheless, one must often do so in lectures, conference presentations, and writing projects. Thus, at the risk of overstating or understating some key elements and of omitting many worthy authors, I believe that treatments of the theology of Lamentations in the past fifty years may be divided into three parts (1954–1989, 1990–1999, and 2000–Present). These time periods feature different, though related,

---

1. Much of what appears in this section is adapted from Garrett and House, *Song of Songs/Lamentations*, 316–23.

concerns. Obviously, the recent trends highlighted in this chapter have roots in the earlier period, but just as obviously, in my opinion, they represent a departure from earlier streams of thought. In what follows I have chosen to feature volumes specifically addressing Lamentations' theology, commentaries in a series with a specifically theological purpose, and key commentaries that have significant sections on the book's theology.

The first era dealt primarily with *theodicy*. Experts attempted to state how Lamentations fits into the Old Testament's discussions of why God acted as he did in Israelite history. Norman Gottwald and Bertil Albrektson wrote the most-discussed works in this period. They deserve credit for setting the stage for subsequent detailed contributions. Stated simply, this era asked, *"How do we explain suffering as it relates to humanity's relationship to God?"*

The second era received impetus from Claus Westermann, who argued that an understanding of theodicy was not all that Lamentations offered its ancient and contemporary readers. For Westermann the book's main contribution was as a vehicle for *expressing pain* for the purpose of relating to God and the world in which we live. He believed that understanding lament better would redeem the genre for current liturgical usage.

This era basically concluded with the publication of Johan Renkema's landmark commentary. While Renkema appreciated Westermann's concerns, he believed that Westermann's emphasis on the original setting of the book undermined his understanding of its theology (see below). Renkema represented other writers who agreed that expressing pain was a vital part of Lamentations' message, yet who also sought its theological import in other areas. As was true in the first era, works in the 1990s tended to utilize standard historical-critical approaches, though Iain Provan noted their limits in his 1991 commentary.[2] Reaction against or beyond historical concerns were part of the reason the next era featured literary approaches. Perhaps a reasonable way of summarizing the second era is to suggest that it focused on the question, *"How do we express our pain to God and one another?"*

The third era gained momentum from several factors. Westermann's volume inspired new work on Lamentations. Three well-known commentary series, Interpretation, the Old Testament Library, and the Word Biblical Commentary, released volumes near the same time. Use of Lamentations to reflect on the Holocaust, the events of September 11, 2001, the bombings in Bali, the killings in Rwanda, and other horrific human events grew. Monographs utilizing a still greater variety of literary methods appeared. Some of these volumes used fairly traditional historical and literary approaches, yet others championed deconstruction and other de-centering methodologies. Some treated female characters more fully than previous works had done. Taken as a whole, these works make it evident that a new and variegated phase of interpretation has begun. To borrow terminology from Tod Linafelt's formative monograph,[3] this era asked, *"How do we survive what God has done?"*

---

2. Provan, *Lamentations*, 7–19.
3. Linafelt, *Surviving Lamentations*.

# GREAT IS THY FAITHFULNESS?

I believe it is possible for insights from all three eras to provide fruitful ground for a new era of holistic analysis, one in which we might ask, *"How do we take on board what we have learned from scholarship and grow in our relationship with God from it?"* After all, theodicy will always remain a significant matter in theology and its formation of life. Furthermore, expressing pain is part of human experience, including human religious experience, and the uses to which one puts such expressions is a vital matter in a dehumanized world. Also, the neglect of some biblical characters, such as the plight of women and children, demands critical and theological redress. Finally, God's character in relationship to our own is the core issue in Biblical Theology, so how we conceive of this relationship will determine much about how we think and how we live our faith. Thus, it seems appropriate to consider how a synthesis of the concerns highlighted in these interrelated eras can offer for consideration a theology of reconciliation and hope.

## *Lamentations and Theodicy (1954–1989)*

As was noted above, the works of two key figures, Norman Gottwald and Bertil Albrektson, are the most important in this era. In his *Studies in the Book of Lamentations,* Gottwald argued that the theology of Lamentations begins with Judah's question of why they suffered so horrendously so soon after Josiah's reforms.[4] He states that Judahites ask this question because they had been led to believe by adherents of deuteronomistic theology that reform would bring relief from Babylonian pressure. Thus, when reform was instead followed by defeat the people sought to know why such things could happen.

So in Lamentations the people utilize themes of reversal to express lost glory and present pain, yet also to state their hope that in the future Yhwh will once again restore their fortunes.[5] By expressing these hopes they affirm their faith in Yhwh and their belief in meaningful history ruled by Yhwh.[6] Lamentations therefore participates in the Israelite prophetic tradition that exposes sin and punishment, yet also promises renewal. It thereby unites the priestly concern for meaningful, results-oriented liturgy with the prophets' desire for future covenantal faithfulness.[7]

Gottwald concludes that Lamentations' theological center is 3:33, where the writer states that Yhwh "does not afflict from his heart."[8] He asserts, "The expression . . . is the high water mark in Lamentations' understanding of God . . . The angry side of his nature, turned so unflinchingly against Jerusalem, is not the determinative factor in the divine purposes. Begrudgingly, regretfully, if there is no other way toward his higher purposes, he may unleash the forces of evil, but 'his heart' is not in it."[9] The reason for Judah's suffering, therefore, lies deep in the heart of human beings, not deep in the heart of Yhwh.

---

4. Gottwald, *Studies in the Book of Lamentations,* 51.
5. Ibid., 53–60.
6. Ibid., 62.
7. Ibid., 114–19.
8. Ibid., 99. Unless otherwise noted, all translations of Lamentations are mine.
9. Ibid.

There is much to commend in Gottwald's groundbreaking volume. His description of the literary and theological traditions the author[10] of Lamentations utilizes is largely accurate. His emphasis on past reversal and current hopes for future renewal are poignant. The book does balance prophetic, priestly, and deuteronomistic emphases. Viewing 3:33 as the book's heart has merit, due to its centrality in the book's structure and its centrality to grasping what the book says about YHWH.

At the same time, Gottwald's volume has one chief weakness, which is Gottwald's underlying historical assumption about the type of theodicy question Judah asks. Unless he believes Lamentations' audience is simply self-deceived, the Old Testament hardly portrays Judah as a society as having been permanently reformed along deuteronomistic lines. Rather, the Old Testament as a whole presents Josiah's reforms as temporary at best, and a government sponsored episode not supported by the people at worst. Furthermore, the speakers in Lamentations never state their pain in terms Gottwald outlines. They state their pain as a fact without asking why it occurs, and they never claim innocence. Still, even if these critiques are valid, Gottwald deserves much credit for initiating the discussion in the manner he did. It is a great deal easier to criticize a pioneer than it is to write pioneering works.

Bertil Albrektson dialogued with Gottwald's volume and extended the discussion of theodicy and Lamentations theology in *Studies in the Text and Theology of the Book of Lamentations*. Albrektson agrees with Gottwald that a deuteronomistic emphasis is apparent in Lamentations; yet he concludes that this strand indicates that the people had reason to expect judgment, not divine approval, for their actions. The book's acquaintance with Deut 28:15–68 reveals this fact.[11]

Besides this basically negative deuteronomistic theme, Albrektson observes a Zion emphasis in the book. He notes that Psalms of Zion, such as Psalms 46, 48, and 76, stress Jerusalem's inviolability, then comments that Lam 2:15; 4:12, 20; and 5:19 contain images similar to those psalms.[12] He then suggests that "[t]he key to the theology of Lamentations" is in fact found in the tension between specific religious conceptions and historical realities: between the confident belief of the Zion traditions in the inviolability of the temple and city, and the actual brute facts."[13] If so, he argues, then the book's many questions related to justice and the descriptions of pain and suffering are evidence of the people's dismay over the broken promise of permanence. He concludes by stating that Lamentations' deuteronomistic and Zion theologies are conjoined by a common interest in the central sanctuary. The loss of this place indicates YHWH's judgment, yet the ongoing prayers of the people indicate they believe YHWH will again choose Zion. What the

---

10. Though I believe it is possible that more than one writer penned one or more of the poems in Lamentations (see the discussion in Garrett and House, *Song of Songs/Lamentations*, 283–303), I think the one-author theory is the most viable option. Thus, when necessary to do so I will refer to "the author" of the book in this chapter.

11. Albrektson, *Studies in the Text and Theology of the Book of Lamentations*, 234–39.

12. Ibid., 220–29.

13. Ibid., 230.

people must do now is cease trusting in a God supposedly enthroned in an inviolable Temple and learn to trust in a God who reigns supreme and unfettered in history.[14]

The main strength of Albrektson's work is the way he brings the Zion materials into the discussion. There can be no doubt that the way the people perceived their situation was in part influenced by what they thought of Jerusalem's past, present, and future position as Yhwh's special city and the Temple as God's special dwelling place. They could not wonder why they have suffered without wondering why Jerusalem fell and why the Temple was razed.

Nonetheless, Albrektson may not distinguish sufficiently between Zion as the exalted and purified future home of Yhwh and his people (see Isa 4:2–6) and Jerusalem as the current physical representation of that future reality. More emphasis on the deuteronomistic strand he notes could balance the discussion, as could the inclusion in his analysis of deuteronomistic passages against the Temple and its cult such as Jeremiah 7 and 26. Like Gottwald, Albrektson recognizes some of Judah's faults, yet he does not seem to believe them as grave as does the book of Jeremiah. Or perhaps he simply does not distinguish sufficiently between the righteous and wicked sufferer. Regardless, more precision would aid the analysis.

Albrektson makes a brief comment that—if fleshed out—would aid his analysis of Lamentations within Old Testament theology. He states that the speaker in Lam 3:40–42 likely echoes Deut 30:2, having already alluded to the consequences for covenant breaking found in Deut 28:15–68 in Lam 3:38. Deut 30:1–10 promises that even after judgment falls the people will return to Yhwh and find forgiveness. Though they have brought judgment on themselves by consistent covenant breaking, they can nonetheless receive pardon in due course. Ps 106:40–48, Dan 9:1–19, and Neh 9:1–38 include prayers with this type of promise in mind. This possibility of renewal after judgment links the Law to the Zion emphasis in the Prophets and Writings, as well as to the hopeful passages related to the Day of Yhwh in Amos 9:1–15, Zeph 3:8–20 and elsewhere. Attention to these linkages would also aid Albrektson's analysis of the basis of future hope in Lamentations.

Albrektson's contribution is considerable. He suggests possibilities that pave the way for other treatments of theodicy in Lamentations and of other theological issues as well. Indeed, his careful textual work, detailed canonical discussions, and fairness when treating other scholars' writings provides an example that those of us who write today do well to emulate. His conclusions invite others to build upon his foundations.

*Lamentations as Expression of Pain (1990–99)*

In his influential 1990 monograph, published in English in 1994 as *Lamentations: Issues and Interpretation*, Claus Westermann writes that the majority of treatments of Lamentations' theology could be summarized in two positions: the book states why the nation suffered and how that suffering may end.[15] He goes on to note that a minority of

---

14. Ibid., 239.

15. Westermann, *Lamentations*, 76. German original: *Die Klagelieder: Forschungsgeschichte und Auslegung* (Neukirchen-Vluyn: Neukirchener Verlag, 1990). He cites as a significant exception to these two categories Re'emi's "The Theology of Hope."

commentators focus on "the immediate impression which the text makes," believing that the author (or authors) of Lamentations write to express pain at the end of a recent horrible experience.[16] In response, Westermann argued that, with the possible exception of Lam 3:26–41, the book offers no explanatory or admonitory function, thereby disagreeing with the majority position.[17] He also disagrees with the minority position, finding that it implies there was no intent in the writing and passing down of Lamentations other than to report what the generation who experienced the fall of Jerusalem in 587 BCE felt.[18]

Westermann's solution to the matter is to offer a nuanced approach to Lamentations' theology. On the one hand, Westermann insists that at least Lamentations 1, 2, 4, and 5 must be read as laments by the people of God written shortly after the fall of 587 BCE, but not read as a means to another goal, such as determining why Jerusalem's people suffered as they did. Only by treating the poems as historical expressions can lament be taken seriously as a form the church should use today.[19] When one takes the book seriously in this manner, one sees that the book must first be read as an expression of grief that is more about survival than about theodicy.[20] On the other hand, taking the theme of survival seriously leads to theological reflection on the goodness of God's nature and on how one may learn from suffering. One's survival resides in Yhwh's goodness. As a lament, the book serves in the liturgy of survivors who worship Yhwh.[21]

As will become evident in the following paragraphs, Westermann's comments are sufficiently subtle to be taken in a variety of directions by subsequent authors. Some interpreters focus on his statements regarding the original audience. Others focus upon lament as a liturgical necessity for the church. Others build on his comments about expressing grief and striving for survival. Others expand his statements about God's nature. Still others interact with varying degrees of success with all of these subjects. Regardless of the responses, Westermann's volume marks a watershed in Lamentations research.

Renkema appreciates Westermann's desire to reclaim the lament as a legitimate form of prayer. But he also thinks that Westermann overemphasizes the original form of the book as immediate expressions of pain and prayer. This overemphasis "prevents him from seeing what actually happened: not distress followed by lament-prayer—as was usually the case—but distress followed by disillusionment!"[22] This disillusionment stemmed from their surprise and outrage at the punishment they received and what they thought they would receive. This difference between expectation and reality caused the people to question what they thought they knew about Yhwh's character.[23] Yet their beliefs about Yhwh's past redemptive deeds and power over all nations provided a frame-

---

16. Westermann, *Lamentations*, 77.
17. Ibid., 78.
18. Ibid.
19. Ibid., 76–80; 106–220.
20. Ibid., 81.
21. Ibid., 221–35.
22. Renkema, *Lamentations*, 60.
23. Ibid., 62.

work for a theology of hope.[24] These beliefs, tested by great adversity, are best revealed in Lam 3, where theology and reality meet as clearly as anywhere in the book.[25] Overall Renkema accepts Westermann's premise about the value of lament, yet disagrees with his conclusions on the original audience's reaction to what they endured.

It should also be noted that Renkema's treatment of the acrostic format of the book aids theological analysis indirectly. Since interpreters tend to base their theological treatments of Lamentations on viewing the book as five separate poems, on treating a specific portion of the book, or on examining the book as a whole, Renkema's insistence on reading the book *as a whole* is important. He demonstrates that the book does not simply consist of four acrostic poems (Lamentations 1–4) and one acrostic-like poem of twenty-two lines (Lamentations 5). Rather the book displays interfacing connections between verses within each poem and across poems. Thus, for instance, catchwords occur in 1:1 and 1:22, in 1:2 and 1:21, and so forth, as well as in 1:1, 2:1, 3:1 and so forth.[26] Thus, in its canonical form the book is presented as an intricately interconnected whole. It is therefore quite in keeping with the book's form to read all five poems *as a book*.

Both Westermann and Renkema make significant contributions to the discussion. Westermann's emphasis on the lament as tool of expressing pain and tool of coming to YHWH moves beyond theodicy issues without minimizing or bypassing them. Renkema's analysis of Judah's disillusionment refines previous understandings of Judah's dismay, which tended to simply deal with innocence and guilt. Both writers testify to the book's literary value and its theological vibrancy for today. Less positively, they may well press the limits of what one can really know about the book's historical background, a point Provan makes independently of Westermann and Renkema's work about other writers who do much the same thing.[27] Nonetheless, they rightly try to anchor their literary comments in actual history and actual historical literary forms.

*Lamentations as Survival, Dialogic, and Protest Literature (2000–Present)*

Recent writers on Lamentations' theology build on older methods and discussions and pursue new directions. They take on board the seminal works on theodicy Gottwald and Albrektson produced. The matter of why YHWH acted as he did remains important. They also retain the interest Westermann, Renkema, Provan, and others show in the literary form of lament and how it expresses pain and asks for renewed relationship with YHWH. Some of these experts have used literary and historical analyses to find new ways to appropriate Lamentations' message for today.[28] Yet others moved away from these older text-based analyses to a type of audience-oriented literary analysis that encourages responding to the text with grief, defiance, or outrage regardless of what the book's author intended or how the book's initial audiences utilized it. Dialogue about survival strate-

24. Ibid., 66–69.
25. Ibid., 70.
26. Ibid., 72–79.
27. Ibid., 15.
28. See, for example, Berlin, *Lamentations*.

gies, discussions about protesting divine activity, and understanding how to deal with a tragic situation are vital subjects of interest.

In his influential monograph Tod Linafelt takes up Westermann's "brief aside" that survival is the main issue in Lamentations and makes this observation the focus of his analysis of Lamentations and the book's reception by later writers.[29] He states that readers need "strategies for surviving the book's harsh and violent, as well as theologically challenging, images and language."[30] To help readers achieve this aim he departs from earlier scholars' focus on Lamentations 3 as the center of the book's theology. Instead, he concentrates on Lamentations 1–2, for he believes that female characters have not received sufficient treatment in biblical studies and that these poems best illustrate the centrality of "survival" in Lamentations.[31] He also stresses complaints by Zion and the absence of any response from Yhwh. Therefore, he treats Lamentations as a book about coping with the loss of divine presence more than as a book about recovering divine presence.

He argues that the survival of Zion's children is a particularly vital subject in Lamentations 1–2, and concludes that pleas for and protests about the conditions of these children, like all other pleas and protests in the book, go unanswered. Thus, for them to survive the children must live on in the afterlife of the book of Lamentations.[32] Linafelt then notes several biblical, ancient non-biblical, and recent witnesses to Lamentations' survival as literature and the concomitant survival of the book's children.[33] He believes these analyses demonstrate the enduring value of Lamentations for a variety of contexts and suggest that more detailed and informed literary analyses of Lamentations are possible and desirable.[34]

Kathleen O'Connor emphasizes the protest and dialogue motifs more than Linafelt. In fact, she writes at some length about "the abusing God," before moving on to more positive comments about Yhwh's character.[35] She claims both good and bad summations of Yhwh's character can be seen in Lamentations because the book offers a "chorus of contradictions" about him that include assertions of his goodness and his willingness to torture and abuse human beings through violence.[36] Given how hard it is to deal with these conflicting images, O'Connor believes that some readers simply ignore divine violence, or deem Yhwh both loving and abusive yet beyond the bounds of justice due to divine sovereignty.[37]

She charts a different path. She reads Lamentations as a book whose power as God's word comes from the community as it dialogues about the book's meaning in our world.

29. Linafelt, *Surviving Lamentations*, 18. See Westermann, *Lamentations*, 81.
30. Linafelt, *Surviving Lamentations*, 18.
31. Ibid., 17–18.
32. Ibid., 61.
33. Ibid., 62–143.
34. See Linafelt's comments in "Surviving Lamentations (one More Time)," 57.
35. O'Connor, *Lamentations and the Tears of the World*, 110–23.
36. Ibid., 111–13.
37. Ibid., 116–19.

## GREAT IS THY FAITHFULNESS?

Here conflicting views find as much harmony and meaning as possible.[38] She believes Lamentations models this communitarian process in its offering of different views of Yhwh. She concludes that Lam 3:33 leaves readers with the hope that God does not judge "from his heart," so she agrees with Gottwald's assessment that this passage contains a major theological tenet of the book.[39]

She finds great hope in this text, for it indicates to her that the "God who does not afflict or grieve willingly may be a God who cannot alter the forces at work in the world. To this possibility I cling as to a life raft upon a turbulent sea. For the time being I look to the God who suffers with the grieved and afflicted, a God whose power and sovereignty are not compromised by human suffering because God cannot prevent it."[40]

She hopes "God's silence veils God's innocence rather than reveals divine calculated destruction. I want it to be so."[41] Indeed, she finds that Lamentations can provide a venue for impassioned prayer,[42] and notes that other biblical passages—most notably Isaiah 40–55—offer a portrait of Yhwh as the comforting God, thereby providing the answer to the protests found in Lamentations.[43] Protest against Yhwh can recede, then, but only if a biblical writer within the ancient community or a current community or a person within it chooses to take this path.

Like O'Connor, Dobbs-Allsopp emphasizes the protest element in Lamentations, yet stops short of declaring Yhwh's character completely suspect. He takes great interest in the subject of violence as it relates to Yhwh. He admits that the ultimate reason for Yhwh's use of violence remains a mystery, yet emphasizes that violence is clearly part of the Bible's witness about God, with Jesus' crucifixion being the chief example of this violence. Readers need to confront this violent streak in God so they can confront it in themselves.[44] He notes that "the complaints of Zion [Lam 1:13–15, 20–22] and the man [Lam 3:1–18], are leveled as accusations, protests against the reality of . . . violation of human bodily integrity, and therefore ultimately serve to delegitimize the violence that so routinely seems to afflict human lives."[45]

Like Linafelt, Dobbs-Allsopp believes that hope resides in the possibility of survival. This survival finds significance in its understanding of the good that each person does in community within the context of harsh conditions.[46] Like O'Connor he finds Lam 3:19–24, 25–39 significant markers of future hope related to Yhwh, but he rightly cautions against using these verses to trivialize terrible events.[47] The book's "theodic and antitheodic poles" make such trivialization impossible. He concludes, "But whether

---

38. Ibid., 121. On this point see also her article "Voices Arguing About Meaning."
39. O'Connor, "Voices," 122.
40. Ibid., 122.
41. Ibid.
42. Ibid., 124–36.
43. Ibid., 137–47.
44. Dobbs-Allsopp, *Lamentations*, 44–45.
45. Ibid., 46.
46. Ibid., 46–47.
47. Ibid., 48.

theodic or antitheodic, hope in Lamentations has but one object, God, and one desire, to see suffering relieved."[48] Thus, he agrees with Jon Levenson that we should follow the book's lead and pray that God would blast away suffering not explain it away.[49] As with O'Connor, he believes that protest can aid understanding of life, yet the key to finding this understanding lies in the ultimate goodness that can be found in a relationship with God and in serving others in a sometimes terribly harsh world.

Carleen Mandolfo agrees with O'Connor and Dobbs-Allsopp that it is important to read Lamentations as a series of differing statements about Jerusalem's situation, as a document providing evidence of divine violence, as a text that offers an unusual opportunity to discuss women characters in the Bible, and as a statement of protest against what Yhwh has done in the world. But she presses yet farther in some of these directions than earlier writers. Using a literary-philosophical methodology taken from Mikhail Bakhtin and Martin Buber respectively,[50] she presents a dialogic hermeneutic that seeks to produce a dialogic theology that will to some extent correct previous approaches to Lamentations. More specifically, since she believes that many earlier treatments of the book accept at face value the prophets' view of Jerusalem as a straying spouse rather than hearing Jerusalem's side of the marital story, and many earlier treatments also take Yhwh's word as final on all matters, she wishes to produce a dialogic approach that decolonizes the text, dethrones Yhwh as final arbiter of all moral issues, and undercuts views of biblical authority that justify divine violence.[51]

To achieve her stated goals, Mandolfo focuses on the Yhwh-Jerusalem marital motif, with an admitted preference for siding with the latter party as a means of correcting past interpretative authoritarianism.[52] She chooses the prophets' comments on the Yhwh-Jerusalem relationship as one pole and Jerusalem's speeches in Lamentations 1–2 as another. She selects these texts not to establish historical dependence, but because "in canonical and literary terms the texts themselves demand them, and because I think others' readings of these texts will be enriched by these associations."[53]

Reading these texts as differing voices allows her to propose a "dialogic theology" that consists of certain key components. First, it is a theology that "goes beyond description to suggest that God is mutable and in process, as are we—that we can author God as surely as he can author us."[54] Second, it is a theology that demands that God be held as accountable as people. She explains, "A dialogic theology thus implies the radical notion that sometimes humans can and must be better than God by calling him into account; and it carries the expectation that God will hear and make the necessary adjustments, but without compromising his own integrity."[55] Thus, divine transcendence is main-

---

48. Ibid., 48.
49. Ibid.
50. Mandolfo, *Daughter Zion*, 1–2.
51. Ibid., 2–6.
52. Ibid., 9.
53. Ibid., 10.
54. Ibid., 20.
55. Ibid., 21.

tained, yet reciprocity of relationship can occur.[56] Third, it rejects divine omnipotence, for affirming God's omnipotence sets up binary distinctions between Yhwh and human beings, thereby leading to violence.[57] Fourth, it treats the Bible as sacred in the sense that it establishes texts that aid in negotiation between God and people. Fifth, it does not embrace a relativistic view of God. Rather, it embraces a "fully relational god."[58] Because of its relational and negotiating nature, marriage provides an excellent metaphor for describing human relationships with the god Mandolfo conceives.[59]

Mandolfo chooses and analyzes several texts she considers representative of "the construction of daughter Zion in the prophets."[60] These texts include passages that indeed paint Zion in a rather unsavory light, such as Ezekiel 16 and 23, Jeremiah 2–3, and Jer 13:20–27. She then presents laments from Psalms and Lamentations 1–2 as counter-testimony from Zion that undercuts the prophetic texts.[61] It is striking that she does not enter any of the most empathetic passages from Jeremiah, for example those in which the prophet risks his own relationship with Yhwh to defend and intercede for the people, as he does repeatedly in Jeremiah 1–20 (see discussion below). Neither does she accept the fact that Zion may simply be a terrible spouse, though she does state that Zion must be accountable for her actions, as must Yhwh.[62]

But Mandolfo admits that the type of interpretation she offers in this monograph does not really seek such balance or objectivity. As she explains, "It is not a claim for 'objective' reading, quite the opposite. It is an intentional reading that focuses on nondominant voices and ideologies. Nondominant does not mean 'right' or 'better'; it means lacking power and authority. My reading expressly chooses to try to redress the imbalances."[63] And she clearly wishes to shift the balance of power more to the human side, even if doing so risks judging in favor of the wrong party in the relationship.

Mandolfo believes that her approach to Lamentations will lead to positive results. It will lead to Bible readers having the balanced relational material needed for a solid divine-human marriage. Its emphasis on reading the Bible as presenting differing perspectives fosters negotiation in life's darkest hours. It allows for divine change and growth while keeping humans humble without forcing them to bow to an all-knowing and all-powerful God, something many people do not wish to do today.

Responding to these recent approaches is not easy given the breadth of what these experts have argued, but a few preliminary positive and negative remarks are appropriate at this point. In my opinion these works have at least five strengths. First, they exhibit that their writers care deeply about the human condition. I am particularly impressed by O'Connor's work in this regard. Second, they deepen our understanding of bibli-

---

56. Ibid., 21.
57. Ibid.
58. Ibid., 22. The lower case 'g' is original to her statement.
59. Ibid., 23–28.
60. Ibid., 29–54.
61. Ibid., 55–101.
62. Ibid., 101, 119.
63. Ibid., 119.

cal characters, particularly female ones. Third, they try to blend historical and literary approaches, with a particular interest in genre and audience. Fourth, they challenge traditional scholars to understand and respond to the current unrest with what people consider God to be doing in the world. Fifth, they rightly emphasize the importance of understanding Lamentations within the canon.

Despite these strengths, in my opinion, these works also have several weaknesses.

1. First, they treat all suffering and sufferers virtually the same. That is, they do not distinguish between sufferers who have not done anything at all to bring suffering upon themselves and those who do. As I will discuss below, not all sufferers are like Job or Tamar. Lack of differentiation in this element (and others, see below) of the book can lead to a blurring of its literary strategies and theological purposes, and thus contribute ultimately to the loss of the book's primary usefulness for today.

2. Second, and related to the first point, they do not distinguish between types of violence. Almost every person believes in some uses of violence. Divine or any other sort of violence may or may not be wicked depending on context.

3. Third, and related to points one and two, they do not treat the diversity within the lament genre with sufficient specificity. By that I mean they tend to treat all lament as if there is no difference between laments of the innocent, or those who claim to be innocent at least, and penitential laments.

4. Fourth, Mandolfo and Linafelt treat Lamentations 1–2 in relative isolation from the rest of the book. One can argue that Lamentations 3 has been treated as if it is the whole of Lamentations' theology, but that does not mean it or chapters 3–5 should be treated cursorily, if at all.

5. Fifth, these works' canonical treatments sometimes pit parts of a larger plot against one another. Pitting hopeful themes in the canon against less hopeful ones sometimes makes as little literary sense as pitting the dismal portion of a comedic plot against its positive ending.

6. Sixth, despite all their best efforts, O'Connor and Mandolfo diminish the biblical portrayal of God to the extent that Mandolfo is correct to switch from writing about God to writing about god. A transcendent, yet slightly better than human god is not likely to dry the tears of the world any more than a domineering harsh judge will. Regardless, the question is what the text yields, not which type of God/god today's audience wants, and the text offers a balanced view of Yhwh that emphasizes justice for the wicked alongside the possibility of grace for the wicked and hope for the faithful.

## A UNITARY LITERARY-THEOLOGICAL READING OF LAMENTATIONS

As noted above, in the past two decades there has been a growing interest in using literary analysis as a methodological basis for making theological assertions from Lamentations.

The literary methods deployed are somewhat eclectic, with some writers using traditional form-critical analysis and others adopting audience-driven methodologies.

What is needed at present, it seems to me, is an approach that takes the totality of Lamentations as well as the totality of the canon into consideration in a way that avoids misrepresenting key characters and avoids oversimplifying suffering and other key themes. It should be as generous as possible to all the book's characters, and it should pay particular attention to the Jerusalem character. It should take notice of how the book's message addresses life now. As a small down payment on this program, this section will examine the book's characterization of Jerusalem in light of Lamentations' historical, canonical, and discrete-book settings to determine if recent characterizations of Jerusalem fit that evidence. It will also analyze briefly the book's genre and rhetorical progression/plot to determine what themes emerge from the book's form and substance. Hopefully, this analysis will lead to relevant and holistic theological observations in the following section of the chapter.[64]

*Jerusalem's Characterization in Historical, Canonical, and Discrete-Book Setting*

One of the fundamental problems with Gottwald's understanding of theodicy as well as the survival-protest readings of Linafelt, Mandolfo, and O'Connor is their handling of the composite character of Jerusalem. Specifically, they seem to interpret Jerusalem's characterization as interpreters normally treat innocent sufferers who appear in the Bible: persons such as Dinah, Joseph, Tamar, Ruth, Naomi, and Esther. This decision has the effect of inverting the book's primary theological import. A brief survey of the book's historical, canonical, and discrete-book settings may help put the book and its characters in clearer perspective. Since Mandolfo, O'Connor, and Linafelt rightly emphasize the centrality of the Jerusalem-Yhwh relationship, what follows highlights these characters.

Viewed from a historical-political perspective it is hard to consider Jerusalem an *innocent* sufferer. Indeed, through the years Jerusalem probably seemed at least as politically fickle to many of its allies as it seemed spiritually fickle to Yhwh and the prophets. By the time Jerusalem fell in 587 BCE, the city, as representative of Judah's government, had supported the policies of large, powerful nations such as Assyria, Babylon, and Egypt depending on whether doing so was politically beneficial to Israel. This changing of allegiances realigned Jerusalem's political relationships with smaller regional neighbors such as Moab, Ammon, and Edom. The fact of the city's destruction indicates that Jerusalem played a dangerous political game and lost that game, having angered allies and deadly foes in the process. Perhaps it was a game that had to be played. Political maneuvering is a way of life in most cultures. But it was certainly neither played the way the prophets advised nor how Babylon, to whom Judah had formerly sworn loyalty, thought it ought to be played.

Both Jerusalem and her allies, who are dubbed Jerusalem's "lovers" Lam 1:19, used one another as they felt was necessary in the decades-long battle for individual national

---

64. For examples of this type of whole canon thematic theology, see Hafemann and House, eds., *Central Themes in Biblical Theology*.

autonomy in the ancient world. Of course, Jerusalem's metaphorical "lovers" fled when Babylon invaded Judah: "I cried out to my lovers; they played me false" (Lam 1:19a). It is hard to blame them. Jerusalem would have done the same to them in this era. Zedekiah was no Josiah on this point (see 2 Kgs 23:28–30).

Politically speaking, then, Jerusalem was hardly an innocent victim of broken treaties and false promises. Like other nations, Judah kept or broke treaties according to circumstances. By international political standards these traits did not make Jerusalem particularly wicked in this era. They simply made her like those around her. By the Mosaic covenant's standards of loyalty to Yhwh and to his prophets, however, these traits look very troubling indeed.

What Jerusalem suffers at the hands of Babylon is terrible and tragic because Jerusalem was once high and is now brought low, and because her children and other innocents have suffered as a result of policies they did not make, not because as a whole she was a political neophyte caught unaware. These observations drawn from history indicate that the book does not ask for sympathy for an innocent bystander, but for a fallen, sometimes crafty player of international politics. As I will argue below, this fact means that readers are asked to care for a type of person or nation many of us judge harshly when we see the evening news reports or read a newspaper. It means readers of Lamentations are asked to believe that Yhwh is a God who receives such characters, who answers these characters' prayers for outrageous demonstrations of grace.

Canonically speaking Jerusalem, as portrayed in Lamentations, is a diversely drawn character, but hardly an innocent one, though many of her citizens are. To reiterate an earlier point, she is not represented like Abel, Dinah, Joseph, Israel during the pre-exodus Egypt years, Jephthah's daughter, Tamar, Uriah the Hittite, Jeremiah, Job, Ruth, Naomi, Esther, or Zechariah. Jerusalem is not then, like a flawed human who certainly did not deserve and/or could not have anticipated what would happen to her. As the writers surveyed above have noted, the Law (Leviticus 26; Deuteronomy 27–28), Prophets (Judges 1–2; 2 Kings 17; Isaiah 1–6; Jeremiah 1–20; etc.), and Writings (Psalms 89; 104–6; Dan 9:1–20; Neh 9:1–37) portray Jerusalem more negatively than the characters just listed. They depict this representative/collective character as a beloved one, yet a beloved one who refused to heed warnings, who broke promises to Yhwh and others, and who thereby put herself and her innocent children—her citizens—in grave danger. She has been a bad mother and a bad wife at this stage of her life. While false accusations against women were made in ancient times[65] and continue to be made today, such is not the depiction here. But her story is not yet complete. Her characterization may change yet again.

In Mandolfo's strategy of pitting Jerusalem against the prophets, it is important to recall the prophets' compassion for Jerusalem. Isaiah 22:1–8; Hos 1:1—3:5; 11:1–9; Amos 7:1–6; Joel 2:12–17; and Hab 1:2—2:1 show great concern for Jerusalem/Judah/Israel. These prophets ask Yhwh to avert disaster or even to explain why disaster must come on his beloved and how long this disaster must last. For example, citing Exod 34:6–7, Joel 2:12–17 relies on Yhwh's kindness and justice as the basis of hope in the aversion of

---

65. At least two passages in the Law know such accusations occur and legislate ways for the woman and her family to refute such claims and get justice on the man making them (Num 5:11–31; Deut 22:13–21).

divine judgment. Moving beyond Joel, the sense of these other passages is that Yhwh has not judged for a very long time in hopes that Israel will return to her previous behavior as a faithful marriage partner, and these writers hope for still more time. The harsh characterization of Jerusalem in other prophetic texts flagged by Mandolfo (especially those in Ezekiel 16, 20, and 23) which I consider the most jarring ones, must be mediated by these prophetic voices that show great care and concern for Jerusalem.

In my estimation, no prophet wrestles with Yhwh's decision to punish Judah/Jerusalem more than Jeremiah. In fact, he boldly prays for Jerusalem even after being told not to do so (Jer 11:14; 14:11; 15:1–2), thus putting his own close relationship with Yhwh at risk. He makes excuses for her actions (Jer 4:10; 8:14–20; 14:13–14) and prays for her in ways that parallel Lamentations 1–2 (Jer 15:15–18; 16:10–13; etc.). Like other prophets he calls for repentance in no uncertain terms. Yet his love for Jerusalem must not be diminished or read over against his warnings, exhibited in characterization of Jerusalem in other portions of the book. Given the hopeful passages about Jerusalem's future in Jeremiah 30–33, Yhwh's love for Jerusalem is as strong as Jeremiah's concern for Jerusalem.

One other canonical matter associated with deuteronomistic theology and Day of Yhwh theology requires notice. Considering this matter may keep one from concluding too quickly that the preceding two paragraphs simply confirm the differing voices approach to canonical reading. As was suggested in the comments on Albrektson's connecting of deuteronomistic and Zion theology, it is important to include passages such as Lev 26:44–45 and Deut 30:1–10 in analyses that highlight these interconnected themes. After all, throughout the canon there is a consistent pattern of renewal following judgment based on a return to Yhwh by the formerly wicked and based on the faithful, who have suffered because of the sins of others, waiting on Yhwh to deal with the wicked. The book of Judges may offer the most repeated examples of divine action along these lines, but Isa 1–12, Zeph 3:6–20, Hos 11:1–19; 14:1–9, Ps 107:1–3 (esp. when read in light of Pss 104–6), Dan 9:1–19, Neh 9:1–38, and 2 Chronicles 36 indicate this pattern as well.

In other words, punishment and renewal are not competing voices. They are the penultimate and ultimate portions of a single plot. What Lamentations probes more specifically than perhaps any other biblical book or portion of a book is how such renewal occurs for both those who have brought down the nation and those who have suffered at the hands of their parents and their leaders. Lamentations plumbs the depths of how people who deserve no grace may receive it anyway and how those who never brought suffering on themselves because of their own sin, but instead suffered because of the normal horrible circumstances of life such as being the child of a neglectful parent and the citizen of a fallen kingdom, may find peace and relief. Lamentations explores how it becomes possible for renewal to follow destruction and what that process looks like at a specific point in time.

As a book in its own right Lamentations itself affirms the historical and canonical data offered above. This observation is particularly true of the book's characterization of Jerusalem in chapters 1–2, the chapters Linafelt and Mandolfo highlight. Though the whole book contains material related to Jerusalem's characterization, at this point I will primarily survey chapters 1–2 and delay further comments on the rest of the book to the treatment of the book's rhetorical progression, or plot.

It is important to note that in the opening part of the poem (Lam 1:1–9a) the narrator shows sympathy for Jerusalem's situation even while stating her role in the catastrophe (Lamentations 1:8–9a), for he emphasizes her lack of anyone comforting her (Lam 1:2, 7c, 9a). He repeats this interest in her receiving comfort in Lam 1:17, and Jerusalem picks up this motif in Lam 1:16, 21. She agrees with the narrator that she has sinned greatly (Lam 1:18) and asserts that what she has endured is nothing less than the Day of Yhwh (Lam 1:21). No claims of innocence appear in this opening chapter.

The narrator continues the Day of Yhwh motif in Lam 2:1–10. Here he makes it equally clear that the Day of Yhwh has come (Lam 2:1–10, 17). The results are terrible, and they include massive suffering by children (Lam 2:11), which brings the narrator back to the theme of the need for comfort (Lam 2:13). When urged to plead for her children, Jerusalem does so, and as in Lam 1:22 asks that her enemies perish. Such relief from enemies would constitute having a comforter.

As is true in the opening chapter, no claims of innocence occur in Lam 2:1–22. But Jerusalem has asked for more than relief for herself, which is her main focus in Lam 1:20–22. She has asked for relief based on her concern for her children (Lam 2:20–22). She realizes that her actions and Yhwh's response to them have caused pain to those for whom she has been responsible. Self-awareness has led to a different sort of complaint and to praying for help. Thus, drawing on the canon's statements about renewal, what is at stake now is whether the conditions for the end of the Day of Yhwh as set forth in Deut 30:1–10 have been met. In other words, Jerusalem has sinned and been punished, but what remains to be seen is if the punishment is over and renewal is beginning.

To summarize, Lamentations 1–2 hardly treats Yhwh as a cosmic terrorist or abusive husband. Strong words are spoken about what has occurred, and the speakers recognize that Yhwh has brought the judgment he warned about for so long, but these comments are hardly the strongest in the Old Testament. One can find harsher things said about Yhwh in Jer 20:7–18 and Job 16:1–22, to name just two prominent examples. Rather, both speakers in Lamentations 1–2 push renewal as far perhaps as one can when innocence is not the issue and the process of renewed relationship is in its early stages. Both speakers seem to count on Yhwh's willingness to see and hear the prayers of one who admits to great wickedness.

This survey of the characterization of Jerusalem reveals a character in need. She has suffered greatly. She has seen the loss of her children. She has lost her comforters, her lovers. She has help in the form of the narrators, but to change her circumstances she must begin a painful journey back to the person she left, Yhwh. His strong, harsh reaction to her adultery and lack of care for her children no doubt could (the text does not say so) make her wonder if he will take her back or if she should risk a relationship with him again. She seems to believe, though, that Yhwh will take her back. She prays as if Yhwh will discount everything that has happened and begin afresh with her. She prays as if grace may naturally follow punishment in the days ahead.

# GREAT IS THY FAITHFULNESS?

## *Genre*

Clearly, the book's setting reveals that a unique situation exists: the Day that Yhwh threatened against Jerusalem has come. But the renewal that Moses and the prophets declare is possible after such judgment has not yet begun. This unusual "in-between-times" setting calls for an unusual literary approach, and the book delivers some of the most adaptive and innovative literature in the Bible. Its genre serves as an instrument for the needed bridge between the past and the future. Thus, Lamentations' genre has historical, canonical, and literary import for understanding the book's theology. It also provides more support for the theory proposed above that the book addresses a different sort of sufferer than the theodic and protest approaches to the book suggest.

Many scholars have discussed the ancient genre of lament and Lamentations' contribution to, and utilization of, that genre tradition. They have noted that the basic form of lament is as follows: address, description of a problem, recalling/reciting of Yhwh's great deeds in the past, and request for deliverance now. They note that statements of wishes about an enemy and a vow of praise often occur as well. They have observed that laments of persons claiming innocence often include statements about innocence and that laments of persons claiming guilt often include long descriptions of sin that an individual or group has committed. They recognize that a poem's setting often leads to an adaptation of the basic pattern of lament, thus creating what seem to be "mixed forms." They have particularly noted parallels between Lamentations and ancient laments over fallen cities (a generic convention that pre-dates Lamentations by several centuries), the presence of both individual and communal lament of the type found in Psalms and other parts of the Bible in the book, and the book's combining of acrostic structure and lament.[66] Thus, they have commented extensively on Lamentations as a hybrid form of lament written for a specific purpose. Yet they disagree on whether the book essentially expresses the prayers of innocent sufferers or the prayers of persons confessing their sins' role in what has happened to them.

For example, Nancy Lee has examined acrostic poems in the Psalter (Psalms 9–10; 25; 33; 34; 37; 38; 94; 111; 112; 119; and 145) in order to compare them to Lamentations.[67] She writes that these psalms "are heavily invested in the idea of retributive justice and accordingly defend God as 'just' or 'righteous'" and that they "reveal a tradition of singers or writers who composed songs espousing retributive justice, a theological 'order' hammered home by every letter (and line) of their acrostic form."[68] She asserts that unlike these psalms, Lamentations "presents dissident singers (and perhaps a dissident scribe/redactor) who in their rebelling against a simplistic retributive understanding of events . . . employ the acrostic structure to *invert* that order of justice," and she views the transposing of the letters *ayin* and *pe* in Lam 2:16–17 as evidence for this inversion.[69] She concludes that Lam 2:18 follows this inversion with the verb "cried out" rather than "was

---

66. For a brief summary of contributions, see House, *Lamentations*, 310–16.
67. See Lee, *The Singers of Lamentation* and Lee, "The Singers of Lamentations."
68. Lee, "The Singers of Lamentations," 43.
69. Ibid., 44.

righteous," when the latter would be expected, thereby indicating a protest against what YHWH has done.[70] This analysis provides insight into acrostic poetry in that it reveals characterization and imagery in poems similar to what one finds in Lamentations. Her treatment of the various speakers in Lamentations, Psalms, and Jeremiah are especially helpful.

Nonetheless, she does not distinguish sufficiently between the setting of the psalms listed and the setting of Lamentations. Most of the psalms noted deal with persons claiming not to deserve retributive justice or to have received it. Thus, the speakers state with confidence that they know there is another explanation for the suffering they have endured. As was noted above, no such claims of innocence appear in Lamentations 1–2. The very subtle potential protest Lee mentions is just as likely to be a poetic device that reflects the reversal of Judah's fortunes brought on by the Day of YHWH, which is the subject matter of Lam 2:16–17. Though she may be correct, it seems to me that the context is clear as it stands. The problem Lee faces is finding protest against retributive justice when that type of protest is simply not clearly present. As she rightly notes, Jeremiah includes strong protest against YHWH's sense of justice based on what he has endured, so it would not be unheard of for Jerusalem to do so if she believed she had been similarly mistreated.

Berlin and Albertz conclude that Lamentations is a unique literary type. Berlin observes that Lamentations has characteristics of a dirge for an individual, of laments over a fallen city, of Zion psalms, and of corporate laments. She believes that this combination of elements creates "the Jerusalem lament," a poem that mourns the death of positive Zion psalms as well as the fall of the city itself.[71] Similarly, Albertz argues that Lamentations is not like typical communal liturgical laments that lay claim to hope based on YHWH's past great acts on Israel's behalf.[72] Rather, Lamentations represents a genre alongside communal laments, one that is non-cultic in nature.[73] He suggests, "With all the foundations of Israel's previous relationship with God destroyed, there had to be a basic dialogue between Israel and YHWH before people could take part in public cultic lamentations. The texts of the book of Lamentations performed this function."[74]

While I do not agree with Albertz's comments about the non-cultic nature of Lamentations' original setting, he and Berlin are accurate in their decision that Lamentations represents a special literary type. They are correct that the connecting of various sorts of lament materials creates something not found elsewhere in the Bible. This genre allows speakers to lead Jerusalem towards reconciliation with YHWH, even as they themselves walk a similar path. This literary type allows both individual and corporate lament. It gives the fallen hope. In other words, it uniquely meets the needs of those who lived in Jerusalem between at least the fall of Jerusalem in 587 BCE and the early stirrings of renewal later in the century.

---

70. Ibid., 44–46.
71. Berlin, *Lamentations*, 22–30.
72. Albertz, *Israel in Exile*, 147–55.
73. Ibid., 155–58.
74. Ibid., 158.

Boda correctly notes that there are similarities and differences between Lamentations and the penitential poems found in Psalms.[75] He then argues that the book as a whole, with Lamentations 3 as a pivot text, provides for the exilic community a "trajectory for the emergence of penitential prayer in which pain is still expressed honestly before God by a sinful community but always in balance with confession and repentance."[76] The import of this opinion, he concludes, is that it helps interpreters see that the book is about divine grace, not solely or even primarily about expressing pain.[77] It also helps interpreters see that the book's genre contributes to this trajectory towards the grasping of grace. Boda's balanced approach allows readers to take both the elements of expressions of pain and statements about hope into account.

Boda's comments indicate that despite the diversity of lament materials in the book, the poems are basically penitential in nature. They are not the poems of one asking why such things have happened when the one praying has been righteous, as is the case in Psalms 3–5, 7 for example. Rather, as the preceding section indicates, these are poems of penitence in the vein of Psalms 6, 32, and 51. Thus, the expressions of pain, the people's complaints, are part of the penitential process. Their purpose is to aid renewal of relationship with Yhwh, which is something quite different than exclusively complaining for the purpose of shifting blame to Yhwh. As Renkema writes in a discussion of the governing verb of Lam 3:39 and its implications,

> A distinction needs to be made in Lamentations between complaints intended as an expression of prayer (to be found, for example, in 1:9c, 11c, 20–22; 2:20–22; 3:55–66; 5:1–22) and complaints which are an expression of dissension and defiance before Yhwh (cf. for example 3:1–18). Such defiance should not be understood as "lament" but would be more appropriately styled "murmuring," a translation which is supported by the only other occurrence of the verb in the OT: Num 11:2.[78]

In his opinion none of Lamentations' speakers simply "murmur." Rather, they all seek the renewal of relationship and subsequent reversal of fortunes they think forgiveness will bring.

If so, then how do these heart-wrenching descriptions of pain aid the restorative process? In penitential psalms these descriptions have several functions, but perhaps three are worth noting for the purposes of this discussion. First, such descriptions highlight the difficult situation the worshipper(s) faces and call forth useful sympathy in readers. Second, they allow the worshipper(s) to indicate that he or she understands that the harsh times have come as a thorough reaction to the worshipper's sins. In this way they take the place of the recollections of Yhwh's past positive acts in psalms relating the plight of innocent sufferers. Third, they help the worshipper(s) acknowledge total dependence on Yhwh for relief for those who have suffered as a result of the sins and

---

75. Boda, "The Priceless Gain of Penitence," 88–90.
76. Ibid., 98.
77. Ibid., 100.
78. Renkema, *Lamentations*, 61–62. Renkema translates this verb as "grumble/murmur" rather than "complain" or "lament." His point is that one laments in a particular way for a particular result. One murmurs simply to rebel against Yhwh, and it is this error that the speaker in Lam 3:39 warns against.

judgment in question. The canonical evidence is that Jerusalem would not turn to Yhwh until all other options have been exhausted. The descriptions of loss provide evidence that Jerusalem knows that all options have been exhausted and that she has nowhere else to turn. If so, then renewal may begin soon.

Given the literary diversity in Lamentations it remains hard to determine *the genre* of Lamentations. Yet it is possible to make some conclusions about its nature. First, its acrostic format imposes unity of structure and comprehensiveness of matter on the book. Second, the book is penitential, confessional, and purposeful in its movement from isolated sorrow to communal prayer. Third, the book is purposeful in its approach to renewing relationship between the people who have sinned and the God whom they expect to forgive them. This movement from sin to punishment to renewal is the plot of much of the Old Testament. Given these conclusions, perhaps it is best to consider Lamentations as "Jerusalem's Penitential Laments," for this term (or one like it) conveys the ones praying, their needs, and the person who can relieve the suffering he has sent due to their actions.

### *Rhetorical Progression/Plot*

Read as an interconnected linguistic whole that includes individual and corporate elements, as Renkema and the analysis offered above indicate is the most viable means of reading,[79] Lamentations relates an unfolding progression from silence and sorrow to communal speaking before Yhwh. The goal is a restored relationship between Yhwh and his beloved people, personified as Jerusalem. This progression mirrors the spiritual needs of the inhabitants of Jerusalem and Judah in light of the Babylonian debacle of 587 BCE. It also corresponds to the scant material we possess on how worship continued in the aftermath of Jerusalem's fall (see Jer 41:5) until the rebuilding of the temple in Haggai and Zechariah's time (c. 520–16 BCE). In Lamentations this progression occurs through the work of persons who aid Jerusalem and through her coming to terms with her need for Yhwh.

In the opening acrostic poem a descriptive narrator writing in the straightforward and sad tone also found in 2 Kings 17 and Jeremiah 39 shows sympathy for Jerusalem's plight (Lam 1:1). This narrator then notes her lack of comforters, in other words nations to deliver her, three times (Lam 1:2, 9, 17). She responds by twice mentioning the same lack of comforters (Lam 1:16, 21). This situation occurs because her former lovers/comforters (Lam 1:2, 19), her political allies, have fled, and because she has sinned greatly against Yhwh by fleeing from him (Lam 1:8–9, 14–16, 18–19). Both speakers conclude that Jerusalem has suffered a Day of Yhwh (Lam 1:12), and that this Day was announced as a warning long before it occurred (Lam 1:21). Both speakers nonetheless hope that Yhwh will yet be a comforter, for Jerusalem asks Yhwh to see her situation (Lam 1:9, 11, 20) and deal with her foes (Lam 1:22). This initial lamenting is penitent and insistent about divine aid. There is no protest of innocence. But there is hope for grace of the type mentioned in Lev 26:44–45, Deut 30:1–10, and in many Day of Yhwh texts (Isa

---

79. See Renkema, *Lamentations*, 72–79, and the analysis of setting and genre above.

2:1–22; Zeph 3:1–20; etc). There is hope that Yhwh may hear, see, and comfort Jerusalem again. They hope in this manner despite knowing Jerusalem cast off Yhwh in the manner Jerusalem's lovers cast her off.

In chapter 2, the speakers are more impassioned than before, but there is still no claim of innocence. As in Lam 1:12, 21 the speakers state they have experienced a Day of Yhwh (Lam 2:1, 22) despite Yhwh's previous warnings that the Day would come (Lam 2:17). In tones and language that remind one of Jeremiah the prophet-priest (see Jer 1:1),[80] the narrative voice mourns the massive destruction he views (Lam 2:1–10; see Jer 39–40). He weeps for the people (Lam 2:11–13; see Jer 8:18—9:3). He blames their troubles on false prophets (Lam 2:14; see Jer 23:9–40). He notes the shame of defeat (Lam 2:15–16), and, like a priest calling people to earnest prayer, exhorts Jerusalem to cry out to Yhwh (Lam 2:17–19). He fastens attention on an issue of justice—in this case the fate of helpless children—as Jeremiah once focused on the unfairness of his having to suffer because of the actions of the wicked (Lam 2:19; see Jer 11:18–23; 20:7–18). Jerusalem responds by again asking Yhwh to see her situation (Lam 2:20). She takes the advice given in Lam 2:19 and highlights the horrifying situation (Lam 2:20–22). She stresses the suffering endured by all her children, regardless of their age or class. Unlike Jeremiah, who stresses his own innocence when persecuted (Jer 12:1–6), she prays for them without claiming innocence on her part.

Indeed, based on 1:20–21, in 2:20–22, she protests their ongoing suffering for her mistakes. She asks that the suffering she has caused cease. She has come to see what her deeds have done and wants punishment's circle of pain to end. This may be her finest moment, for she takes responsibility for her own actions and intercedes for others.

Lamentations 3 offers the statements of one speaker, who identifies himself simply as "the man who has seen affliction" (Lam 3:1). His first-person testimony parallels speeches by individuals in Job, Proverbs, and Ecclesiastes. Perhaps his wisdom-oriented confession stands in contrast to the unhelpful wise men Jeremiah mentions (see Jer 8:8–10). He joins the narrators of chapters 1–2 as one trying to aid Jerusalem's restoration of relationship with Yhwh. But unlike the other narrators he admits to sin (Lam 3:1–18), as Jerusalem has already done. Yhwh has punished him, just as he has punished Jerusalem. The result was that he lost hope for a time, just as Jerusalem has lost hope (Lam 3:18).

At this low point of despair the speaker took theological stock. He recalled that Yhwh's covenant-based love and mercy are renewed every morning (Lam 3:19–22). This active linking of his situation to the Lord's characteristics (found particularly in Exod 34:6–7)[81] reminded him that Yhwh's faithfulness is great, which led him to hope again based on the fact that Yhwh is his "portion" (see Num 18:20) in life (Lam 3:23–24). He then recalled that Yhwh is good to those who wait for him (see Ps 37:1–11), so he accepted his situation quietly (Lam 3:25–30), a progression of thought also found in Ps 73:1–26. He concluded that Yhwh does not judge "from his heart" (Lam 3:33), so he waits for justice to be restored (Lam 3:31–39).

---

80. For an excellent treatment of the similarities between Jeremiah and this speaker, see Lee, *The Singers of Lamentation*, 132–62.

81. See House, "God's Character and the Wholeness of Scripture."

With these notions in place, he calls on his fellow sufferers to return to Yhwh and to cry out until Yhwh sees their situation in light of their change of heart (Lam 3:40–51). He confesses that Yhwh has so heard and acted in the past, and he asks Yhwh to punish his foes now (Lam 3:52–66). Thus, he embraces Jerusalem's confessions of sin and concludes his poem with the same sentiments as Lam 1:20–22 in the same strong emotional language as Lam 2:20–22.

This central poem has stated more about Yhwh's character and Jerusalem's situation than its predecessors. But like his predecessors this speaker has not spoken with certainty that relief is now on the way. Lamentations 4 settles this matter. This narrator is prophetic, for he asserts that Zion's punishment has been completed, and that of Jerusalem's enemies, embodied here in Edom, is about to begin (Lam 4:22). The prayers of Lam 1:20–22; 2:20–22; and 3:52–66 have begun to be answered. Before making this conclusive statement the narrator gives as bleak a description of Jerusalem's present as the book offers (Lam 4:1–16). Jerusalem affirms the accuracy of the description (Lam 4:17–20) before the actual prediction is given (Lam 4:21–22). Both the narrator and Jerusalem speak of Yhwh, the former to state that divine wrath stands behind Jerusalem's woes (Lam 4:11, 16), the latter to note that "Yhwh's anointed," the Davidic heir, has gone into captivity (Lam 4:20). The end of judgment unveils the possibility of renewal, just as Deut 30:1–10 states. The end of judgment signals the renewal of relationship and eventual reversal of fortunes may begin. All the people may share the hope the speaker of Lam 3:19–24 has found.

Lamentations 5 presents all the book's speakers addressing Yhwh together, corporately. With the time of punishment over (Lam 4:22) the people can take the wisdom speaker's advice and return as one to Yhwh (Lam 3:40–42). They can begin the long road to recovery. In this communal lament, the group asks Yhwh to remember them (Lam 5:1), to see what they have suffered (Lam 5:2–18) because of their sins (Lam 5:16), and to restore them even though he has been justifiably angry over what they have done (Lam 5:19–22).[82] The community admits as much about their sins as did the individuals who have spoken in the previous chapters. They also ask for as much, for they ask for renewal of relationship and reversal of fortunes despite what they have done.

As has already been noted, such renewal after this type of sin is possible according to the canonical witness and the testimony of the narrators in Lamentations. They know the canonical emphases of sin, punishment, and renewal found in passages like Lev 26:44–45, Deut 30:1–10, and Isa 6–12. They are probing to find if this renewal can begin. They seek grace beyond their sin and sorrow. Thus, the book ends with the whole community reaching out to Yhwh, who has promised through Moses and the prophets to take them back even though they do not claim to merit such favor. In short, they pray that new acts of grace will remove the results of old acts of unfaithfulness.

This analysis of the book's plot leads to three basic conclusions. First, Jerusalem is not portrayed as an innocent victim. Second, nonetheless, she is not treated as a despicable woman who must be tossed on the dustbin of life. Her change in behavior from

---

82. For a discussion of options concerning the translation and interpretation of the book's last two verses and a defense of this reading, see House, *Lamentations*, 470–72.

faithful one to unfaithful one—and concomitant tragic outcomes associated with such transformation—are to be mourned. Her comfort matters to the narrator and her restoration is integral to the book. Third, Yhwh is willing to hear and restore. This willingness is part of the biblical plot in such circumstances. It seems hard for the characters in Lamentations to know *when* such renewal may begin, but their hopes are all pinned on the plot taking shape. Only a resolute God could punish one so beloved after delaying judgment so long, and only a forgiving God could take such a spouse back again.

### *Theological Synthesis: Outrageous Demonstrations of Divine Grace*

Clearly, there has been a great deal of fine work done on Lamentations' artistry and theology. Since much of this work has dealt with Lamentations as a discrete book there is room for fresh synthetic treatments of the book as part of the whole Bible. In particular, I believe that the book needs to be read in light of two passages, Exod 34:6–7 and Gen 1–3, that probe Yhwh's nature and his relationship with human beings. Exodus 34:6–7 reveals that Yhwh is inherently both forgiving and unwilling to clear the guilty at the same time. Genesis 1–3 reveals human beings as made in God's image and capable of both great acts of good and great acts of wickedness at the same time. Both passages express Yhwh's willingness to forgive human beings and begin afresh with them, yet also indicate that this grace cannot be taken for granted. Yhwh dispenses justice, but he also offers outrageous demonstrations of divine grace for those who have sinned. Belief in such grace spurs the prayers of the characters in Lamentations. They are aware of their sin and the severity of their punishment, which makes their prayers for renewal all that much more dependent on Yhwh's grace.

Lamentations reveals profound belief in Yhwh's self-description in Exod 34:6–7: "Yhwh, Yhwh, a God compassionate and gracious, slow to anger, and full of covenant-type[83] mercy and faithfulness, keeping covenant-type mercy for thousands [of generations], forgiving iniquity and transgression and sin, but who will by no means clear the guilty, visiting the iniquity of fathers unto sons, even unto the sons of the sons unto the third even unto the fourth [generation]." The two key elements of this description—Yhwh's mercy regarding sinners and his ultimate unwillingness to affirm sin—are at the heart of all Biblical Theology.[84] Given common misunderstandings of the verse just quoted, it is important to note that in the context of Exodus and of this passage the sons mentioned are sons who have sinned in the manner of their fathers.[85]

When the speakers in Lamentations affirm that their sins have brought disaster they are recalling the fact that Yhwh does not clear the guilty. They echo the confession of Nah 1:2–8, which quotes Exod 34:6–7, claiming that Yhwh's actions towards Nineveh are justified. They thereby connect their lives to the reality of the prophets' teaching about the Day of Yhwh. They also affirm Yhwh's truthfulness about his own character. They

---

83. For a defense of this translation see House, "God's Character and the Wholeness of Scripture," 6.
84. See ibid., 4.
85. For a discussion of this matter, see ibid., 7–8.

confirm Yhwh's personal integrity and aversion to allowing sin to take over the lives of his people on a permanent basis.

When the speakers declare hope they also do so on the basis of Yhwh's character. The speaker in Lam 3:1–66 states that Yhwh's "covenant-type mercies," the acts of kindness he does because Israel is his beloved nation, "never cease" (Lam 3:22a). He states that Yhwh's acts of compassion "never end" (Lam 3:22b). Indeed, God's covenant mercy and compassion are "new every morning" (Lam 3:23). They cannot be exhausted, though sinners must not take them for granted. The words translated "covenant-type mercies" and "compassion" also occur in Exod 34:6–7, where Yhwh forgives Israel and restores his covenant with them after the golden calf incident and Moses' resultant intercession on their behalf. The speaker in Lam 3:19–24 has come to realize that God's capacity for kindness, compassion, and forgiveness is immense.

The inevitable conclusion that the speaker must draw from his reflection on Exod 34:6–7 and from his own experience is that God's lack of kindness or covenant memory is not the problem. The problem must lie elsewhere, and in the context of the whole of the book of Lamentations it resides in the sins of the covenant people. The people praying in Lam 5:1–22 concur, for they admit their sin and ask for mercy. What they know about Yhwh's core character leads them to ask for the outrageously generous forgiveness they require.

As for the depiction of human beings, the book parallels Genesis 1–3 in many ways. On the one hand, as in Gen 1:26–31, in Lamentations one can easily see evidence of the potential for human greatness. The book's artistry, the level of compassion the speakers show, and the intelligent reversal of flawed patterns of behavior all speak well of human beings. On the other hand, Jerusalem breaks faith with Yhwh, as do the man and the woman in Gen 3:1–15. Indeed, Jerusalem's long-term unfaithfulness to her covenant spouse, her concurrent neglect of her children, and her slow response to the realities around her are ugly reminders of human ability inverted against itself. She is portrayed as a serial adulterer, a negligent mother who places her children in danger through criminal neglect, and a self-seeking ally. She is the sort of spouse one leaves, the sort of mother who loses her children by court order, and the sort of friend that one cannot count on in troubled days. Similarly, the speaker in Lam 3:1–66 admits willful and ongoing sin in his life. According to his own testimony, it took terrible circumstances for him to realize his situation (Lam 3:1–18). In short, he was foolish. He admits he was the sort of wisdom teacher one avoids. These sorts of activities are aspects of the human condition the book exposes.

Yet the Bible emphasizes over and over again that Yhwh receives people like these—and worse. In the Old Testament Yhwh receives and forgives flawed people like Adam, Eve, Abraham, Sarah, Isaac, Rebekah, Rahab, David, Bathsheba, Jonah's Ninevites, and a host of others. In the New Testament Jesus teaches parables of God forgiving the worst sort of son (Luke 15:11–23), of God accepting people at the last hour (Matt 20:1–16), and of God receiving persons from many nations (Luke 13:22–30). Like the prophets, he does so while warning of coming judgment and the need for repentance (see Matt 4:17). Unlike the prophets he offers himself as the sacrifice for the sins the people have committed and a relationship with himself as the key to a relationship with Yhwh (Matt 11:20–30; John 14:1–11).

In the Bible over and over again Yhwh offers forgiveness after judgment based on repentance and promise of faithfulness. His ability to trust anew in light of contrary evidence is astounding. He does what people rarely do if they wish to be safe: he takes the people back who give only their word and their heart—two proven unreliable sources—in pledge of a restored relationship that reverses the consequences of a willfully faithless person. Yhwh takes this risk with his reputation.

The biblical canon helps us know how the people praying in Lam 5:1–22 will be received. Yhwh will take them back as he promised in Leviticus 16, Deut 30:1–10, and several other passages. Indeed, the presence of Ezra-Nehemiah, Haggai and Zechariah, and Psalm 107 attest that the prayers were answered. Yhwh performed yet another outrageous act of grace in post-exilic times. Frankly, we may have to decide if we like this God more than we would like one who judges such people and leaves them to their own devices. Seen this way Lamentations is more like the parables Jesus tells about the God who receives people at the last moment than it is about how God is overly severe.

## CONCLUSION

This reading of Lamentations has several practical implications. First, one should be very careful when applying situations of victimization or innocent suffering (like the Holocaust, genocide in Rwanda, or pedophilia) to Lamentations. It is important to recall that Lamentations is a book written by people who confess to suffering due to their long lasting defiance of Yhwh, neglect of the prophetic words sent to them, and historical amnesia concerning the wisdom of trusting local allies against major nations. Again, the main speakers in Lamentations are not "innocent sufferers" in the normal sense of that phrase, though they speak of innocent sufferers—namely, their children. Thus, I personally found it odd, for example, to hear a national news presenter lead the network broadcast on September 12, 2001, with a quotation of Lam 1:1. I guessed the presenter would be horrified to learn that a contextual reading of Lam 1:1 would place him in league with preachers who claimed that the events occurred because God was angry with the United States. Of course, if he did believe that the United States suffered for whatever it was that angered God then he had the correct book.

Second, those of us who blame Yhwh for all the world's suffering need to stop feeling self-righteous about how he has acted when we realize how little we like serial adulterers, inept politicians, corrupt priests, and parents whose action, (in)action, or rebellion could lead to their children's deaths. Most of us want them stopped, and they rarely stop on their own, thereby forcing society to restrain or correct their actions. It is these very people for whom the narrator in Lamentations 1–2 feels such sympathy. It is these very people the speaker in Lamentations 3 encourages to trust Yhwh's kindness. It is these very people who receive the promise that their captivity has ended in Lamentations 4 and who come to pray in Lam 5. Lamentations concludes that Yhwh is the sort of God who takes such people back.

Third, we need to embrace Lamentations' realistic view of the divine-human relationship. It describes humanity at its best and worst, and it describes Yhwh's response. It describes the human feeling of the yawning absence of Yhwh in passionate detail. It expresses how real people feel in really terrible situations. Yet more to the point, it describes how people who have brought these terrible situations on themselves should think, act, and pray. It describes how persons suffering alongside others reach out to fellow sufferers, and it describes how those who trust Yhwh most believe he will take back the most horrible type of sinner. Coupled with the Bible's teachings on innocent suffering, this realistic reading will give holistic understandings of a very confusing world.

Lamentations asks us to look at, then reach out to wicked, judged persons and see hope. Their tears can be dried and our self-righteousness negated. The truly outrageous nature of Yhwh's patient mercy and unwillingness to judge will sustain those who wait for faithfulness each morning. It will sustain those who wait with them. It will thereby aid a biblical understanding of theodicy, expressing pain, and protesting suffering without diminishing God's character.

## Bibliography

Albertz, Rainer. *Israel in Exile: The History and Literature of the Sixth Century B.C.E.* Studies in Biblical Literature. 3. Atlanta: Scholars, 2003.

Albrektson, Bertil. *Studies in the Text and Theology of the Book of Lamentations.* Lund: Gleerup, 1963.

Berlin, Adele. *Lamentations.* Old Testament Library. Louisville: Westminster John Knox, 2002.

Boda, Mark. "The Priceless Gain of Penitence: From Communal Lament to Penitential Prayer in the 'Exilic Liturgy of Israel.'" In *Lamentations in Ancient and Contemporary Contexts*, edited by Nancy C. Lee and Carleen Mandolfo, 81–102. SBL Symposium Series, 43. Atlanta: Scholars, 2008.

Dobbs-Allsopp, F. W. *Lamentations.* Interpretation. Louisville: John Knox, 2002.

Garrett, Duane, and Paul R. House. *Song of Songs/Lamentations.* Word Biblical Commentary, 23B. Nashville: Thomas Nelson, 2003.

Gottwald, Norman K. *Studies in the Book of Lamentations.* Rev. ed. Studies in Biblical Theology. Series One, 14. London: SCM, 1962.

Hafemann, Scott J., and Paul House, eds. *Central Themes in Biblical Theology: Mapping Unity in Diversity.* Grand Rapids: Baker, 2007.

House, Paul R. "God's Character and the Wholeness of Scripture." *Scottish Bulletin of Evangelical Theology.* 23 (Spring 2005) 4–17.

Lee, Nancy C. *The Singers of Lamentations: Cities under Siege, from Ur to Jerusalem to Sarajevo.* Biblical Interpretation Series, 60. Leiden: Brill, 2002.

———. "The Singers of Lamentations (A)Scribing (De)Claiming Poets and Prophets." In *Lamentations in Ancient and Contemporary Contexts*, edited by Nancy C. Lee and Carleen Mandolfo, 33–46. SBL Symposium Series, 43. Atlanta: Scholars, 2008.

Linafelt, Tod. *Surviving Lamentations: Catastrophe, Lament, and Protest in the Afterlife of a Biblical Book.* Chicago: University of Chicago Press, 2000.

———. "Surviving Lamentations (one More Time)." In *Lamentations in Ancient and Contemporary Contexts*, edited by Nancy C. Lee and Carleen Mandolfo, 57–66. SBL Symposium Series, 43. Atlanta: Scholars, 2008.

Mandolfo, Carleen. *Daughter Zion Talks Back to the Prophets: A Dialogic Theology of the Book of Lamentations.* Semeia Studies, 58. Atlanta: Society of Biblical Literature, 2007.

O'Connor, Kathleen. *Lamentations and the Tears of the World.* Maryknoll, NY: Orbis, 2002.

———. "Voices Arguing about Meaning." In *Lamentations in Ancient and Contemporary Contexts*, edited by Nancy C. Lee and Carleen Mandolfo, 27–32. SBL Symposium Series, 43. Atlanta: Scholars, 2008.

Provan, Iain. *Lamentations.* New Century Bible Commentary. Grand Rapids: Eerdmans, 1991.

Re'emi, S. P. "The Theology of Hope: A Commentary on the Book of Lamentations." In *God's People in Crisis: A Commentary on the Book of Amos and a Commentary on the Book of Lamentations*, by R. Martin-Achard and S. P. Re'emi, 73–134. International Theological Commentary. Grand Rapids: Eerdmans, 1984.

Renkema, Johan. *Lamentations.* Translated by Brian Doyle. Historical Commentary on the Old Testament. Leuven: Peeters, 1998.

Westermann, Claus. *Lamentations: Issues and Interpretation.* Translated by C. Muenchow. Minneapolis: Fortress, 1994.

Soundings
in Jewish Reception History

# A

## Lamentations in Isaiah 40–55

Lena-Sofia Tiemeyer

### INTRODUCTION

INNER-BIBLICAL ALLUSIONS ARE A well-known phenomenon. One biblical text alludes to another earlier text and, as a result, the interpretation of both texts is modified. This chapter looks at the ways in which the author(s) of Isaiah 40–55 *consciously* made use of and interacted with the laments of Lamentations.[1] Other types of inter-textuality will not be considered.[2] In particular, we shall explore how these later Isaianic authors furnished the laments in Lamentations—texts characterized by God's silence—with divine answers.

### INNER-BIBLICAL TEXTUAL ALLUSIONS

When dealing with inner-biblical textual allusions, three key factors must be established. First, we need to decide the *direction* of the allusions: which is the source text and which is the alluding text? Secondly, we need to ascertain that we are dealing with actual *dependency* rather than merely shared outlook and vocabulary. Thirdly, we need to determine that the alluding text had *access* to the source text.

---

1. I shall refer to Isaiah 40–55 as one textual corpus, as the many shared theological and stylistic factors indicate that these sixteen chapters form a distinct literary corpus. I make, however, no claim of original unity of these chapters. Likewise I shall use the singular term "author" for the sake of convenience, without making any claim of authorial unity of Isaiah 40–55. There is virtually no textual support within Isaiah 40–55 of a prophetic individual. In view of this, it is preferable to assume that Isaiah 40–55 was composed by a group of authors belonging to the same prophetic tradition.

   More extensive discussions of much the material in this articles can be found in my two previous articles "Geography and Textual Allusions" and "Two Prophets, Two Laments, and Two Ways of Dealing with Earlier Texts."

2. For further discussion of textual allusions, their form and their use, and the main differences between inter-textuality and textual allusions, see Sommer, *A Prophet Reads Scripture*, 6–10, with cited bibliography.

In the particular case of Lamentations and Isaiah 40–55, both texts can be dated to roughly the same time period (ca 586–22 BCE). There is, however, little doubt that Isaiah 40–55 is the later composition. It is likely that many, if not all, of the laments in Lamentations were composed before 540 BCE.[3] In contrast, it is doubtful that any text in Isaiah 40–55 was written long before 539 BCE.[4] In addition, as we shall discuss further below, Isaiah 40–55 actively interacts with and sometimes also reverses statements in Lamentations. This phenomenon points not only to the direction of the allusions but also suggests actual dependency of Isaiah 40–55 upon Lamentations. In fact, although running the risk of circularity, more than one scholar uses the allusions to Lamentations in Isaiah 40–55 as a tool for determining the *terminus ad quem* of Lamentations.[5] Finally, given the likely liturgical use of Lamentations (cf. Zech 7:3, 5), it is reasonable to assume that the author of Isaiah 40–55 had access to Lamentations, although not necessarily in its final form.

We further need to determine the *types* of and the *reasons* for the use of Lamentations by the author of Isaiah 40–55. There are several ways in which one text can refer to another text consciously (allusion, influence, echo, and exegesis).[6] In the case of the textual interaction between Isaiah 40–55 (the alluding text) and Lamentations (the source text), the term "allusion" is the most fitting. From the reader's perspective, the reader of Isaiah 40–55 recognizes a "marker," i.e., an identifiable element or pattern from the source text, in this case Lamentations. The same reader then brings certain elements of Lamentations to bear on the understanding of Isaiah 40–55. From the author's perspective, the author of Isaiah 40–55 reuses vocabulary and themes from Lamentations in order to establish a link to the former text.

A textual allusion may serve the purpose of establishing the authority of the alluding author or, *vice versa*, to bolster the authority of the existing tradition of the source text. Alluding can also simply give pleasure to the author and reader alike, giving both the chance to display their erudition. Alternatively, a later text can use textual allusions polemically in an attempt to replace the source text.[7] In the particular case of Lamentations and Isaiah 40–55, the nature of the allusions can be termed polemical insofar as the latter text aims to provide positive answers to the laments in the former. At the same time, the allusions to Lamentations enhance the message of Isaiah 40–55 in that they affirm the place of Isaiah 40–55 within the same textual tradition.

---

3. See the recent discussion in Berlin, *Lamentations*, 33–35. Berlin argues against regarding the vividness of the descriptions of the destruction of Jerusalem as a compelling reason for dating Lamentations close to 586 BCE. At the same time, she maintains that the Hebrew of Lamentations renders an exilic dating of the texts likely. It is possible that Lam 3 was composed later (see, e.g., Westermann, *Lamentations*, 54–66, 66–67, 104–5 // Westermann, *Die Klagelieder*, 56–57, 65–66, 95–96).

4. I regard Isaiah 40–55 to have been written over a brief period of time, ranging from shortly before 539 BCE to around 520 BCE, although it is possible that some passages date to even later periods. For an up-to-date discussion in English of the various theories pertaining to the dating of Isaiah 40–55, see Albertz, *Israel in Exile*, 376–433.

5. See Berlin, *Lamentations*, 34; Westermann, *Lamentations*, 104–5 // Westermann, *Klagelieder*, 95–96.

6. See discussion in Sommer, *Prophet*, 10–18.

7. See discussion in ibid., 18–31.

## THE MESSAGE OF THE ALLUSIONS

Scholars, going all the way back to Jewish midrash (*Lam. Rab.* 1:21), have long recognized the textual links between Lamentations and Isaiah 40-55. Among early critical scholars, Löhr in particular noted the shared vocabulary,[8] and his insights were later developed by Gottwald.[9] More recently, Sommer discusses the similarities in vocabulary and, in recognizing direct allusions in Isa 51:17-22 to Lam 2:13-19, argues for dependency of Isaiah 40-66 upon Lamentation 1-4.[10] In a more extensive investigation, Willey maintains that there are allusions throughout all of Isaiah 49:1—54:17 to numerous verses in all five chapters of Lamentations. Rather than bolstering the claims made by the laments, however, these allusions serve "to answer them, to dispute, reverse, and reinvent them."[11]

How, then, do these allusions in Isaiah 40-55 answer, dispute, reverse, and reinvent the laments in Lamentations? In most cases, Isaiah 40-55 picks up the speech of Lamentations and, using the same vocabulary, responds to it. In other cases, Isaiah 40-55 reuses a key motif in Lamentations, again in order to proclaim the very opposite. To illustrate this, we shall look at six representative examples.[12]

First, Lamentations lament that God has abandoned and forsaken the people of Judah and/or Zion-Jerusalem. He never *comforts* them (Lam 1:2, 9, 16, 17, 21; 2:13 etc.) and he *forgets* them and *forsakes* them (Lam 5:20). Isaiah 40-55 responds positively to these charges, often echoing the exact vocabulary of Lamentations. First, God indeed *comforts* Jerusalem. Isaiah 40-55 opens with the famous command to "comfort, comfort my people, speak to the heart of Jerusalem" (Isaiah 40:1), and the idea of comfort continues to reverberate throughout the whole text (e.g., Isaiah 49:13a; 51:12). Secondly, God also *remembers* them. Isa 49:14 lets the lamenting speech of Zion-Jerusalem echo that of Lam 5:20. The following verse 15b then contradicts her claim: no, God will not *forget* her.

Secondly, Lam 2:10 states how the elders of *daughter* Zion *sits* on the *ground*, and how they cast up *dust*. Isa 47:1 reverses the imagery by replacing Zion with Babylon. Now *daughter* Babylon *sits* and descends upon the *dust* and upon the *ground*. By using the same words—"daughter," "sitting," "dust"—as well as the opposites—"cast up" (*Hiphil* of עלה) versus "descend" (*Qal* of ירד)—Isa 47 is creating a poignant picture of divine retribution where the former misery of Zion will befall her former enemy.

Thirdly, Lam 2:11-12; 4:1-10 states that her *children* are dead or left as orphans or lead away into captivity by their enemies. Although using few exact literary parallels, Isa

---

8. Löhr, "Der Sprachgebrauch es Buches der Klagelieder," 42-43, 44, 47, and 48.

9. Gottwald, *Studies in the Book of Lamentations*, 44-45.

10. Sommer, *Prophet*, 127-30. He notes that there are no allusions to Lamentations 5 which to him suggests that Deutero-Isaiah (defined by Sommer as the author of Isaiah 40-66) did not know that chapter. This can be taken to mean that either the chapters of Lamentations were circulated individually or that Lamentations 1-4 formed a single scroll to which Lamentations 5 was added later.

11. Willey, *Remember the Former Things*, esp. 265. See also O'Connor, "Speak Tenderly to Jerusalem," esp. 286-92.

12. For a more detailed discussion, see the research by especially Sommer, Willey, and O'Connor.

49:17–23 responds with a contrasting vision where living children are being led back to Jerusalem by the same enemy.

Fourthly, Lam 2:19 and 4:1, 9–11 speak of fainting children lying scattered at "the head of every street." Isa 51:20–23 not only reuses this imagery—thus clearly evoking the memory of Lamentations (v. 20a)—but also provides a response (v. 23) by stating that those responsible for Jerusalem's situation will be punished.

Fifthly, along similar lines, Lam 2:22 and 4:21 use the image of a *drinking cup* to symbolize God's wrath against Jerusalem and her share of affliction. Isaiah 51:17–23 picks up this imagery but then turns it around: Jerusalem has indeed drunk the cup of God's wrath but now God has removed that cup from her, promising that she will never have to drink from it again.

Finally, Lam 4:13–16 speaks about the leaders of the people, holding them accountable for the fall of Jerusalem. Notably, verse 15 states that people are calling out behind these leaders: "go away," "impure," "do not touch." By using similar vocabulary and similar syntax, Isa 52:1, 11 creates a contrasting picture between *then* (Lamentations) and *now* (Isaiah 40–55). No impure person will henceforth be let into Zion-Jerusalem (v. 1). Furthermore, the leaders are transformed from being carriers of sin and blame to carriers of holy vessels, and their impurity is reversed as they are leaving their uncleanness behind in the form of the foreign land of their exilic sojourning (v. 11).

## ZION AND THE SUFFERING SERVANT

In addition to the types of allusions mentioned above, there are other literary connections between Lamentations and Isa 40–55. In particular, the alternating imagery of Zion (Isa 49:13—50:3; 51:12—52:12; 54:1–17) and the Suffering Servant (Isa 49:1–12; 50:4–11; 52:13—53:12) in Isaiah 40–55[13] recalls the respective figures of Zion in Lamentations 1–2, 4–5 and the "suffering male" (Hebrew גֶּבֶר) in Lam 3. This latter chapter stands out in Lamentations in that it is uttered in the first person singular ("I") and in that it expresses the suffering of the community in less urgent tones than does the rest of Lamentations. In particular, it reasserts positive characteristics of God with particular reference to divine salvation and vision.[14]

For Willey, the singular "male" in Lam 3 becomes Zion's counterpart, a figure who, like Zion, embodies the suffering of many. Unlike her, however, who cries out her pain and her anguish to God without restraint, and who holds God accountable for her suffering, demanding an explanation, the "male" expresses reasons to hope. Moreover, he serves as a model for the suffering servant in Isa 52:13—53:12.[15] Along similar lines, Middlemas argues that Lam 3 formulates an alternative response to the catastrophe that is less angry, less accusing, and also less heartfelt than that is the rest of Lamentations and more in

---

13. For further discussion of the imagery in Isaiah 40–55, see, e.g., Wilshire, "The Servant-City"; Sawyer, "Daughter of Zion and Servant of the Lord," esp. 99–101; Korpel, "The Female Servant of the Lord in Isaiah 54"; O'Connor, "Speak Tenderly to Jerusalem," 287; Linafelt, *Surviving Lamentations*, 68–72; Berges, "Personification and Prophetic Voices of Zion in Isaiah and Beyond," esp. 70–72.

14. See further Middlemas, "Did Second Isaiah Write Lamentations III?" 505–7.

15. Willey, *Remember the Former Things*, 214–28. See also Seitz, *Words Without End*, 133–34.

line with what Middlemas calls "a sanctioned way to respond faithfully to disaster." The "male" in Lam 3 waits silently and patiently and expectantly for divine restoration accomplished by a sovereign and all-seeing God. The distinct character of Lamentations 3, both in terms of themes and in terms of theology, combined with its uncertain date of origin, raises questions as to the direction of the allusions. Contrary to Willey, Middlemas therefore argues for the opposite relationship: it is the suffering servant of Isaiah 40–55 who forms the backdrop of the "male." For her, both Isaiah 40–55 and Lamentations 3 are of exilic origin. As such, both the suffering servant in Isa 52:13—53:12 and the "male" in Lamentations 3 personify *exiled* Israel.[16]

## JUDAH AND EXILE

This brings us to the next issue, namely the communities responsible for the texts of Lamentations and Isaiah 40–55. There is something as rare as a near scholarly consensus pertaining to the Judahite origin of Lamentations, with the possible exception of Lamentations 3 (cf. above).[17] In the case of Isaiah 40–55, the situation is more complicated. While most Anglo-Saxon scholars regard all of Isaiah 40–55 as stemming from the exilic community in Babylon,[18] most Continental scholars argue in favor of a core text written in Babylon—limited to parts of Isaiah 40–48—and subsequent redactional layers written in Judah.[19] In addition, a few scholars place all of Isaiah 40–55 in Judah.[20] In my view, much favors the two latter positions. On the one hand, there is little explicit textual evidence of a Babylonian setting of Isaiah 40–55. On the other hand, especially the pervading focus on Zion-Jerusalem suggests a Judahite setting of at least Isaiah 49–55, if not all of Isaiah 40–55.

Nonetheless, although nearly all of the allusions to Lamentations can be found in Isaiah 49–55, much of the discussion about these allusions has taken for granted a cross-cultural setting. Gottwald, for example, argues that the similarities between Lamentations and Isaiah 40–55 suggest that Lamentations circulated in the Babylonian exile.[21]

More recently, scholars have focused on the ways in which the exilic author of Isaiah 40–55 adopts and reverses the language of the Judahite Lamentations. Zion-Jerusalem

---

16. Middlemas, "Did Second Isaiah Write Lamentations III?" 522–24.

17. See further Westermann, *Lamentations*, 55, 105 // Westermann, *Klagelieder*, 57, 96; Middlemas, *The Troubles of Templeless Judah*, 177–78.

18. Nuanced and well argued positions are held by especially Goldingay and Payne, *Isaiah 40–55*, 30–37, and Blenkinsopp, *Isaiah 40–55*, 102–4.

19. E.g., Kratz, *Kyros im Deuterojesaja-buch*; Steck, *Gottesknecht und Zion*, 47–59, van Oorschot, *Von Babel zum Zion*; Berges, *Jesaja 40–48*, 36–37.

20. E.g., especially Barstad, *The Myth of the Empty Land* and Barstad, *The Babylonian Captivity of the Book of Isaiah*. See also Loretz, "Mesopotamische und ugaritisch-kanaanäische Elemente," 288; Kiesow, *Exodustexte im Jesajabuch*, 55–56; Vincent, *Studien zur literarischen Eigenart und aur geistigen Heimat von Jesaja*, 216–17, and Goldingay, "Isaiah 40–55 in the 1990s," 241–42. Goldingay adds, however, that the audience is both the Jerusalem community and that in Babylon

21. Gottwald, *Lamentations*, 45. Cf. Middlemas, "Did Second Isaiah Write Lamentations III?" 24, who argues, based on her interpretation of Lamentations 3, that there was cross communication between the exilic community in Babylon and the community in Judah.

thus becomes a symbol of hope for the exilic community. Gottwald argues that the Judahite community is nowhere present in Isaiah 40–55. Rather Isaiah 40–55 preserves only the voice of the former Judahite ruling elite in Babylon, serving as a weapon in their struggle to preserve their socio-cultural identity. In contrast, the book of Lamentations speaks on behalf of the community in Judah.[22]

Newsom modifies Gottwald's statement about the absence of the people of Judah in Isaiah 40–55. She argues that rather than being absent, their speech is present in Isaiah 40–55 through the allusions to the Judahitie composition of Lamentations. Yet their speech is reaccented in Isaiah 40–55, "infused with the perspectives and intentions of the exilic community," and betraying their interests. The exiles in Isaiah 40–55 thus represent themselves in terms drawn from Judahite speech. The reason for this is an awareness of the difficulties that are likely to await those exiles returning to Judah. By reusing the speech of Lamentations, Isaiah 40–55 thus provides the exilic community with a symbolic narrative within which they can imagine themselves being welcomed home. It is possible that this also betrays a need for a common language and an appeal to the people of Judah to welcome the exiles home. This rearranging of the speech of Lamentations is done through a strategic selection and recasting of images and expressions. In particular, Isaiah 40–55 simplifies the portrayal of Zion-Jerusalem. She ceases to be a multifarious entity of living people and physical structures (Lamentations) and becomes the personified destination of the returning exiles (Isaiah 40–55).[23]

Noting that the exiles have left Babylon in Isa 48:20, Linafelt, following Newsome's line of thinking, argues that the following text (Isaiah 49–55) is concerned with the re-entry of the exiles into Judah. In alluding to Lamentations, all Judahite speech has thus been subsumed under the figure of personified Zion, symbolizing the destination of the exiles. The answer in Isaiah 40–55, promising the restoration of Zion's exiled children, does therefore not really respond to Judah's lament in Lamentations. In other words, rather than responding to Zion herself, Isaiah 40–55 focus only on the returning children. "The figure of Zion has been co-opted to serve a role in the ideology of [Isaiah 40–55]."[24]

In my view, Newsom's portrayal of Zion-Jerusalem in Isaiah 40–55 is an oversimplification. Jerusalem is referred to throughout Isaiah 40–55, as having physical attributes such as ruins (44:26; 49:19; 51:3; 52:9) and walls (49:16). Isaiah 54:11–12, for example, speaks of its stones, its foundations, its shields, its gates, and its walls. Moreover, the city is going to be rebuilt (44:28; 49:17). Furthermore, its human population is referred to explicitly in 44:26 and probably also in 48:2. Moreover, in response to Linafelt, Zion-Jerusalem is often addressed concerning matters that have no direct connection to the return of the exiles (e.g., Isa 40:1–2, 40:9;[25] 51:16; 52:7). There is thus little justification in saying that Zion-Jerusalem is reduced to the destination of the exiles. Rather the city

22. Gottwald, "Social Class and Ideology in Isaiah 40–55," 43–57.

23. Newsom, "Response to Norman K. Gottwald." See also O'Connor, "Speak Tenderly to Jerusalem," 293.

24. Linafelt, *Surviving Lamentations*, 62–79.

25. Reading ציון מבשרת as "messenger to Zion."

remains a city of flesh and blood and mortar, just as in Lamentations. It is instead preferable to follow Seitz who, accepting the possibility of a Judahite setting of Isaiah 40–55, argues that the affinity between Isaiah 40–55 and Lamentations are best explained as the result of shared religious circumstances, date, and actual setting, i.e., life in Jerusalem following the destruction of Jerusalem.[26] I thus consider it likely that the answer in Isaiah 40–55 was first and foremost intended for the community in Jerusalem, the one responsible for the laments in Lamentations.

## ISAIAH 40–55: AN ADEQUATE ANSWER TO LAMENTATIONS?

We have until now focused on the ways in which Isaiah 40–55 responds to Lamentations. There is, however, one final aspect that needs discussion and that is whether or not the answers provided by Isaiah 40–55 are adequate or even acceptable. Following in the footsteps of especially Linafelt (above), Mandolfo argues that rather than responding to Zion's particular accusations in Lamentations, Isaiah 40–55 has its own agenda. God is doing nearly all the talking, thus overshadowing Zion's own speech. According to Mandolfo, much of the effort of Isaiah 40–55 addresses Zion's plea for vengeance upon her enemies in Lam 1:22, exemplified especially by Isaiah 47. In doing so, however, God sidetracks the real issue for Daughter Zion, namely God's culpability for her torment. Zion's claim in Isa 49:14 that God has forsaken her is thus never really answered in the following response in Isa 49:15–23. Yes, children are coming home (i.e., the returning exiles), but Zion's own children, those people of Judah who speak in Lamentations, are irrevocably lost. God's rhetoric aims to win Zion over—heart and mind—rather than to give her firm answers. In view of this, Zion's own silence in Isaiah 40–55 is striking. Is she not convinced or is she not allowed to speak more, as her voice would subvert God's speech? God finally takes responsibility for Zion's suffering in Isa 54:7–8. Mandolfo concludes by acknowledging that the answer to Lamentations by Isaiah 40–55 is profoundly beautiful and moving, as well as psychologically adept and therapeutic. Yet there is a lingering sense that *the* question of Lamentations, namely why God has brought the destruction upon Jerusalem, is never fully addressed. The Bible is always theodic. As such the answers in Isaiah 40–55 are in the end insufficient. Is God really contrite? Is his desire for reconciliation genuine? Does he have an agenda beyond the good of Daughter Zion?[27]

Mandolfo is right in her critique: God's answers in Isaiah 40–55 do not respond *fully* to the laments in Lamentations. At the same time, the answers in Isaiah 40–55 are all we have got. Whether we like it or not, the question of why calamities strike that appear to be out of proportion to any sin that the victims have committed will always be with us. In the meantime, God's tender words of love and wooing in Isaiah 40–55 may ultimately not be a bad thing to live on.

---

26. Seitz, *Words Without End*, 130–49.
27. Mandolfo, *Daughter Zion Talks Back to the Prophets*, 103–19.

## BIBLIOGRAPHY

Albertz, Rainer. *Israel in Exile: The History and Literature of the Sixth Century B.C.E.* Translated by D. Green. Studies in Biblical Literature. Atlanta: Society of Biblical Literature, 2003.

Barstad, Hans M. *The Babylonian Captivity of the Book of Isaiah: "Exilic" Judah and the Provenance of Isaiah 40–55.* Oslo: Instituttet for Sammenlignende Kulturforskning, 1997.

———. *The Myth of the Empty Land: A Study in the History and Archaeology of Judah during the "Exilic" Period.* SOFS 28. Oslo: Scandinavian University Press, 1996.

Berges, Ulrich. *Jesaja 40–48.* HThKAT. Freiburg: Herder, 2007.

———. "Personification and Prophetic Voices of Zion in Isaiah and Beyond." In *The Elusive Prophet: The Prophet as a Historical Person, Literary Character, and Anonymous Artist.* OTS 45. Leiden: Brill, 2001.

Berlin, Adele. *Lamentations: A Commentary.* OTL. Louisville: Westminster John Knox, 2002.

Blenkinsopp, Joseph. *Isaiah 40–55.* AB 19A. New York: Doubleday, 2000.

Goldingay, John. "Isaiah 40–55 in the 1990s: Among Other Things, Deconstructing, Mystifying, Intertexual, Socio-Critical, and Hearer-Involving." *BibInt* 5 (1997) 226–46.

———, and David Payne. *Isaiah 40–55*, Volume 1. ICC. London: T. & T. Clark, 2006.

Gottwald, Norman K. "Social Class and Ideology in Isaiah 40–55: An Eagletonian Reading." *Semeia* 59 (1992) 43–57.

———. *Studies in the Book of Lamentations.* SBT 14. London: SCM, 1954.

Kiesow, K. *Exodustexte im Jesajabuch: Literarkritische und motivgeschichtliche Analyses.* OBO 24. Fribourg: Éditions Universitaires, 1979.

Korpel, Marjo C. A. "The Female Servant of the Lord in Isaiah 54." In *On Reading Prophetic Texts: Gender-Specific and Related Studies in Memory of Fokkelien van Dijk-Hemmes*, edited by B. Becking and M. Dijkstra, 153–67. Leiden: Brill, 1996.

Kratz, Reinhard G. *Kyros im Deuterojesaja-buch.* FAT 1. Tübingen: Mohr Siebeck, 1991.

Linafelt, Todd. *Surviving Lamentations: Catastrophe, Lament, and Protest in the Afterlife of a Biblical Book.* Chicago: University of Chicago Press, 2000.

Löhr, Max. "Der Sprachgebrauch es Buches der Klagelieder," *ZAW* 14 (1894) 42–43.

Loretz, O. "Mesopotamische und ugaritisch-kanaanäische Elemente im Prolog des Buches Detuerojesaja (40,1–11)." *Or* 53 (1984) 284–96.

O'Connor, Kathleen M. "Speak Tenderly to Jerusalem: Second Isaiah's Reception and Use of Daughter Zion." *The Princeton Seminary Bulletin* 20 (1999) 281–94.

Mandolfo, Carleen. *Daughter Zion Talks Back to the Prophets: A Dialogic Theology of the Book of Lamentations.* SBL Semeia Studies 58. Leiden: Brill, 2007.

Middlemas, Jill. "Did Second Isaiah Write Lamentations III?" *VT* 56 (2006) 505–25.

———. *The Troubles of Templeless Judah.* OTM. Oxford: Oxford University Press, 2005.

Newsom, Carol A. "Response to Norman K. Gottwald, 'Social Class and Ideology in Isaiah 40–55.'" *Semeia* 59 (1992) 73–78.

Oorschot, Jürgen van. *Von Babel zum Zion: Eine literarkritische und redaktionsgeschichtliche Untersuchung.* BZAW 206. Berlin: de Gruyter, 1993.

Sawyer, John F. A. "Daughter of Zion and Servant of the Lord in Isaiah: A Comparison." *JSOT* 44 (1989) 89–107.

Seitz, Christopher R. *Words Without End.* Grand Rapids, Eerdmans, 1998.

Sommer, Benjamin D. *A Prophet Reads Scripture: Allusion in Isaiah 40–66.* Contraversions. Stanford, CA: Stanford University Press, 1998.

Tiemeyer, Lena-Sofia. "Geography and Textual Allusions: Interpreting Isaiah xl–lv and Lamentations as Judahite Texts." *VT* 57 (2007) 367–85.

———. "Two Prophets, Two Laments, and Two Ways of Dealing with Earlier Texts." In *Die Textualisierung der Religion*, edited by J. Schaper, 185–202. FAT. Tübingen: Mohr Siebeck, 2009.

Vincent, J. M. *Studien zur literarischen Eigenart und aur geistigen Heimat von Jesaja, Kap. 40–55.* Beiträge zur biblischen Exegese und Theologie 5. Frankfurt: BET, 1977.

Westermann, Claus. *Die Klagelieder: Forschungsgeschichte und Auslegung.* Neukirchen, Germany: Neurkirchener, 1990.

———. *Lamentations: Issues and Interpretations.* Translated by C. Muenchow. Minneapolis: Augsburg Fortress, 1994.

Willey, Patricia T. *Remember the Former Things: The Recollection of Previous Texts in Second Isaiah*. SBLDS 161. Atlanta: Scholars, 1997.

Wilshire, Leland E. "The Servant-City: A New Interpretation of the 'Servant of the Lord' in the Servant Songs of Deutero-Isaiah." *JBL* 94 (1975) 356–67.

# B

## The Character and Significance of LXX Lamentations

Kevin J. Youngblood

### INTRODUCTION

THE SEPTUAGINT VERSION OF Lamentations (hereafter LXX Lam) represents not only the first written translation of the Hebrew parent text but also its first written interpretation. The Italians have a proverb that says, "Traduttore, traditore" meaning "a translator is a traitor." The point of the proverb is that distortion is inherent to translation. Translation always includes interpretation that, either wittingly or unwittingly, adds to or subtracts from the text's meaning. One must remember, however, that if something is lost in translation, something is also gained. The translation serves as a window into the world that produced it: its emphases, biases, and interpretive framework. Such is certainly the case for LXX Lam, but the clues it offers are complex and require a careful eye and a broad awareness of the text's transmission and translational character. This essay offers a brief introduction to these issues as an aid to those interested in what LXX Lam reveals about Second Temple Jewish interpretation.

The following characterization is based on Joseph Ziegler's critical edition with a few minor modifications.[1] The first modification is the inclusion of the alphabetic strophe labels present in the best manuscripts as original to the translation.[2] Due to the presence of these labels, which preserve in Greek some sense of the acrostic structure of Lamentations, a few of Ziegler's textual decisions must be reconsidered. For example, Ziegler omits Lam 3:22–24, the entire *hēt* stanza in the third acrostic poem, on the basis of nineteen manuscripts. Had he accepted the alphabetic strophe labels as original, however, he probably would have retained the verses. The translator's attention to the acrostic structure of the first four poems makes the omission of an entire strophe unlikely. The

---

1. Joseph Ziegler, *Ieremias, Baruch, Threni, Epistula Ieremiae*.
2. See the translation in the appendix. For a full discussion of the case for the originality of these labels see Albert Pietersma, "The Acrostic Poems of Lamentations in Greek Translation."

omission is much more likely to have occurred in the transmission of the Greek text than in the Hebrew tradition or at the hands of the translator.[3]

A similar situation exists for Lam 3:29, a verse which Ziegler also omitted. Given the tight structure of the third acrostic, however, it is unlikely that this omission occurred in the Hebrew text tradition or at the point of translation.[4] Therefore, for the purposes of this characterization, the verse is considered original.

## CHARACTER OF LXX LAM AS A TRANSLATION

Having clarified what the original text of LXX Lam is likely to have been, we can turn our attention to a characterization of this translation. Scholars have long recognized that the translator responsible for LXX Lam adhered very closely to the Hebrew text. Perhaps the best characterization of the translator's general method is that of quantitative formal equivalence. This means that the translator attempted, as far as possible, to represent every element of the Hebrew text with a corresponding element in Greek. The result was often awkward but almost never incomprehensible. One might think of it as a kind of interlinear translation designed to acquaint Hellenistic Jews with the traditional Hebrew text.[5]

The discovery of the Greek Minor Prophets Scroll from Nahal Hever (hereafter GMP), composed sometime in the first century BCE, significantly advanced understanding of the development of the LXX tradition and of LXX Lam in particular. Dominique Barthélemy concluded, after a detailed analysis of translation technique, that the GMP was not an original translation but a thorough revision of the LXX in alignment with an emerging standard Hebrew text. This insight led to the identification of a group of pre-Christian recensions and translations within the LXX tradition that share the same translation technique and goal of GMP. Barthélemy suggested that LXX Lam might belong to this group of translations and revisions on the basis of a number of features that it shares with other members of this group, such as the use of stereotyped lexical equivalents and the tendency to translate the Hebrew particle גם or וגם (*gam*, "also, indeed," whether with or without the conjunction *wāw*) with καίγε (*kaige*, "and indeed").

Barthélemy proposed that this group of recensions/translations was the result of a movement or school under the leadership of the reviser Theodotion, characterized by a reliance on rabbinic principles of interpretation. Thus he referred to these translations and revisions as the *Kaige*-Theodotion Group after their shared tendency to render *gam* or *wĕgam* with *kaige* and its similarity to the translation technique of revisions attributed to Theodotion.[6]

Subsequent research has confirmed Barthélemy's identification of the *Kaige*-Theodotion Group, though many have pointed out that his theory of the movement's origin has led to overestimations of the degree of homogeneity shared by the individual

---

3. Pietersma, "Acrostic Poems," 196.
4. Gentry, "Lamentations," 932.
5. This analogy is used by Albert Pietersma. See Pietersma and Wright, "To the Reader of NETS," xiv.
6. Barthélemy, *Les devanciers d'Aquila*.

members of the group. Isabel Assan-Dote and Kevin Youngblood have each independently confirmed that LXX Lam belongs to the *Kaige*-Theodotion group.[7] By identifying LXX Lam as a member of the *Kaige*-Theodotion group, Barthélemy fixed the date of its translation squarely within the first century BCE. Assan-Dote, on the other hand, argues for a later date (between 70 and 100 CE) on the basis of a questionable interpretation of LXX Lam 2:8 (see discussion below). A careful comparison of LXX Lam's translation technique with other members of the *Kaige*-Theodotion group, other non-*Kaige* translation units within the LXX tradition, and later revisers such as Aquila suggests that LXX Lam fits somewhere between 50 BCE and 100 CE. Regardless of the dating scheme one adopts, LXX Lam fits squarely within the period of Second Temple Judaism when reflection on the significance and meaning of the Jewish Scriptures in the light of Israel's post-exilic situation was at its height.

## LXX LAM'S INTERPRETATIVE AND THEOLOGICAL CONTRIBUTIONS

Despite the translator's close adherence to the Hebrew text, a few notable differences do exist between the LXX and MT. First, a few additions are found in the LXX that are not present in the MT. Most of these are glosses added for the sake of clarification. For example, the MT of Lam 2:20b reads, "Should women eat their fruit?" The phrase "their fruit" (פרים, *piryām*) is clearly a reference to children as indicated by the following phrase "healthy children" (עללי טפחים, *'ōlĕlê ṭippuḥîm*) The translator of LXX Lam, however, clarified the phrase by adding the word "womb" thus translating "fruit of their womb" (καρπον κοιλίας αυτῶν, *karpon koilias autōn*). Doubtless the translator was influenced by the similar wording of Deut 28:53, the covenantal curse that is realized in Lam 2:20b. The translator probably felt compelled to clarify the phrase because he misunderstood and mistranslated the following phrase in the Hebrew which reads, "healthy children" but which he translated "a butcher made a gleaning."[8]

One of these additions, however, is more substantial and hermeneutically significant. The translator added the following prologue as an introduction to the Greek rendition of Lamentations. It reads: "And it happened after Israel was exiled and Jerusalem was desolated that Jeremiah sat weeping and he voiced this lament over Jerusalem and said, . . ." This brief prologue appears to be the translator's own composition since no underlying Hebrew text is extant. It represents a clear attempt on the part of the translator to shape tradition regarding Lamentations in a number of ways. First, it connects Lamentations to the book of Jeremiah as a kind of appendix. The prologue serves as the canonical tissue for this connection, and it justifies Lamentation's placement with other additions to the book of Jeremiah. As a result, we are invited to read LXX Lam in the light of the Jeremiah tradition. Therefore, these five poems have a historical, narrative, and canonical context in Greek that they do not have in Hebrew.

---

7. Assan-Dote, *Baruch, Lamentations, Lettre de Jérémie* and Youngblood, "Translation Technique in the Greek Lamentations."

8. The word for "healthy" (טפח) and the word for "butcher" (טבח) are distinguished by only one letter. Furthermore, the word for "child" (עולל) and "gleaning" (עולל) are identical. Whether this was the translator's mistake or a corruption in the Hebrew text from which he translated is impossible to determine.

Naturally the alternative placement of Lamentations in the Greek canon facilitated by the prologue significantly impacts interpretation. For example, from a reading of the Hebrew text we assume that the first person pronouns in chapter 1 mark the direct speech of personified Jerusalem. The prologue in the Greek text, however, complicates matters by leaving the impression that at least some of these first person references are the voice of Jeremiah rather than the voice of personified Daughter Zion. Thus, when we read LXX Lam 1:13, for example, we see a clear connection with Jer 20:9 which becomes the backdrop for interpretation.

> From his height, he sent fire in my bones; he brought it down. He spread a net for my feet; he turned me to the things behind me. He gave me up as one removed from his sight, enduring pain all day long (LXX Lam 1:13)

> And I said, "I will never again name the name of the Lord, and I will never again speak in his name." And it became like a fire, burning, consuming in my bones, and I am weak all over, and I cannot endure it (LXX Jer 20:9)[9]

A similar phenomenon occurs in LXX Lam 3. The Hebrew text of the third acrostic introduces an anonymous masculine voice that expresses the community's disillusionment with God and leads them to acceptance of divine judgment and repentance. The Hebrew gives the impression that this is a masculine Davidic voice introduced to balance the feminine voice of personified Daughter Zion.[10] The prologue of the Greek version, however, predisposes the reader to identify the first person voice with Jeremiah resulting in a very different understanding of the text. For example, the references in LXX Lam 3 to the Lord shutting out the speaker's prayers recall the Lord's prohibiting Jeremiah from interceding on behalf of his people (Jer 7:16; 11:14; 14:11). The Hebrew text, however, leaves the impression that the Lord is rejecting the prayers of his worshipping people who, through abuse of the temple cult, forfeited their access to God (cf. 1 Kgs 8:30).

A final consideration regarding LXX Lam's unique hermeneutical and theological contribution has to do not with additions to the text but with translational decisions that betray the translator's assumptions and theological biases. For example, the translator consistently rendered verb forms derived from the root עלל with Greek verbs meaning "to glean" despite the fact that, in context, the word clearly requires a meaning such as "to treat badly, deal harshly with." A comparison of LXX Lam 2:20 with MT Lam 2:20 illustrates the point.

> Look, Lord, and observe whom you *gleaned* in this manner! Will women eat the fruit of their womb? A butcher made a gleaning. Will you kill in the Lord's sanctuary priest and prophet? (LXX Lam 2:20)

> Look, LORD, and observe whom you have *treated* this way. Should women eat their own fruit, healthy children? Will you kill in the Lord's sanctuary priest and prophet? (MT Lam 2:20)

---

9. All translations are the author's unless otherwise noted.
10. Dempster, *Dominion and Dynasty*, 209.

Whether the translator only knew the one meaning for the root עלל or he chose this meaning to introduce a metaphor not already present in the text, the end result is a text that reads quite differently, especially in light of this equivalent's repeated occurrence (Lam 1:22; 2:20; 3:51). The translator, either intentionally or unintentionally, connected these texts to numerous others that compare Judah to a vineyard and her exile to a gleaning (cf. Isa 17:5–6; 24:13; 27:12; Jer 5:10–11; 6:9; 49:9; Obad 1:5; Mic 7:1). Readers are thus invited to interpret these texts in the light of this prophetic metaphor.

Some scholars have gone so far as to see a pesher style of interpretation behind some of the renderings in LXX Lam. Pesher interpretation is an attempt to apply a biblical text prophetically to a new situation with minimal consideration of its original, intended meaning. As an example, note LXX Lam 2:8:

> The Lord *returned* to destroy the wall of Daughter Zion. He stretched out a measuring line; he did not withdraw his hand from destruction, and rampart and wall grieve; together they faint (LXX Lam 2:8)

> The LORD *planned* to destroy the wall of Daughter Zion. He stretched out a line; he did not remove his hand from annihilation. Rampart and wall grieve; together they faint (MT Lam 2:8)

The translator mistook the Hebrew form חשב (*ḥāšab*, "he thought, planned") for the similar form השיב (*hēšîb*, "to bring back, to reverse") which he rendered with the verb ἐπέστρεψε (*epestrepse*, "to turn something, to return"). Since the Greek verb can convey the idea of repetition, of doing something a second time, Isabelle Assan-Dote construes this rendering as a deliberate reference to the destruction of the second temple in 70 CE.[11] Her conclusion, however, stretches the evidence. While such an interpretation is possible, it is by no means necessary. The Targum of Lamentations may connect this text with 70 CE, but LXX Lam does not make a clear connection.

One does, however, detect a hint of second temple eschatology in the translator's rendering of Lam 5:20.

> Why do you forget us *until the (final) victory*? Will you abandon us days without end? (LXX Lam 5:20)

> Why do you forget us *forever*? Will you forsake us days without end? (MT Lam 5:20)

The Hebrew text contains the temporal modifier לנצח (*lěneṣaḥ*) meaning "forever." LXX Lam, however, reflects a later meaning attested in the Dead Sea Scrolls: εις νικος (*eis nikos*) meaning "until victory."[12] This term came to be associated in Second Temple Judaism with the eschatological victory of God and his people over their enemies. The text then betrays the more developed eschatology of Second Temple Judaism and expresses faith in the vindication of God's people at the end of time.

---

11. Assan-Dote, *Baruch, Lamentations, Lettre de Jérémie*, 169.
12. Elisha Qimron, *The Hebrew of the Dead Sea Scrolls*, 111.

## CONCLUSION

Though this introduction to LXX Lam offers only a sampling of its character, perhaps it is sufficient to indicate the complexity of ancient translations. On the one hand, LXX Lam almost slavishly adheres to the Hebrew text often at the expense of Greek style. On the other hand, it undeniably adds a layer of tradition and interpretation consistent with the concerns of Second Temple Judaism.

## BIBLIOGRAPHY

Assan-Dote, Isabelle. *Baruch, Lamentations, Lettre de Jérémie.* La Bible D'Alexandrie Vol. 25.2. Paris: Cerf, 2005.

Barthélemy, Dominique. *Les devanciers d'Aquila.* Supplements to Vetus Testamentum 10. Leiden: Brill, 1963.

Dempster, Stephen G. *Dominion and Dynasty: A Theology of the Hebrew Bible.* New Studies in Biblical Theology. Downers Grove, IL: InterVarsity, 2003.

Gentry, Peter J. "Lamentations." In *A New English Translation of the Septuagint,* 932–41. New York: Oxford University Press, 2007.

Pietersma, Albert. "The Acrostic Poems of Lamentations in Greek Translation." In *VIII Congress of the International Organization for Septuagint and Cognate Studies,* edited by Leonard Greenspoon and Olivier Munnich, 183–201. SBL Septuagint and Cognate Studies. Atlanta: Scholars, 1995.

Pietersma, Albert, and Benjamin G. Wright. "To the Reader of NETS." In *A New English Translation of the Septuagint,* xiii–xx.. New York: Oxford University Press, 2007.

Qimron, Elisha. *The Hebrew of the Dead Sea Scrolls.* Harvard Semitic Studies. 29. Atlanta: Scholars, 1986.

Youngblood, Kevin J. "Translation Technique in the Greek Lamentations." PhD diss., The Southern Baptist Theological Seminary, 2004.

Ziegler, Joseph. *Ieremias, Baruch, Threni, Epistula Ieremiae. Septuaginta: Vetus Testamentum Graecum Auctoritate Societatis Litterarum Gottingensis editum,* vol. 15. Göttingen: Vandenhoeck & Ruprecht, 1957.

# C

# Targum Lamentations

Christian M. M. Brady

## INTRODUCTION

The term "Targum" (pl. "Targumim") simply means "translation" in Hebrew and Aramaic and the term may used to refer to any translation.[1] By the rabbinic period, however, the term "Targum" acquired the specific meaning of an Aramaic translation of the Bible (Tanakh) and when Aramaic had become the *lingua franca* for much of the ancient Near East (particularly for those Jews who remained in Babylon after the decree of Cyrus in 538 BCE) these translations were vital for a community which no longer understood Hebrew.

There is much debate as to the precise origins and uses of the Targumim but rabbinic sources tell us that there were three main contexts wherein the Targumim were used.

1. In private devotion[2] the Targum would be read alongside the biblical text in preparation for services.

2. In the *Beyt haSefer* (Elementary School), where the primary subject was the learning of Torah, the Targumim were apparently studied, perhaps as a "crib" to help children learn Aramaic.

3. The primary setting of the Targumim, however, was in the synagogue. Mishnah Megilah 4.4[3] tells us that the Torah should be read one verse at a time with the

---

1. See, for example, Ezra 4:7, "And in the days of Artaxerxes, Bishlam and Mithredath and Tabeel and the rest of their associates wrote to King Artaxerxes of Persia; the letter was written in Aramaic and translated."

2. *b Ber.* 8a

3. "One who reads the Torah [in synagogue] should read not less than three verses, and he should not read to the translator (מתורגמן) more than one verse [at a time]. In a Prophet, however, [he may give him] three at a time. If the three verses constitute three separate paragraphs, he must read them [to the translator] one by one. The reader may skip [from place to place] in a prophet but not in the Torah" (Danby, *The*

translator (*Meturgeman*) rending verse by verse after the lector. The rules were established primarily to ensure that there would be no confusion between the Written Torah and its translation. But Targum is far more than a simple translation of the Bible.

Among the various versions of biblical texts the Targumim stand apart. The Septuagint (LXX) translates the text into Greek and the Peshitta (P) translates the text into Syriac, but the Targum, while it translates the biblical text into Aramaic, also provides an embedded commentary. Targum is not a paraphrase, but it is also not a literal translation. It is, in fact, *sui generis*, without peer and comparison. A Targum will have a word-for-word rendering of the Hebrew into Aramaic, representing the biblical text in order and without repetition.[4] Yet at the same time a Targum will incorporate commentary into its rendering, the result is a "translation" of the biblical text which can, and often does, completely transform the meaning and structure of the original. The Targum to the Book of Lamentations is particularly rich in aggadic, or interpretative, additions as a result of the Targumist's attempt to wrestle with this emotive and confrontational text.

## THE THEOLOGY OF TARGUM LAMENTATIONS

The Book of Lamentations challenges the reader, especially those who read it from within Jewish or Christian faith traditions, because it is a challenge to God. This raw and emotive text lays bare the poet's soul and confronts the horrors of war and the tragedy of struggling to survive. The poet[5] does not shy away from naming God as Israel's enemy who has completely ravaged Jerusalem. The language used is evocative and disturbing. Mothers boil their young in order to stave off starvation and the royalty cling to dung heaps. Most scholars agree that the Book of Lamentations contains the words of an eyewitness as he struggles to come to terms with his horrifying experience. At times the poet looks forward, trying to perceive if there is a future, but for the most part the poet speaks of pain and grief endured. Moments of confession occur and are quickly overcome by the magnitude of the punishment that was visited upon them by God. And it *is* God who has done this to Zion. The poet does not waver in that belief. Quite the contrary, it is vigorously asserted that it is the *Lord* who has rejected, humiliated, and "destroyed without mercy" (Lam 2:2).

The poet of Lamentations was responding to the very real events of his life. He had suffered, watched others die, and now sought to live into the future. The Targumist, on the other hand, is not responding to a personal experience. He is not even directly responding to the destruction of 586 BCE or of 70 CE, although he does, of necessity, deal with both. The Targumist is primarily concerned with responding to the *text* of

*Mishnah*, 200). All translations of the Mishnah are from Danby unless otherwise noted.

4. There are, of course, exceptions, but they are few in number. Many such exceptions, however, are present in Targum Lamentations.

5. Or poets. There is no real consensus concerning the number or identity of the author. It is likely that there was more than one poet; chapter 3 seems to at least indicate the kind of reflection that can only come with the passage of time, but for simplicity I will merely refer to the author or poet in the singular.

# GREAT IS THY FAITHFULNESS?

Lamentations itself. Where the Book of Lamentations is an expression of grief and an outpouring of pain with little concern for maintaining a systematic theology, Targum Lamentations (TgLam) is concerned with vindicating God, acquitting the Lord of any perceived guilt, and bringing Lamentations into line with contemporary rabbinic theological beliefs. It also sought to direct its audience to proper rabbinic worship through repentance and the study of Mishnah and Torah. In so doing, TgLam reveals itself as a pastoral (if polemic) work.

Gottwald has argued that the key to the theology of the Book of Lamentations is "the tension between Deuteronomic faith and historical adversity."[6] The authors of Lamentations, according to Gottwald, have sought to interpret the reality of their current historical situation in light of the statements found in the Book of Deuteronomy, especially Deut 28, that declare God's punishment against an unfaithful people. While Gottwald's interpretation of the center of Lamentations' theology has not met with universal agreement,[7] it is certain that the Targumist holds this view of Lamentations and renders his version of the book accordingly.

Through translation and interpretation the Targumist puts forward a wide variety of reasons to explain how Israel, as a nation, had sinned against God and brought upon itself the punishment meted out by God through the hand of Nebuchadnezzar. I will focus briefly on three key ways in which the Targumist re-presents Lamentations for his audience, the Congregation of Israel that gathers together on Tisha b'Av to commemorate the destruction of Jerusalem and the Temple.

## THEOLOGICAL PROLOGUE

TgLam begins with a massive expansion of the first four verses of Lamentations,[8] the purpose of which is to place the Targum into an interpretive context. While Lam 1:1 begins with the lament of Jerusalem's fallen state ("How lonely sits the city that once was full of people")[9] the Targum inserts an extended discourse between Jeremiah and the Attribute of Justice.[10] TgLam goes on to outline the history of Israel's rebellion against God beginning with Adam and Eve, moving on to Israel's refusal to accept that God would deliver Canaan into their hands (an allusion to Numbers 14), and continuing down to the time of the destruction itself.

The combination of these additions to the text serves to create a theological prolegomenon to Lamentations. This reframes the entire Book of Lamentations providing the Targumist's audience with what the Targumist believes to be the proper context within which they are to interpret the text. The massively expanded first four verses thus ensures

---

6. Gottwald, *Studies in the Book of Lamentations*, 525–26.

7 See Westermann, *Lamentations*, 76–81.

8. See Appendix for the text and translation of TgLam. For detailed discussion of this passage see Brady, "Targum Lamentations 1.1–4."

9. All biblical quotations in English are from the *New Revised Standard Version* (Oxford: OUP, 1989) unless otherwise noted.

10. For more on the Attribute of Justice see Brady, "The Role of מדת דינא in the Targumim."

that the audience would not come to erroneous conclusions, such as that God was impotent to stop the Babylonians or that he had acted capriciously in destroying Jerusalem.

## DRAMATIC HEIGHTENING

Another technique employed by the Targumist to cope with the graphic and challenging text of Lamentations is unexpectedly *to intensify it*. This technique, which may be called "dramatic heightening," appears to be unique among the Targumim. It is not uncommon to find that the Targumim (and rabbinic literature in general) soften the language of a biblical text where it appears to present views which were contrary to contemporary notions. Given the graphic and accusatory nature of Lamentations it would be reasonable to expect TgLam to interpret the harsh passages of Lamentations (e.g., Lam 2:4–5, 20) in such a way that they would no longer be offensive or challenging to the commonly held rabbinic views. It is therefore quite surprising to find that not only does our Targumist retain references to God "as an enemy," but he even introduces vivid and graphic imagery to passages which were otherwise relatively banal.

The most startling example of this is in the interpretation of Lam 1:15. The biblical text describes God as proclaiming a time when both the young men and women of Judah would be destroyed. The language of this verse is quite strong, it is the Lord himself who has "trodden" the "virgin daughter Judah," but the language of the Targum is much more dramatic: "The Lord has crushed all my mighty ones within me; he has established a time against me to shatter the strength of my young men. The nations entered by decree of the *Memra*[11] of the Lord and defiled the virgins of the House of Judah until their blood of their virginity was caused to flow like wine from a wine press when a man is treading grapes and grape-wine flows." The biblical text describes the Lord as *rejecting* the warriors of Judah, but the Targumist intensifies the image by describing the Lord as *crushing* them. God no longer treads on the virgin daughter Judah, but instead the Targum tells us that it is "the nations" who act by "the decree of the *Memra* of the Lord." The most startling change to this verse, however, is the nature of the calamity that befalls Judah. In the biblical verse Jerusalem is personified as "the virgin daughter Judah" and she has been laid low, "trodden," by the Lord. In the Targum, however, the metaphorical "virgin daughter Judah" becomes the "virgins of the House of Judah" who are raped by the invading nations so viciously that the "blood of their virginity" flows freely.

In a similar manner, although not nearly so graphic, the Targumist's audience is told repeatedly that it was "because of the greatness of the rebellious sin" that Zion was destroyed. In seven separate instances, most of which are found at the beginning of the Targum,[12] the Targumist has *added* references to Israel's rebellion as the cause of their downfall. The Targumist not only retains the biblical text's confession of sin found in verses such as Lam 1:5, 8, 14, 22; 2:14; and 3:42, but amplifies both the nature of their sin and the resulting punishment. In so doing the Targumist makes it explicit for his audi-

---

11. Memra is Aramaic for "word" and is used in the Targums to distance God from anthropomorphisms. Thus it is the "word" of the Lord which utters the decree rather than the Lord himself.

12. See TgLam 1:1, 4, 7–9; 3:28, 39.

ence that the national tragedy that befell Judah was not the capricious act of a vengeful God, but was the just punishment against a sinful people.

Beneath this all lays the fundamental assumption that God is ultimately responsible. Rather than distance God from these actions, the Targumist makes it clear that their entire history is controlled by God: it is he alone who determines when and how Israel will be punished. But while God controls history he also gave Israel the freedom to disobey so that when he does act against his people, he acts in righteousness to bring judgment upon them. As TgLam 1:15 elucidates, the nations entered at his command, his *Memra*, and he showed no mercy.

## RABBINIC COMMUNITY

In spite of this clear condemnation of Israel and vindication of God's actions, TgLam retains a pastoral focus. It is intended to guide the community in worship on Tisha b'Av in their reading of Lamentations and to direct them in proper worship and belief. The use of the phrase כנשתא ("Congregation"), where other translations of the Hebrew בת ("daughter") would have been possible, engages the audience by encouraging them to identify with the experience of those who sinned and suffered in the Book of Lamentations. Those gathered in mourning and commemorating the destruction of the Temples by listening to the recitation of Lamentations and its Targum hundreds of years after the events being described are also the "congregation of Israel dwelling in exile" (TgLam 2:19). TgLam has been crafted so that future readers and worshippers will find themselves in its words and that through its reception, they will remember and be moved. But the Targumist does not seek simply to evoke emotions. The congregation dwelling in exile is called to busy itself "with Mishnah in the night, for the *Shekinah* of the Lord is dwelling before [them]" (TgLam 2:19). They are called to repentance and proper worship of the God of Israel. This worship is thoroughly rabbinic in nature.

At the structural center of TgLam, beginning with TgLam 3:25, is an exhortation to the audience to adhere to fundamental rabbinic principles and practice. Those who desire to have the favor of the Lord bestowed upon them are to wait patiently for his salvation as they bear the yoke of the commandments and the yoke of heaven, through the recitation of the *Shema*. All of this is so that they might be accepted into the world to come. They are to hope for salvation (TgLam 3:25, 26, and 28) and turn in repentance (v. 40) before the Lord "whose *Shekinah* is in heaven above" (v. 41). While they seek God's instruction (v. 25) and obey Torah (v. 27), they are also to accept the chastisement from God for the sake of his name (v. 28) and "for the sake of the fear of the Lord" (v. 30). These corrections will, in turn, result in their being accepted by God in the world to come (v. 28) as the Lord has mercy upon his people (vv. 28, 31, and 32).

The general statements of chapter 3, such as "the Lord is good to those who wait for him" (Lam 3:25), are transformed for the audience into clear directions of the proper rabbinic response to suffering and persecution. The language, concepts, and practices described are all rooted within the rabbinic culture, as described in the classical sources, both midrashic and halakhic. The purpose is to provide guidance to the community, now far removed both historically and geographically from the events of 586 BCE, on how to respond to the text that they have heard. It is similar to the way in which the Targumist establishes the framework within which the book of Lamentations is to be understood and interpreted by presenting the litany of Israel's sins throughout her history. Now, however, the congregation sitting upon the floor or stools of the synagogue, hearing the text and its Targum recited, find themselves within this *Heilsgeschichte*.

In TgLam 2:19 and TgLam 3:25–30, the Targumist provides what might be called the application of the Targum, as he tells his audience what is expected of them. They are part of this great, often difficult, history of Israel and they too have a unique and special relationship with God. So what is their response to be when reflecting upon the tragedies of Jewish history? When trapped within their own moments of despair and anguish? The Targum offers guidance and directs the community to study Mishnah, to patiently take upon themselves the yoke of Torah as a witness to the unity of the Lord, and to pray in the synagogue. This is how the Jewish community is to commemorate Tisha b'Av and this is how it is to respond to its own crises.

The challenge of the Book of Lamentations—its strong language, emotions, accusations against God, and its potential threat to orthodox understanding of God and his relationship with is people—is thus tempered and forged into what is, for the rabbinic Targumist, a powerful tool for encouraging his community. The Targumist's audience exists in the middle of this sweeping flow of history he has woven into Lamentations. As the community gathers in worship on Tisha b'Av and looks back, remembering Israel's sins of the past as well as God's faithfulness, they also look forward to the coming of the Messiah and God's final deliverance of Israel (TgLam 4:22). The community exists within this *Heilsgeschichte*, in the present before God. So the Targumist calls them to take part in the "holy history" of Israel by repenting of their sins and committing themselves once again to right, rabbinic worship and obedience to the Lord their God. Thus their mourning and that of Lamentations will be turned into dancing.

## BIBLIOGRAPHY

Alexander, Philip S. *The Targum of Lamentations.* Collegeville, MN: Liturgical, 2007.

———. "Textual Tradition of Targum Lamentations." *Abr-Nahrain* 24 (1986) 1–24.

Albrektson, Bertil. *Studies in the Text and Theology of the Book of Lamentations with a Critical Edition of the Peshitta Text.* Vol. 21. Studia Theologica Lundensia. Lund: Gleerup, 1963.

Brady, Christian M. M. *The Rabbinic Targum of Lamentations: Vindicating God.* Studies in Aramaic Interpretation of Scripture. Vol. 3. Leiden: Brill, 2003.

———. "The Role of מדת דינא in the Targumim." In *The Interpretation of Scripture in Early Judaism and Christianity: Studies in Language and Tradition,* edited by Craig A. Evans, 364–74. Studies in Scripture in Early Judaism and Christianity 7. Sheffield: Sheffield Academic, 2000.

———. "Targum Lamentations 1.1–4: A Theological Prologue." In *Targum and Scripture: Studies in Aramaic Translations and Interpretation in Memory of Ernest G. Clarke,* edited by Paul V. M. Flesher, 175–83. Studies in Aramaic Interpretation of Scripture, 2. Leiden: Brill, 2002.

Danby, Herbert. *The Mishnah.* Oxford: Oxford University Press, 1989.

de Lagarde, Paulus. *Hagiographa Chaldaice.* 1873. Reprint. Osnabrück: Seller, 1967.

Gottwald, Norman K. *Studies in the Book of Lamentations.* Studies in Biblical Theology, 14. London: SCM, 1962.

Greenup A. *The Targum on the Book of Lamentations.* Sheffield: Greenup, 1893.

Levine, Étan. *The Aramaic Version of Lamentations.* New York: Hermon, 1976.

———. *The Targum to the Five Megillot: Codex Vatican Urbanati 1.* Jerusalem: Makor, 1977.

Sperber, Alexander. *The Bible in Aramaic Vol. 4A. The Hagiographa: Transition from Translation to Midrash.* Leiden: Brill, 1968.

———. *The Bible in Aramaic Vol. 4B. The Targum and the Hebrew Bible.* Leiden: Brill, 1973.

Van der Heide, Albert. *The Yemenite Tradition of the Targum of Lamentations.* Studia Post-Biblica 32. Edited by J. C. H. Lebram. Leiden: E. J. Brill, 1981.

Westermann, Claus. *Lamentations: Issues and Interpretation.* Translated by Charles Muenchow. Minneapolis: Augsburg Fortress, 1994.

# D

## Lamentations Rabbati

JACOB NEUSNER

### EDITORS' INTRODUCTION

THE HEBREW WORD USED by ancient rabbinic authorities for biblical interpretation was *midrash*. Many different exegetical techniques were used by the Rabbis to derive deeper meanings from the biblical text thus making it ever-fresh and relevant for the Jewish community.

The rabbinic midrashim were originally preserved orally but, beginning in the second century CE, they began to be written down. The interpretative comments in the midrashic collections come from a variety of rabbinic authorities, dating from different periods, and offering a range of interpretative possibilities.

There are two major collections of midrashim—the *Mekhilta* ("rules of interpretation") dating from about 300 CE and *Midrash Rabbah* ("the Great Midrash") dating from about the end of the fifth century CE. *Lamentations Rabbati* belongs to the latter.[1]

### THE THEME

The theme of *Lamentations Rabbati* is Israel's relationship with God, and the message concerning that theme is that the stipulative covenant still and always governs that relationship. Therefore everything that happens to Israel makes sense and bears meaning; and Israel is not helpless before its fate but controls its own destiny. This is the one and whole message of our compilation, and it is the only message that is repeated throughout; everything else proves secondary and derivative of the fundamental proposition

---

1. The following summary of the content of Lamentations Rabbah was originally published in Jacob Neusner, *Introduction to the Midrash Compilations of the Sixth and Seventh Centuries: An Introduction to the Rhetorical Logical, and Topical Program. I. Lamentations Rabbah*. Atlanta: Scholars, 1990. It is reproduced here with kind permission of the copyright holder, Jacob Neusner. A sample Jacob Neusner's translation of *Lamentations Rabbati* can be found in Appendix 3.

that the destruction of the Temple in Jerusalem in 70 CE, as much as in 586 BCE, proves the enduring validity of the covenant, its rules and its promise of redemption.

*Lamentations Rabbah*'s is a covenantal theology, in which Israel and God have mutually and reciprocally agreed to bind themselves to a common Torah; the rules of the relationship are such that an infraction triggers its penalty willy-nilly; but obedience to the Torah likewise brings its reward, in the context envisaged by our compilers, the reward of redemption. The compilation sets forth a single message, which is reworked in only a few ways: Israel suffers because of sin, God will respond to Israel's atonement, on the one side, and loyalty to the covenant in the Torah, on the other. And when Israel has attained the merit that accrues through the Torah, God will redeem Israel. That is the simple, rock-hard, and repeated message of this rather protracted reading of the book of Lamentations. Still, *Lamentations Rabbah* proves nearly as much a commentary in the narrowest sense—verse by verse amplification, paraphrase, exposition—as it is a compilation in the working definition of this inquiry of mine.

What holds the document together and gives it, if not coherence, then at least flow and movement, after all, are the successive passages of (mere) exposition. All the more stunning, therefore, is the simple fact that, when all has been set forth and completed, there really is that simple message that God's unique relationship with Israel, which is unique among the nations, works itself out even now, in a time of despair and disappointment.

The resentment of the present condition, recapitulating the calamity of the destruction of the Temple, finds its resolution and remission in the redemption that will follow Israel's regeneration through the Torah—that is the program, that is the proposition, and in this compilation, there is no other.

## TOPICAL PROGRAM

Israel's relationship with God is treated with special reference to the covenant, the Torah, and the land. By reason of the sins of the Israelites, they have gone into exile with the destruction of the Temple. The founders of the family—Abraham, Isaac, and Jacob—also went into exile. Now they cannot be accused of lacking in religious duties, attention to teachings of the Torah and of prophecy, carrying out the requirements of righteousness (philanthropy) and good deeds, and the like. The people are at fault for their own condition (I:i.1–7). Torah-study defines the condition of Israel, e.g., "If you have seen [the inhabitants of] towns uprooted from their places in the land of Israel, know that it is because they did not pay the salary of scribes and teachers" (II.i).

So long as Judah and Benjamin (meaning, in this context, the surviving people, after the northern tribes were taken away by the Assyrians) were at home, God could take comfort at the loss of the ten tribes; once they went into exile, God began to mourn (II:ii). Israel (now meaning not the northern tribes, but the remaining Jews) survived Pharaoh and Sennacherib, but not God's punishment (III:i). After the disaster in Jeremiah's time, Israel emerged from Eden but could come back (IV:i). God did not play favorites among the tribes; when any of them sinned, he punished them through exile (VI:i). Israel was punished because of the ravaging of words of Torah and prophecy, righteous men, religious duties, and good deeds (VII:i). The land of Israel, the Torah, and the Temple are ravaged, to the shame of Israel (Jer. 9:19–21) (VIII:i). The Israelites practiced idolatry, still more did the pagans; God was neglected by the people and was left solitary, so God responded to the people's actions (X:i). If you had achieved the merit (using the theological language at hand), then you would have enjoyed everything, but since you did not have the merit, you enjoyed nothing (XI:i).

The Israelites (throughout referring to the surviving Jews, after the northern tribes were taken into exile) did not trust God, so they suffered disaster (XIII.i). The Israelites scorned God and brought dishonor upon God among the nations (XV:i). While God was generous with the Israelites in the wilderness, under severe conditions, he was harsh with them in civilization, under pleasant conditions, because they sinned and angered him (XVI:i). With merit one drinks good water in Jerusalem, without, bad water in the exile of Babylonia; with merit one sings songs and Psalms in Jerusalem, without, dirges and lamentations in Babylonia. At stake is peoples' merit, not God's grace (XIX:i). The contrast is drawn between redemption and disaster, the giving of the Torah, and the destruction of the Temple (XX:i). When the Israelites went into exile among the nations of the world, not one of them could produce a word of Torah from his mouth; God punished Israel for its sins (XXI:i). Idolatry was the cause (XXII:i). The destruction of the Temple was possible only because God had already abandoned it (XXIV:ii). When the Temple was destroyed, God was answerable to the patriarchs for what he had done (XXIV:ii). The Presence of God departed from the Temple by stages (XXV:i).

The Holy One punishes Israel only after bringing testimony against them (XXVII:i). The road that led from the salvation of Hezekiah is the one that brought Israel to the disaster brought about by Nebuchadnezzar. Then the Israelite kings believed, but the pagan king did not believe; and God gave the Israelite kings a reward for their faith, through Hezekiah, and to the pagan king, without his believing and without obeying, were handed over Jerusalem and its Temple. (XXX:i). Before the Israelites went into exile, the Holy One, blessed be he, called them "bad." But when they had gone into exile, he began to sing their praises (XXXI:i). The Israelites were sent into exile only after they had defied the Unique One of the world, the Ten Commandments, circumcision, which had been given to the twentieth generation [Abraham], and the Pentateuch (XXXV:ii, iii). When the Temple was destroyed and Israel went into exile, God mourned in the manner that mortals do (XXXV:iv). The prophetic critique of Israel is mitigated by mercy. Israel stands in an ambiguous relationship with God, both divorced and not divorced (XXXV:vi, vii).

Before God penalizes, he has already prepared the healing for the penalty. As to all the harsh prophecies that Jeremiah issued against the Israelites, Isaiah first of all anticipated each and pronounced healing for it (XXXVI:ii). The Israelites err for weeping frivolously, "but in the end there will be a real weeping for good cause" (XXXVI:iv, v). The ten tribes went into exile, but the Presence of God did not go into exile. Judah and Benjamin went into exile, but the Presence of God did not go into exile.

But when the children went into exile, then the Presence of God went into exile (XXXIX:iii). The great men of Israel turned their faces away when they saw people sinning, and God did the same to them (XL:ii). When the Israelites carry out the will of the Holy One, they add strength to the strength of heaven, and when they do not, they weaken the power of the One above (XL:ii). The exile and the redemption will match (XL:ii). In her affliction, Jerusalem remembered her rebellion against God (XLI;i).

When the gentile nations sin, there is no sequel in punishment, but when the Israelites sin, they also are punished (XLII:i). God considered carefully how to bring the evil upon Israel (XLVIII:i). God suffers with Israel and for Israel (L:i), a minor theme in a massive compilation of stories. By observing their religious duties the Israelites became distinguished before God (LIII:i). With every thing with which the Israelites sinned, they were smitten, and with that same thing they will be comforted. When they sinned with the head, they were smitten at the head, but they were comforted through the head (LVI:i). There is an exact match between Israel's triumph and Israel's downfall. Thus: Just as these (the people of Jericho) were punished through the destruction effected by priest and prophet (the priests and Joshua at Jericho), so these (the people of Jerusalem in the time of the Babylonian conquest) were subject to priest and prophet (Jeremiah). Just as these who were punished were penalized through the ram's horn and shouting, so Israel will be saved through ram's horn and shouting (LVII:ii).

God's relationship to Israel was complicated by the relationship to Jacob, thus: "Isn't it the fact that the Israelites are angering me only because of the icon of Jacob that is engraved on my throne? Here, take it, it's thrown in your face!" (LVII:ii). God is engaged with Israel's disaster (LIX:ii).

The Israelites did not fully explore the limits of the measure of justice, so the measure of justice did not go to extremes against them (LX:i, LXI:i). God's decree against Jerusalem comes from of old (LXIV:i). God forewarned Israel and showed Israel favor, but it did no good (LXIX:i). God did to Israel precisely what he had threatened long ago (LXXIII:i). But God does not rejoice in punishing Israel. The argument between God and Israel is framed in this way. The Community of Israel says that they are the only ones who accepted God; God says, I rejected everybody else for you (LXXIX:ii). Israel accepted its suffering as atonement and asked that the suffering expiate the sin (LXXV:i).

God suffers along with Israel, Israel's loyalty will be recognized and appreciated by God, and, in the meantime, the Israelites will find in the Torah the comfort that they require. The nations will be repaid for their actions toward Israel in the interval. Even though the Holy One, blessed be he, is angry with his servants, the righteous, in this world, in the world to come he goes and has mercy on them (LXXXVI:i). God is good to those that deserve it (LXXXVII:i). God mourns for Israel the way human mourners mourn (LXXXVIII:i). God will never abandon Israel (LXXXIX:i). The Holy Spirit brings about redemption (XCV:i). It is better to be punished by God than favored by a gentile king, thus: "Better was the removing of the ring by Pharaoh [for the sealing of decrees to oppress the Israelites] than the forty years during which Moses prophesied concerning them, because it was through this [oppression] that the redemption came about, while through that [prophesying] the redemption did not come about" (CXXII:i).

The upshot here is that persecution in the end is good for Israel, because it produces repentance more rapidly than prophecy ever did, with the result that the redemption is that much nearer. The enemy will also be punished for its sins, and, further, God's punishment is appropriate and well placed.

People get what they deserve, both Israel and the others. God should protect Israel and not leave them among the nations, but that is not what he has done (CXXIII:i). God blames that generation for its own fate, and the ancestors claim that the only reason the Israelites endure is because of the merit of the ancestors (CXXIX:i). The redemption of the past tells us about the redemption in the future (CXXX:i). "The earlier generations, because they smelled the stench of only part of the tribulations inflicted by the idolatrous kingdoms, became impatient. But we, who dwell in the midst of the four kingdoms, how much the more [are we impatient]!" (CXXXI:i).

God's redemption is certain, so people who are suffering should be glad, since that is a guarantee of coming redemption; thus "For if those who outrage him he treats in such a way, those who do his will all the more so!" So if the words of the prophet Uriah are carried out, the words of the prophet Zechariah will be carried out, while if the words of the prophet Uriah prove false, then the words of the prophet Zechariah will not be true either. "I was laughing with pleasure because the words of Uriah have been carried out, and that means that the words of Zechariah in the future will be carried out" (CXL:i). The Temple will be restored, and Israel will regain its place, as God's throne and consort, respectively (CXLI:i).

Punishment and rejection will be followed by forgiveness and reconciliation (CXLII:i). The Jews can accomplish part of the task on their own, even though they throw themselves wholly on God's mercy. The desired age is either like that of Adam, or like that of Moses and Solomon, or like that of Noah and Abel; all three possibilities link the coming redemption to a time of perfection, Eden, or the age prior to idolatry, or the time of Moses and Solomon, the builders of the Tabernacle and the Temple, respectively (CXLIII:i). If there is rejection, then there is no hope, but if there is anger, there is hope, because someone who is angry may in the end be appeased. Whenever there is an allusion to divine anger, that too is a mark of hope (CXLIV:i).

Israel's relationship with the nations is treated with interest in Israel's history—past, present, and future—and how that cyclical is to be known. But there is no theory of "the other," or the outsider here; the nations are the enemy; the compilers find nothing of merit to report about them. Israel's difference from the other, for which God is responsible, accounts for the dislike that the nations express toward Israel; Israel's present condition as minority, different and despised on account of the difference, is God's fault and choice. Israel was besieged not only by the Babylonians but also the neighbors, the Ammonites and Moabites (IX:i), and God will punish them too. The public ridicule of Jews' religious rites contrasts with the Jews' own perception of their condition. The exposition of Ps 69:13 in terms of gentiles' ridicule of Jews' practices (the Jews' poverty, their Sabbath and Seventh Year observance), is followed by a re-exposition of the Jews' practices, now with respect to the ninth of Ab (XVII:i). Even though the nations of the world go into exile, their exile is not really an exile at all. But as for Israel, their exile really is an exile. The nations of the world, who eat the bread and drink the wine of others, do not really experience exile. But the Israelites, who do not eat the bread and drink the wine of others, really do experience exile (XXXVII:i).

The Ammonites and Moabites joined with the enemy and behaved very spitefully (XLIV:i). When the Israelites fled from the destruction of Jerusalem, the nations of the world sent word everywhere to which they fled and shut them out (LV:i). But this was to be blamed on God: "If we had intermarried with them, they would have accepted us" (LXIX:i). There are ten references to the "might" of Israel; when the Israelites sinned, these forms of might were taken away from them and given to the nations of the world. The nations of the world ridicule the Jews for their religious observances (LXXXIII:i). These propositions simply expose, in their own framework, the same proposition as the ones concerning God's relationship to Israel and Israel's relationship to God. The relationship between Israel and the nations forms a subset of the relationship of Israel and God; nothing in the former relationship happens on its own, but all things express in this mundane context the rules and effects of the rules that govern in the transcendent one. All we learn about Israel and the nations is that the covenant endures, bearing its own inevitable sanctions and consequences.

# E

# Introduction to Rashi's Commentary on Lamentations

MAYER I. GRUBER

THE NAME RASHI is an acronym for Rabbi Solomon Izhaqi, i.e., Rabbi Solomon son of Isaac. Born in 1030 or 1040 CE in the city of Troyes, which was the capital of the province of Champagne, Rashi died there in 1105. Rashi wrote the standard Jewish commentaries on most of Hebrew Scripture and the greater part of the Babylonian Talmud, the two most important sacred writings of Judaism. Because Rashi's commentaries on Hebrew Scripture were the ones most commonly read by Jews, Christians studied those commentaries to understand how the Old Testament was understood by the members of the faith community that had composed that corpus.

While the spoken language of the Jews of Troyes in the time of Rashi was Old Northern French, the language of virtually all of their prose writings, including Rashi's biblical and Talmudic commentaries, was a form of Mishnaic Hebrew. Rashi often clarifies the meanings of obscure words in Biblical Hebrew by citing the precise equivalent in Old Northern French or other European languages with which his readers may have been familiar. In fact, Rashi's Commentary on Lamentations includes nineteen Old French glosses. Within a very short time after their composition, Rashi's commentaries were copied and studied all over the world from Spain and North Africa in the West to Persia in the East and from the Germanic lands in the North to Yemen in the South.

Rashi's commentary on the Pentateuch was especially popular because of the holy obligation incumbent upon every Jew to read each week of the year the assigned section of the Pentateuch together with either the ancient Aramaic translation or the commentary of Rashi.

Next in popularity to Rashi's Commentary on the Pentateuch were Rashi's commentaries on the Five Scrolls, i.e., Canticles, Ruth, Lamentations, Ecclesiastes, and Esther. While the obligation to read the Book of Esther publicly in the synagogue is discussed already in the third century CE Mishnah (Rosh ha-Shanah 3:7; Megillah 1–2), the obligation to read the Scroll of Lamentation on the Fast of the Ninth of Av is first attested in the eighth century CE in Tractate Sopherim 18:4. The popularity of Rashi's Commentary on the Five Scrolls is reflected in the fact that the most popular super-commentary on

## GREAT IS THY FAITHFULNESS?

Rashi's biblical commentaries—Siphte Hakahim "The Lips of the Wise" by Shabbetai Bass (1641–1718)—covers Rashi's commentaries on both the Pentateuch and the Five Scrolls.

The twenty-four hour Fast of the Ninth of Av commemorates primarily the destruction of the First Temple (586 BCE) and the Second Temple (70 CE) as well as other tragedies including the divine decree to sentence the Israelites to a forty year sojourn in the wilderness of Sinai as punishment for their having accepted the negative report concerning the land of Israel presented by ten of the twelve spies sent by Moses (see Numbers 13–14; Deuteronomy 1; and see Rashi at Lam 1:2).

Rashi's commentaries on biblical narratives, best exemplified by his commentary on Genesis, serve not only to elucidate vocabulary, grammar, and syntax but also to summarize Rabbinic stories based upon biblical stories. Rashi's commentaries on biblical law, exemplified by his commentary on the Decalogue and the Covenant Code (Exodus 21–24) likewise serve not only to elucidate the biblical text but also to explain the meaning which legal statements in the Pentateuch are given in the major Rabbinic law corpora—Mishnah, Mekhilta, Sifra, Sifre, and the Babylonian Talmud. The Book of Lamentations contains neither law nor narrative although it alludes both to the violation of divine law (Lam 1:9) by the people of the generation of the First Exile (586 BCE) and to events known from biblical narratives. For example, Rashi finds in Lam 5:13 an allusion to the exiles' being marched across the desert to Babylonia carrying burdens. Moreover, Rashi finds in Lam 4:21—"Rejoice and exult, Fair Edom, Who dwell in the land of Uz. To you, too, the cup [i.e., the poison draught as a means of judicial punishment] shall pass"—a prophecy concerning the aftermath of the fall of the Second Temple, which was destroyed by the Romans, who are given the epithets "Edom/Edomites" in Rabbinic literature.

By-and-large Rashi's commentary on Lamentations attempts to elucidate obscure words and phrases for the benefit of a target audience that wanted to understand the Book of Lamentations both because of its place in the worship service on the eve of the Ninth of Av and because the informed reading of this book constitutes for Jews an act of "Study of Torah," which is the functional equivalent of Protestant "Bible Study." Most of Rashi's Commentary on the Book of Lamentations is philological. This is to say that, for the most part, Rashi explains the meaning of rare words by recourse to cognates in the Hebrew Bible and, when necessary, in Mishnaic Hebrew or Aramaic. The principle sources which Rashi often explicitly cites are Lamentations Rabbah and the dictionary of Biblical Hebrew called Mahberet composed by Menahem Ibn Saruq (tenth-century Cordova). On very rare occasions (in the commentary on Lamentations only at 4:7), Rashi will write, "I say," suggesting that he is expressing an original view as to the meaning and/or etymology of a Biblical Hebrew word or phrase.

In addition, in his commentary at Lam 1:1 Rashi writes, "And there are many aggadic midrashim, but I have come to explain the language of the Bible according to its literal meaning." This comment reminds one of Rashi's frequently quoted remarks at the beginning of his commentary on Canticles and in his commentary on Gen 3:8 and his comment on Ps 2:1. Critical Jewish biblical exegetes in modern times often expressed disappointment that Rashi seems not to have followed through on his promise to present only the literal meaning of Scripture insofar as his commentaries on biblical narrative are replete with stories that have no basis in the literal meaning of the biblical text while his commentaries on legal texts incorporate halakhic interpretations, which appear to be anachronistic. Naturally, many critical Jewish biblical exegetes delight in Rashi's commentaries on the prophetic books and Lamentations, which offer very few digressions from pure philological commentary and which clearly bracket most of the digressions with expressions such as "an aggadic midrash states."

Rashi begins his commentary on Lamentations with a discussion of the book's authorship and the composite nature of the book at hand. Rashi's introduction to Lamentations reminds one of Rashi's introduction to the Book of Psalms where he indicates that the latter book contains at least ten genres, which correspond numerically to ten psalmists listed in Midrash Tehillim at Ps 1:1 and in Babylonian Talmud, Bava Batra 14b–15a. Summarizing a Rabbinic text found in Lamentations Rabbah, Rashi contends that Jeremiah wrote the Book of Lamentations. This must be a Second Temple tradition as it is reflected in Josephus' Antiquities, the Septuagint, and the Vulgate, all of which place the Book of Lamentations after the Book of Jeremiah. In fact, the Vulgate labels the Book of Lamentations "the Lamentations of Jeremiah."

Inspired by Lamentations Rabbah, Rashi states that the Scroll of Lamentations as we know it is (1) the scroll, which was burnt by King Jehoiakim according to Jer 36:21–25 and which was rewritten by Baruch the scribe as dictated by Jeremiah (Jer 36:32) with additional material. What more could we want from a medieval commentator who, like modern critical exegetes, claims to be interested only in what the Bible actually says than a declaration that the book we have in front of us was written by Jeremiah but with additions, exactly what most modern commentators on the Book of Jeremiah say about that book as well? The comment, which Rashi copies out from Lamentations Rabbah goes further. It states that originally the Book of Lamentations consisted of the three lamentations in the form of alphabetical acrostics that constitute chapters 1, 2, and 4 of the Scroll of Lamentations. Rashi explains that Jeremiah subsequently added chapter 3, which is a three-fold alphabetical acrostic. It should be noted, furthermore, that when the Scroll of Lamentations is sung from a printed book or from a handwritten parchment scroll on the eve of the Ninth of Av, chapters 1, 2, 4, and 5 are sung to the identical tune while the chapter 3 is sung to an entirely different tune. Moreover, in his commentary on Lam 4:1 Rashi, basing himself on Lamentations Rabbah, states that Lam 4:1 actually existed independently of the scroll twice copied out by Baruch (see Jer 36 cited above) for it was originally composed as the funeral dirge on the occasion of the tragic death of King Josiah. The source for the assertion that Jeremiah composed and sang a lamentation or funeral dirge on the occasion of the death of King Josiah is 2 Chr 35:25. Rashi's assertion that Lamentations 4 was originally a funeral dirge composed in honor of King Josiah is more than an innocent piece of proto-source criticism, which can and will be utilized by modern Jewish exegetes, who seek both ancient and medieval pedigrees for atomizing Scripture and evidence that Rashi should be recognized as a critical exegete who supported the atomization of Scripture. In fact, the assertion that Lam 4 was the lament composed on the death and burial of Josiah by Jeremiah the Prophet supplies a brilliant answer to the exegetical question as to what happened to the lament referred to in 2 Chr 35:25, which was said to have been part of the standard curriculum studied by men and women who learned to sing lamentations at funerals. However, in the hands of Rashi the assertion that Lam 4 had a life of its own before it was incorporated into the scroll burnt by King Jehoiakim and then re-dictated and re-copied with various additions provides an answer to an exegetical question, which occupies Rashi in his commentary on Ps 2:1; 84:10; and 105:15, namely, who is the *mashiah*, i.e., the anointed king to whom Hebrew Scripture refers? Christian commentators saw in all of these verses references to Jesus Christ. Rashi endeavored to show that biblical philology undermined that interpretation. Not surprisingly, therefore, in his commentary at Lam 4:20—"The breath of our life, the LORD's anointed, was captured in their traps"—Rashi comments, "He is Josiah in accord with what is stated in Chronicles (2 Chr 35:25), 'And Jeremiah composed a lament for Josiah.'"

The most important Rabbinic source utilized by Rashi in writing his commentary on Lamentations is the text we now call Lamentations Rabbah or Eichah Rabbah. Rashi mentions this source explicitly only twice (2:6; 4:17), and he calls it Midrash Qinot, which means "The Midrash of Lamentations." Rashi thus employs both for the midrash and for the biblical book the older designation qinot "lamentations," which is reflected also in the Greek, Latin, and English titles of the biblical book. In Judaism in modern times, however, the word *qinot* "lamentations" designates the post-biblical dirges sung on the Ninth of Av. The biblical book of Lamentations and the Rabbinic midrash, on the other hand, are designated by the first word of the biblical book, *eichah*, which is an exclamation meaning "How!" Similarly, the biblical book of Genesis is commonly referred to in Hebrew by the first word bereshit, and the biblical book of Leviticus is commonly referred to in Hebrew by the first word *wayiqra*.

Interestingly, while Rashi mentions in his introduction to Lamentations that chapters 1, 2, and 4 are alphabetical acrostics and that chapter 3 is a triple alphabetical acrostic, he does not discuss the structure or lack of it in Lamentations 5. Rashi's source in Lamentations Rabbah 1:1 does intimate that the assertion that the Book of Lamentations is essentially the scroll that was dictated by Jeremiah and copied out by Baruch son of Neriah (after a previous scroll had been burnt by King Jehoiakim) and included also many additions (Jer 36:32) refers to the fact that the final chapter of Lamentations, chapter 5, is an add-on in that it does not follow the alphabetical acrostic arrangement of the earlier chapters. Significantly, Rashi does not comment on this even at the beginning of Lam 5. In fact, his commentary on Lam 5 begins only with v. 4.

Most of Rashi's commentary on Lamentations supplies the definitions of words. In two places (1:17 and 4:15) he explicitly cites Menahem ben Jacob Ibn Saruq. In two instances (1:14; 4:8) he notes that the word under discussion is an *hapax legomenon* within the corpus of Hebrew Scripture. On five occasions he utilizes a cognate from Mishnaic Hebrew to clarify the meaning of a word in Biblical Hebrew (1:14, 17, 20; 3:16, 43). In one instance he utilizes an Aramaic expression from the sixth century CE—Pesiqta deRav Kahana (1:14)—and on one occasion (3:10) he uses the expression *leshon gemara* to designate Babylonian Jewish Aramaic found in the Babylonian Talmud. In only one instance (4:7) does he claim originality for an interpretation.

A fully annotated edition and/or translation of Rashi's Commentary on Lamentations should focus primarily on evaluating Rashi's contribution to biblical lexicography with specific reference to the question as to the extent to which Rashi's idiosyncratic interpretations should be adopted.

## BIBLIOGRAPHY

Catane, Moche. Ozar ha-La'azim. Jerusalem: Gitler, 1990. [In Hebrew.]
Gruber, Mayer I. Rashi's Commentary on Psalms. Brill Reference Library of Judaism, 18. Leiden: Brill, 2004.
Zohory, Menahem. The Sources of Rashi's Halakhic and Aggadic Midrashim in His Commentaries: The Five Scrolls. Jerusalem: Cane, 1993. [In Hebrew.]
———. Grammarians and their Writings in Rashi's Commentaries. Jerusalem: Cane, 1995. [In Hebrew.]

# F

## Lamentations in Jewish Liturgy

ELSIE R. STERN

THE BOOK OF LAMENTATIONS is the scriptural centerpiece for Tisha b'Av (Ninth of Av), the holiday which commemorates a collection of catastrophes in the Jewish historical and mythical past. A tradition recorded in the Mishnah (a third-century rabbinic legal collection) states, "On the 9th of Av it was decreed that our ancestors would not enter the land; the first and second Temples were burned; Betar was captured and the city was destroyed" (*m. Ta'an.* 4:6). In the medieval and modern periods, Tisha b'Av was designated as the day of commemoration for additional tragedies in Jewish history, including the expulsions of Jews from England and Spain.

Lamentations is the lectionary text for the service on the eve of the holiday. The book is chanted to a haunting and plaintive melody and its performance is accompanied by dramatic signs of mourning. In many traditional synagogues, the curtain is removed from the Torah ark before the service and congregants remove their shoes if they are made of leather. During the performance of Lamentations itself, congregants sit on the ground or on low stools, in accordance with traditional Jewish mourning practice. The recitation of Lamentations is often followed by medieval poems of lament (*kinnot*). In many congregations, contemporary readings that relate to the theme of the day are recited as well.

Needless to say, the choice of Lamentations as the liturgical centerpiece for this holiday makes topical sense. While Tisha b'Av theoretically commemorates the host of tragedies enumerated above, the destructions of the first and second Temples serve as epitomes for the larger litany of catastrophes. Since Lamentations is the Bible's most direct and sustained response to the destruction of the first Temple, it seems an obvious lectionary choice for the holiday.

At the same time, however, the choice of Lamentations shapes the tone of the holiday in ways that are unusual within the larger Jewish liturgical context. Within the broader corpus of Jewish statutory liturgy, God is portrayed primarily as a fair and merciful sovereign who merits praise and supplication. The liturgy repeatedly states that God loves and favors the people of Israel and yearns for the repentance of both individuals and the community. While the liturgy certainly attributes enormous power to God, it focuses on past and potential deployments of that power that are beneficial to Israel and the members of the worshipping community. Within the daily liturgy, there is a section that begs God to address the community's misfortunes (*tachanun*) and also requests that God restrain God's legitimate anger in order to mobilize the essential divine mercy and compassion on Israel's behalf.

Lamentations presents a stark contrast to these dominant liturgical themes. Though Lamentations contains scattered expressions of a deuteronomic theology of sin and punishment (e.g., Lam 1:5, 8), its dominant tone is one of pain and devastating rupture. Within the poem, the suffering of Zion and the raging violence of God are the most powerful and prominent themes: "YHWH has destroyed without mercy all the dwellings of Jacob. He has torn down in his wrath the strongholds of the daughter of Judah. He has cut down in fierce anger the horn of Israel. He has drawn back his right hand from before the enemy. He has burned in Jacob like a flaming fire, consuming all around" (Lam 2:2–3). This portrait of a furiously destructive God is certainly at odds with the just and loving God of the larger Jewish liturgy.

The portrait of Zion as an abandoned and sympathetic victim is also central to the poem. "What can I compare to you? To what can I liken you, oh daughter Jerusalem? What can I compare to you that I might comfort you, maiden daughter Zion? For as vast as the sea is your ruin: who can heal you?" (Lam 2:13).

Although Lamentations 3 articulates a more familiar covenantal optimism, the book as a whole ends with a cry of anguished rupture and despair: "Rather, you have utterly rejected us; raged against us exceedingly" (Lam 5:22). The logic of Jewish prayer depends on the ongoing relationship of God and Israel. While the worshipper might acknowledge divine judgment or temporary feelings of estrangement, the threat of permanent rupture is totally foreign to the liturgical worldview. If God were to reject Israel utterly, prayer would be futile.

If one imagines the possible range of liturgical stances toward catastrophe, Lamentations' perspective becomes even more striking. A community might commemorate past catastrophes with assertions of a deuteronomic worldview, with penitential vows, statements of defiance or commitments toward activism and change. Lamentations does none of these. Rather, its central mode is one that testifies to Israel's pain and suffering and gives full expression to the experience of God as a fierce, irrational, and destructive enemy. Despite its nods to the deuteronomic theology, its primary message isn't "We have sinned and have been punished," but rather is "Pay heed to my suffering which is too extreme to ever have been deserved."[1]

Whilst the text and rituals of Tisha b'Av encourage the congregation to immerse itself in feelings of sadness, alienation, loss, and despair, this experience is embedded

---

1. The Aramaic translation to Lamentations (Targum) differs significantly from the Hebrew original by repeatedly identifying Israel's suffering as punishment for its sins. It is not clear whether this translation was used widely in synagogue settings. If it was, it would have tempered Lamentations' radical stance of lament with a more conventional justification of the nation's suffering. See Christian Brady's chapter on the Targum Lamentations in this volume.

within a larger cycle that is ultimately redemptive and reconciliatory. The recitation of Lamentations on Tisha b'Av serves as the fulcrum for a lectionary sequence that extends from the seventeenth of Tammuz to Rosh Hashanah. For most of the year, the Sabbath lectionary reading from the Prophets (*haftarah*, or plural, *haftarot*) is linked lexically or thematically to the week's Torah portion. For example, the first Torah portion of the year (Gen 1:1—6:8) is paired with Isa 42:5—43:10, which begins with a reference to God's creation of the heavens and the earth. For the three weeks preceding Tisha b'Av and the seven weeks following, however, the *haftarot* form a sequence that is independent of the Torah portions. The readings for the three Sabbaths before Tisha b'Av (Jer 1:1—2:3; 2:4-28; Isa 1:1-27) are known as the *haftarot* of rebuke and the seven following the holiday (excerpts from Isaiah 40-63) are known as the *haftarot* of consolation. In the first three, Israel is harangued for its sinfulness and is warned of the terrible consequences it will trigger. The reading of Lamentations on Tisha b'Av functions as the fulfillment of those dire prophecies. Through the recitation of Lamentations, the worshipping community is given license to articulate the pain, suffering, and most importantly, the alienation from God that the text expresses. The *haftarot* for the seven weeks following the holiday chart a process of reconciliation and consolation in which God deploys a wide range of strategies to console Israel and bring her back into relationship. This pattern was noticed by the fourteenth-century liturgical commentator, Abudarham, who interprets the first verses of each *haftarah* as the lines in a dialogue between God and Israel:

> It says in the Midarash . . . that they decided to begin the *haftarot* of consolation with *Comfort, comfort my people* (Isa 40:1) which is to say that the Holy one, blessed be He, says to the prophets: *comfort comfort my people*. The congregation of Israel responds to this: *And Zion says YHWH has abandoned me* (Isa 49:14). Which is to say, I am not appeased by the consolations of the prophets . . . And in the places where they recite *Unhappy storm tossed one, uncomforted* (Isa 54:11) . . . this is to say that the prophets respond and say before the Holy One, Blessed be He: "Behold the congregation of Israel is not pacified by our consolations." To this the Holy One Blessed be He replies: *I, I, am he who comforts you (Isa 51:12)*. And he says further, *Rejoice barren one who has not given birth* (54:1) and he says: *Arise, shine for your light comes* (Isa 60:1). To this, the congregation of Israel responds, *I will greatly rejoice in YHWH (61:10)* which is to say, now I have reason to rejoice and be happy.

While Abudarham cites only the first lines of each *haftarah*, the full liturgical experience is even more intense. For six weeks, Israel is the recipient of repeated attempts at divine consolation that focus on God's abiding love for Israel and God's promises of imminent and permanent reconciliation. After six weeks of proffered (and implicitly rejected) consolation, Israel, speaking through the prophetic texts, accepts divine consolation (Isa 61:10). This acceptance of reconciliation occurs on the Sabbath before Rosh Hashanah, the holiday that focuses on God's role as king and ushers in the season of repentance and atonement. For many Jews, especially those who only attend synagogue on Rosh Hashanah and Yom Kippur, the intensity of the hierarchical royal language and the judgment language on Rosh Hashanah can be quite alienating. However, if one understands Rosh Hashanah not only to be the beginning of the new year and the fall festival season, but also the *culmination* of the lectionary story that began on the seventeenth of Tammuz, the holiday's language resonates very differently. In this context, God's enthronement and judgment on Rosh Hashanah are predicated on, and prefaced by, Israel's free re-entry into the divine-human relationship.

Thus, within the Jewish liturgy as a whole, Lamentations' role is a paradoxical one. It enables the worshipping community to articulate feelings of despair and alienation that are fiercer, more extreme, and more unmitigated than those that are liturgically scripted at any other point of the year. At the same time, this experience serves as the starting point for a liturgical and lectionary process in which God seeks the consolation and reconciliation of Israel and it is ultimately up to the community to grant it.

## BIBLIOGRAPHY

Linafelt, Tod. *Surviving Lamentations: Catastrophe, Lament and Protest in the Afterlife of a Biblical Book.* Chicago: University of Chicago Press, 2000.

Stern, Elsie R. *From Rebuke to Consolation: Exegesis and Theology in the Liturgical Anthology of the Ninth of Av Season.* Brown Judaic Studies, 338. Providence, RI: Brown Judaic Studies, 2005.

Abudarham, David ben Yosef. *Sefer Abudarham Hashalem* (various imprints).

# G

## Lamentations in Modern Jewish Thought

ZACHARY BRAITERMAN

Two interrelated distances leave an acerbic taste to the book of Lamentations in twentieth-century liberal Jewish thought. The first is the historical distance between self-identifying modern readers and any ancient text. For readers influenced by historicism, the poetic images in Lamentations sit at an immense historical divide separating two distinct cultural worlds. The crisis torn image-world of Lamentations reflects nothing of the quotidian quality of modern Jewish life. The second distance that besets the book of Lamentation is the ontological distance between image and reality. Readers influenced by modern and postmodern aesthetic theory will note the distance that the poetic image takes from lived reality, and then seek out the operation by which the poetic imagination seeks to preserve, close, and preserve that gap. To ignore either distance is to forget one's place in the world, courting what Jacob Neusner calls "vicarious Judaism" or what the great mid-century American art critic Clement Greenberg might have called "kitsch."[1]

My intention in these few pages is to explore how the book of Lamentation works as an assemblage of images at a critical distance in relation to lived middle-class reality in the modern West. I begin by isolating three broad types of image in our text:

(1) *Grotesque images:* the image of an enemy God, the image of Fair Zion, and the terrible things he has done to her and that she has suffered—rape, destruction, death, and the cannibalization of children. The abject interminable crying of Fair Zion in chapters 1–2 and kindred laments throughout the entirety of the text lends itself to this paraphrase: God did this to us, to me; God is a cruel enemy; look at what God has done to us, to me. The great medieval commentator Rashi concludes in his commentary on Lamentations that even if God's people have sinned, "You should not have raged as much as You raged."[2]

---

1. For Neusner on vicarious Judaism, see for instance, *The Religious Renewal of Jewry*, 108–10; Clement Greenberg, "Avant-Garde and Kitsch," 34–49.

2. Rashi, Lamentations 5:22. For more information on Rashi, see Gruber's "Rashi's Commentary on Lamentations" in this volume.

(2) *Pious images:* the figure of repentance evoked by the man of suffering in chapter 3, whose purpose may or may not be to restore meaning and reconcile the reader to God. Tod Linafelt argues that although most Christian (as well as non-Christian) readers consider this confidence to be the center of our text, the poet's hope may only be relative at best.[3] The contemporary modern orthodox thinker Irving Greenberg wryly notes the same: "the memory of God's past kindness restores [the poet's faith]—barely."[4] In this vein, Ed Greenstein observes that the faith declared in the middle of chapter 3 is followed in both this chapter and the next by more bitterness (God looks down from heaven at my ceaseless tears; do not shut your ear; you have seen; vindicate *my* right). Greenstein identifies the small concentration of theodicy in chapter 3, its scarce presence in chapters 1 and 5, and its total absence in chapters 2 and 4. He maintains that there is no reason to search for the text's meaning at its center (chapter 3), and points instead to more frequent motifs and to the text's conclusion.[5]

(3) *The ironic image:* the final image in chapter 5, of God on his throne sitting above or beyond the suffering of the people. This image testifies to the God upon whom the poet's misery depends. Looked at carefully, the onus of our repentance seems not to rest upon our own decision to act; God instead is challenged to make the first move. Compare this with how the prophet Malachi hears God charge the errant people, "Turn to me and I will turn back to you" (Mal 3:7); or with our own poet who tentatively declares at a more pious moment in the text, "Let us examine our ways and turn back to Lord" (Lam 3:40); the onus would rest upon the people. Exactly opposite is the im/pious upshot of our text's conclusion, the poet's imperative communication, "Turn us back, O Lord, to you and we will return" (Lam 5:22). This final position would resemble Christian grace (reconciliation depends upon God, not human works) were it not for the challenge implicit in the call for God to turn back and repent. But no matter how one reads it, piously or impiously, the entire image constellation projected in Lamentations remains distant from liberal-secular twentieth-century Jewish sensibilities.

## FAIR ZION

The problematic quality of Lamentations in the secular motivation driving modern Zionist and Israeli thought has been explored by the prominent Israeli student of modern Jewish philosophy Eliezer Schweid in *The Jewish Experience of Time*. The original impetus behind this study of the traditional liturgical year was to introduce Jewish cultural content to secular Israelis distant from and not untypically hostile to tradition and to the images of exile that permeate its post-biblical articulation.[6] As a cultural Zionist, Schweid's response is to focus on historical time and national memory. In his presentation, religion is a type of monument or album in which the holidays constitute "the im-

---

3. Tod Linafelt, *Surviving Lamentations*, 3.
4. Irving Greenberg, *The Jewish Way*, 297.
5. Greenstein, "The Wrath at God in the Book of Lamentations," esp. 29–31.
6. Schweid, *The Jewish Experience of Time*, 376, 385.

pressions of the history of the Jewish people."[7] The fast day of Tisha b'Ab, during which the book of Lamentations is traditionally read, becomes a national day of mourning to commemorate the destruction of Judea and the Temple and the historical suffering of a people in exile.[8] Viewed as cultural memory, Lamentations is an "ancient anguish" that teaches the modern Zionist lesson against exilic existence.[9]

As much as there is an attempt to hold on to Lamentations as historical-national memory, one finds in Zionist culture (indeed in all forms of modern Jewish culture) an even stronger desire to let go of it. This is poet Hayyim Nachman Bialik's radical posture in his classic *b-'Ir ha-Haregah*, "In the City of Slaughter" (1906). Recalling the Kishinev pogrom of 1903, the poet assumes the mantle of the prophet of a God in whom the poet no longer believes, a God who communicates the poet's contempt for the folk religion of reward, punishment, and repentance, "Ululating, lachrymose/Crying from their throes/ *We have sinned* and *Sinned have we*."[10] Instead of lamentation, this pauper God would rather see fists flung like stones against his own heavenly throne. About Bialik's modernist prophet, Schweid writes, "Awe in a situation that actually calls for rage appears sacrilegious to the poet because it trivializes the name of God through mendacity."[11] Despite his own more pronounced respect for religious belief and tradition, for Israeli thinkers like Schweid, the answer to the problem of Jewish suffering is Zionism, whose liberal articulation is said to frame universal, mutual responsibility in the face of evil.[12]

## THE MAN OF SUFFERING

Bialik's secular revolt against the tradition of theodicy enters mainstream, American post-Holocaust religious thought in the 1960s and 1970s. Thinkers like Richard Rubenstein, Eliezer Berkovits, Emil Fackenheim, and Irving Greenberg affirmed the protest of Job and metaphysical confusion instead of theodicy. Our text is virtually absent at this juncture for thinkers who insist that the Holocaust remains a unique catastrophe in the history of Jewish and even human suffering that swamps both the first and second destruction of the Temple.[13] The only way into the book of Lamentations for the generation of Jewish activists and scholars that grew up in this spiritual milieu was through modernist literature. Indeed, two studies stand out from the mid-1980s: *Ḥurban* and *Against the Apocalypse*. The former is a study of Hebrew literature by Alan Mintz and the latter is a study of Yiddish literature by David Roskies.[14] Both studies draw attention to the long proem 24 of *Lamentations Rabbah*, in which God puts his people Israel on trial only to find himself put on trial, found guilty, and forced, as it were, to repent. In these two

7. Ibid., 21, 379.
8. Ibid., 220.
9. Ibid., 238–39.
10. Bialik, "The City of Slaughter."
11. Schweid, *The Jewish Experience of Time*, 264.
12. Ibid., 275–77.
13. For discussion of these figures, see Braiterman, *(God) After Auschwitz*.
14. Mintz, *Ḥurban*; Roskies, *Against the Apocalypse*.

scholarly studies, the way back to Lamentations and to Jewish religion was collective solidarity with a suffering people.

## THE IRONIC IMAGE

The post-Holocaust moment and its angry, hurt pathos have long since waned in contemporary Jewish discourse, which no longer seems to be interested in any "antitheodicies" or ironies that may surface in the book of Lamentations for the careful reader. And while contemporary liberal Jews might be happy to be done with the inscrutable God of reward, punishment, and repentance, the anger that attends the image of an unjust and inscrutable God remains problematic still; not just because we live in an American consumer-driven therapeutic culture in which, as Dana Kaplan comments, a premium is placed on "feeling good,"[15] but also, more simply, because this anger no longer speaks to the lived reality of most American Jews. In traditional Jewish religious culture, the book of Lamentations is showcased in a summer (off-season) fast that most liberal Jews have never heard of; and even for those who are familiar with the fast day and its text, Lamentations presents an image world that most liberal Jews want to leave.

A case in point is Naomi Seidman's autobiographical "Burning the Book of Lamentations," the searing recollection of a young woman who in her rebellion against an Orthodox upbringing has almost "forgotten Jerusalem."[16] The title of Seidman's essay recalls a story told by a woman of her acquaintance in the community, identified as "someone's mother," about a town in Poland where the Tisha b'Ab liturgy and its sad poems were thrown into a bonfire, because, after all, the Messiah is always coming this year. Absorbed by the story, Seidman herself is not sure that Lamentations is her story.[17] Revolted and exhausted by the violent imagery, the memory of the Holocaust, the claustrophobia of a tightly knit family and community, and the sweltering summer fast, she longs for the bonfire in Poland. She wants to "join in the end-of-lamenting dance" that is the whirling, starry hipster image of New York City circa the late 1980s, early 1990s.[18]

For all its rebellion, Seidman's radical gesture is reflected across the spectrum of liberal-leaning Jewish thought. Arthur Waskow, a leading figure in the Jewish renewal movement, also associates the fast and its biblical text with searing sensation and the promise of change. While Waskow's unabashed and even pious, joyful confidence in renewal contrasts against Seidman's more ironic detachment, his account still ends with a neo-hasidic tale. Like Seidman, Waskow also dreams about the last Tisha b'Ab and the end of lamentation. This tale is set in Jerusalem. The Messiah has come, and Jews and Muslims on the Temple Mount are on the verge of Armageddon. Suddenly and inexplicably, they are moved to throw their weapons down into a pile out of which they

---

15. Kaplan, *American Reform Judaism*, 58.
16. Seidman, "Burning the Book of Lamentations," 279. Note Thomas' "Feminist Interpretation(s) of Lamentations" in this volume.
17. Seidman, "Burning the Book of Lamentations," 285.
18. Ibid., 288.

construct their own bonfire,[19] just like the one in Seidman's account. It seems that no one wants to lament. For his part, even Greenberg laments lamentation, the way in which "the whole tone of Judaism became more somber and sorrowful" after the destruction of the Temple and exile from the Land. Israel represents for Greenberg the "overcoming" of Tisha b'Ab (as with Schweid), and with almost all modern Jewish thinkers, Greenberg eagerly awaits the end of mourning.[20]

Although this lamentation-fatigue would seem to leave our text in the past, over and over we see the same temporalizaton of Lamentations across large swaths of modern Jewish thought on the part of those who want to keep to the text. Lamentations turns into a book of cultural memory and personal recollection. Greenberg, who, despite the desire to be done with claustrophobic grief, seeks out a more profound sense of the past that he believes only the tragic can provide; he thinks we "should fight for the recovery of memory."[21] For Schweid, we have seen, Lamentations is a monument, "an undertaking of memory and hope."[22] Amir Eshel has explained this impulse well. Regarding Israeli Holocaust poetry and the tradition of Jewish literature on catastrophe, Eshel observers this attempt to create continuity with the past by creating "a unique textual space, one in which 'the past' is always close at hand and the dead are never rendered silent."[23] Seidman too cannot seem to let go of the past; if she were truly done with Lamentations, she would not have written the essay; our text allows her to recall from her present home in Berkeley California her own past girlhood in Brooklyn.

## CONCLUSION

In closing, I would recommend the future tense as an alternative temporalization to melancholy and nostalgia. In this view, associated by Schweid with paganism, "[t]he past is a future that may recur, and the future is a past that is about to recur, just as the present has already been and shall be."[24] Perhaps the power of Lamentations, perhaps of all religious imagery, lies not in its power to re-present the past or create cultural memory as much as the way it anticipates future possibilities. Let us assume for the moment, with W. C. Gwaltney, that the book of Lamentations' authorship is late, that it belongs to the period of restoration, and that one purpose of lamentation is to avoid ruin.[25] With its eye on a past that might very well recur, Lamentations is a platform from which to consider future disasters of our own making, wrought by God that only God can suspend, the destruction of the Second Temple or, in our own times, a nuclear explosion in New York City or Tel Aviv. Recalling ancient Jerusalem reminds us that our own cities hang on the

---

19. See Waskow, *Seasons of Our Joy*.
20. Greenberg, *The Jewish Way*, 302–3.
21. Ibid., 301.
22. Schweid, *The Jewish Experience of Time*, 17.
23. Eshel, "Eternal Present," esp. 143.
24. Schweid, *The Jewish Experience of Time*, 17.
25. Gwaltney, "The Biblical Book of Lamentations in the Context of Near Eastern Lament Literature," 256, 258.

verge of destruction. Lamentations foments terrible premonitions, whose only cognitive resolution rests upon the image of a God who must "turn," a theological irony so subtle as to avoid the notice of readers preoccupied or repelled by the text's own surface pieties, both the traditional piety of sin-repentance-reconciliation and the modern piety of meaning-memory-hope.

## BIBLIOGRAPHY

Bialik, H. N. "The City of Slaughter." In *Complete Poetic Works of Hayyim Nahman Bialik. Vol. 1*, edited by Israel Efros, 129–43. New York: Histadruth Ivrith of America, 1948.

Braiterman, Zachary. *(God) After Auschwitz: Tradition and Change in Post-Holocaust Jewish Thought*. Princeton: Princeton University Press, 1998.

Eshel, Amir. "Eternal Present: Poetic Figuration and Cultural Memory in the Poetry of Yehuda Amichai, Dan Pagis, and Tuvia Rübner." *Jewish Social Studies* 7.1 (2000) 141–66.

Greenberg, Clement. "Avant-Garde and Kitsch." *Partisan Review* 6.5 (1939) 34–49.

Greenberg, Irving. *The Jewish Way: Living the Holidays*. New York: Simon and Schuster, 1993.

Greenstein, Ed. "The Wrath at God in the Book of Lamentations." In *The Problem of Evil and Its Symbols in Jewish and Christian Tradition*, edited by Henning G. Reventlow and Yair Hoffman, 29–42. London: T. & T. Clark, 2004.

Gwaltney, W. C., Jr. "The Biblical Book of Lamentations in the Context of Near Eastern Lament Literature." In *Essential Papers on Israel and the Ancient Near East*, edited by Frederick E. Greenspahn, 243–65. New York: New York University Press, 1991.

Kaplan, Dana. *American Reform Judaism*. New Brunswick, NJ: Rutgers University Press, 2003.

Linafelt, Tod. *Surviving Lamentations: Catastrophe, Lament and Protest in the Afterlife of a Biblical Book*. Chicago: University of Chicago Press, 2000.

Mintz, Alan. *Ḥurban: Responses to Catastrophe in Hebrew Literature*. Syracuse, NY: Syracuse University Press, 1996.

Neusner, Jacob. *The Religious Renewal of Jewry*. Judaism in Cold War America, 5. Bloomington, IN: Indiana University Press, 1993.

Roskies, David. *Against the Apocalypse: Responses to Catastrophe in Modern Jewish Culture*. Cambridge: Harvard University Press, 1984.

Schweid, Eliezer. *The Jewish Experience of Time: Philosophical Dimensions of the Jewish Holy Days*. Translated by Amnon Hadary. Northvale, NJ: Aronson, 2000.

Seidman, Naomi. "Burning the Book of Lamentations." In *Out of the Garden: Women Writers on the Bible*, edited by Christina Büchmann and Celina Spiegel, 278–88. New York: Fawcett Columbine, 1995.

Waskow, Arthur. *Seasons of Our Joy: A Handbook of Jewish Festivals*. New York: Bantam, 1982.

Soundings
in Messianic Jewish Reception History

# H

## Holocaust Theology in the Light of Yeshua?

*Messianic Jewish Reception of* Eikah

RICHARD HARVEY

### INTRODUCTION

A MESSIANIC JEWISH RECEPTION of Lamentations? For some the very notion of seems anomalous. Jacob Neusner, in the series foreword to his translation of the midrash on Lamentations, draws up the interreligious dividing lines which would preclude the possibility of such an approach: "It is clear, while 'Judaism,' 'Christianity,' and 'Islam' encompass religious systems of considerable diversity, all Judaisms differ from all Christianities and all Islams in their reading of those Scriptures."[1]

Nevertheless, Messianic Jews claim to be both a "Judaism" and a "Christianity," not only reading the Scriptures from within both traditions, but also contributing to them. Their belief in the Messiahship of Yeshua (Jesus) and their affirmation of the ongoing election of Israel (the Jewish people) are the two epistemic priorities from which their theological interpretation of the Scriptures flow.[2] The purpose of this chapter is to demonstrate how a Messianic Jewish reception of *Eikah,* situated in the interstitial space between Jewish and Christian interpretation, allows the text to speak afresh to Jew, Christian, and Messianic Jew alike.

The reception of Lamentations within Messianic Judaism has been sporadic but not without significance. The first translation of the book into Yiddish was made by the sixteenth-century Swiss Hebrew Christian, Michael Adam.[3] David Stern's *Complete Jewish Bible* paraphrases and adds Jewish glosses to the text.[4] H. L. Ellison's commentary

---

1. Neusner, *Israel after Calamity,* ix.
2. Harvey, *Mapping Messianic Jewish Theology.*
3. Bernstein, *Some Jewish Witnesses for Christ,* 75.
4. Stern, *Complete Jewish Bible,* 1061–74.

reflects on the relationship between the destruction of the Temple, the exile, and the death of Yeshua (Jesus).[5] Paul Re'emi uses the text for reflection on the Holocaust.[6] In addition, materials by Messianic Jews focus on a Messianic exegesis of the text, and liturgical and reflective use of the book. Finally, the recent renewal movement within Messianic Judaism, "Hashivenu," styles itself from the liturgical use of 5:21.

## MESSIANIC EXEGESIS

Messianic Jewish commentator Tsvi Sadan is typical of Messianic Jews whose christological exegesis finds support from both Jewish midrashic and Christian apologetic readings. In his "Hundred Names of the Messiah" Sadan refers to the Midrash Rabbah on Lam 1:16 and the name of the Messiah. "Comforter" (Hebrew, *Menahem*) as one of the names of the Messiah is mentioned in the Talmud in Sanhedrin 98–99. This well-known passage, which discusses the signs of the Messiah's coming, also gives him names that reveal his unique characteristics.

> The name Menahem for the Messiah was also based upon the prophet Jeremiah's words: "For these things I weep; my eyes flow with tears; for a comforter is far from me, one to revive my courage" (Lam 1:16). Some say this comforter was the son of King Hezekiah or the child promised by Isaiah to King Ahaz (Isa 9:6). The mysterious disappearance of a comforter caused great despair, leading some Sages to declare that the Messiah would never appear.
> 
> But in Jewish mystical writings, there is one named Menahem, son of Imiel (God with me), and it is this "Comforter, son of God with me" who is considered to be the one who will eventually defeat Israel's enemies. In one such mystical text, *The Book of Zerubbabel*, Menahem is described as a bruised vagabond who reveals to Zerubbabel how and when the Messiah will come. Upon hearing Menahem's message, Zerubbabel is greatly comforted.
> 
> Zerubbabel is given eyes to see the glory of this vagabond: "He looked to me like a child with incomparable beauty and pleasantness." However, when Menahem revealed himself to the Sages of Israel as "the Messiah sent by God to preach the good news to you and to save you from your enemies . . . they looked at him and despised him."
> 
> Menahem as one of the names of the Messiah highlights Israel's lack of concern for him, as revealed in the Book of Lamentations. "For a comforter is far from me" were the words of those who acknowledged that he is far because of Israel's sin. Tragically, Menahem is the one who seeks to comfort, to bring the good news, but is shunned by those to whom he wishes to offer them.[7]

Alfred Edersheim, a Hebrew Christian of the nineteenth century, found references to the Holy Spirit bringing repentance in 2:19; the name of the Messiah (*Shiloh—she-lo*) in 1:16.[8] Using the Midrash on 3:49 Edersheim refers to the remark that it is one of the

---

5. Ellison, "Lamentations."

6. Re'emi. "Lamentations."

7. Sadan, "100 Names of the Messiah, 'Menahem'" (online, no page numbers).

8. Edersheim, *The Life and Times of Jesus the Messiah*. "Midr. on Lam. i. 16, to the Messiah, with this curious remark, implying the doubt whether He was alive or dead: 'The king Messiah, whether He belong to the living or the dead, His Name is to be David, according to *Ps. xviii.* 50.'"

three passage in which mention of the Holy Spirit follows from mention of redemption. The Targums on 2:22—"Thou wilt proclaim liberty to thy people, the house of Israel, by the hand of the Messiah"—and 4:22—"And after these things thy iniquity shall cease, and thou shalt be set free by the hands of the Messiah and by the hands of Elijah the Priest"—are also discussed.

Whilst Edersheim and Sadan access the midrashic materials for their own apologetic and illustrative purposes, a more sustained engagement with Lamentations can be found in the works of two Hebrew Christian commentators of the previous century.

## BIBLE COMMENTARY

### Harry Ellison

H. L. Ellison's commentary on Lamentations describes the book as a "funeral dirge over an irrecoverable past."[9] The key theological concern is the "problem of national suffering." While there is "no effort to minimize Israel's sin, the writer is clearly overwhelmed by the greatness of her doom."[10] Yet the suffering is caused by God himself, and Ellison links the imponderable nature of the suffering with that of Calvary.

Ultimately there are depths in God's actions that finite man cannot grasp. God's revelation in word and act consistently show his justice and covenant love; yet there is always a residue of human experience that demands our bowing to a wisdom too high for our understanding.[11]

Then Ellison makes his christological move, plumbing the mystery of Calvary for insights into God's sovereign will. "This finds its supreme example in the cross and in the cry of Jesus in Mark 15:34. This is why every facile theory of the atonement has failed to satisfy for long, for there are depths concealed in Golgotha that pass human understanding. Only when in glory we see free will and predestination reconciled will we also grasp how God's sovereign will is compatible with his justice and covenant love to his people."[12]

Ellison's commentary follows the standard lines of conservative evangelical exegesis, but adds from his own Hebrew Christian heritage insights into the Jewish experience.[13]

He sees anti-Semitism stirring in the laughter of 1:7: "The glee of Jerusalem's enemies came doubtless from the same motive that underlies some aspects of modern anti-Semitism—viz., a human reaction to Israel's claim to be God's elect."[14]

On the familiar reflection on the Passion of Christ found in 1:11: "It would be pedantic to object to the use of the first two lines of this verse in a meditation on our Lord's

---

9. Ellison, "Lamentations," 697.

10. Ibid., 698.

11. Ibid., 699.

12. Ibid.

13. H. L. Ellison was a second generation Hebrew Christian from Poland, who worked with the Mildmay Mission to the Jews, and taught the Old Testament at London Bible College (now London School of Theology). For biography and bibliography see Lewis, ed. *Torah and Other Essays*.

14. Ellison, "Lamentations," 705.

passion. For all that, there is no connection; and a careless use of this verse could lead to a false theory of the atonement."[15]

For Ellison the "sheer impact of physical disaster is overwhelming; it is only later that the shame of it all is seen as something worse."[16] He avoids the anti-Judaism that some Christian commentators have leveled at 2:14: "Just as the majority of preachers are so obsessed with the holiness of the church that they have not been able to take the church's shortcomings seriously: so it was in Israel. It took the shock of the Babylonian exile to break the power and influence of the prophets and to discredit them finally."[17]

On the hope of 3:21 Ellison is realistic: "The 'hope' that the writer expresses here is not created by denying or minimizing suffering and misery. Rather, these are transformed when the mind is turned to God."[18]

He follows a traditional Christian approach to the call for restoration of 5:21: "Suddenly there was the overwhelming realization that true repentance is possible only as initiated by an act of God (cf. Jer 31:18, 33–34; Ezek 36:26–27). This is a foreshadowing of the NT doctrine of regeneration. Unfortunately it was grasped by few at the time. Normative Judaism lays very great stress on the importance of repentance but has always regarded it as something essentially within man's control."[19]

In his concluding comments, Ellison finds it strange that "one who could so pour out his heart to God should receive so little consolation." There was not even the burning hope of return and restoration that had been voiced by Jeremiah and Ezekiel. The simple fact is that the people of Israel—with few exceptions—had so failed to grasp God's revelation that an experience parallel to the bondage in Egypt and a new exodus were needed to prepare Israel for the appearance of her Messiah and the world's Savior.[20]

### *Paul Re'emi*

A second Messianic Jewish commentary is that of Paul Re'emi.[21] Re'emi's commentary—"a short but carefully written commentary with theological leanings"[22]—is more exploratory. The commentary contains paraphrase, biblical quotation, textual comment, and a

---

15. Ibid., 707.
16. Ibid., 710.
17. Ibid., 714.
18. Ibid., 720.
19. Ibid., 732–33.
20. Ibid., 733.

21. Clärli Re'emi, "Samuel Paul Re'emi: a tribute, as told to Lo Kaye-Wilson. Born Samuel Wieselthier in 1912 in Podwoloczyska, Poland, Re'emi's training in Hebrew and Law at the University of Lemburg led him to further legal studies in Strasbourg, and a doctorate in Toulouse. He survived the Nazis, living in the French free zone, whilst his grandparents, parents, sister, aunts, nephews, and friends all perished in the Holocaust. He would be haunted for the rest of his life with the nightmares of his family being seized. In 1944 he moved to Israel, joined the Church of Scotland in Jerusalem in 1956, and was ordained in 1962. As a member of the Hebrew Christian Alliance he led services in Hebrew in Tiberias, compiled an analytical concordance to the Delitzch edition of the New Testament, and translated books into Hebrew and wrote several commentaries."

22. R. B. Salters. *Jonah and Lamentations*, 65.

strong sense of identity with the Jewish poet which one reviewer described as "reminiscent, in fact, of some 11th–12th century Jewish biblical exegesis (a comment which is not intended as a slur by any means)."[23]

According the Re'emi, the book "served the survivors of the catastrophe in the first place as a means of expressing their grief and horror."[24] As a holocaust survivor he wrote: "The best way for men to live through the grief and shock of a calamity is by facing it, by measuring its dimensions, by finding words to order and express their feelings."[25] It also brought a note of hope, reminding Israel of their past glory, which "brought a gleam of light into their darkness and humiliation."

Secondly, the book is also a confession of sin. "The poet recognizes, as none before him had done so completely, that God waits until his disloyal people are at last aware that of themselves they are nothing, and that they cannot rescue themselves from the pit into which they have sunk. Yet God's purpose and plan for the world through them will continue—but by grace alone."[26]

Re'emi makes clear reference to the Shoah throughout: "Is it nothing to you, all you who pass by" (1:12) "could have been the cry of despair of those who, dumped into cattle trucks, passed through flowering fields and gardens to the concentration camps of Auschwitz or Buchenwald."[27]

Re'emi refers to Holocaust theologians: Elie Wiesel refuses to relieve God from responsibility for the Holocaust, and Eliezer Berkovitz finds it "difficult to explain the disaster that befell God's chosen people in view of God's goodness and omnipotence, except by faith." Quoting another Messianic Jew, Jacob Jocz, Re'emi responds to the problem of suffering: "Even if no answer can be found, we would still be left with the only alternative with which Job was left, i.e. contending with God, while trusting him, of questioning while believing, inquiring in our minds, yet knowing in our hearts."[28]

With some overstatement Re'emi applies the language of sacrifice both to Israel and her Messiah. "But now the daughter of Zion was herself to be the sacrifice! She herself had become the *olah*—the 'whole offering'; not even just a part offering when only portions of the sacrificial animal went up to the Lord—for 'none escaped or survived'. And so Israel is now meeting with that ultimate horror, known absolutely to Jesus on the Cross (when he quoted Ps 22:1), of being abandoned by God himself."[29]

Tod Linafelt sees Re'emi's use of the cross of Christ as a hermeneutical key that "tightly governs how one reads a text."[30] However, Re'emi's reading goes beyond the simple use of Christ as a hermeneutical key. Linafelt does not refer to the more nuanced

---

23. Review in *Journal for the Study of the Old Testament* 35 (1986), 126.
24. Re'emi, "Lamentations," 76.
25. Ibid.
26. Ibid.
27. Ibid., 88.
28. Jacob Jocz, "Israel after Auschwitz." In *The Witness of the Jews to God*, edited by David Torrance, 60–61. Edinburgh: Handsel, 1988, cited in Re'emi, "Lamentations," 88.
29. Re'emi, "Lamentations," 98 on 2:18–20.
30. Linafelt. *Surviving Lamentations*, 8.

understanding that links the Holocaust and the death of Yeshua to the catastrophe of the fall of Jerusalem. God himself has offered Israel as an "extraordinary sacrifice." "In declaring as much, our poet has this laid his finger on that ultimate reality which is true for all times and which we have see exemplified in our generation in the Holocaust of Auschwitz. For then, to use instead the language of Acts 2:23, God's own child, his chosen people, 'delivered up according to the definite plan and foreknowledge of God, *you* crucified and killed by the hands of lawless men.' We can see this New Testament exposition exemplified clearly in Hitler and his Nazis."[31]

Re'emi then asks the rhetorical question, "Was this suffering of Israel, this immolation of a whole people by God himself in fact vicarious suffering? Had it all happened for the sake of the world?" Just as the Qumran community saw their suffering as continuing the tradition of a small group of consecrated saints suffering on the part of others, so Re'emi admits the possibility. But "at this point of history, viz. 587 B.C., our poet has no theological interpretation to give to the events he is living through. They stand as historical fact for later generations to seek to understand in the light of God's later intervention in the history of his people in the Cross of Christ."[32]

For Re'emi the "inner dynamic of this book" is summarized in the repeated *Hashivenu* of 5:21 and 23: "The poet leads the people step by step to make this mighty discovery, that through wrath and judgment, acknowledgment of sin and repentance, Israel may discover that 'God's steadfast love never ceases, and his mercies are new every morning—for great is his faithfulness.'"[33]

Re'emi notes that the fall of Jerusalem had "as we would say today, unique eschatological significance."[34] Whilst Ellison's commentary reflects the shock of the Shoah, Re'emi takes a more reflective tone, factoring in the sacrifice of Yeshua and the theodical questions of Jewish theologians. These are brought to life also in the perennial period of mourning and reflection on Lamentations in the Messianic Jewish calendar.

## TISH B'AV AND THE LECTIONARY CYCLE

Tish B'av (the Ninth of Av), is commemorated by Messianic Jews as part of the Jewish liturgical calendar, linking the destruction of the Temple with the tragedy of the Holocaust and the death of Yeshua. "This Tisha B'av, as our Jewish people mourn the series of tragedies in Jewish history, followers of Yeshua can make it a time to reflect on how God the Father took a great tragedy of His own and turned it into the victory of the Resurrection."[35]

The article also refers to Bernstein's Jeremiah Symphony, precluding a "tidy answer to tragedy." When he was twenty-four years old, Jewish composer and conductor Leonard Bernstein wrote his first symphonic effort, the Jeremiah Symphony. In the third move-

---

31. Re'emi, "Lamentations," 99.
32. Ibid., 99 on 2:18–20.
33. Ibid., 132 on 5:22.
34. Ibid., 97 on 2:13.
35. http://www.jewsforjesus.org/publications/realtime/13/mourning (accessed July 2009).

ment, he incorporated part of the text of Lamentations, with the soprano singing the traditional melody used on Tisha be-Av. Bernstein explained that the symphony offered "comfort, not a solution." He knew that he could not offer a tidy answer to tragedy.[36]

Russ Resnick, President of the Union of Messianic Jewish Congregations, sees the exile, the Shoah, and the spiritual and physical rebirth of the nation, in the grief poured out over "Zion's pain."

> On Tisha B'Av my fathers sat
> by gravesides and memorial,
> intent on grief,
> on a Polish mound under iron skies
> to stalk their prey.
> Overtaken, its bitter yield,
> salted by tears for their sins
> and Zion's pain,
> strengthened them for exile's task
> and nourished hope.
>
> They looked up from their graveside,
> and far in the east
> Zion arose from her hidden bed
> and arrayed herself for her Lover's eyes.
> And they, the attendants,
> the Bridegroom's men,
> sat watching for His joy.[37]

The book of Lamentations plays a prominent role in Messianic Jewish lectionaries, the cycle of readings used in Messianic Syngagogal worship, as Mark Kinzer explains:

> The cycle reaches its climax, with the narrative of Yeshua's death, between the 17th of Tammuz and the 9th of Av, when the Jewish calendar enters a period of mourning for the destruction of the temple, and three haftorahs of admonition are read. It reaches its joyful conclusion with seven readings related to Yeshua's resurrection, corresponding to the seven Sabbaths between the 9th of Av and Rosh Hashanah, when haftorahs of consolation from the latter chapters of Isaiah are read. The cycle thus points us to the truth that Yeshua, as the King of Israel and its representative, embodies in his person the meaning of the temple, the holy city, and Jewish history as a whole. His suffering sums up and purifies Israel's suffering, and his resurrection will bring about Israel's ultimate restoration.[38]

Janie-Sue Wertheim explains the tradition of fasting: "Our people fast from sunset to sunset on Tisha b'Av and read the book of Lamentations. It was written by Jeremiah whose heart was broken by the destruction of Jerusalem and the first Temple. Years later,

---

36. Ibid.
37. Russ Resnick. *Graveside Poem*. Online: http://www.jewsforjesus.org/publications/issues/10_3/graveside (accessed July 2009).
38. Kinzer, *Introduction to "Chayyei Yeshua Besorah* Reading Cycle."

Yeshua would weep over Jerusalem just as Jeremiah did. He still grieves over people who've rejected His sacrifice for their sin."[39]

The Union of Messianic Jewish Congregations (UMJC) similarly focuses in intercessory prayer as a keynote that emerges from the reading of Lamentations on Tisha B'Av:

> Tisha b'Av is the anniversary not only of the beginning of exile, but of many tragic events during the exile, culminating in the expulsion of the once-glorious Jewish community of Spain in 1492. Paradoxically, the convergence of so many similar tragedies on this date provides a note of hope, because there appears to be a divine pattern behind it all. The exile is not a meaningless turn of history, but is part of the much larger plan of redemption. Thus, one tradition has it that Messiah will be born on Tisha b'Av.
>
> How are we to respond to this hope? Not passively, but with intercessory prayer. As we stand in solidarity with our people on this day, we can pray for victory over our sins, for the end of exile, and for the restoration of Jerusalem that is a key to the restoration of the whole earth. The conclusion of the Book of Lamentations that we read aloud on Tisha B'Av provides the words of intercession: *Hashivenu Adonai elecha v'nashuva chadesh yameinu ki-kedem*. "Turn us again, O Lord, to you and we shall return; renew our days as of old!"[40]

## *HASHIVENU*—POST-MISSIONARY MESSIANIC JUDAISM

It is with the cry for renewal of 5:21 that the reception of Lamentations in the Messianic Judaism can be summarized. Whilst the early Hebrew Christian forms of Messianic Judaism in the nineteenth and twentieth centuries were happy to mine the book for apologetic and Christological material, the "Postmissionary Messianic Judaism" of Mark Kinzer and the *Hashiveny Forum* looks for a more nuanced reading of such texts.[41] In "Toward a Mature Messianic Judaism" the authors state:

> With the cry "*Hashivenu*" the Torah service concludes, imploring God to bring us back to himself. It is our conviction that HaShem brings Messianic Jews to a richer knowledge of himself through a modern day rediscovery of the paths of our ancestors—*Avodah* (liturgical worship), *Torah* (study of sacred texts), and *Gemilut Chasadim* (deeds of lovingkindness).
>
> Our goal is a mature Messianic Judaism. We seek an authentic expression of Jewish life maintaining substantial continuity with Jewish tradition. However, Messianic Judaism is energized by the belief that Yeshua of Nazareth is the promised Messiah, the fullness of Torah. Mature Messianic Judaism is not simply Judaism plus Yeshua, but is instead an integrated following of Yeshua through traditional Jewish forms and the modern day practice of Judaism in and through Yeshua. Messianic Judaism will only attain maturity when it has established communal institutions

---

39. Wertheim and Shapiro, *Walk with Y'shua through the Jewish Year*, 59.
40. "Tisha B'av." http://umjc.net/content/view/399/40/ (accessed July 2009).
41. Kinzer, *Postmissionary Messianic Judaism*.

which are capable of expressing its ideals and transmitting them effectively to ourselves, to our children, and to a skeptical world.[42]

Messianic Jews have thus received and reflected on Lamentations benefitting from two traditions of which they are a part. Their hermeneutical methods have been eclectic, and a systematic reflection has yet to emerge. But somewhere between Zion, Auschwitz, and Golgotha, the lament can still be heard.

---

42. http://www.hashivenu.org/core_values.htm (accessed July 2009).

# BIBLIOGRAPHY

Bernstein, A. *Some Jewish Witnesses for Christ*. London: Operative Jewish Converts Institution, 1909.

Ellison, H. L. "Lamentations." In *The Expositor's Bible Commentary, Vol. 6*, edited by Frank E. Gaebelein, 695–736. Grand Rapids: Zondervan, 1986.

Harvey, Richard. *Mapping Messianic Jewish Theology: A Constructive Approach*. Milton Keynes, UK: Paternoster, 2009.

Kinzer, Mark. *Introduction to "Chayyei Yeshua* (Life of Yeshua) *Besorah Reading Cycle."* Congregation Zera Yisrael. Ann Arbor, MI, 2008.

———. *Postmissionary Messianic Judaism: Redefining Christian Engagement with the Jewish People*. Grand Rapids: Brazos, 2005.

Lewis, Ronald L., ed. *Torah and Other Essays: A Symposium in Honour of the 80th Birthday of H. L. Ellison*. Ramsgate: International Hebrew Christian Alliance, 1983.

Linafelt, Todd. *Surviving Lamentations: Catastrophe, Lament, and Protest in the Afterlife of a Biblical Book*. Chicago: University of Chicago Press, 2000.

Neusner, Jacob. *Israel after Calamity: The Book of Lamentations*. Valley Forge, PA: Trinity, 1995.

Re'emi, Clärli. "Samuel Paul Re'emi: A Tribute, as Told to Lo Kaye-Wilson." *The Messianic Jew and Hebrew Christian* LXIX.4 (Dec 1996–Feb 1997) 91–94.

Re'emi, Paul. "Lamentations." In *Amos and Lamentations: God's People in Crisis*. International Theological Commentary Series, 73–134. Edinburgh: Handsel, 1984.

Sadan, Tzvi. "100 Names of the Messiah, 'Menahem.'" http://www.zvisadan.com/?103,comforter (accessed July 2009).

Salters, Robin B. *Jonah and Lamentations*. JSOT Old Testament Guides. Sheffield: JSOT, 1994.

Stern, David. *Complete Jewish Bible*. Jerusalem: Jewish New Testament Publications, 1998.

Wertheim, Janie-Sue, and Kathy Shapiro. *Walk with Y'shua through the Jewish Year*. San Francisco: Purple Pomegranite, 1998.

Soundings
in Christian Reception History

# I

# Lamentations in the Patristic Period

HEATH A. THOMAS

## INTRODUCTION

LAMENTATIONS GENERALLY DOES NOT share the pedigree of other OT books and therefore did not receive the amount of attention as Isaiah, Genesis, the Psalter, or even Job in the patristic period. Still, it has its place. The Fathers quote Lamentations at various points and in various ways. Each of these receptions of the book fit within the overall approach of patristic interpretation of the OT: Christological, prophetic, and oriented toward the life of the church.[1]

By the "patristic period" this brief essay intends a general timeframe between the second and seventh century CE. This is somewhat artificial, as the tenets of medieval interpretation do not differ greatly from those of patristic hermeneutics. Nonetheless it is useful to describe the reading practices of the church on Lamentations in the period before the Carolingian Renaissance. In this essay the timeline will be framed by the works of Irenaeus (120–202 CE) and Gregory the Great (540–604 CE).[2] More than in any other way, Lamentations was seen as an important prophetic witness to the person of Jesus in this era. This is most prevalently seen in the reading of Lam 4:20, which will be addressed below. Besides this, Lamentations provides moral guidance for the people of God.

## READING LAMENTATIONS IN THE PATRISTIC PERIOD

To begin, it is helpful to delineate precisely the text traditions, commentaries, or any other major resources (if any) that were used to aid interpretation of this book. To the first

---

1. For the approach of patristic interpretation of the OT, see Heine, *Reading the Old Testament with the Ancient Church*; Jeanrond, *Theological Hermeneutics*, 18–26. Reventlow, *History of Biblical Interpretation: Vol. 1*, 118–99; Reventlow, *History of Biblical Interpretation: Vol. 2*, 3–136.

2. A useful distillation of patristic commentary on Lamentations may be found in Wenthe, ed., *Jeremiah, Lamentations*, xix–xxviii, 273–328. A useful index of references to Lamentations in the patristic literature may be found in *Biblia Patristica*.

question, early patristic interpretation was rooted in Greek translations of Lamentations, although it remains a complicated process to decipher which Greek text-type was used in the first century of the patristic period (ca. 100–200 CE). The LXX Lamentations belongs to the *kai-ge* recension dated likely to the first century CE[3] and was available to the Fathers and was used by them. Aquila and Symmachus was also used by some of the Fathers. Origen apparently used the LXX as well as Aquila and Symmachus in his rendering of Lamentations in his Hexapla (230–40 CE). So these three Greek text traditions, as well as Origen's Hexapla, were influential.

It is in place to mention as well the Old Latin text, which was translated from the Septuagint. This corpus preceded Jerome's Vulgate and it was influential on some of the earliest fathers' reading of Lamentations. Tertullian apparently was dependent upon this version and it may have impacted his reading of Lamentations. But as this Old Latin text leaned heavily upon the LXX the echo of this Greek text resounds predominantly in the Latin. Ziegler goes so far as to identify the Old Latin version as the "Septuagint in Latin clothing."[4] So the Greek heritage looms large over the reading of Lamentations in the early patristic period. In later times Jerome's Latin Vulgate figured prominently and became the set text for the church's reading of the book.

LXX, Aquila, and Symmachus were used in the formulation of Origen's now-lost commentary on Lamentations, the earliest Christian commentary on the book. This work is likely one of the first of Origen's commentaries (ca. 222–25 CE), and while tragically lost it still may be reconstructed in part from Byzantine catenae.[5] This commentary employs the same hermeneutical approach that one finds throughout Origen's other works: discussion on the literal interpretation of the book that grounds the deeper, truer, spiritual meaning of the text as it reveals Christ and the church.

For example, note Origen's discussion of Lam 1. He reads this chapter against the backdrop of Josephus' account of the fall Jerusalem in 70 CE; he does so to establish an analogy between the destructions of Jerusalem in 587 BCE and 70 CE. This literal and grammatical meaning of the text then establishes an entrée into its spiritual meaning. In his discussion on Lam 1:10, Origen suggests that Jerusalem in captivity to Babylon spiritually signifies the soul's (church's) captivity to demonic power. Demons/Babylonians invade the reason/sanctuary of the believer/Jerusalem, where God dwells. Because of this invasion, confusion follows in the heart and life of the believer. Throughout his commentary, Origen blends the literal and spiritual, so that Lamentations becomes instructive for the heart and soul of the believer.[6]

After Origen's works, the major influence of Lamentations interpretation in the later patristic era is Jerome. He completed his *magnum opus* of translation, the Vulgate, between 393 and 406 CE. Jerome's rendering of Lamentations was not just a transla-

---

3. See Youngblood, "The Character and Significance of LXX Lamentations" in this volume.

4. Quoted in Wurthwein, *The Text of the Old Testament*, 90.

5. For Greek version(s) of Lamentations, see Youngblood's article in this volume. Cf. Barthelemey, *Les davanciers d'Aquila*. For an English translation of Origen's reconstructed commentary, see Trigg, *Origen*, 73–85. For the critical edition of the reconstructed original, see Klostermann, ed., *GCS*, vol. 6: 235–78.

6. Trigg, *Origen*, 80–82.

tion but also a significant interpretation. Like the LXX (and the Targum), he introduced Lamentations with a carefully rendered preface that links Lamentations with Jeremiah the prophet, and the book with the fall of Jerusalem. This, of course, is absent from the Hebrew text tradition. Jerome distinguishes that his introduction, although like the LXX, is not in the Hebrew original but is the product of the "seventy interpreters" (the translators of the LXX Lamentations) "to give the reader to understand upon what occasion Lamentations was published." Additionally, Jerome utilized the alphabetic acrostic in his translation, acknowledging its importance in the Hebrew original. So each line begins with a Latinization of the Hebrew letters: "aleph," "beth," "gimel," etc.

There is a good reason why Jerome influenced Lamentations interpretation in the late patristic and medieval periods. It was not only due to his rendering of the book in the Vulgate, but also his interpretation of the acrostic in his Letter to Paula (Epistle 30), which was available to later interpreters. Jerome may well have used the epistolary medium as a vehicle to promulgate particular scriptural teaching to others in addition to addressing more quotidian affairs.[7] At any rate, Matter goes so far to say that this letter became the standard resource by which to govern Latin interpretations of Lamentations in the late patristic age and into the medieval period.[8]

In this letter, he argues that each letter of the alphabet in the alphabetic poems of the Bible actually signifies something higher, deeper, and spiritual. Amongst the various meanings of the letters, Jerome notes that "aleph" indicates doctrine, "beth" indicates the house, "gimel" indicates plenitude, etc. From his analysis of the twenty-two alphabetic letters, Jerome distinguishes seven major spiritual teachings that ought to be embraced from them. In his approach to the acrostic, the spiritual meaning of each letter governs the reading process: to adduce the meaning of Lamentations one looks to teaching of the acrostic first rather than the text. The outcome of this is that the book, through the alphabet, teaches about living under God's rule and this derives primarily from doctrine. By meditating upon God's word in this way, the reader benefits and plumbs the wisdom of God.[9] This process opens the allegorical meaning of Lamentations in a way that is fertile for the church as well. This is especially so because the first two major teachings of the seven deal with living under God's word and understanding that the Scriptures preeminently reveal Christ. His influence is seen in the medieval commentaries of Hrabanus Maurus, Paschasius Radbertus, Thomas Aquinas, and Gilbert of Auxerre.[10]

A final major resource for reading Lamentations in the patristic age is Gregory the Great's *Moralia in Job*. Within this influential work, Lamentations is quoted at least seventeen times. Gregory follows Origen's allegorical approach and renders the literal

---

7. Cain, *The Letters of Jerome*, 81–82.

8. Matter, "The Lamentations Commentaries," 141. For a full translation of Jerome's Epistle 30, see Columbia University's Columbia Center for New Media Teaching and Learning (CNMTL), particularly the web-based repository *Epistolae: Medieval Women's Latin Letters* (accessible at: http://epistolae.ccnmtl.columbia.edu/). Jerome's Epistle 30 to Paula is archived in both Latin and English and accessible at: http://epistolae.ccnmtl.columbia.edu/letter/278.html.

9. Matter, "The Lamentations Commentaries," 141.

10. Matter, "The Legacy of the School of Auxerre." Cf. Matter, "The Lamentations Commentaries."

meaning of Lamentations along with the spiritual. Note, for example, Gregory's interpretation of Lam 3:1, "I am the man who beholds my poverty by the rod of His indignation." Gregory sees in this verse Jeremiah's pain over banishing any love of the present life in favor of riches of the heavenly kingdom. Gregory says, "But because all the Elect continually behold that they have fallen into the present life from that faculty of innate strength, it is well said, 'I am the man who beholds my poverty.' For whoever still longs after these visible things, understands not the mystery of his pilgrimage [suffering over the Christian's constant denial of the earthly world and longing for the riches of the heavenly kingdom], and has not the skill to see the very evil which he is suffering."[11] In Gregory's interpretation, Lamentations becomes a resource that teaches the church how to let go of this world and await God's coming heavenly kingdom. Lamentations is a vehicle for the church's spiritual formation. This approach to the book is typical in Gregory's *Moralia*.[12] Because it was so influential and widely read, Gregory's approach to the book in *Moralia* impacted the church's understanding of Lamentations in later times.

## PROPHECY AND THE SUFFERING OF CHRIST

In light of the resources that were used in reading Lamentations, how precisely was it interpreted? It is to this question I now turn. As indicated above, Lamentations signaled Christ and gave insight into the spiritual formation of the church.

The Fathers read Lamentations as a prophetic text concerning Jesus. To expose OT prophetic witness to the suffering of Jesus, Irenaeus combines a series of texts from Isaiah with Lam 3:30: "He will give his cheek to the smiter; he will be filled with reproach." Irenaeus can conclude, then, by saying, "All these things Christ suffered."[13] Irenaeus links the experience of the suffering man in Lamentations with the experience of Christ in his passion; moreover, this linkage is not typological or allegorical but *prophetic* at root. So by the early second century, Lamentations was recognized as a prophetic witness to the suffering of Jesus.

Likewise, by the fourth century, Rufinus exploited Lamentations as a prophecy concerning Jesus. Again, the third poem comes into view. In his "Commentary on the Apostles' Creed," Rufinus expounds upon the suffering Jesus experienced at his point of death and burial. He marshals a number of OT texts from Isaiah and the Psalter to highlight the OT "foretelling" of Jesus' death and burial, but embedded in his discussion is a citation from Lam 3:53: "They have cut off my life from the pit and have laid a stone upon me."[14] After his citation, Rufinus concludes that the text prophesies about the burial of Jesus.

Despite these indicators, by far the most quoted portion of the book in this period is Lam 4:20. From the second to the seventh century CE, this text is used in reference to

---

11. Gregory the Great, *Morals on the Book of Job: Volume III, Part 2*, 622. See all three volumes of the work: Gregory the Great, *Morals on the Book of Job: Volumes I–III*.

12. Cf. Matter, "The Lamentations Commentaries," 142–43.

13. Irenaeus, *The Demonstration of the Apostolic Preaching*, paragraph 68, 129–30.

14. Ibid., paragraph 70, 131–32; *NPNF 2*, vol. 3: 553.

Jesus. Lam 4:20 serves as a witness to the spiritual and divine natures of Christ (Irenaeus, Ambrose, Tertullian),[15] a prophecy of Christ's coming (Eusebius),[16] and a prophecy concerning Christ's Lordship and death (Augustine, Rufinus).[17] A major factor influencing the common patristic understanding that Lam 4:20 refers to Jesus derives in fact from the heavy dependence upon the Greek and Latin versions of the OT. The Greek of the verse translates the Hebrew word "messiah" explicitly with *christos* in the phrase "the Christ of the Lord," and most Greek manuscripts actually read both nouns in the nominative case: *christos kurios*, "Lord Christ."[18]

Jerome's Vulgate follows this Greek pattern as well, but alters the noun relationship to produce a blatant christological meaning: *Christus Dominus* or "the Lord Christ."[19] These translation factors certainly inform the reading of Lam 4:20 as an explicit christological prophecy, but by no means was translation the only factor in such interpretations. The general hermeneutic for reading the OT was christological and prophetic in the first place. So even if Jerome was looking at the Hebrew construct chain that should be rendered "the messiah of the Lord," his rendering of Lam 4:20 in the Vulgate exemplifies the conviction that this text ultimately concerns Christ.

## LAMENTATIONS AND THE SPIRITUAL FORMATION OF THE CHURCH

Alongside this emphasis upon the prophetic suffering of Christ, as indicated above the Fathers saw Lamentations as a resource for the church. Regularly the Fathers highlight for the church the themes of penitence and asceticism in the face of sin. In this way, Lamentations speaks to the practice of mourning, repentance, fasting, and confession. Lamentations serves as a medium of spiritual formation.

Tertullian reads Lam 3:40–41 as instructive for the practice of asceticism. In his treatise "On Fasting," Tertullian argues that for spiritual development, the body must be brought under subjection, so as to deny the self and feed the soul. Fasting plays an important role in this regard. Instead of fattening up the body, one should fatten up the soul and be edified by this self-denial. This was, for Tertullian, the practice of Moses, who "lifted up" his heart to God rather than succumbing to the desires of his body. The language here is evocative of Lam 3:40–41: "Let us lift up our hearts over our hands to the God of heaven." As a result, Tertullian teaches, through Lamentations, Moses' practice of spiritually feeding on the Lord through fasting. The church, then, should do likewise.[20]

More common in the patristic age is to see in Lamentations a powerful invitation to repentance and confession for the church. In his *Confessions*, Augustine uses Lam 3:48 to signify his repentance over sin when confronted with the work of Christ. Indeed, he

---

15. *NPNF 2*, vol. 10: 107, 325, 351; *ANF* vol. 3: 610.
16. *NPNF 2*, vol. 1: 86.
17. *NPNF 1*, vol. 2: 379; *NPNF 2*, vol. 3: 553.
18. Cf. Albrektson, *Studies in the Text and Theology*, 193.
19. See Alexander, *The Targum of Lamentations*, 48–49.
20. *ANF* vol. 4: 105.

weeps "rivers of tears" and turns to Christ.[21] Additionally, John Cassian speaks of different kinds of conviction that leads to weeping. Some tears are produced by virtue, but some tears, he argues, are produced from conviction over sin. Along with Ps 6:7, Cassian draws in Lam 2:18: "Let tears run down like a torrent day and night: give yourself no rest and let not the apple of your eye cease [from weeping]." The point is that Lamentations reveals the kind of weeping that is necessary when confronted with sin. The appropriate response to "the pricks of our sins smiting our heart" ought to be penitence and weeping over sin.[22] Gregory the Great in his "Book of Pastoral Rule," teaches the importance of weeping over sin in an act of penitence to God. In fact, Gregory here teaches the importance of singling out sins through meditation on the sinner's waywardness. As with Augustine, Lam 3:48 is cited, but here Gregory states, "Whence it is well said through Jeremiah, when the several transgressions of Judaea were being considered, 'Mine eye hath shed divisions of waters' [Lam 3:48]. For indeed we shed divided waters from our eyes, when to our several sins we give separate tears."[23]

Finally, it is appropriate to note the way in which Eusebius draws attention to Lam 2:1–2 to rebuke the church for division and warring in her midst. In fact, in his *Ecclesiastical History*, Eusebius argues that the state of the church in his day is a result of leaders fighting one another, casting aside "the bond of piety," and instead acting like "tyrants eagerly endeavoring to assert their power."[24] He then quotes Lam 2:1–2 to show the great reversal from the honorable church to the debased church. As Parry says, "Clearly Eusebius saw situations in which churches suffer *for their iniquity* much as Jerusalem did in Lamentations."[25] Here Lamentations serves as an open rebuke to God's people, a summary statement of its sin, and the explanation for persecution. In each of these examples (and more could be given)[26] one notes the use of Lamentations as a means for spiritual formation, particularly in terms of penitence and even open correction.

## CONCLUSION

Although not central in the construction of its Christian identity, Lamentations was still read and used in the life of the church. Indeed, Lam 4:20 served as a major text that identified the death and burial of Christ. Additionally, the church found in Lamentations a guide for spiritual formation, particularly through its instruction on penitence, fasting, and mourning sin. Reading Lamentations as a Christological and a formative text (especially teaching penitence) set a trajectory of understanding for the book certainly throughout the medieval period, but the reformation as well.

21. *NPNF 1*, vol. 1: 159.
22. *NPNF 2*, vol. 11: 397.
23. *NPNF 2*, vol. 12: 60.
24. *NPNF 2*, vol. 1: 324.
25. Parry, *Lamentations*, 219.
26. See John Chrysostom's "Homily 15" which uses Lam 3:27 to signify the value of God's discipline on those he loves and is shaping for his service (*NPNF 1*, vol. 3: 253); Jerome's rebuke in a letter to Domino to desist in complaining and instead to sit alone in silence (Lam 3:28) as a faithful and penitent monk (*NPNF 2*, vol. 6: 81).

# BIBLIOGRAPHY

Albrektson, Bertil. *Studies in the Text and Theology of the Book of Lamentations*. Studia Theologica Lundensia, 21. Lund: Gleerup, 1963.

Alexander, Philip S. *The Targum of Lamentations*. The Aramaic Bible, 17B. Collegeville, MN: Liturgical, 2007.

*Biblia Patristica: Index des Citations et Allusions Bibliques dans la Littérature Patristique*. 7 Volumes. Centre d'Analyse et de Documentation Patristique. Edited by J. Allenbach, A. Benoit, et al. Paris: Centre National de la Recherche Scientifique, 1975–2000.

*Ante Nicene Fathers: Translations of the Writings of the Fathers down to A.D. 325*. 10 Volumes. Edited by Alexander Roberts and James Donaldson. Revised by A. Cleveland Cox. Edinburgh: T. & T. Clark, 1867–85.

Barthélemey, Dominique. *Les davanciers d'Aquila*. Vetus Testamentum Supplements, 10. Leiden: Brill, 1963.

Cain, Andrew. *The Letters of Jerome: Asceticism, Biblical Exegesis, and the Construction of Christian Authority in Late Antiquity*. Oxford Early Christian Studies. Oxford: Oxford University Press, 2009.

Gregory the Great. *Morals on the Book of Job: Volumes I–III*. Library of Fathers of the Holy Catholic Church. Oxford: Parker, 1844–50.

Heine, Ronald E. *Reading the Old Testament with the Ancient Church*. Grand Rapids: Baker Academic, 2007.

Irenaeus. *The Demonstration of the Apostolic Preaching*. Translated and Introduced by J. Armitage Robinson. London: SPCK, 1920.

Jeanrond, Werner. *Theological Hermeneutics*. London: SCM, 1994.

Klostermann, Erich, ed. *Die griechischen christlichen Schriftsteller der ersten drei Jahrhunderte*. Band 6. Leipzig: Heinriche, 1901.

Matter, E. Ann. "The Lamentations Commentaries of Hrabanus Marus and Paschasius Radbertus." *Traditio* 38 (1982) 135–63.

———. "The Legacy of the School of Auxerre: Glossed Bibles, School Rhetoric, and the Universal Gilbert." *Temas Mediev* 14 (2006) 85–98. Accessible online: http://www.scielo.org.ar/scielo.php?pid=S0327-50942006000100004&script=sci_arttext.

Parry, Robin A. *Lamentations*. The Two Horizons Old Testament Commentary. Grand Rapids: Eerdmans, 2010.

Reventlow, H. G. *History of Biblical Interpretation: Volume 1, From the Old Testament to Origen*. Resources for Biblical Study, 50. Translated by Leo G. Perdue. Atlanta: Society of Biblical Literature, 2009.

———. *History of Biblical Interpretation: Volume 2, From Late Antiquity to the End of the Middle Ages*. Resources for Biblical Study, 61. Translated by Leo G. Perdue. Atlanta: Society of Biblical Literature, 2009.

*Select Library of Nicene and Post-Nicene Fathers of the Christian Church*. First Series. 14 Volumes. Edited by Philip Schaff. Edinburgh: T. & T. Clark, 1886–89.

*Select Library of Nicene and Post-Nicene Fathers of the Christian Church*. Second Series. 10 Volumes. Edited by Philip Schaff. Edinburgh: T. & T. Clark, 1890–1900.

Trigg, Joseph W. *Origen*. Early Church Fathers. London: Routledge, 1998.

Wenthe, Dean O., ed. *Jeremiah, Lamentations*. Ancient Christian Commentary on Scripture: Old Testament, 12. General Editor, Thomas C. Oden. Downers Grove, IL: InterVarsity, 2009.

Würthwein, Ernst. *The Text of the Old Testament*. 2nd ed. Translated by Erroll F. Rhodes. Grand Rapids: Eerdmans, 1995.

# J

# Christian Interpretation of Lamentations in the Middle Ages

David S. Hogg

## A GENEALOGY OF INTERPRETATION

There are certain books in the canon of Christian Scripture that are the focus of attention in almost every generation. Lamentations is not one of those books. Quite apart from the relative abundance of deliberation on this significant, albeit brief, portion of Scripture in our contemporary age, it did not garner much interest for at least the first half of the Middle Ages.

Although fragmentary comments can be found in early medieval exegesis, the first extensive treatment of Lamentations in the Middle Ages was made by Gregory the Great. Even here, however, Gregory did not produce a volume on Lamentations itself, but incorporated his reflections throughout his *Moralia in Iob*.[1] It was not until the Carolingian period (ninth century CE) that any self contained commentary appears. The first to produce such a volume was Rabanus Maurus, Archbishop of Mainz. Among his voluminous corpus of Old Testament commentaries, Rabanus added a commentary on Lamentations at the end of his work on Jeremiah that evinces a knowledge of and familiarity with Gregory's work, yet demonstrates originality of thought.[2]

The first treatment of Lamentations in its own right came from the pen of Paschasius Radbertus in the mid-ninth century.[3] The significance of Radbertus' commentary over that of his predecessors is that his forms the basis for much of what would eventually be included in the twelfth-century *Glossa Ordinaria*. The dominance of Radbertus' work both on its own and as part of the *Gloss* appears to have served as an impetus for further reflection on this heretofore neglected scriptural text. Among those applying their inter-

---

1. Magni, *Moralia in Iob*.
2. Andrée, *Gilbertus Universalis*, 54.
3. Radberti, *Expositio in Lamentationes*.

pretive skills to Lamentations are Guibert de Nogent[4] (one of Anselm of Canterbury's more famous students), Hugh of St. Victor[5] (prolific author and esteemed leader of the Victorines in Paris) and Rupert of Deutz[6] (controversial yet influential theologian whose work on the Eucharist garnered interest in the sixteenth century).

## THE SIGNIFICANCE OF THE *GLOSSA ORDINARIA*

As just noted, the most prominent Christian interpretation of Lamentations in the European Middle Ages was that contained in the *Gloss*. Setting to the side the tangled but fascinating history of how the *Gloss* was produced, the section on Lamentations was largely the work of Gilbert the Universal, who drew heavily on the work of Radbertus.[7] In addition to following the work of Radbertus, Gilbert also maintained the same hermeneutical method and the one that was most popular in the Middle Ages. For each discreet section, the *Gloss* provides an historical, allegorical, and moral interpretation. Generally, the historical interpretation addresses the original setting as it can be determined from, mainly, other biblical material. The allegorical interpretation reflects on how the text relates to the church, and the moral interpretation focuses on how the text under consideration applies to the life of contemporary Christians.

From the outset, the *Gloss* on Lamentations identifies the description of the city of Jerusalem as applying both to the actual city itself and to the church.[8] In other words, Gilbert and Radbertus, along with other medieval interpreters, saw Lamentations as a work of prophecy that resonated as true for Israel in exile, but its proper or final fulfillment lies with the church. It is on account of this perspective that the *Gloss* is able to include cross-references to the New Testament that may seem somewhat improbable to the modern day reader. However, not all intertextual comments can be easily dismissed as misguided.

Take, for example, the commentary on Lam 1:3 as given in the *Gloss*. The text reads, "Judah has migrated on account of affliction and great servitude. She has lived among the Gentiles, but has not found rest. All her persecutors have overtaken her in the midst of straits." The historical interpretation progresses through a standard explanation that Judah is being punished for her sin and that in such a situation no one should expect to find rest but rather continuing strife. At this stage there is a reference to Matt 11:29–30 where Jesus calls people to cease struggling under the yoke of sin and to take his yoke which is easy and through which rest may be found.

Here, one might be tempted to think that jumping straight into the New Testament is unwarranted, but consider the point to which both Lamentations and Jesus are directing their audience. Granted, Lamentations takes longer to resolve the dilemma of suffering for sin than Jesus' succinct statement, but the aim is the same. As the reader discovers

---

4. Migne, *Patrologiae Latina*, vol. 156, 451–87.
5. Migne, *Patrologiae Latina*, vol. 175, 255–322.
6. Tuitiensis, *De Sancta Trinitate et Operibus Eius*, 1591–642.
7. Andrée, *Gilbertus Universalis*, 20.
8. Ibid., 172.

in Lam 3, the yoke of judgment may be heavy, but the yoke of God's redemption is light because it comes with compassion and loving-kindness. Well may the *Gloss* comment that, "For justly are they oppressed by hard affliction who have fled from under the light yoke of the Lord, and have despised the liberty promised in Christ. They rightly labor under the affliction of servitude"[9]

This example is instructive because in it we see not only the *Gloss*' interest in connecting texts from both testaments that have a similar focus, but also that medieval historical interpretation included a christological perspective. Understanding Christ to be at the heart of the Old Testament was not considered by medieval theologians as a matter of *eis*egesis but of *ex*egesis. To comprehend Christ as the center of revelation was to recognize the purpose of the revelation of God from start to finish. Thus, in the commentary on Lam 1:3, to speak of "the liberty promised in Christ" is to admit that the freedom gained through God's salvation under the old covenant remains utterly consistent and congruent with divine salvation through Christ in the new covenant. Biblical scholars in the Middle Ages did not see this as anachronistic but as a necessary principle endemic to Scripture itself.

In his *Didascalion*, Hugh of St. Victor guides his students through the study of theology by defining more precisely what is meant by the literal or historical meaning. "If, however, we use the signification of this term in a broader sense, e.g., to say that 'history' is 'not only a telling of things accomplished, but the primary signification of any telling that is expressed using words,' there is no problem; I think that all the books of both Testaments involve this broader acceptation [ . . . ] with regard to the reading in the literal sense."[10]

Approximately a half century earlier, Isidore of Seville had written about the literal sense that biblical history has two parts. On the one hand, its purpose is to tell us of past actions; on the other hand, its purpose is to make known divine precepts.[11] Thus, in the case of our example in Lam 1:3, the precept of burdens for those under condemnation is matched by the precept of a lighter burden through submission to God's plan of salvation.

This pattern of interpretation is characteristic of the chief medieval Christian commentary on Lamentations. It sometimes jumps too far, too fast (as in the case of identifying Jerusalem with the church). But it is also mixed with some refreshingly thoughtful insights (as in the case of tying together Jesus' lighter yoke with the heavy yoke of sin) and rich theological interpretation.

## LAMENTATIONS IN THE LITURGY

Apart from a consideration of the place of Lamentations in the history of biblical interpretation, there is a tradition stretching back at least to the eighth-century Carolingian

---

9. "Iure enim, qui leve iugum Domini fugerant, dura afflictione premuntur et, qui libertatem in Christo promissam vilipendebant, affliction servitutis merito laborabant." (Andrée, *Gilbertus Universalis*, 188).

10. Cited in de Lubac, *Medieval Exegesis*, 41.

11. de Lubac, *Medieval Exegesis*, 42.

church where selections from Lamentations were read as part of the liturgy of Holy Week. On Maundy Thursday Lam 1:1–14 was read; on Good Friday Lam 2:8–10 and 3:1–9 was read; on Holy Saturday Lam 3:22–30, 4:1–6 and 5:1–11 was read.[12] These selections were read during the night office of Tenebrae. At this evening service, candles inside the church were slowly and systematically snuffed out until, by the end of the service, the church was in total darkness (apart from a single candle that remained lit for the reader).

It appears that time and distance kept this part of the liturgy from maintaining uniformity. By the late medieval period in England, for example, the office of Tenebrae was observed on Wednesday, Thursday, and Friday of Holy Week and appears to have lost some of its popularity among the laity.[13] Nevertheless, the office was still practiced and the significance still explained to devoted practitioners of Holy Week liturgy. In a collection of homilies by Johannes Mirkus, for instance, we find the following explanation of Tenebrae: "For when Christ was nailed foot and hand, hanging on the cross, the hours of the day from noon until three in the afternoon, the son withdrew its light and was dark through the world, shewing that the maker of light paid that time to death."[14]

Along similar lines, though adding a new dimension, we discover the following explanation in another collection of fifteenth century homilies:

> And they call the office Tenebrae because it is a sign of the dark hearts of the Jews that saw Christ that was the light of all the world and would not trust in him. Another explanation why the office is called Tenebrae is that it is a sign of the dispersion or departing that the apostles made when they forsook and fled their master in the night of his passion, and also as a sign of the death and burying of Christ, when he was dead and buried and so withdrew his presence whereby all the world was lightened.[15]

When we place these homilies side by side we see that there was a double reference in the symbolism of the snuffed out candles. The first referent was to the abandonment of the disciples, one by one, on the night of Christ's betrayal. The second, and more significant, referent was to the death of Christ on Good Friday. When that final candle was snuffed out during this night office, the point could hardly be more profound that the light of the world had departed his creation, leaving it in total darkness. If ever there was a time for lamentation in the history of humanity it was in the days between the death and resurrection of the Messiah.[16]

---

12. Ibid., 52.
13. Duffy, *The Stripping of the Altars*, 23.
14. Mirk, *Mirk's Festial*, 117–18.
15. Weatherby, ed. *Speculum Sacerdotale*, 101–2.
16. For further reading on the development and use of Lamentations in the medieval western church see Edmund Bishop, *Liturgica Historica*. Further insight will be gained from Tyrer, *Historical Survey of Holy Week*. For a brief but informative introduction to this aspect of western medieval liturgy consult Reynolds, "Holy Week." For a more general survey consult Heffernan and Matter, eds., *The Liturgy of the Medieval Church*.

## BIBLIOGRAPHY

Andrée, Alexander. *Gilbertus Universalis Glossa Ordinaria in Lamentationes Ieremie Prophete, Prothemata et Liber I*. Acta Universitatis Stockholmiensis Studia Latina Stockholmiensia, 52. Stockholm: Almquist & Wiksell, 2005.

Bishop, Edmund. *Liturgica Historica: Papers on the Liturgy and Religious Life of the Western Church*. Oxford: Clarendon, 1962.

Duffy, Eamon. *The Stripping of the Altars: Traditional Religion in England 1400–1580*. New Haven: Yale University Press, 1992.

Heffernan, Thomas J., and E. Ann Matter, eds. *The Liturgy of the Medieval Church*. 2nd ed. Kalamazoo, MI: Medieval Institute, 2005.

de Lubac, Henri. *Medieval Exegesis: The Four Senses of Scripture*. Vol. 2. Translated by E. M. Macierowski. Edinburgh: T. & T. Clark, 2000.

Magni, S. Gregroii. *Moralia in Iob*. Edited by Marci Adriaen. Corpus Christianorum Series Latina, 143/143A. Turnholt, Belgium: Brepols, 1979.

Migne, J.-P. *Patrologiae Latina*. Vol. 156. Paris: Garnier Fratres, 1880.

———. *Patrologiae Latina*. Vol. 175. Paris: Garnier Fratres, 1879.

Mirk, John. *Mirk's Festial: A Collection of Homilies by Johannes Mirkus*. Edited by T. Erbe. London: EETS, 1905.

Radberti, Pascasii. *Expositio in Lamentationes Hieremiae Libri Quinque*. Edited by Beda Paulus. Corpus Christianorum Continuatio Mediaeualis, 85. Turnholt, Belgium: Brepols, 1988.

Reynolds, Roger E. "Holy Week." In *Dictionary of the Middle Ages*, Vol. 6, edited by Joseph R. Strayer, 276–80. New York: Scribner's Sons, 1985.

Tuitiensis, Ruperti. *De Sancta Trinitate et Operibus Eius*. Edited by Hrabanus Haacke. Corpus Christianorum Continuatio Mediaeualis, 23. Turnholt, Belgium: Brepols, 1972.

Tyrer, John Walton. *Historical Survey of Holy Week, Its Services and Ceremonial*. London: Oxford University Press, 1932.

Weatherby, E. H., ed. *Speculum Sacerdotale*. Oxford: EETS, 1971.

# K

# John Calvin's Interpretation of Lamentations

Pete Wilcox

## INTRODUCTION

Calvin's *Commentary on Lamentations* (1563) was nothing of the sort. But then, none of his expositions of the prophets were "commentaries" in any conventional sense. These works were not written by him, but were compiled by friends from lectures he gave in the Academy in Geneva. The story has been told before.[1] The stenographers were sufficiently skilled to achieve a word for word record of what Calvin said. They even captured his asides, as well as the prayers with which Calvin finished each lecture.[2] If a modern scholar publishes a Bible commentary based on material previously delivered as lectures, the lectures are generally invisible: the commentary is revised so thoroughly that there is no trace of the audience originally addressed. In Calvin's lectures, however, the published text is still clearly addressed to hearers, not readers.[3]

Calvin's *Commentary on Lamentations* is a series of eighteen lectures delivered between Monday 21 September 1562, and Tuesday 19 January 1563.[4] His basic routine was to speak on Monday to Wednesday mornings,[5] alternating a week of preaching with a week of lecturing. This was, however, a period close to the end of his life, when he was suffering considerable ill health. As a result, a series of lecture that ought to have taken only three months, in fact required four.

---

1. See, for example, Wilcox, "Calvin as Commentator on the Prophets" and Wilcox, "The Lectures of John Calvin and the Nature of his Audience."

2. For example, at the end of Lecture 9, he says, "I am surprised at the hour striking so soon; I hardly think that I have lectured a whole hour" (Calvin, *Commentaries*, 408).

3. As, for example, when he says at the end of Lecture 18 (with reference to his colleagues in the Company of Pastors), "As it has seemed good to the brethren, I will begin tomorrow the explanation of Ezekiel" (ibid., 518).

4. *Calvini Opera*, 21.93, 95.

5. This accounts for the repeated references to "yesterday" (Calvin, *Commentaries*, 311, 385, 397, etc.), "tomorrow" (ibid., 359, 384, 432, etc.), "the next lecture" (ibid., 492) and "the last lecture" (ibid., 408, 420).

# GREAT IS THY FAITHFULNESS?

Calvin's lectures lasted exactly an hour. His friend and biographer, Nicholas Collodan, states that he spoke without notes, on the back of only about an hour of preparation, and taking nothing with him into the auditorium except a Hebrew Bible.[6] He would read out a short passage of Hebrew Scripture, translate it into Latin, and then (in Latin) expound a verse or a series of verses.

Like all his expositions of the prophets, the *Commentary on Lamentations* was rushed into print. It was the last of Calvin's commentaries to be published within his lifetime.

## THE PURPOSE OF LAMENTATIONS ACCORDING TO CALVIN

Calvin introduces his *Commentary* with a discussion of the book's historical context and of what he regards as Jeremiah's purpose. "We must inquire when the Book was composed by the Prophet, and also what was the object of the author," he says.[7]

On the first point, he is dismissive of the opinion of Jerome, that these Lamentations are the ones referred to in 2 Chron 35:25 and date from the time of king Josiah. Jerome was, he says, "grossly mistaken." He sees "nothing in this book which relates to Josiah. There is indeed mention made in one place of a king, but what is said there cannot be applied to Josiah; for he was never driven into exile, but was buried at Jerusalem with his fathers." Rather, he asserts, "From the whole contents of the Book we may justly conclude, that it was written after the city was destroyed, and the people led into exile."[8] Nevertheless, he accepts without question that these lamentations were composed by the prophet Jeremiah.

On the second point, Calvin urges that the really remarkable thing about this book is the fact that it contains an unusual kind of prophecy. It is easy enough, he says, to prophesy in prosperity, when everything is going well and there is every reason to feel confident about the future. It is a much more remarkable thing, he maintains, when a prophet continues to prophesy, "when things are in a state of despair, and God seems to have forsaken his Church." Here in this book, Jeremiah is found still to discharge his office, "when the kingdom had fallen, when the king with all his children was exposed to extreme disgrace, when in short the covenant of God seemed wholly abolished."[9] And in this circumstance, Calvin draws attention to four points:

1. the prophet, he suggests, was led "to speak first of God's judgments;
2. secondly, to exhort the people to repentance;
3. thirdly, to encourage them to hope;
4. and lastly, to open the door for prayer to God, so that the people in their extremities might venture to flee to God's mercy; which could not have been done without faith.

---

6. *Calvin Opera* 40.23–24; 42.189–90.
7. Calvin, *Commentaries*, 299.
8. Ibid.
9. Ibid., 300.

It is for this reason that "this Book was written by Jeremiah: his object was to shew that though nothing in the land appeared but desolation, and the Temple being destroyed, the Covenant of God appeared as made void, and thus all hope of salvation had been cut off, yet hope still remained, provided the people sought God in true repentance and faith."[10] The emphasis on "repentance and faith" is absolutely characteristic of Calvin's biblical expositions, whether Old or New Testament. It is an emphasis that recurs at frequent intervals throughout the exposition.[11] In the process, Calvin asserts, Jeremiah "constructed some sort of building out of the ruins."[12]

## THE HUMANIST STYLE OF CALVIN'S EXEGESIS

Calvin's humanist ambitions are well known. He was self-consciously part of a movement in reaction to the philosophical and hermeneutical scholasticism of previous centuries. In the interpretation of texts, "humanism" exhibited a particular interest in context and authorial intention. Calvin experienced some ambivalence about whether or not his lectures contributed to the cause. He was acutely aware that his written works achieved far greater "brevity" and "clarity" (two of the watchwords of the movement); but he was persuaded by his friends and publisher that even these *ex tempore* expositions demonstrated the values to which the humanists aspired.

There is some debate about the extent of Calvin's facility in Hebrew.[13] He certainly knew a *hilphil* when he saw one and could distinguish it from a *hithpael*.[14] But if his ability as a linguist is open to question, his aim to engage as far as possible with the original language is in no doubt. At each new section of biblical text, Calvin offers his own translation, justifying it and commenting on alternatives. Occasionally, he isolates a particular Hebrew word and explores its etymology: he is not always accurate when he does so; but in terms of his humanist ideals, it is the attempt itself that is significant. He strives to establish the plain or simple sense of the text, as opposed to what is *coactum* (forced) or *frigidum* (lifeless) or *durum* (harsh). At the end of this exercise, Calvin frequently concludes, "Now we understand the meaning of the prophet." To postmodern ears, this sounds like an extraordinary claim; but this was only the second generation of printing, and quite possibly the very first time that Calvin's hearers had been exposed to the text of Lamentations in anything other than the Latin Vulgate text.

The genre of his text matters to Calvin. He notes that Lamentations is a series of acrostic poems. Oddly, this is not until Calvin embarks on the exposition of chapter 3, when the literary form changes: "The letters of the alphabet are tripled in this chapter, which I had omitted to mention," he says. "In the first two chapters each verse begins with the successive letters of the alphabet, except that in the last chapter there is one instance

---

10. Ibid., 300.
11. E.g., "To conversion, he adds prayer; for we cannot be reconciled to God unless he buries our sins; nor can repentance be separated from faith," ibid., 433.
12. Ibid., 301.
13. Engammare: "Iohannes Calvinus trium linguarum peritus?"
14. See for example Calvin, *Commentaries*, 329, 431.

of inversion, for Jeremiah has put p, phi, before e, oin; or it may be that the order has been changed by the scribes; but this is uncertain. Here then, as I have said, each letter is thrice repeated. Then the first, the second, and the third verse begins with a aleph; and the fourth begins with b, beth, and so he goes on to the end."[15] There is something remarkably modern about such a degree of literary sensitivity and critical candor.

On the other hand, Calvin does not attempt to explore what possible theological or pastoral reason there might have been for this acrostic scheme. He does note, in relation to chapter 4, that here Jeremiah "follows the order of the alphabet the fourth time"; and in relation to chapter 5 he wonders whether "this prayer ought to be read as unconnected with the Lamentations, for the initial letters of the verses are not written according to the order of the Alphabet."[16]

It is similarly a mark of Calvin's humanist instincts that he refers in the course of the commentary not only to biblical but also to classical authors. He quotes three pieces of poetry by Virgil in the second lecture, and refers again to Virgil as well as to Horace in the penultimate one.[17] Such references are especially impressive, if we are to assume they were made from memory.

## CALVIN'S ENGAGEMENT WITH OTHER INTERPRETERS AND APPLICATION OF THE TEXT

A striking feature of Calvin's exposition of Lamentations (typical, in fact, of his practice) is the lack of specific references to other expositors. The lectures are littered with vague and impersonal allusions to "some interpreters," "many" and "others," which do suggest that Calvin had access to either ancient or contemporary commentaries and had studied them. But the only commentator named by Calvin in this series of lectures is Jerome; and all eight of these references are critical. It is not possible to tell whether Calvin was unfamiliar with the work of other church fathers, such as Origen, or simply chose not to refer to them. It is, however, difficult to imagine that he did not have access to the expositions of contemporaries such as Oecolampadius or Peter Martyr Vermigli. In their case, it is probable that he did not refer to them because he did not wish to appear disloyal to his reforming colleagues, by disagreeing with them. On the other hand, there are also no references to Roman Catholic opponents as "Papists," "Romanists" or "scholastics," usually common in his expositions.

Similarly (and again this is in keeping with Calvin's usual practice in his expositions of the Bible), there are few references to contemporary events or situations. There is a single reference to the Papacy in his comments on 3:41.[18] There is presumably an allusion to the experience of many of his hearers, exiles from France, when he says that "when God afflicts his Church, however grievous it may be to see innocent men slain, blood

---

15. Ibid., 389–90.

16. Ibid., 455, 492.

17. In Lecture 2, the references are to the *Aeniad* 2 (twice, ibid., 317) and 3 (ibid., 318). In Lecture 17, the references are to Horace, *Ode* 6.1 and to Virgil, *Eclogues & Georgics*, book 1 (ibid., 499).

18. Ibid., 433.

shed promiscuously, the sexes, men and women, killed indiscriminately, and although it be a sad spectacle, to see houses robbed and plundered, fields laid waste, and all things in a confusion, yet when all these things are compared with the abolition of God's worship . . . all these things ought to appear light to us."[19]

On the whole, the theological applications Calvin derives from the text are very general. In these terms however, Calvin regards the message of the prophet as directly relevant to his hearers. Such applications are frequently heralded by Calvin's use of the word *doctrine*: "from this we derive a useful doctrine," he will say, before proceeding to apply a text. Most of the applications are of two kinds. First, he sees the destruction of Jerusalem and its temple as the just vengeance of God upon a disobedient people, and takes it for granted that from time to time it may be the purpose of God to afflict his church. It is only the ungodly "who murmur and think that God is unjust and cruel."[20] What the Jews experienced, the church may also discover: "as, then, we see that the Jews . . . so when we . . ."[21] Perhaps the fullest example occurs in Lecture 2, when he says, "We may hence gather a useful doctrine; for what the Prophet relates of Jerusalem is seen almost in all mankind; but we must beware lest this should be true of us . . . Let us now, then, take heed lest we become stupid while God deals liberally with us; but, on the contrary, let us learn to appreciate the blessings of God, and consider the end for which they have been given us, otherwise what is said here of Jerusalem will happen to us."[22]

Similarly, secondly, he regards the words and disposition of the prophet (in his perseverance in prayer, his struggles against despair, his meekness yet boldness) as model of Christian obedience and discipleship. Indeed, most surprisingly, Calvin asserts that Jeremiah provides a model even in protest against God: "The Prophet then dictates for all the godly such complaints as they might, so to speak, pour forth confidently and freely into the bosom of God."[23]

It is, however, above all in the extemporary prayers with which Calvin concludes each lecture, that he makes the step of application. They almost all include the words "as at this day." A typical example is the prayer at the end of Lecture 2: "Grant, Almighty God, that as at this day we see thy Church miserably afflicted, we may direct our eyes so as to see our own sins, and so humble ourselves before thy throne, that we may yet cease not to, entertain hope, and in the midst of death wait for life; and may this confidence open our mouth, that we may courageously persevere in calling on thy name, through Christ our Lord. Amen."[24]

---

19. Ibid., 309.
20. Ibid., 311.
21. Ibid., 483.
22. Ibid., 314–15.
23. Ibid., 400.
24. Ibid., 324.

## BIBLIOGRAPHY

Baum, Guilielmus, August Eduardus Cunitz, and Eduard Reuss, eds. *Corpus Reformatorum: Ioannis Calvini Opera Quae Supersunt Omnia, vols. 29–87*. Brunswick: Schwetschke, 1863–1900.

Calvin, John. *Commentaries on the Book of the Prophet Jeremiah and the Lamentations*, vol. 5. Translated and edited by John Owen. Edinburgh: Calvin Translation Society, 1855.

Engammare, M. "Iohannes Calvinus trium linguarum peritus? La Question de l'Hebreu." *Bibliotheque de Humanisme et Renaissance* 58 (1996) 37–39.

Wilcox, Pete. "Calvin as Commentator on the Prophets." In *Calvin and the Bible*, edited by Donald McKim, 107–30. Cambridge: Cambridge University Press, 2007.

———. "The Lectures of John Calvin and the Nature of his Audience." *Archive für Reformationsgeschichte* 87 (1996) 136–48.

# L

## Lamentations for the Lord

*Great and Holy Friday in the Greek Orthodox Church*

Eugenia Scarvelis Constantinou

Although the Book of Lamentations is not utilized liturgically in the Orthodox Church, the articulation of lament is thoroughly incorporated into Orthodox Christian worship and forms a natural and frequent part of liturgical expression. The matins service always begins with the reading of six psalms, four of which are psalms of lament.[1] The key psalm in the Orthodox vespers service is also lamentful in character, "Lord, I have called upon Thee, hear me."[2] But perhaps the most common expression of lament is found in the recurrent use of Psalm 50,[3] ("Have mercy upon me, O God, according to thy great mercy") which is read or chanted halfway through every matins service. This psalm is also recited by the priest quietly during every liturgy and is utilized as a familiar feature in many other divine services. The "uncompromisingly happy" attitude which Robin Parry describes in the present volume as a feature of evangelical worship is certainly not the Orthodox tradition. Praise, joy, and glorification are frequently expressed but not to the exclusion of other sentiments and realities. Lament psalms incorporated in Orthodox worship express the great range of human emotion and experience. Parry ponders whether Christians ought to be encouraged to lament as an alternative to "uncompromisingly happy" worship and whether an "aspiration to misery" is appropriate.[4] But the Orthodox use of lament psalms would never be considered an expression of misery, nor would a personal feeling of misery be required for such to be considered "authentic" expressions. Lament fills a spiritual need which Parry eloquently identifies and articulates as absent in the "uncompromisingly happy" nature of evangelical worship. Lament psalms are expressions of repentance, an attitude which is not reserved for sacramental confession or for grave sins, but which is part of

---

1. Psalms 3, 37/38, 62/63, and 87/88.
2. Psalm 140/141.
3. Psalm 51 in the West.
4. Robin Parry, "Wrestling with Lamentations," 175.

Orthodox daily prayer and spirituality. Lament psalms are not perceived as mournful or depressing but express our genuine longing for God, an awareness of the inadequacy of the self, regret for our failures and a desire for healing and renewal.

## HOLY WEEK IN THE ORTHODOX CHURCH

No Orthodox service encapsulates the complex emotions of lamentation more than the evening service on Great and Holy Friday ("Good Friday" in the West).[5] The actual title of the service itself in the Greek Orthodox Church is "Epitaphios Threnos" ("Lamentations on the Tomb"), but the service is popularly referred to as *Ta Egkomia* for the singing of panegyric-style lamentations. The most popular service of the liturgical year for Greek Orthodox Christians may well be the evening of Great and Holy Friday. Despite the length of the service,[6] "The Lamentations" draws large crowds of faithful who are especially attracted by participation in the "funeral procession" for Christ and the cherished singing of traditional lamentations. The biblical book of Lamentations is not incorporated in the festal traditions of the Greek Orthodox Church in the way that it is in the Western liturgical traditions associated with "Holy Week."[7] Still, despite the fact that the book is not employed in the liturgy, some similarities in general tone and theology in the celebration of Great and Holy Friday in the Eastern Orthodox Church mirror the tone of mourning and lamentation that accompany Western Christian traditions. Likewise, the christological focus of lament in both the Western and Eastern traditions remains similar. For this reason, it is appropriate to elucidate the practice of "The Lamentations" (*Ta Egkomia*) in this volume focused upon the biblical book of Lamentations.

Holy Week in the Orthodox Church actually begins the day before Palm Sunday,[8] and the week in its totality is a profoundly theological and spiritual journey and engagement in the Passion and Resurrection of Christ. At least two services are held most days of Holy Week and each service is entirely unique, with its own particular themes and hymns. The goal and culmination of the week is the Resurrection service, celebrated at midnight on Saturday. The service of "The Lamentations" can only be properly understood contextually, within the totality of the services of Holy Week and the general liturgical perspective in the Orthodox Church.

The services are "experienced" as the faithful "participate" in the event, not as re-enactments or as mere remembrance of past events, but in a true, mystical connection to the event. This is quite typical of Orthodox spirituality and liturgy, which evinces a strong conviction that as members of the timeless church we participate in such events in a timeless manner. Mystically connected to one another, not only globally at the present moment as the church militant, but to the past and even the future, as both human

---

5. The term "Good Friday" is not used by Eastern Christians. Instead the day is known as "Great and Holy Friday," emphasizing the importance and character of the day.

6. At least three and a half hours. Only one service exceeds it in length: Great and Holy Thursday evening.

7. See the articles by David Hogg, Andrew Cameron-Mowat, and Robin Parry in this volume.

8. "Saturday of Lazarus," in which the church remembers the raising of Lazarus and recognizes that event as the reason for the triumphal reception of Christ into Jerusalem on the following day, Palm Sunday.

and angelic members of the church triumphant in the kingdom of heaven join us as a "cloud of witnesses."[9] Throughout Holy Week, as well as during the entire liturgical year, the hymns often express what happened on that day not as something which took place long ago but as something which we experience *now*.[10]

During the course of Holy Week, expectation of the Passion grows until the crucifixion of Christ is commemorated on Great and Holy Thursday evening "by anticipation."[11] Twelve long Gospel selections are read, narrating the events of the Passion, interspersed with prayer petitions, psalms, and hymns. The night is highlighted by a solemn procession through the darkened church in which a large icon of Christ crucified[12] is carried through the church by the priest after the fifth Gospel reading. The procession comes to the front of the congregation and the cross with the icon of Christ crucified is placed upright in the center of the solea[13] where it stands throughout the remainder of the service until the next afternoon.

The following day, Great Friday morning, women and girls come to the church early to decorate the "tomb" of Christ with flowers.[14] The "tomb" is represented by a wooden structure called the *kouvouklion*,[15] which is akin to a platform, approximately four feet wide by two feet deep, with an ornately carved wooden canopy which arches over the platform supported by four wooden posts in the corners. This sits on a wooden rectangular base of the same size, and is higher than a table so that the "tomb" can be seen by the congregation. The entire structure is about seven or eight feet high and the top half is removable from the base. The women of the parish spend the entire day elaborately decorating the *kouvouklion* with greenery and hundreds of flowers so that the *kouvouklion* is usually entirely covered with flowers. The result is always beautiful, and often spectacular, depending on the artistry and skill of the ladies, as well as the number and variety of flowers available to them.

9. Hebrews 12:1.

10. This is emphasized by the use of the word "today" in Orthodox hymnography. When Christ is betrayed, a hymn states: "*Today* Judas betrays the Master." When he is crucified the priest chants: "*Today* is hung upon the Tree He who suspended the earth in the midst of the waters." When he is buried another hymn reflects on that mystery and personifies Hades receiving Christ as dead: "*Today* Hades cries out groaning, 'I should not have accepted the man born of Mary.'"

11. The various services of Holy Week are performed earlier than one might expect "by anticipation." The service of Thursday night is technically the matins service for Friday morning. Following the ancient Jewish custom, the ecclesiastical day begins at sunset in the Orthodox Church. Therefore, a service for the following day can be performed any time after sunset the night before. For practical and pastoral purposes the matins services of Holy Week are done the night before.

12. The icon is large, three to four feet high, and shaped like the crucified Christ. The icon is detachable from the cross itself, which, of course, is even larger.

13. The solea is the space between where the congregation sits or stands and the iconostasis (the icon screen) that separates the nave from the sanctuary.

14. Although the services of Holy Week are basically the same for all Orthodox Christians, the decoration of the "tomb" of Christ is typically more elaborate and involved among the Greek and Arab Orthodox, and less so among the Russians and other Orthodox of the Slavic tradition. Other minor traditions also sometimes differ.

15. The *kouvouklion* is often mistakenly called *the epitaphios*, which is actually the name of the icon which will be placed upon the *kouvouklion*.

## GREAT IS THY FAITHFULNESS?

The women only have a few hours to complete their task. They must finish decorating the *kouvouklion* by mid-afternoon Great Friday since the next service, the *Apokathelosis*, usually takes place at 3:00 p.m. At the *Apokathelosis*, (which literally means, "taking down"), the body of Christ is taken down from the cross. The detachable wooden icon of Christ crucified, which had been carried in procession the night before, is removed from the cross by the priest who represents Joseph of Arimathea. The crucified Christ is wrapped in a white sheet, representing the linen shroud, and placed in the sanctuary by the priest. The priest then emerges from the sanctuary with another icon, this time a cloth icon, which is an elaborately embroidered depiction of the dead Christ. This cloth icon is called the *epitaphios*, literally "on the tomb," because it will be placed on the *kouvouklion*. After a solemn procession through the church with the *epitaphios*, which recalls Jesus being carried to the tomb to be buried by Joseph of Arimathea, the priest places it on the floral decorated tomb of Christ.[16] The service concludes shortly thereafter.

The depiction of the dead Christ on the *epitaphios* can differ somewhat stylistically, but certain features of the *epitaphios* are consistent. Christ is always shown dead, lying flat on his back with his arms at his sides and his head on the left side of the scene. Usually his mother is depicted on the far left and is embracing his head, while other women mourners are also portrayed along with angels, Nicodemus, Joseph of Arimathea, and the apostle John. The words of a Great Friday hymn are always embroidered around the four sides of the *epitaphios*:

> The noble Joseph, when he had taken down your most pure body from the Tree, wrapped it in fine linen and anointed it with spices and placed it in a new tomb.

After Christ has been taken down from the cross and placed in the tomb at the afternoon *Apokathelosis* service, everyone goes home. They return at night for the long-anticipated service of "The Lamentations." The service begins with psalms, prayers, and other hymns. Everyone holds a lit candle and the church is ablaze in brilliant candlelight. The flower-bedecked *kouvouklion* stands in the center of the solea before the congregation with the icon of the dead Christ atop a bed of flowers like a bier with a floral canopy covering. The *kouvouklion*, usually decorated primarily with white flowers and artistically embellished with red, purple, or other colors, glows in the candlelight as the congregation sings the lamentations. There are three different "stanzas," (meaning three different melodies), for the lamentations. The verses for the first melody are sung before the congregation continues with the verses of the second stanza, and then the third. In total there are approximately two hundred verses for all three stanzas combined. In most Greek American parishes not all two hundred verses are sung.

After singing the lamentations inside the church, the "funeral procession" for Christ begins. The flower-covered *kouvouklion* with the embroidered icon of the dead Christ is lifted off its base and taken outside and around the church, usually into the streets of the city. The *kouvouklion*, which can be somewhat heavy and awkward, is carried by four to

---

16. Orthodox Christians of the Slavic tradition usually do not have a *kouvouklion* but only a simple bier on which the *epitaphios* is placed. It is decorated with far fewer flowers than is typical of the Greek or Arab Orthodox.

six men of the congregation who have been chosen for this honor as bier bearers. The *kouvouklion* is accompanied by the priest, acolytes carrying processional fans and a large processional cross, the choir, chanters, and the faithful who follow the procession holding their lit candles and singing lamentations. In the course of the procession the priest stops three times to offer prayer petitions. In large metropolitan areas where another Orthodox Church is nearby, parish processions often meet in a central square to offer prayers jointly before returning to their respective churches for Scripture readings and the conclusion of the service.

The lamentations hymns themselves are beautiful, poetic, deeply meaningful, and greatly loved. The first two stanzas sound quite lamentful, especially the second melody, which is very dramatic. The third melody is much brighter, almost happy in tone, and seems to reflect a mood of expectation for the resurrection. The content of the different verses is quite varied. Orthodox hymns typically are theological and rarely emotional or sentimental. The lamentations for Christ, however, do express the sentiments of the congregation and of those who historically participated in the burial of Christ, yet they are always infused with theology. A common theological motif in the lamentations expresses the defeat of death by death, voicing the paradox of Life Himself lying dead in the tomb, the Creator buried by his creatures, etc.

> How, O Life, can You die? How can You dwell in a grave?
> But You now destroy the kingdom of death,
> and You make the dead of Hades rise.

A number of lyrics express the scene at Christ's burial, describing Joseph taking down the body and Nicodemus, or the women, bringing spices. For example:

> From the cross the Arimathean brought You, and in a grave he laid You.

Or another:

> Joseph is entombing, along with Nicodemus, the body of his Creator.

Some verses voice the lament of the Virgin Mary:

> O light of my eyes! O my sweetest Child!
> How are you now covered in the grave?

Or

> "I am rent with grief and my heart within is crushed and broken,
> as I see them slay You unjustly," so bewailing him his grieving mother cried.

Other verses describe the shocked reaction of the angels at seeing Christ dead:

> In a grave they laid You, O my life, my Christ,
> And the armies of the angels were so amazed as they glorified Your condescension.[17]

---

17. *Synkatabasis*, often translated "condescension," is a very common word in the patristic tradition and Orthodox theology. It refers to the love and humility of God who willingly deigned ("condescended") to become human and die on the cross. It does not express distain or contempt.

## GREAT IS THY FAITHFULNESS?

Some lyrics personify the reaction of creation:

> The earth shook with trembling and the sun concealed its face, O Savior,
> For the unwaning light that shines from You has sunk with Your body into darkness and the grave.

Many lamentations express the feelings of the worshippers, mostly praising Christ and glorifying his condescension:

> Now we magnify You, O Lord Jesus, our King,
> And we honor Your passion and burial
> For by it You have delivered us from death.

Or

> Every generation comes to Your grave, O Christ, bringing dirges of praise.

No one "pretends" they do not know the outcome of the death of Christ, and the hymns of Holy Week typically anticipate the resurrection, even among those who have already died and are awaiting the general resurrection:

> Rise, O Lord of Mercy, raising us up also, who languish deep in Hades.

It should be noted at this point that many scholars have observed that the commemoration of the burial of Christ in the Greek Orthodox Church bears some similarity to the ancient rites for the burial of the god, Adonis. Some scholars, beginning perhaps with James Frazer,[18] have either suggested or stated expressly that the Orthodox Christian practice is simply the direct continuation of the Adonis rite in Christianized form with the worship now transferred to Christ. It is true that many practices of the Orthodox Church are extremely ancient. However, the rituals connected with the burial of Christ in the Orthodox Church developed during the middle ages and have no connection to the Adonis rite, either directly or indirectly.[19]

Great Friday services commemorating the death of Christ in the first centuries of Christianity involved the singing of psalms, not lamentations. Psalms were sung for or-

---

18. James Frazer, *The Golden Bough: A Study in Comparative Religion*, (1890, reprinted in one volume as *The Golden Bough: The Roots of Religion and Folklore*, 1981). Frazer wrote, "The whole custom . . . is probably nothing but a continuation, under a different name, of the Adonis worship" (ibid., 295–96). This notion was explored by Margaret Alexiou in *The Ritual Lament in Greek Tradition*. Alexiou does not entirely reject this notion, although she focuses primarily on the continuation of cultural customs from antiquity. See also Pilitsis, "The Gardens of Adonis in Seres Today." Although Pilitsis acknowledges that "mere existence of parallels and similarities does not prove continuity" he proceeds to say that "certain details of the Good Friday rituals . . . may suggest pagan origin, influences and/or transformation of the ancient cult into Christian forms" (ibid., 156).

19. The resemblance between Great Friday rituals for Christ and the ancient rituals for Adonis are actually quite minimal and any likeness between them is not religious but the result of social and cultural continuity with ancient Greece. The similarities are limited to actions that would have typically been performed at a Greek funeral for any person: the singing of lamentations, a funeral procession with the body, and flowers for decoration of the tomb. This was done for Adonis in antiquity because it was already the practice for the funerals of ordinary Greeks before the cult of Adonis developed.

dinary Christian burials as well[20] and psalms remain a large part of the Orthodox Holy Week services, including Great Friday. In the earliest centuries, Great Friday services for the "burial" of Christ reflected what was done by the church for the burial of ordinary individuals: psalms were sung, not lamentations. The singing of actual lamentations was disapproved of by church leaders, probably because of the extreme and dramatic actions of women mourners which were considered unseemly and inappropriate by Christian standards, including wailing, tearing of hair, and other excesses which had accompanied lamentations in Greek antiquity.[21] Yet the custom of singing lamentations for the dead in homes and cemeteries continued as a cultural practice even though this custom was not part of the church's funeral service.

Eventually, actual lamentations were composed for Christ and first appear in ecclesiastical service books for the Greek Orthodox Church by the thirteenth or fourteenth century.[22] Around this time, other Great Friday rituals developed for Christ as we know them today. The cloth icon depicting the dead Christ was already in common use as a liturgical cloth known as the *aer*, and was adapted during this period for use in Great Friday services and became the *epitaphios*.[23] It was no longer used liturgically as an *aer* and the *aer* developed into a very plain cloth which no longer depicts the dead Christ. These developments and others during the middle ages confirm that the Orthodox rituals of Great Friday have no connection to the ancient worship of Adonis but developed organically and naturally as an expression of love and piety by the faithful for Christ.

## CONCLUSION

The sights, sounds, smells, and actions of the Orthodox Lamentations Service of Great Friday involve rituals that predate the church but express the theology of the ancient church. Not mere re-enactment, nor recollection of events in the distant past, The Lamentations service speaks of the events of Christ's death and burial in the present tense, as a lived-liturgy thousands of years old yet always new for each generation. Although the Greek Orthodox Liturgy does not draw particularly from the biblical book of Lamentations in its worship, the association of Christ's death and burial for the forgiveness of sin with the book of Lamentations is readily appropriated in the Western Church, as demonstrated in Parry's and Cameron-Mowat's essays in the present volume. The liturgical use of Lamentations, then, in the Western Church finds resonance in the Lamentations Service of Great and Holy Friday in the Eastern Church. Together both celebrate in their own ways the death of Christ, and anticipate the moment of resurrection, both in the life of Christ and the life of the church.

---

20. See the description of Macrina's funeral by her brother, Gregory of Nyssa, in *de Mortuis*.
21. See Alexiou, *Ritual Lament*, 27–31.
22. Moraites, "Epitaphios Threnos," 794.
23. Tomadakes, "Epitaphios," 793.

## BIBLIOGRAPHY

Alexiou, Margaret. *The Ritual Lament in Greek Tradition*. 2nd ed. Oxford: Rowman and Littlefield, 2002.

Frazer, James. *The Golden Bough: The Roots of Religion and Folklore*. New York: Crown, 1981.

Gregory of Nyssa. *de Mortuis*. In *Patrologia Graeca*, vol. 46, edited by Jean Paul Migne, 46.993A. Paris: Garnier, 1863.

Moraites, Dimitris. "Epitaphios Threnos." In *Threskeytike kai Hethike Egkyklopaideia* [Encyclopedia of Religion and Ethics], vol. 5, edited by Athanasios Martinos, 794–95. Athens, 1964.

Pilitsis, George. "The Gardens of Adonis in Seres Today." *Journal of Modern Greek Studies* 3 (1985) 145–66.

*The Lenten Triodion*. Translated by Mother Mary and Archimandrite Kallistos Ware. The Service Books of the Orthodox Church. London: Faber and Faber, 1978.

Tomadakes, N. B. "Epitaphios." In *Threskeytike kai Hethike Egkyklopaideia* [Encyclopedia of Religion and Ethics], vol. 5, edited by Athanasios Martinos, 792–93. Athens, 1964.

# M

## Lamentations and Christian Worship

Andrew Cameron-Mowat SJ

In the current Roman Catholic ordo, the text of Lamentations is used at Mass only on Saturdays of the twelfth week of ordinary time, in the second of the two cycles of readings. The selection is from Lam 2:2, 11–14, 18–19, and speaks of the predicament of the people who have been punished for their sins. This text is coupled with the Gospel passage of Matthew (Matt 8:5–17) in which the centurion pleads for the life of his paralyzed servant. Jesus takes the opportunity to condemn those who fail to accept his teaching and will be "turned out into the dark, where there will be weeping and grinding of teeth" (v. 12).

The most significant use of Lamentations, however, was in the traditional service known as "Tenebrae," which was the service of Matins and Lauds that was celebrated on Thursday, Friday, and Saturday of Holy Week. The service took place late at night, or very early in the morning, and so in the hours of darkness. An array of fifteen lit candles would be placed in the view of everyone on a candelabrum known as a "hearse." The service began with a silent Our Father, Hail Mary, and Creed, followed by three psalms with an antiphon for each. As each psalm or canticle finished, one of the candles was extinguished. The third psalm and antiphon was followed by a versicle and a response, and another silent Our Father. At this point Scripture would be proclaimed or chanted, with a response at the end of each section. Thus concluded the first of a set of three "nocturnes." From this service of Matins the ceremony would move immediately to Lauds, with another series of Psalms and antiphons. During the singing of the *Benedictus* the six candles on the altar were extinguished. Eventually only one central candle was left. This candle was removed and held out of sight until after the singing of *Christus factus est* and the *Miserere* (Ps 50), followed by a final prayer. At this point, there would a great banging of seats, books, and other materials for a short while, known as the *strepitus*, to commemorate the earthquake from the narratives of the Passion, until the lit candle was returned to view. This was the signal for the end of Tenebrae. The dramatic and musical content of the service was very attractive and so it was a popular part of the celebration of the Holy Week liturgies in parishes with the musical resources to celebrate it properly.

## GREAT IS THY FAITHFULNESS?

The service grew less popular when it was moved to mornings in the 1955 reform of Holy Week, and it fell out of use in most places after the renewal of the liturgy after the Second Vatican Council.

The proclamation of the Lamentations took place during the first Nocturn on each of the three days. The common practice was that members of the choir would sing in a particular order, beginning with the youngest voice. The great composers of the late Middle Ages and the Renaissance created significant settings of these Lamentations texts, and also of the responsories between each portion of the Lamentation texts.

There was, therefore, a triple context into which the text of the Lamentations was placed.

1. First, there was the importance of the days themselves at which these texts were proclaimed: the first day, with the commemoration of the Lord's Supper and his Agony in Gethsemane; the second day with the betrayal, trial, and crucifixion of Christ; and finally Saturday, with Christ in the tomb and the world awaiting his resurrection.

2. Secondly, there was the context of the psalms which would be chanted before the Lamentation text.

3. Finally, there was also the immediate context of the sung responsory after each Lamentation text, which told the story at each stage of the Passion narrative.

Thursday: Pss 68, 69, and 70 were chanted, and the Lamentation texts were from Lam 1:1–5, 6–9, and 10–14. The set psalms are themselves very much of the genre of lament: cries of distress and anguish, which speak of the shame of the psalmist, of the insults and pain inflicted, of the sackcloth and the vinegar (Ps 68). There is a cry for rescue and for shame to be brought against those who attack the psalmist (Ps 69). This is repeated in Ps 70, which ends with words of hope and expectation of rescue. It would have been a relatively simple matter for participants to connect the predicament of the psalmist with those of Christ at this crucial moment in his life. The Lamentation texts for this service speak of the affliction that has come to the city as a result of the crimes of the people, ending with an appeal to Jerusalem to return to the Lord. After verses 1 to 5 the responsory speaks of Christ on the Mount of Olives, overlooking the city. After verses 6 to 9 we hear of the betrayal by Judas, and after verses 10 to 14 the words of the Suffering Servant ("surely he has borne our griefs and carried our sorrows", etc., Isa 53) are used to make clear that both Isaiah and Jeremiah speak prophetically of the sufferings of Christ.

Friday: The psalms for the first Nocturn were 2, 21, and 26, and the texts of Lamentations were from Lam 2:8–11, 12–15 and from Lam 3:1–9. Again, there would be an understandable connection made by participants with the sufferings of Our Lord. Psalm 2 speaks of those who plot against the Lord and his anointed one. In Ps 21, the psalmist expresses the pain and suffering of someone who feels abandoned by God. This psalm was also chanted during the solemn stripping of the altar at the end of the Holy Thursday ceremonies, so there would have been resonances with the dramatic connotations of that event. The words in the first verse, "My God, my God, why have you forsaken me?" are the same as those spoken by Christ during his final agony. Other verses are also charged with prophetic references: "they divide my garments among them and cast lots for my clothing" (Ps 21:18), "the whole world will remember and return to the Lord" (Ps 21:27). Ps 26 proclaims trust in the Lord and prays that God will not abandon his servant. The Lamentation texts for this day speak eloquently of the misery that has come upon the people of the city, with particular attention paid to the plight of women. Attention then moves to the suffering one, afflicted, broken, and enclosed by stone—words that would be particularly resonant on the day of the commemoration of Christ's Passion and death. After Lam 2:8–11 the responsory speaks of the abandonment suffered by the Lord, treated as a common criminal, and given vinegar to drink. After Lam 2:12–15 we hear of the moment of the death of Christ: the veil in the temple is torn in two, the earth quakes, and the thief cries out. After Lam 3:1–9 the people are asked why they have turned against the Lord and released Barabbas.

Saturday: Psalms for the first Nocturn were 4, 14, and 15. The Lamentations texts were from Lam 3:22–30, Lam 4:1–6, and from Lam 5:1–11 (also called the "Prayer of Jeremiah"). In Ps 4, the psalmist speaks of trust in God, and lies down to rest in peace at the last, secure in the knowledge of God's protection. Ps 14 asks who is worthy to dwell on God's holy mountain. Ps 15 prays for God's protection for the one who now rests: he will not be abandoned or see the abyss—perhaps this expresses Messianic hope in resurrection. The texts from the Lamentations here remind us of the importance of patient hope and trust, even in the face of peril and destruction, ending with the prophet's prayer to God for help in a despairing situation. After Lam 3:22–30, the responsory speaks of the suffering Servant, the lamb who does not speak but who brings life to the people. After Lam 4:1–6, Jerusalem is commanded to wear sackcloth in grief for the killing of its savior. The responsory after Lam 5:1–11 is a more extended and grief-stricken lamentation at the death of the savior, calling forth crying and howling.

Although for most parishes the full celebration of Tenebrae in its most solemn and elaborate form is difficult to arrange, there are still places where the services are a much cherished part of liturgical life. The words of the Lamentations contribute a great deal to the spirit of tragedy and grief felt by Christians who mourn the death of Christ, conscious that their sins contribute to the sufferings of our Lord. Surrounded, as these texts are, by sympathetic psalms and responsories, participants could not fail to grasp the depths of the suffering of Christ for us, nor the language of hope and trust in God that they also proclaim.

Soundings
in Artistic and Contemporary Reception

# N

# Musical Responses to Lamentations

F. JANE SCHOPF

MANY COMPOSERS HAVE SET the *Lamentations* either as a complete text following the layout and order of the services for Holy Week or have set certain sections.[1] I am going to look at three settings of the *Lamentations* spanning a period of almost four hundred years. Each of the works has a unique purpose: ecclesiastical, personal, public. The composers, the Spanish Tomas Luis de Victoria (c. 1548–1611), the Austrian Ernst Krenek (1900–1991), and the Russian Igor Stravinsky (1882–1971), use contemporary compositional techniques to respond personally and dramatically to the texts.

Since each composer is dealing with a text concerned with pain and sorrow, it is not surprising to find a commonality in basic musical language. Traditionally music expressing sorrow, anguish, despair, or pain utilizes discords:[2] the nature of these discords varies according to the historic period in which the piece is written—the closer to modern times the more extreme and continuous they can become.

## TOMAS LUIS DE VICTORIA

Victoria[3] wrote at a time when the ecclesiastical compositional style was more rigid than that for secular works. Frequently the outcome was stylized pieces not necessarily reflect-

---

1. Those who set complete or partial liturgical texts include: Pierre de la Rue (c.1452–1518), Carpentras (c. 1470–1548), Claudin de Sermisy (c. 1490–1562), Morales (c. 1500–1553), Thomas Tallis (c.1505–1585), Palestrina (c.1525–1594), Lassus (1532–1594), Robert White (c. 1538–1574), William Byrd (1543–1623), Ferrabosco the Elder (1543–1588), Nanino (c.1543–1607), Ingegneri (c. 1547–1592), Victoria (1548–1611), Francois Couperin (1668–1733), Igor Stravinsky (1882–1971), Ernst Krenek (1900–1991), Alberto Ginastera (1916–83), Leonard Bernstein (1918–90), and James MacMillan (b. 1959).

2. In pre-tonal music the interval of the fourth (C-F); later the minor seventh (C-B Flat) and its more pungent form the major seventh (C-B); the ninth (C-D) and its pungent form the minor ninth (C-D Flat).

3. Tomás Luis de Victoria studied at Avila Cathedral under the leading composers of the day and at Rome, possibly under Palestrina. He is considered the greatest Spanish Renaissance composer and his music for Holy Week is generally acknowledged his crowning achievement. John IV of Portugal noted in his *Defensa de la musica* (1649), "there is much in his Holy Week volume (1585) that exactly suits the text" (Sadie, ed., *New Grove Dictionary*, 705).

ing the actual texts set. However, Victoria utilizes the most modern aspects of the style to respond to the text in a very personal, dramatic way, illustrating in sound the essence of the words. His setting of the Lamentations, *Officium Hebdomadae Sanctae*, 1585, comprises works from earlier editions including *O vos omnes* from 1572.

In the sixteenth century there were strict rules governing the use of intervals[4] and chords.[5] Victoria worked within these to create a poignant dramatic setting of the text, aurally as graphic of pain and despair as was then possible. He used "forbidden" intervals and chords by creating discords through suspensions[6] to illustrate the text.

In his setting of *O vos omnes*[7] Victoria uses the following structure:

| A | O vos omnes qui transitis per viam, attendite et videte | O, all you who pass this way, pay attention and see | set for all four voices. |
|---|---|---|---|
| B | si est dolor similis sicut dolor meus | if there is any sorrow like my sorrow | set using all four voices |
| C | attendite universi populi, et videte dolorem meum | pay attention people of the world and see my sorrow | set for the three highest voices |
| B | si est dolor similis sicut dolor meus | if there is any sorrow like my sorrow | set using all four voices |

The B section focusing on suffering is repeated, thus drawing the audience's attention to it as the textual voice requests. Victoria uses discords in this passage in a rather ingenious way by writing a passage of five dovetailed suspensions on long notes—thereby gaining the maximum aural effect. This concentration allows Victoria to wring every possible ounce of emotion from this highly graphic section. The treatment of the similar text at the end of section C is less intense with only four suspensions and with notes half the duration, thus making less impact but still maintaining the image of suffering.

In addition, the whole piece predominantly comprises phrases which descend in pitch—again a traditional construct denoting resignation and acceptance.[8] The reflexive rising semi-tone (e.g., G-A Flat-G) is commonly found in music expressing sorrow (the musical equivalent of a groan) and is used here both at the beginning of section A and at the close of section B. Victoria uses every available construct for aural illustration.

---

4. The distance between two notes.

5. When two or more notes are sounded together.

6. This technique permitted notes to be held over from one chord into the succeeding chord where they did not harmonically belong to produce a discord provided they were 'resolved' in the subsequent chord where they did fit harmonically and the sound was concordant.

7. "O all you who pass this way," Lam 1:12.

8. Deryck Cooke refers to descending motion as "oppressive" (Cooke, *Language of Music*, 35). Lawrence Kramer makes the distinction between Liszt's music for Faust and that for Gretchen noting that the latter's themes "consist wholly of descending phrases" (Kramer, *Music as Cultural Practice*, 106) indicative of her literary role.

## ERNST KRENEK

Krenek[9] wrote his *Lamentatio Jeremiae Prophetae* Op. 93 in 1941–1942 for mixed choir, adhering to the format found in the *Liber Usualis* for the services of Passion Week. He noted in his journal that it was a purely personal composition, not intended for public performance.[10]

As Jeremiah wrote about his beloved Jerusalem, so Krenek wrote about his beloved Austria explaining that he chose the Catholic Tenebrae texts "because this selection was sanctified by the authority of the institution that made it, an institution into which I was born and to which I developed an intense allegiance ever since Nazi-dominated Germany began to threaten with extinction my native country, Austria."[11] As an artist fleeing his homeland he would have had a very personal sense of the cries for help. He sets the full nine lessons ending each with a plea to Jerusalem to return to her old ways, each time increasing the number of voices by one, culminating in nine separate parts.

There is a deliberate attempt to recapture the past glories of church music and, perhaps metaphorically, the past of a unified and untroubled Austria. Krenek clearly sees his composition within the rich tradition of Western church music even though it is in a modern style derived from serialism.

Serialism, created by Matthias Hauer (1883–1959) and Arnold Schoenberg (1874–1951), treats the twelve chromatic notes of the scale in a set pattern ("row"); the notes of the row not being repeated until all have been sounded either vertically in chords, or horizontally in melodic contours. To give variation various techniques of transposition,[12] inversion, and retrograde are employed. Krenek's unique method within this system was not to treat the twelve tones in such a proscriptive manner but to divide the row—which he derived from the plainsong intonation found in the *Liber Usualis*—into half rows of six notes arranged in a scale-like pattern[13] and use his own method of "rotation"[14] rather than the traditional transposition used by other composers.[15] These techniques create a

---

9. Ernst Krenek was born in Vienna but emigrated to America in 1938 and became a lecturer in music at Malkin Conservatory. His compositional style encompasses the whole gamut of techniques, he was hailed as a "one-man history of twentieth century music" (quoted in Schmidt, *Ernst Krenek*, 17).

10. "The fact that something is written for no practical purpose whatsoever," he noted in his journal on December 2, 1941, "seems to favour the quality of the writing, because the excellence of the job is the only justification for its being done and the only source of satisfaction for the maker. I wonder if I am not much more fussy [sic] about certain details in the Lamentations because I know that no living person will sing or hear them, than I would be in a composition ready for consumption" (Stewart, *Ernst Krenek*, 239).

11. Stewart, *Ernst Krenek*, 237.

12. Putting at different pitches.

13. "The purpose of the operation was not so much to make the serial design stricter, but rather to relax it, insofar as the wide variety of available six-tone patterns made it possible to remain within the frame of reference of the twelve-tone serial technique without constantly having to use complete twelve-tone rows." (Krenek in Lang, ed., *Problems of Modern Music*, 75).

14. This involved taking the first note of each set of six and moving it to the end creating a varying set of melodic intervals unlike the static intervals of traditional row transposition.

15. Whereby the entire row is transposed a semitone at a time through the twelve tones.

work that simultaneously combines of a number of half rows both vertically and horizontally giving a greater freedom and variety of harmonic color.

Krenek was an early music scholar and in his book on Ockeghem in 1953 he talks about Ockeghem's compositional technique being rooted in the individual melodic lines, harmony arising only as a by-product of their congruence—the same approach he used in the *Lamentatio*. Another early music practice adopted by Krenek is the absence of bar lines, which he felt gave an abnormal rigidity to phrases when applied to flowing contrapuntal lines.[16]

Krenek positions his whole response within techniques that show his reverence for the past. These include: Gregorian chants[17] (the opening plainsong "incipit" informs his setting of the Hebraic letters and the pleas to Jerusalem); *Canti Firmi*;[18] unaccompanied voices; structural devices such as canon and mirror canon;[19] *nota cambiata*;[20] the absence of dynamic markings; word painting (e.g., "aqua"[21]) and tone rows reflecting the old Church Modes.[22] These historical techniques sit alongside modern harmonic devices such as 7th and 9th chords and tritones. The reflexive turn of the Gregorian intonation for the Hebraic letters link these settings, just as 7ths and 9ths consolidate the overall musical fabric.

Like Victoria, the focus in Krenek's setting of *O vos omnes* is suffering. He sets the full text repeating the words "attendite" three times,[23] illustrative, perhaps, of his concern for the events occurring in central Europe which were as unprecedented as Jerusalem's suffering at the hands of the Lord.

The dissonances Krenek wrote for the cry "attendite" epitomise the anguish felt as they are extreme, being interlocked sevenths and ninths (e.g., E Flat, A, G, F; E, G, B, C#, A, C; C, G#, B, F#; F, C#, E, G, B Flat, D, A). This interlocking occurs again on the words "dolor meus," illustrating the text. The discords used for the closing words, "furoris sui,"[24] utilize single discords, mostly sevenths which, whilst illustrative,[25] nevertheless are less pungent than the interlocking ones saved for the plight of the "Christ" voice earlier or, for Krenek, Austria. The impact of the "attendite" discords is further heightened by setting them homophonically (in contrast to the counterpoint in the rest of the piece) which focuses attention on them.

16. See Krenek, *Johannes Ockeghem*, 45.

17. Synonymous with plainchant—the music of the early church: "Throughout the Middle Ages . . . the centre and core of all serious art music" (Krenek, *Johannes Ockeghem*, 23).

18. A melodic line derived from plainsong presented in equal long notes around which other voices weave their independent melodic lines.

19. This form of imitation where each voice imitates each other exactly was a favorite compositional technique of the period 1650–1750.

20. A melodic formula where a descending line jumps down a third from a non-harmonic note before returning to the harmony note e.g., D C A B (the harmony note being B).

21. Krenek, *Horizons Circled*, 67.

22. The scales which informed music up until the emergence of tonality during the Renaissance.

23. Twice antiphonally between female and male voices and once with all voices together.

24. "His anger."

25. During the whole section there are only eight chords that are not discordant.

## IGOR STRAVINSKY

Stravinsky's *Threni* (1958) uses instruments as well as solo and choral voices. It was commissioned not by a church but by the North German Radio, Hamburg. Although its performance stage, the concert hall, was secular the composer said a religious understanding of the text was necessary in order to set it.[26] Stravinsky wrote *Threni* as a "challenge" to what he saw as a decline in "the Church as a musical institution" and a "protest against the Platonic tradition . . . of music as anti-moral."[27] Only selected verses from chapters 1, 3 and 5 are set and there are no divisions for the Holy offices.

Like Krenek's setting, *Threni* is a serial work which creatively veers from the conventional serial writing of Schoenberg, but, unlike Krenek and Schoenberg, exhibits tonal leanings in that the combination of the various transpositions of the row create chords with tonal affiliations[28] as Stravinsky uses thirds and fifths within the row.[29] Unlike Krenek, Stravinsky uses the standard twelve-note row and writes in a vertical, not horizontal, contrapuntal manner.

Stravinsky too was influenced by the past—even though when asked "Did you model your *Threni* on the *Lamentations* of any old master?" he replied: "I had studied Palestrina's complete service, and the *Lamentations* of Tallis and Byrd but I don't think there is any 'influence' of these masters in my music"[30]—as he uses the old contrapuntal form of canon (in the second Elegy) where he dispenses with bar lines to achieve, as Krenek, metrical authenticity.[31]

Stravinsky's response to the text exhibits other similarities to Krenek as both were composers in the twentieth century: both use pungent discords—minor ninths and major sevenths. *Threni* opens with both a minor ninth and a major seventh and "wailing" dynamics—loud fading to quiet on each chord.[32] Dynamics play an important role in this piece adding greatly to the overall effect.

---

26. In conversation with Robert Craft Stravinsky said: "I had hoped my *Mass* would be used liturgically, but I have no such aspiration for the *Threni*, which is why I call it not *Tenebrae Service,* but *Lamentations*" (Craft, *Stravinsky in Conversation*, 136).

27. Ibid., 136–37.

28. Tonality was established at the end of the Renaissance and lasted until the turn of the last century. The "rules" of tonality are based on principles where certain sounds progress to closure. The fundamental interval for this type of music is the interval of the fifth (e.g., C-G) and the Perfect Cadence (ending formula) going from the fifth of the scale, the dominant, to the first, the tonic. It was this construct which Serialism strenuously avoided.

29. Robert Craft asked Stravinsky about this aspect of this work:
R.C. "Do you think of the intervals in your series as tonal intervals; that is, do your intervals always exert tonal pull?"
I.S. "The intervals of my series are attracted by tonality; I compose vertically and that is, in one sense at least, to compose tonally" (Craft, *Stravinsky in Conversation*, 38).

30. Ibid., 35–36.

31. "The voices are not always in rhythmic unison. Therefore, any bar lines would cut at least one line arbitrarily. There are no strong beats in the canons, in any case, and the conductor must merely count the music out as he counts out a motet by Josquin. For the same reasons I have also written half notes rather than tied notes over bars. This is perhaps more difficult to read, but it is a truer notation" (ibid., 35).

32. Roman Vlad has called the opening of *Threni* "a series of groans and deep sighs" (Vlad, *Stravinsky*, 211).

Stravinsky uses rhythmic speaking in the chorus for both the narrator and supplicant in the first Elegy, possibly reflecting monks chanting. The use of the rows in *Threni* has an hypnotic effect as repetitions are frequent.[33] Krenek continued the ecclesiastical tradition of unaccompanied voices but Stravinsky only follows this in the second Elegy, elsewhere he incorporates orchestral instruments producing a rich kaleidoscope of color enhanced by detailed dynamics.

Stravinsky's setting is bound more to the serial technique than to a detailed illustrative response to the text. There are virtually no examples of musical illustration as found with the other composers, even the drop of a twelfth on the words "ut contereret sub pedibus suis"[34] is reused for different texts thus removing any sense of illustrative function. However, Stravinsky does capture the overall sense of despair by the use of general dissonance, deftly graded dynamics and instrumental color.

The first two composers we considered show a very detailed response to the text by using musical conventions to illustrate words and recreate emotions. The reasons behind all three compositions were different: Victoria was a church musician whose job was to compose music for ecclesiastical use; Krenek wrote his piece from a personal need to express despair at the events he saw unfolding in his home country, and Stravinsky wrote his setting in protest of the decline of the church's musical tradition. By bringing the text into the secular domain, Stravinsky empowered it with a completely different expectation to the settings of Victoria and Krenek. Uniquely in the musical history of this text, Stravinsky made a personal selection divorced from any religious function—a public statement *about* the church not *for* the church, turning the text in on itself by having it challenge the institution which had for so long used it to challenge the outside world.

---

33. For instance in "Quomodo sedet" one row, the retrograde inversion, appears either in its entirety or in fragments thirteen times within twenty bars.

34. "To crush under his feet."

# BIBLIOGRAPHY

## Primary Sources

Krenek, Ernst. *Lamentatio Jeremiae Prophetae*. Kassel, Germany: Bärenreiter, 1957.

Stravinsky, Igor F. *Threni*. London: Boosey & Hawkes, 1958.

Victoria, Tomás Luis de. *Tenebrae Responsories*. Edited by Bruno Turner. London: Chester Music, 1960.

## Secondary Sources

Cooke, Deryck. *The Language of Music*. London: Oxford University Press, 1959.

Craft, Robert. *Stravinsky in Conversation with Robert Craft*. London: Pelican, 1962.

Kramer, Lawrence. *Music as Cultural Practice 1800–1900*. Berkeley, CA: University of California Press, 1990.

Krenek, Ernst. *Horizons Circled: Reflections on My Music*. Berkeley, CA: University of California Press, 1974.

———. *Johannes Ockeghem*. London: Sheed & Ward, 1953.

Lang, Paul Henry, ed. *Problems of Modern Music: The Princeton Seminar in Advanced Musical Studies*. New York: Norton, 1960.

Sadie, Stanley, ed. *The New Grove Dictionary of Music & Musicians, vol. 19*. New York: Grove, 1980.

Schmidt, Matthias, ed. *Ernst Krenek Zeitgenosse des 20. Jahrhunderts*. Vienna: Wiener Stadt-und Landesbibliothek, 2000.

Stewart, John L. *Ernst Krenek*. Berkeley, CA: University of California Press, 1991.

Strimple, Nick. *Choral Music in the Twentieth Century*. Cleckheaton, UK: Amadeus, 2002.

Vlad, Roman. *Stravinsky*. 3rd ed. Oxford: Oxford University Press, 1978.

Walsh, Stephen. *The Music of Stravinsky*. London: Routledge, 1988.

# O

## Lamentations in Rembrandt van Rijn

### "Jeremiah Lamenting the Destruction of Jerusalem"

HEATH A. THOMAS

THE RECEPTION OF LAMENTATIONS in the visual arts is, by and large, dominated by associating the book with the prophet Jeremiah. This is likely due to the close connection between the prophet and the book in Jewish and Christian tradition.[1] And both traditions trace the authorship of Lamentations to Jeremiah via 2 Chr 35:25. With this tradition firmly entrenched, apparently artists have recognized and "read" Lamentations through it in their work.

The present sounding focuses upon one major reception of Lamentations in the visual arts: "Jeremiah Lamenting the Destruction of Jerusalem" (1630) by Rembrandt van Rijn. His great interest in rendering biblical scenes is well established, but this work remains unique in that it represents a major reception that focuses upon Lamentations, which is somewhat rare in the visual arts.[2] Moreover, this work is selected because of the paradigmatic manner in which it focuses upon the prophet, the Torah, and melancholy.

It would be interesting to see a reception of Lamentations in the visual arts with an explicit emphasis upon the persona of Daughter Zion but such work is unknown. There is one work that moves slightly in this direction: Marc Chagall's "Jeremiah's Lamentations" (1956), where one may note suggestions of a motherly metaphor at work, imagining Jeremiah the prophet as a "mother" for his children, the people of Jerusalem. As such, the metaphor of Daughter Zion as mother in Lamentations is suggestive, and perhaps not so far off in this twentieth-century Russian reception of the book. But even here, following traditional reception of Lamentations, Jeremiah remains as the dominant figure.

---

1. See the contributions "LXX Lamentations," "Targum Lamentations," and "Lamentations Rabbati" in this volume.

2. See also Marc Chagall's "Jeremiah" (1956) and "Jeremiah's Lamentations" (1956). These latter pieces both derive from Chagall's Bible Series prints (1931–56).

## "JEREMIAH LAMENTING THE DESTRUCTION OF JERUSALEM" (1630)

Rembrandt van Rijn painted the biblical scene of Jeremiah lamenting Jerusalem in his early career, while living in Leiden prior to moving to Amsterdam. In this period he painted a number of biblically-themed pieces,[3] especially from the Old Testament. His fascination with Old Testament themes accords with a number of Dutch painters in the period who gained inspiration from the Old Testament, rich as it is with imagery and emotion.[4] "Jeremiah Lamenting the Destruction of Jerusalem," which Durham hails as Rembrandt's "biblical masterpiece from the Leiden years,"[5] is a fine example from this cultural milieu.

The work depicts the prophet in a cave or grotto, looking downward with head on hand, sitting upon a rock that also has upon it dull golden implements (likely from carried away from the sacked temple in the background), extravagant robes which spill down the rock, a Torah-cover and a codex (upon which Jeremiah rests his elbow, upon which he leans). The codex bears an inscription "BiBeL."[6] Behind Jeremiah is a large pillar and to left of him is the mouth of the cave, out of which we see a scene of destruction in the distance. A city, presumably Jerusalem, is in flames, with black smoke filling the sky. Soldiers enter through a gate while an inhabitant looks away in horror. A building with a dome, likely the temple due to the two pillars in front of it (analogous to Jachin and Boaz, the two pillars of Solomon's temple described in 1 Kgs 7:15-22), one of which is broken down. All of this is suggestive of the destruction of Jerusalem.[7]

---

3. Among them in these early years are: "David Presents the head of Goliath to King Saul" (1627), "Samson and Delilah" (1628), "David Playing the Harp for Saul" (c. 1629), "Judas Repentant, Returning the Pieces of Silver" (1629), "Jeremiah Lamenting the Destruction of Jerusalem" (1630), "The Presentation of Jesus at the Temple" (1631), "The Raising of Lazarus" (1631–1632), "Christ in the Storm" (1633), and "The Raising of the Cross" (c. 1633). Rembrandt was inspired by the stories of the Bible throughout his career. For further study, see Bell, *Rembrandt van Rijn*; Bockemühl, *Rembrandt*.

4. Nadler, *Rembrandt's Jews*.

5. Durham, *The Biblical Rembrandt*, 96.

6. Durham suggests this is likely inserted by another hand after Rembrandt's time to clarify the message of the painting: destruction is in accord with God's Word (ibid., 99). Whether or not this is the case, it is clear that the codex is a representation of the Scriptures.

7. For a full discussion, see the helpful description of ibid., 95–100.

*Jeremiah Lamenting the Destruction of Jerusalem* (1630), Rembrandt van Rijn. Oil on panel, 58.3 x 46.6 cm. Rijksmuseum, Amsterdam.

This scene, however, is not explicitly on display in the text of Lamentations. So in what way is this painting a reception of this book? Durham for one does not equate this work with a reception of Lamentations but rather of 2 Mac 2:4–5. Other texts may have been a source of inspiration as well (2 Kgs 25; 2 Chr 36:11–21; Jer 21:1–10; Pss 74 and 79), but it is the passage from 2 Maccabees that Durham finds as the biblical source for the painting:

> It was also contained in the same writing, that the prophet, being warned of God, commanded the tabernacle and the ark to go with him, as he went forth into the mountain, where Moses climbed up, and saw the heritage of God. And when Jeremy [Jeremiah] came thither, he found an hollow cave, wherein he laid the tabernacle, and the ark, and the altar of incense, and so stopped the door. (2 Mac 2:4–5, KJV)

Durham believes that the "hollowed out place" mentioned in the text above is the cave depicted in Rembrandt's painting. And yet the geography, as he admits, remains problematic for this view: on the 2 Maccabees account, the place where Jeremiah places the temple implements is at Mount Nebo, some twenty-five miles east of Jerusalem. It is possible that Rembrandt had no knowledge of Palestinian geography, as Durham argues, or it may be that the cave or grotto from Rembrandt's painting does not derive from the 2 Maccabees account. While there are presumably implements in Rembrandt's painting, there is no depiction of the Ark of the Covenant nor altar of incense, and the stopping of the mouth of the cave is not in view at all. Nor in the passage from 2 Maccabees is the scene of Jerusalem's destruction in view, which it clearly is in Rembrandt's work. So some difficulties emerge from Durham's interpretation.

Another possibility is that Rembrandt reacted to a series of texts, among them Lamentations.[8] A number of indicators link Rembrandt's painting to this text. The flames in the background recall Lam 2:3, "He [God] has burned in Jacob like a flame of fire; it has consumed everything." The only things not consumed by fire are the natural enclaves around Jerusalem, like the one in which Jeremiah sits in Rembrandt's painting. In the background, the Temple and city lay in ruins, as in Lam 2:2, "The Lord swallowed, he did not pity, all the habitations of Jacob. He tore down, in his rage, the strongholds of Daughter Judah. He brought down to earth, he profaned, kingdom and her princes." This scene of destruction fit well the overall depiction in Rembrandt's vision. Also the implements resting beside Jeremiah are tarnished and dull, as in Lam 4:1, "How the gold has become dim; the finest gold changed."

Moreover, in Rembrandt's work, Jeremiah's gaze directs the eye downward to the destruction of the city. He does not directly look at the sacking of the city but rather glances towards it, unable to look directly into the carnage. In this way, Jeremiah becomes the central figure reflecting upon the devastation—and yet he remains an external observer of the tragic scene. The characteristic of external observation of destruction is a hallmark of the third person speech in Lamentations, particularly in Lam 1. The external

---

8. Rembrandt clearly was familiar with biblical texts and scenes (see n. 4, above), and so it is not at all apparent, as Durham supposes (ibid., 96), that he would not have had a number of texts in mind when creating "Jeremiah Lamenting the Destruction of Jerusalem." And it is not inconceivable that he had Lamentations in view as well.

observer (in Rembrandt's painting, Jeremiah) witnesses the city's downfall at a distance, detached, to a degree, from it.

However, in neither work, does the distance save the observer from experiencing grief. Jeremiah is central in the painting; his posture sits broken and melancholy, despite the gold, Torah, and Temple garments beside him. Rembrandt's construction of the prophet's posture becomes important, as Bockemühl rightly states:

> It is only from the posture of the figure [of Jeremiah] that the observer grows aware of the action—that of brooding itself. It is at this point that the manner in which Rembrandt makes use of the possible effects of the posture upon the observer becomes crucial. It is not only a question of the observer's registering intellectually the inner activity of the figure in the picture through the posture with which he is confronted. Having grasped the content of this contemplation or this mourning, he then begins himself to ponder over what it is that the person portrayed is meditating upon—the apostle's letter, the destruction of Jerusalem.[9]

What does the prophet contemplate? In the painting, Jeremiah reflects upon the disaster itself and God's Word. More to the point, his city is destroyed precisely because of the "BiBeL," an anachronism in Rembrandt's painting to be sure (there was no "Bible" as such in Jeremiah's day), but nonetheless, a sense of the execution of God's word of destruction for covenant disobedience. In the words of Lam 1:5, "The Lord afflicted her on account of the greatness of her transgression." Or later, "The Lord is right; for I have rebelled against his mouth" (Lam 1:17). Now to my mind this latter verse is spoken by the voice of personified Zion, but in Rembrandt's reception, he likely hears the prophet Jeremiah's speech here (following tradition), speaking in solidarity with rebellious Jerusalemites.

Note, however, that Jeremiah does not directly look at the burning city nor does he look at the Torah. He looks indirectly between them towards a blank space on the canvas. This indirect gaze opens space for the observer to reflect upon reasons for the city's destruction and how God's word has been met. Through the figuration of Jeremiah, the prophet observes and reflects upon disaster and all the while the viewer participates with him in the deep emotion of loss and suffering.

Interestingly what is lacking in Rembrandt's painting, which is ever present in Lamentations' poetry, is a call upon God in prayer.[10] Jeremiah broods without approaching the deity to make sense of the devastation, complaint, or petition—all of which occur in the poetry of Lamentations. The action in Rembrandt's work is set in the midst of disaster, while Lamentations is set after the destruction, rehearsing it.

The disparity between these perspectives enables Rembrandt to centre upon the suffering of the moment as well as the horror and loss that accompany it. Jeremiah then becomes paradigmatic of his popular namesake—the "weeping prophet." He reflects upon the disaster all around him—in the painting, literally to the left and in the background. The stance and expression of Jeremiah is akin to Michelangelo's representation of the

---

9. Bockemühl, *Rembrandt*, 23.
10. Lam 1:9, 11, 20–22; 2:20–22; 3:55–66; 5.

prophet in the Sistine Chapel—brooding, melancholy, and despondent. Michelangelo's Jeremiah does not visually look upon disaster while Rembrandt's glances toward it, almost unable to look directly into the face of war. If Rembrandt would have, with Lamentations, represented prayer, the focus may have shifted away from the emotion and experience of loss by directing this grief to the Lord with the hopes of some sort of reversal. This second action requires a psychological shift beyond the experience of grief and channels it toward God. Rather by focusing upon the reality of destruction through the central figure of the prophet, Rembrandt foregrounds the grief of the present moment, enabling the observer to embody the pain with Jeremiah the prophet.

## CONCLUSION

This exploration reveals the fecundity of Lamentations as an intertext to Rembrandt's painting, and that further, Rembrandt may well have had Lamentations in mind when creating this work. The question remains, however, how Rembrandt's rendering intersects directly with the poetry and theology of Lamentations.

At the heart of Rembrandt's vision of Lamentations lay a meditation upon God's word and the experience of historical disaster, mediated by the central figure of the prophet. His posture and gaze invites the observer to reflect with him upon the horror at disaster, its relation to the painful reality of God's promised word of covenant curse for disobedience (Jeremiah significantly rests his elbow on the Torah without looking at it), and the raw experience of pain and grief. In this vision, Rembrandt touches upon some, but certainly not all, theological themes at work in Lamentations' own horizons.[11]

Yet Rembrandt does not engage the issues of prayer, loss of human life, or even the ambivalence at work in Lamentations. Engaging these issues may have been impossible for Rembrandt—he may not have actually read Lamentations closely enough to do so—or, more charitably, it may be that doing so would have detracted him from focusing upon the experience of human grief at work in his painting. He does, however, follow tradition in reading Lamentations through the experience of the prophet and thereby provides an essentially one-sided reception in what is multi-voiced poetry—within Lamentations we hear the voices of an observer, Zion, and enemies.

---

11. See the essay by Paul House in this volume.

## BIBLIOGRAPHY

Bell, Malcolm. *Rembrandt van Rijn*. London: Bell & Sons, 1901.

Bockemühl, Michael. *Rembrandt: The Mystery of the Revealed Form*. Translated by Michael Claridge. Köln: Taschen, 2000.

Durham, John I. *The Biblical Rembrandt: How Rembrandt Experienced the Bible*. Macon, GA: Mercer University Press, 2005.

Nadler, Steven. *Rembrandt's Jews*. Chicago: University of Chicago Press, 2003.

# P

# Psychological Approaches to Lamentations

Paul M. Joyce

## INTRODUCTION

It was when I was living and working in a seminary that I first came across the insights of pastoral psychology, particularly the work of Elisabeth Kübler-Ross on death and dying and Yorick Spiegel on grief and bereavement.[1] A change of job found me in a university setting, having to teach the biblical book of Lamentations as a Hebrew set text. As I wrestled with this profound work that nonetheless seemed so full of inconsistencies and ambiguities and so lacking in coherent theological closure, suddenly I was reminded once again of the insights of Kübler-Ross and Spiegel. I was led to consider whether psychological insights might provide a framework within which the inconsistencies and ambiguities of the book might better be understood.[2]

Both Spiegel and Kübler-Ross' insights have at their heart a radical experience of loss. Spiegel's paradigm assesses the psychology of bereavement by highlighting a range of stages: shock; controlled grief (often expressed through mourning rites); regression (involving withdrawal to childlike behavior); and adaptation (adjustment to bereaved condition where new start on life can be made). Kübler-Ross suggests five stages experienced by those who are dying: denial and isolation; anger; bargaining (often including pleading for relief of pain and the prospect of death); depression; and acceptance (quiet detachment in recognition of impending death). It is important to note that both writers observe that the stages they outline can be encountered in varying sequences, that one can "get stuck" at a particular stage or indeed regress to earlier ones, and that elements of different stages can co-exist. All too often biblical criticism has been hampered by the unrealistic assumption that people react to events with a single consistent emotion or

---

1. Spiegel, *Der Prozess des Trauerns*; Kübler-Ross, *On Death and Dying*.
2. Joyce, "Lamentations and the Grief Process." Elsewhere I have set this approach in the context of a range of ways of taking emphasis off historical questions in reading Lamentations: Joyce, "Sitting Loose to History."

opinion. Spiegel and Kübler-Ross help us see that a person can experience and express a whole gamut of emotions within a short space of time. Reimer subsequently applied Kübler-Ross' insights even more precisely to the book of Lamentations, arguing that her psychological analysis provides a description of the contents and structure of the book and that it offers a trajectory for theological reflection.[3]

## A RANGE OF PSYCHOLOGICAL APPROACHES

Pursuing my enthusiasm for such an approach, I discovered that it was not quite as new as I had thought. There were earlier commentators in the history of interpretation, including Augustine and Ignatius Loyola, for whom psychological insights, albeit differently expressed, certainly had an important place. Nor was psychological interpretation as far removed from so-called "mainstream" biblical criticism as I had assumed. Modern historical criticism of the Bible first flourished in the very age in which Freud was doing his groundbreaking work and in the same geographical and cultural context, namely that of German-speaking central Europe. It is striking how many shared features these two enterprises have. For example, both speak of aetiology when addressing questions of origins and causation, and both apply a "hermeneutic of suspicion." And indeed in our own time, Moore had already done important work relating Lamentations to psychological analysis, arguing that Lamentations is a cathartic expression, an artistic outlet to voice pain.[4]

The range of ways in which Lamentations may be illumined from psychology is great. For example, Linafelt employs Freudian psychoanalysis in his reading of Lamentations,[5] specifically Freud's distinction between mourning and melancholia.[6] Freud was perhaps the first to distinguish between mourning and melancholia. Mourning is a positive process that brings a sense of resolution to suffering. Melancholia, on the other hand, prevents the possibility of resolution in mourning. Linafelt foregrounds the protest of personified Jerusalem in Lam 1 and 2, resisting the predominant theological impulses of Lam 3. He thus highlights the rhetoric of melancholia over the possibility of resolution in mourning, arguing that the poetry functions to perpetually confront God and interminably express pain.

Pyper develops Linafelt's work in this area, albeit in a different direction.[7] Using Freud's article "The Ego and the Id,"[8] Pyper argues that the surviving voice in Lamentations turns the anguish of survival into an attack on the mother, personified Zion, reinforced by wider biblical motifs that juxtapose women, food, and death. Ultimately, hope is projected onto the continued violence of the father, God, which is justified at the expense of the mother.

3. Reimer, "Good Grief?"
4. Moore, "Human Suffering in Lamentations."
5. Linafelt, *Surviving Lamentations*, 141–43.
6. Freud, "Mourning and Melancholia."
7. Pyper, "Reading Lamentations."
8. Freud, "The Ego and the Id."

In a rather different mode, Labahn applies insights from John Archer's *The Nature of Grief*[9] to Lamentations and argues that here mourning actually paves the way towards a positive future with God.[10] Archer argues that humans cope with grief in different ways, of which he highlights two in particular, a "loss-orientated" process as well as a "restoration-orientated" process. The theological tensions in the book are explained by Labahn through these differing perspectives of "loss-orientated" and "restoration-orientated" styles of coping with grief. She suggests that Lamentations evinces both styles identified by Archer but it finally emphasizes the "restoration-orientated" style. Lamentations 1, 2, 4, and 5 exemplify the "loss-orientated" style and reflect an extreme sense of loneliness and pain. However, the prominent central position of Lam 3:21–39a draws significant attention to the "restoration-orientated" coping process, and here she locates the overall purpose of the book.

Smith-Christopher explores Lamentations through the psychological insights of refugee studies and Post-Traumatic Stress Disorder (PTSD).[11] PTSD disorients those who experience it, through recurrent intrusive memories, dreams, feelings of repetition of the destruction and violence, debilitating depression, detachment, and estrangement. Moreover these symptoms persist to the degree that they can appear years after the event or events that triggered them, instigating a "cross-generational passing of PTSD symptomatology" from parents to children. Smith-Christopher recognizes the serial trauma that Lamentations depicts and relates this to PTSD. Recurring memories of destruction and brutality crop up in Lamentations, indicative of "intrusive memories," including cannibalism (Lam 1:11; 2:12; 4:4, 9–10), famine (Lam 2:11–12; 4:4–10), rape (Lam 1:10; 5:11), and slaughter (Lam 1:1; 2:21). Further, the sense of isolation (the lack of comfort in Lam 1:2, 9, 16–17, 21) and depression (Lam 1:20; 2:11) evidenced in the poetry are also PTSD symptoms. Smith-Christopher concludes that reading the book through the lens of PTSD "is once again to recover Lamentations as a measure of the psychological and spiritual crisis of the exile."[12]

A valuable recent contribution is that in which Heath Thomas relates prayer and pain through reflection on psychological analysis and Lamentations research.[13] Surveying applications of psychological insights to the study of the book, he notes a recurrent shortcoming. While useful in identifying and assessing pain in the poetry, these approaches undervalue, he argues, the crucial indicators of prayer. This leads him on to investigate the relationship between prayer and pain in the poetry by exploring the connections between Lamentations and the psychology of prayer.

---

9. Archer, *The Nature of Grief*.
10. Labahn, "Trauern als Bewältigung."
11. Smith-Christopher, *A Biblical Theology of Exile*, 75–104.
12. Ibid., 104.
13. Thomas, "Relating Prayer and Pain."

## CONCLUSION

Psychological approaches to the book of Lamentations are then proving both profound and fruitful. Of course, such work should be seen in the context of a wider application of psychological insights across the field of biblical studies in recent years. This can involve drawing upon the range of psychoanalytic and other psychological approaches, including behavioral or cognitive therapies as well as non-therapeutic kinds of psychology, such as experimental and social psychology, not least in the areas where these overlap with social anthropology.[14] But there are grounds for believing that both in terms of insights already achieved and also potential for further valuable work the book of Lamentations is a particularly rich field for this approach.

---

14. Kille, *Psychological Biblical Criticism*; Ellens and Rollins, eds., *Psychology and the Bible*; Rollins and Kille, eds., *Psychological Insight into the Bible*.

## BIBLIOGRAPHY

Archer, John. *The Nature of Grief: The Evolution and Psychology of Reactions to Loss*. London: Routledge, 1999.

Ellens, J. Harold, and Wayne G. Rollins, eds. *Psychology and the Bible: A New Way to Read the Scriptures*. 4 Volumes. Westport, CT: Praeger, 2004.

Freud, Sigmund. "The Ego and the Id." In *On Metapsychology: The Theory of Psychoanalysis*, 350–408. Penguin Freud Library, 11. Harmondsworth, UK: Penguin, 1991.

———. "Mourning and Melancholia." In *On Metapsychology: The Theory of Psychoanalysis*, 245–68. Penguin Freud Library, 11. Harmondsworth, UK: Penguin, 1991.

Joyce, Paul M. "Lamentations and the Grief Process: A Psychological Reading." *Biblical Interpretation* 1 (1993) 304–20.

———. "Sitting Loose to History: Reading the Book of Lamentations without Primary Reference to its Original Historical Setting." In *In Search of True Wisdom: Essays in Old Testament Interpretation in Honour of Ronald E. Clements*, edited by Edward Ball, 246–62. JSOTSupp, 300. Sheffield: Sheffield Academic, 1999.

Kille, D. Andrew. *Psychological Biblical Criticism*. Guides to Biblical Scholarship: Old Testament Series. Minneapolis: Fortress, 2001.

Kübler-Ross, Elisabeth. *On Death and Dying*. New York: Touchstone, 1969.

Labahn, Antje. "Trauern als Bewältigung der Vergangenheit zur Gestaltung der Zukunft. Bemerkungen zur anthropologischen Theologie der Klagelieder." *Vetus Testamentum* 52 (2002) 513–27.

Linafelt, Tod. *Surviving Lamentations: Catastrophe, Lament, and Protest in the Afterlife of a Biblical Book*. Chicago: University of Chicago Press, 1998.

Moore, Michael S. "Human Suffering in Lamentations." *Revue Biblique* 90 (1983) 534–55.

Pyper, Hugh S. "Reading Lamentations." *Journal for the Study of the Old Testament* 95 (2001) 55–69.

Reimer, David J. "Good Grief? A Psychological Reading of Lamentations." *Zeitschrift für die alttestamentliche Wissenschaft* 114 (2002) 542–59.

Rollins, Wayne G., and D. Aandrew Kille, eds. *Psychological Insight into the Bible: Texts and Readings*. Grand Rapids: Eerdmans, 2007.

Smith-Christopher, Daniel. *A Biblical Theology of Exile*. Overtures to Biblical Theology. Minneapolis: Fortress, 2002.

Spiegel, Yorick. *Der Prozess des Trauerns: Analyse und Beratung*. Munich: Kaiser, 1973.

Thomas, Heath A. "Relating Prayer and Pain: Psychological Analysis and Lamentations Research." *Tyndale Bulletin*. 61 (2010) 183–208.

# Q

## Feminist Interpretation(s) and Lamentations

HEATH A. THOMAS

### INTRODUCTION

AT PRESENT FEMINIST ANALYSIS is gaining currency in Lamentations scholarship. One should note, however, there is no *one* feminist *interpretation*, but rather diverse feminist *interpretations*, as will be demonstrated below. Nonetheless, as Doob Sakenfeld notes, "A feminist, broadly speaking, is one who seeks justice and equality for all people and who is especially concerned for the fate of women—all women—in the midst of 'all people.'"[1] This chapter explores her characterization of "feminist interpretation" as well as its varieties of the same in Lamentations research.

### FEMINIST APPROACHES

To begin it may prove useful to distinguish between "feminist," "female," and "feminine," for these three terms are not coterminous. Moi explains that the first represents a political position, the second is a matter of biology, and the third is a social and cultural construct; collapsing the second and third terms comprises substance for some feminist discourse.[2] Each of these terms, then, has a part to play in the discussion. For example, Barry argues that feminist criticism of the 1970s especially went into exposing "mechanisms of patriarchy, that is, the cultural 'mind-set' in men and women which perpetuated sexual inequality."[3]

In this way, what was culturally reckoned to be "feminine" was equated with "female," and this conflation may come with disastrous effects, namely the degradation, subjugation, or oppression of women. Recognizing this is crucial for Schüssler Fiorenza, whose outline for feminist biblical interpretation springs from the experience of women's

---

1. Sakenfeld, "Feminist Perspectives on Bible and Theology," 5.
2. Moi, "Feminist, Female, Feminine."
3. Barry, *Beginning Theory*, 122.

liberation from oppression, particularly in terms of patriarchal coercion.[4] Such feminist approaches are figured as inherently *liberative*, and accord with Trible's designation of feminism: rather than a narrow focus upon women as such, feminism—and thereby feminist interpretation—is inherently social and political, functioning as "a critique of culture in light of misogyny [hatred or distain for women, whether implicit or explicit]."[5] A feminist approach in this vein then redresses such degradation or eclipse and works to liberate the woman's perspective from oppression. In this thread of feminist interpretation, the issue of *justice* lay central—the interpreter perceives misogyny in a biblical text or in the reception of a biblical text that has led to the eclipse, obfuscation, or oppression of women or women's voices.

Whilst the above description remains viable, it should not be transformed into a caricature of *all* feminist approaches. Some feminist analysis investigates the place of women writers in the academic guild (and women's place in the literary canon); others explore distinctive characteristics of women's creativity, style, and imagination. Finally, some feminist studies endeavor to formulate distinctively feminine theories of text and gender-based textualities.[6]

In terms of Lamentations research, some interpreters exhibit the first variety, identifying misogyny in the book and explicitly reading against the text, working to excise such oppression from cultural currency. Still others simply hear from feminist approaches, allowing the political edge that arises from them to inform their understanding of Lamentations as a whole, whatever their critical methodology. One also may note an approach that reads the biblical text not with resistance but fidelity; the difference here is that the reading practice is done expressly from the standpoint of a "woman's perspective."[7] As such, neglected feminine images and metaphors are explored more fully and integrated into a more coherent interpretation of the book.

These categories do not exhaust feminist approaches to be sure, and at present in the discipline there is a drive to expand the horizons and semantics of "feminist analysis," differentiating objectives on the basis of class, ethnicity, and social location, among other categories. The impetus behind this lies in the desire to lay emphasis upon varieties and contestations of "feminism" as a concept and discipline as well as ideologies of varieties and contestations of the category of "woman." This is true especially in literary theory,

---

4. Schüssler Fiorenza, *In Memory of Her*, 32.

5. Trible, *God and The Rhetoric of Sexuality*, 7.

6. Richter, "Feminist Literary Criticism." Richter states that these three approaches are considered by some to present an evolutionary sequence, the last of which representing the last phase of development. He rightly argues, however, that this developmental view remains deficient on a number of grounds (ibid., 1064). The history of feminist approaches is less tidy than this. For analogues in biblical criticism, see Brenner and van Dijk-Hemmes, eds., *On Gendering Texts*, 1–13; Brenner and Fontaine, eds., *A Feminist Companion to Reading the Bible*.

7. So argue Clark Kroeger and Evans, "Preface," xiii. Inevitably, this enterprise becomes problematic, as a "woman's perspective," identified as such, becomes a boundary marker that may serve to solidify inherent patriarchal norms—this is at least a critique from a distinctive feminist perspective. Moreover, the notion of "woman" can easily be reduced to a naive essentialism. See the recent work by Moi, "I am not a woman writer."

social theory, political theory, and some forms of biblical interpretation.[8] In terms of feminist scholarship on Lamentations up to the present, such detailed critical engagements on the relationship between the discipline and the biblical book are lacking—these works are generally related to the discovery and denial of patriarchal oppression and the exploring problems and possibilities of women or women's voice in Lamentations.

## RESISTANT FEMINIST INTERPRETATIONS OF LAMENTATIONS

Explicitly *feminist* interpretations of Lamentations exemplify highly political readings of its poetry, reading against the text and advocating that the poetry stands as unjust and immoral literature. The logic follows that reading against the (Hebrew) Bible is necessary because: (1) it exploits and abuses the feminine in its poetry, or (2) it promotes an ideology that justifies and exemplifies female abuse via the (Hebrew) Bible's place as Holy Scripture in both Jewish and Christian traditions—such exploitation and abuse become, in effect, "God's word." In light of these realities, feminist approaches, in turn, resist and contravene divine vindication.

Seidman's represents a Jewish exploration of Lamentations that ultimately resists its message and theology. The supposed divine complicity in violent destruction of the personified feminine city of Jerusalem leads her to state of God: "If we forgive him, it is because we are too exhausted to do otherwise."[9] Her ultimate desire is not to forgive God but, in a sense, to abandon him. She protests against God's violence, and her perception that Lamentations justifies his abuse leads her to wish for a bonfire into which all the books of lamenting and violence, destruction and abuse—the book of Lamentations included—could be thrown. From this she gains the title of her essay, "Burning the Book of Lamentations." In Seidman's work one notes the lack of critical feminist discourse; rather hers is an inscribed testimony of her experience as a Jewish woman dealing with the liturgy of Tisha b'Av and Lamentations. Thus the borders of what qualifies as "feminist" blurs to a degree.

Guest's analysis of theology in Lamentations derives from her concern to counter what she sees as a cycle of degradation of the feminine in the book. Guest's work is scholarly and critical; she judges that the justification of divine violence (theodicy), as well as masculine concealment behind the naked, abused, raped, and humiliated image of the woman, persists in the ideology of the author of Lamentations, the history of (mostly male) commentary of the book, as well as in God himself. This must be contravened.[10]

Hers is an addition to the well-known discussion in "porno-prophetics," which turns on the view that in the (Hebrew) Bible God justifies himself at the expense of women, in that the people of Israel is often negatively portrayed in the prophetic books as a "whore" thereby legitimizing God's violent treatment of them. Guest traces how personified Jerusalem is depicted as battered and the object of blame in Lamentations: she

---

8. For a very useful discussion on this point, with bibliography, see Aichele, Castelli, et al., eds. "Feminist and Womanist Criticism"; Brenner and van Dijk-Hemmes, eds., *On Gendering Texts*.

9. Seidman, "Burning the Book of Lamentations," 288.

10. Guest, "Hiding," 413.

is raped (Lam 1:10), she is accused of guilt (Lam 1:5, 8), and she confesses guilt (Lam 1:14, 18, 20). So the author of Lamentations confirms the image of a battered woman to advance its rhetoric about Jerusalem's sin. She sees that mostly male commentators have reduced the pain and violation of the feminine, especially the rape in Lam 1:10, to advance the theology of just punishment: Jerusalem got what she deserved because of her sin. God too is implicated in abusing the feminine to advance the rhetoric of the city's sinfulness. Within the account of rape of Lam 1:10, Guest argues that God is implicated in this violation and justified for it through a form of theodicy: YHWH is justified, even in rape, because the city deserved punishment for sin.

The persistence of justified violence toward the feminine in Lamentations and in the commentary tradition leads Guest to read against the text, invalidating its claims. She argues, "an appropriate response to the personification of Zion/Woman in Lamentations is one of resistance to the text and a female solidarity" with ancient women in the situation of oppressive abuse.[11] She reads against those who created the metaphor of a personified city as female because she feels that these patriarchal "masterminds" justify their own oppressive worldview at the expense of the female, making "Zion/Woman the elected victim, the offering given up on their behalf" in Lamentations.[12]

This abuse of the female can then extend outward, to those who read and comment on the text. As a result, Guest concludes that the image of Jerusalem as a battered and abused city, the very personification itself, "must be rejected: literary oppression of women should not be continued."[13] Thus Guest sees in Lamentations' theology a clear affirmation of the city's sinfulness, only to read against it.

Guest rightly brings attention to the pain and destructiveness presented in the book; however, she paints far too monochrome a portrait of the book's theology. For instance, Guest under-reads the complexity of the issue of "blame" by placing it *directly* upon the female scapegoat, Jerusalem personified. She is certainly correct that Lam 1 and 2 present the feminine personification of the city as battered, isolated, and abused. Even so, if one evades blame by hiding behind the female figure in Lamentations, then there are other persons behind whom the poet hides as well. Blame for the disaster is spread around quite a bit and the feminine is not singled out. The man (גבר) of Lam 3 is also to blame for the punishment, especially in 3:39: "Why should a living human being, a man [גבר], complain about his punishment for sin?" Lee argues that this works to implicate the "man" in blame for the punishment of exile.[14] Lee further argues that Lam 4:13–15 contains an extended tirade against the leaders of Jerusalem—the priests and prophets—who are defiled and impure because they shed innocent blood, enraging the deity; the poetry blames the *male* leadership for the downfall of Jerusalem here.[15] A similar critique is leveled at the male prophets in Lam 2:14, in which they have "seen for you [Jerusalem] false and deceptive visions; they did not expose your iniquity so as to

11. Ibid., 427.
12. Ibid., 430.
13. Ibid., 444.
14. Lee, *The Singers of Lamentations*, 175.
15. Ibid., 186–89.

restore your fortunes. They saw oracles that were false and misleading." Thus blame is spread around, not completely isolated to the female figure, though the female figure of Dear Zion certainly is implicated. So if one argues oppression and abuse as something to be excised, one must discard more than Guest does.

In addition, the theological presentation of theodicy is not as straightforward as Guest supposes. The Lord is not necessarily justified *carte blanche* at the expense of the feminine. Rather, there is a strong protest element at work in the theology of the book. Lam 2:20 at the very least sees Dear Zion confronting the deity in his activity: "Look, O LORD, and consider to whom you have done this! Is it right that mothers consume their own fruit, little ones raised to health? Is it right that priests and prophets be killed in the sanctuary of the Lord?" The protest impulse weaves into the fabric of verse and raises questions about the justice of God rather than affirming it. The poetry is not so unequivocally oriented towards theodicy that the feminine city must be "re-membered" as Guest suggests. While helpfully elucidating the anguish and pain witnessed in Lamentations as well as a masculine bias in the commentary tradition, Guest obscures the complexity and ambiguity of the book's theology.

And yet both Guest and Siedman's interpretations of Lamentations are figured to be in some way liberative and accord with resistant feminist interpretations, as discussed above. Thus the politics and social dynamics at work in the creation and reception of Lamentations create an oppressive situation for women, a situation that must be contravened by surfacing the subjugation. The desire to expose this, however, may come at the price of under-reading the poems and censoring their ambiguity and force *qua* poetry.

## OTHER FEMINIST APPROACHES TO LAMENTATIONS

Other contributions in Lamentations research are concerned with recognizing gender bias and the implications that arise hermeneutically and theologically therefrom (O'Connor), learning from feminist criticism and incorporating it into their own fabric of analysis (Mandolfo), or simply trying to read Lamentations with a "women's perspective" and from the perspective of (evangelical) Christian faith (Snow Flesher).[16] With the exception of the monographs of Mandolfo and O'Connor, these works do not carry the level of sophistication of Guest's article nor do they evince critical awareness of feminist discourse. This is, of course, an immediate drawback, but to be fair they do not aim (except in the case of the monographs) at the level of scholarly critical discourse. O'Connor's and Snow Flesher's articles appear in one-volume women's Bible commentaries, where brevity is a necessity. The monographs, however, present an interesting mix of receptions of feminist discourse. O'Connor's *Lamentations and the Tears of the World* is clearly aware of feminist discourse, but does not exhibit resistant feminist analysis *per se*. Rather, she attempts to formulate theology by reading Lametnations critically, but with fidelity: theology may only be constructed after working through the feminine voice and its abuse in Lamentations.

---

16. O'Connor, "Lamentations"; O'Connor, *Lamentations and the Tears of the World*; Mandolfo, *Daughter Zion Talks Back to the Prophets*; Snow Flesher, "Lamentations."

O'Connor warns readers to be aware that "[b]iases against women appear in the book's imagery and in its structure," and these biases reflect and affirm an inherent subordination of women. One example demonstrates her view. The term "Daughter Zion"—a personification of the city of Jerusalem as a woman, used prevalently in Lamentations—conveys overtones of dignity (associated with the loftiness of the capital city and Temple therein), but also conceptually subordinates the female city to the male deity (whether as daughter or as wife). Furthermore, in Lamentations, Daughter Zion is scorned, raped, and said to be complicit in these experiences. These features, argues O'Connor, remain inherently harmful for women.[17]

Further, O'Connor sees in the structure of Lamentations gender bias. In its poetry, the concept of "hope" necessarily filtered through a prism of masculinity and androcentrism. She argues that where the masculine figure of the "suffering/strong man" of Lam 3 appears and speaks (the central chapter of the book), hope begins to surface in the poetry. Likewise, when the community speaks in Lam 5 (the final chapter of the book), the feminine voice of Lam 1 and 2 recedes. Here O'Connor sees an inherent gender prejudice that stifles feminine voice in Lamentations.[18]

And yet in spite of these indications, O'Connor is able to develop a theology of "witness" from Lamentations, especially from the voice of Daughter Zion. In *Lamentations and the Tears of the World*, she argues the poetry begs God to witness their pain and situation of disaster. O'Connor marks Lam 2:20, where Daughter Zion stridently questions and protests God's justice in his acts of slaughter and punishment. Far from allowing what she terms as Jerusalem's "abuse" to go unchecked, O'Connor argues that:

> the book's speakers stand up, resist, shout in protest, and fearlessly risk further antagonizing the deity. They do not accept abuse passively. They are voices of a people with nothing left to lose, and they find speech, face horror upon horror, and resist unsatisfactory interpretations offered by their theological tradition. From the authority of experience, they adopt a critical view and appraise and reappraise their situation. The result is a vast rupture in their relationship with God, yet they hold on to God, and in that holding they clear space for new ways to meet God."[19]

The fearless contestation of Daughter Zion against the LORD's activity provides the means by which modern women may pray and use Lamentations. Different to Guest and Siedman, O'Connor attempts to rehabilitate Lamentations into the life of faith via her theology of "witness" through the voice of Daughter Zion. In this way, hers is not a *resistant* interpretation of Lamentations, but rather an approach that attempts to critically read the book with fidelity, arrived at only and through a reading that accounts for the abuse and possibilities of the feminine voice in the book.

Mandolfo does not attempt to apply a feminist hermeneutic to her interpretation of Lamentations, but rather learns from the political edge of feminist analyses to inform her reading. In this way, feminist approaches are her "conversation partners"

---

17. O'Connor, "Lamentations," 188–89.
18. Ibid., 189–90.
19. O'Connor, *Lamentations and the Tears of the World*, 123. See also O'Connor, "Lamentations," 190–91.

in the attempt to elucidate "dialogic theology" in Lamentations.[20] Methodologically, Mandolfo employs the literary theory of Russian theorist Mikhail Bakhtin, who argued that texts speak beautifully when they speak with many voices (polyvalence) rather than with one voice (monologism). The interaction of the many voices in a work of art is "dialogism." Mandolfo teases out how this dialogic quality might be worked out in the prophets (Ezekiel, Jeremiah, the prophets of Isa 40–66), who speak for God (the father/husband), and Lam 1–2, whose speech is that of Daughter Zion (the daughter/wife).

Mandolfo sees in Lamentations fertile ground to work out this program, as she sees Lamentations as actually doing this in its feminine, resistant voice against God (Lam 2:20, for example). Her aim is not to overturn the Bible or do away with it *per se*, but rather to refigure concretized, essentialist, notions of justice and contest them, as Daughter Zion does in her protests. She says, "If we care about justice, we must be careful not to approach the Bible, in Bakhtinian terms, as the monologic 'word of the father' that in the end justifies divine violence."[21]

Mandolfo explores, like O'Connor, the use of the marriage metaphor in Lamentations, its tacit power relations (male subjugates female), and ultimately aims to dethrone biblical authority as presently construed as the "word of God" and reify a new vision of biblical authority as the "words of God."[22] Lamentations 1–2 are marked by divine silence to the cries of Daughter Zion, as explored above; rather than simply affirming this reality, Mandolfo figures Lamentations as Daughter Zion's response to God's voice heard in the prophets that accuse her of wantonness and sin. By doing so and attending to the feminine voice in Lamentations in dialogic interaction with the prophets, a full-fledged voice is constructed and "woman" attempts to reclaim her agency. Daughter Zion, then, in Lamentations subverts the voice of God in the prophets, exposing the unjust construction of Zion therein and challenging it.[23] By doing so, Mandolfo, with recent feminist analysis, destabilizes the objectification of "woman" and restores "woman" to a cogent subject, a responsible agent.[24]

Finally, one may see a rather different kind of feminist analysis in Snow Flesher's work on Lamentations. According to Catherine Clark Kroeger and Mary Evans, the commentary in which Snow Flesher writes is "written by women of faith who believe that all Scripture is inspired by God and given for the benefit of humanity. The contributors have examined the difficult texts from a 'hermeneutic of faith,' a conviction that the Scriptures are meant for healing rather than hurt, for affirmation of all persons, especially those who are oppressed."[25]

---

20. Mandolfo, *Daughter Zion Talks Back to the Prophets*, 3.
21. Ibid., 5.
22. Ibid., 3–28.
23. Ibid., 81–102.
24. Ibid., 82–83. For corollary in feminist discourse, see Aichele, Castelli, et al., eds., "Feminist and Womanist Criticism," 234–44.
25. Clark Kroeger and Evans, "Preface," xiv.

From this perspective, the differences between this work and those of Mandolfo, O'Connor, Guest, or Siedman become apparent. Yet with a concern for a commentary written with the chosen perspective of that of "women," the editors immediately fragment naïve essentialism to a degree, emphasizing the different *kinds* of voices present in "women's perspective": different social locations, ethnicities, and ecclesiastical backgrounds. Thus theirs cannot be identified as naïve, but rather guided by a view of the Bible that sees it as fundamentally helpful, especially when received in the context of (a community of) women and interpreted in that light.

Snow Flesher, like O'Connor, takes note of the feminine imagery in Lamentations. However, she argues differently that the imagery of Daughter Zion in Lamentations is a means to persuade God to deliver Jerusalem from distress, rather than a means to shame the people to repentance (as in the prophets).[26] Counter to Guest and Siedman in particular, Snow Flesher reads Lamentations as a means of fidelity to God: faithful interpretation of Lamentations will read with Daughter Zion and cry out to God on behalf of suffering—even if the deity has caused it. However, whilst Guest and Siedman reject such masculine abuse, Snow Flesher's conclusion is akin to, though not identical with, O'Connor's. Her approach runs counter to Mandolfo's program, for Snow Flesher embraces the biblical text of Lamentations as authoritative and helpful *as is*, while Mandolfo wants to *recast* Lamentations' (and the prophets') "word of the father" and its nature as biblical authority, though without discarding them as does Siedman.

## CONCLUSION

Feminist interpretations of Lamentations highlight the difficulties associated with pinning down the nature of feminist discourse in general. Aims and methods vary, and with this diversity, it becomes apparent that a set of pre-theoretical philosophical and theological constructs affect outcomes. For instance, Mandolfo's concern for "justice" is admirable in her interpretation of Lamentations; but the meaning of "justice" remains contested, especially in light of the difference between hers and Snow Flesher's deployments of "feminist analysis": A "just" interpretation for Snow Flesher reads with the grain of the text (as "God's word") while Mandolfo's "just" interpretation must necessarily read beyond it. Again, Guest's approach assumes that Lamentations is destructive and harmful, while Clark Kroeger and Evans assume that the Bible promotes help and healing. O'Connor's approach, too, reads the text with critical fidelity.

Future work may press "feminist analysis" to expose presuppositional elements in play and the hermeneutical similarities and differences that eventuate as a result of them. In short, an ecology of (pre)understanding affects the varieties of feminist interpretations of Lamentations, and the environment is affected by philosophy, ethics, and social theory, among other factors. As these elements are explored, greater clarity may be gained in terms of similarities of feminist approaches, and where they diverge. In the case of reading the Bible, some of the divergence will arise from theological issues—among them the nature of Scripture, the role of experience in theological construction

---

26. Snow Flesher, "Lamentations," 392.

and hermeneutics, and the place of reason in theology, as Schüssler Fiorenza recognized early on in her groundbreaking *In Memory of Her*.

## BIBLIOGRAPHY

Aichele, George, Elizabeth A. Castelli, et al., eds. "Feminist and Womanist Criticism." In *The Postmodern Bible: The Bible and Culture Collective*, 225–71. New Haven: Yale University Press, 1995.

Barry, Peter. *Beginning Theory: An Introduction to Literary and Cultural Theory*. Manchester: Manchester University Press, 1995.

Brenner, Athalya. "Pornoprophetics Revisited: Some Additional Reflections." *Journal for the Study of the Old Testament* 70 (1996) 63–86.

———, and Carol Fontaine, eds. *A Feminist Companion to Reading the Bible*. Sheffield: Sheffield Academic, 1997.

———, and Fokkelien van Dijk-Hemmes, eds. *On Gendering Texts: Female and Male Voices in the Hebrew Bible*. Biblical Interpretation Series, 1. Leiden: Brill, 1993.

Clark Kroeger, Catherine, and Mary J. Evans, eds. "Preface: Why a Women's Bible Commentary?" In *The IVP Women's Bible Commentary*., edited by Catherine Clark Kroeger and Mary Evans, xiii–xv. Downers Grove, IL: InterVarsity, 2002.

Guest, Deryn. "Hiding Behind the Naked Women in Lamentations: A Recriminative Response." *Biblical Interpretation* 7 (1999) 413–48.

Schüssler Fiorenza, Elizabeth. *In Memory of Her: A Feminist Theological Reconstruction of Christian Origins*. London: SPCK, 1983.

Lee, Nancy C. *The Singers of Lamentations: Cities under Siege, from Ur to Jerusalem to Sarajevo*. Biblical Interpretation Series, 60. Leiden: Brill, 2002.

Mandolfo, Carleen. *Daughter Zion Talks Back to the Prophets: A Dialogic Theology of the Book of Lamentations*. Semeia Studies. Atlanta: Society of Biblical Literature, 2007.

Moi, Toril. "Feminist, Female, Feminine." In *The Feminist Reader: Essays in Gender and the Politics of Literary Criticism*, edited by Catherine Belsey and Jane Moore, 115–32. London: Macmillan, 1989.

———. "'I am not a woman writer': About Women, Literature and Feminist Theory Today." *Feminist Theory* 9 (2008) 259–71.

O'Connor, Kathleen. "Lamentations." In *The Women's Bible Commentary*. Expanded Edition. Edited by Carol A. Newsom and Sharon Ringe, 187–91. Louisville: Westminster John Knox, 1998.

———. *Lamentations and the Tears of the World*. Maryknoll, NY: Orbis, 2002.

Richter, David H. "Feminist Literary Criticism." In *The Critical Tradition: Classic Texts and Contemporary Trends*, edited by David H. Richter, 1063–78. Boston: Bedford, 1989.

Sakenfeld, Katherine Doob. "Feminist Perspectives on Bible and Theology: An Introduction to Selected Issues and Literature." *Interpretation* 42 (1988) 5–18.

Seidman, Naomi. "Burning the Book of Lamentations." In *Out of the Garden: Women Writers on the Bible*, edited by Christina Büchmann and Celina Spiegel, 278–88. New York: Fawcett Columbine, 1995.

Snow Flesher, Leanne. "Lamentations." In *The IVP Women's Bible Commentary*, edited by Catherine Clark Kroeger and Mary J. Evans, 392–95. Downers Grove, IL: InterVarsity, 2002.

Trible, Phyllis. *God and the Rhetoric of Sexuality*. Overtures to Biblical Theology. Minneapolis: Fortress, 1978.

# 3

# Wrestling with Lamentations in Christian Worship

ROBIN A. PARRY

## INTRODUCTION

The book of Lamentations was birthed in order to bring a deep and profound grief before the throne of Yhwh in the context of communal worship. It found ongoing relevance for the people of God in the worship of Jewish and Christian communities over the centuries and, if it is to function as Holy Scripture today, it must do so by finding a place in the ongoing worshipping life of synagogue and church. This chapter offers some reflections on Christian theological interpretation of Lamentations in doxological contexts.

## LAMENTATIONS IN LITURGICAL CONTEXT

### Lamentations in the Worship of Ancient Israel

Biblical scholars have devoted considerable attention to the question of the original life setting of the poems that make up Lamentations. While there is much disagreement on such issues, the almost unanimous view of biblical scholars is that the poetry of Lamentations was composed as a liturgical response to the Babylonian destruction of Jerusalem in 587 and its aftermath.[1] The poems, in other words, were written for use in public worship. It may well be that they were used in services held on the ruined temple site although we cannot be certain of this.

The evidence for the use of Lamentations in public worship is mainly internal. Both the form and content of the poems are strongly suggestive of a liturgical function for the book (or, at least, its component parts). The poems of Lamentations have strong formal similarities to numerous Psalms and also some similarities to ancient Near Eastern city laments both of which strongly suggest a public use for the poetry.[2] In terms of content

---

[1]. Even if, with a few scholars, one questions the traditional dating (e.g., Provan, "Reading Texts") that does not affect one's conclusions regarding the liturgical function of the book.

[2]. On the debate about links between Lamentations and ANE city laments see Kramer, *Lamentation*; Michalowski, *Lamentation*; Dobbs-Allsopp, *Weep, O Daughter of Zion*.

we could note that the communal prayers in the book, for instance, seem to have little use outside of a communal worship setting. The fact that later Jewish tradition came to employ Lamentations for liturgical use on the 9th of Av only reinforces these impressions.

There are numerous issues debated amongst scholars regarding the formal classification of the different poems. Chapter 5 is the most straightforward—the majority of scholars see it as more or less a communal lament. It contains a complaint in the face of disaster, a request that God rescue his suffering people, and a self-reproach for the arising of the situation. Middlemas, while seeing no hope communicated through the content of the poem (I take a more positive approach towards the content), does see hope embodied in the poetic form because communal lament was motivated by the hope that God might act to redeem.[3]

Chapter 3 is the least straightforward poem to analyze, being a unique combination of elements from a range of literary genres unlike any other in the Old Testament. Consequently suggestions regarding its prehistory prior to inclusion in the book or of its specific liturgical function are heavily speculative.

Chapters 1, 2, and 4 combine forms. To take chapter 1 as an example; since the work of Jahnow in 1923[4] and Gunkel in 1929[5] most commentators recognize elements from the funeral dirge in the poem. These include the mournful cry "Alas!" (איכה, 1:1), the description of misery that follows it (2a, 4c), and the presence of the reversal motif (1:1, 6). Clearly the dirge form has been modified because certain elements, such as the announcement that someone has died, are missing while alien elements, such as the plea to Yhwh and the confession of guilt, are present. Westermann, on the other hand, argues that Lam 1, especially the second section, is primarily a communal lament.[6] He sees the following major elements from the communal lament in the poem: (a) the community's direct complaint (1:9c, 11c, 20a), (b) the accusation against God (1:12c–15), (c) the complaint about enemies (1:5a, 9c, 21b). He also thinks that the following minor elements are drawn from the communal lament form: (d) the acknowledgement of guilt (1:14a, 18a, 22b), (e) the plea for Yhwh to take heed (1:9c, 11c, 20a), (f) the plea for reprisal on the enemies (1:21–22) and, (g) the motif of God's justification (1:18) set over against the accusation against God (1:12c–15). However, there are also elements from the communal lament form, such as the expression of trust, that are missing in Lam 1. Also our poem does not always follow the expected order of elements in the communal lament. Westermann sees this as resulting from the pressure of the acrostic form but even if this were the case the form is still disrupted. Whether we see Lam 1 as a dirge modified by elements from the communal lament or vice versa we must concede that it is not a pure form. This poem includes some, but not all, elements from both forms and blends them

---

3. Middlemas, *Troubles*, 222, 226.
4. Jahnow, *Das Hebräische*.
5. Gunkel, "Klagelieder Jeremiae."
6. Westermann, *Lamentations*, 114–19. Eissfeldt, while seeing a dirge in 1:1–11 and 17, maintains that 9c, 11c, and 12–16 are in the form of an *individual lament* (Eissfeldt, *The Old Testament*, 501–5. See also Re'emi, "The Theology of Hope," 79).

in a unique way. We need to adequately respect the uniqueness of the poem as well as what it shares with other poems.[7]

For our purposes, however, we do not need to settle all the controverted questions debated by modern biblical scholars, nor can we afford to spend all our time in their august company, because the context within which we need to read Lamentations is far wider than that with which biblical scholars are normally concerned.

All sacred texts are inherited by worshippers within a living tradition of reception that informs the ongoing use of the text though a process of sedimentations and innovation.[8] The poems of our book were created for worship and have been used within worship throughout Jewish and Christian history and this should inform their ongoing reception within both synagogue and church. If these poems are to function as Scripture for believers then they can only do so within doxological contexts.

Now academic biblical scholarship plays a constructive role in the hermeneutical enterprise by enabling a relative "distancing of horizons" between a text and its modern interpreter. This allows texts to stand over against us and surprise us and in that way it helps us avoid domesticating them. As such it can serve to limit the range of legitimate meanings that a text can have. But if we leave biblical texts in the hands of scholars without returning them to their natural habitat those texts have ceased to function as Scripture.

### *Lamentations in the Worship of the Synagogue*

As Elsie Stern points out in her chapter, Lamentations has long occupied an important place in the Jewish liturgical calendar. It strikes me that there are at least five things of critical importance that the churches can learn from the Jewish tradition here. First, the text of Lamentations is used as a means for reflecting on other catastrophes that have touched the Jewish people. In this way the text is allowed to be read in the presence of horrors not considered by its author(s), thereby opening up new horizons of meaning and ways in which the text finds ongoing significance within a community.

Second, while the Jewish tradition allows the text to interpret, and be interpreted by, catastrophes other than that which occasioned its creation, the original historical referent is not eclipsed in the process. That is to say that the Jewish tradition has always used Lamentations to remind the community of the original Babylonian destruction of Jerusalem. This event may serve as a model for other, later horrors thereby allowing the words of the text to encompass that which its authors did not see, but the text is emphatically not dehistoricized. Its embeddedness in the ongoing story of the people of God is

---

7. Renkema, *Lamentations*, 91–93. Tod Linafelt proposes that it is not a coincidence that the elements of the dirge form cluster in the narrator's speech while elements of the lament cluster in Lady Zion's speech. The narrator's speech is dominated by the overtones of death even though Zion is not dead. Zion, however, is a survivor and when she speaks it is a lament straining towards life, and not a dirge looking back to death, that she employs. Thus the very form of her speech indicates a resistance to her fate not found in the narrator's speech, the form of which suggests a mournful resignation (Linafelt, *Surviving*, 35–43).

8. The metaphor is that of Paul Ricoeur. See Ricoeur, *Time and Narrative*, 68–70. See also Parris, *Reception Theory*.

affirmed. In fact, it is precisely this affirmation that guides the creative extension of the textual significance.

Third, it is clear from the above that the Jewish practice of reading Lamentations alongside other, later events is not ad hoc but hermeneutically controlled. Most obviously the destruction of Herod's temple finds a parallel in the destruction of Solomon's. But, more than that, the community suffering in Lamentations are the ancestors of the Jewish people and so it is natural to make links between the plight of those in the texts and later Jewish sufferings. Now Lamentations can speak to sufferings beyond those of Jewish communities—indeed it can only function as Christian Scripture if this is the case; but, as Paul House points out in his chapter, such applications of Lamentations need to have hermeneutical controls. And, more specifically, we need to be able to provide a biblical-theological rationale for such extensions in application.

Fourth, as Elsie Stern so helpfully shows, the use of Lamentations on 9th of Av must be understood as located within a broader liturgical context spanning from the 17th of Tammuz to Rosh Hashanah. Its community-shaping role must be located within that wider liturgical framework. Stern helpfully shows how this works with the Sabbaths before 9th of Av (focusing on Israel's sin), Tisha b'Av itself (with its reading of Lamentations attending to the terrible consequences of that sin), and the Sabbaths that follow charting "a process of reconciliation and consolation" in which God comforts Israel and restores her to himself. This tradition allows liturgical space for the sorrow and despair of Lamentations to be expressed without being crushed by the premature arrival of "good news." Yet, at the same time, it does not allow Lamentations the last word. In this way lament and rejoicing and held in balance and in place.

Fifth, the Jewish tradition has offered not simply liturgical room for the text of Lamentations within the ongoing life in the community but has also offered guides to its interpretations. In this book we have explored how Targum Lamentations, Lamentations Rabbah, and Rashi's commentary all served this function within the context of private and/or public Jewish devotion. These guides serve different functions. The Targum, for instance, is concerned in part to vindicate God's justice and to guard against what its authors may perceive as impious "readings" of Lamentations. Lamentations Rabbah importantly aimed to situated the text within the ongoing covenant relationship between God and Israel (as well as vindicating God). Rashi, is concerned to explain problematic words in order to help people understand better the literal meaning of the book. These interpretative samplings have ongoing importance for Jewish reception of the text, though not in the sense that a reading that departed from them ceases to be Jewish. Some contemporary Jewish hearings of the scroll, out of respect for the content of the text itself, have objected that the classical interpretative tradition, in its eagerness to vindicate God, has domesticated Lamentations by stifling the book's more critical edge. They argue that we should be less keen to fit Lamentations into neat theological categories. Stern's and especially Braiterman's chapters point in this direction. But Jewish interpretation was never univocal. The midrashic tradition was always multi-vocal, dialogical, and incomplete. It was never about imparting the single, correct Jewish interpretation.

Christians have no influential reception traditions for interpreting Lamentations because the book has not featured as a major text in the way that it has for Judaism (a situation that is not going to change, for the Gentile section of the ekklesia at any rate). If Christians are to grant Lamentations a place in public worship, however, then we would be well advised to mine our own historical traditions to uncover the oft-forgotten insights of past readers. Some of the chapters in this volume begin the task of doing precisely that. On top of that, Christians would be well advised to listen closely to the historic Jewish interpretations. Gentile believers in Jesus need to appreciate afresh that this is a book, in the first instance, addressing the sufferings of Israel. Gentile Christians thus hear it over the shoulder of Israel, through union with Yeshua the Messiah.

## *Lamentations "Outside In"—In the Worship of the Church*

So Gentile Christ-believers need to hear the text as a word addressed, in the first instance, by the people of Israel to Yhwh, and written down for the people of Israel. Christians instinctively read the texts as insiders—we hear our own voices in the anguished words of those in pain. This is right but I want to propose that there is a place for a different, far more unsettling reading stance vis-à-vis the text.

The book speaks of the brutal violence of the nations against Israel and it is sobering for Gentile Christians to read the text not from the position of suffering-Israel, but in the role of the oppressive nations. Read in this way the book serves to invite the communities that have persecuted Israel to listen to the voices of their victims. Even a glancing familiarity with the shocking treatment of Jews by Christians through the ages goes a long way towards indicating the potential power of such a reading strategy.

But, someone may protest, surely this is not to read Lamentations as Christian Scripture for it puts Christians on the outside looking in (in contrast to Paul's indication that Israel's Scriptures were written for the church; cf. 1 Cor 9:10). So long as this is not the only stance that Christian readers take to the text I must beg to differ.

In this dangerous, almost prophetic, mode the word of God comes as a harsh word of rebuke, a shocking exposure of an oft-forgotten crime, a call to the painful task of listening to one's victims, and an invitation to repentance. In this way, the text of Lamentations fleshes out part of the function of Scripture as a prescient "rebuke" to believers (2 Tim 3:17). Christian oppression of Jewish people may have been at its worst in times past but it is certainly not a thing of the past. Christians live with the ever-present temptation to think that since the Messiah came God has abandoned the Jewish people in favor of the church.[9] This, to my mind, represents a fundamentally unbiblical ecclesiology but it has been the theology at the root of a lot of anti-Semitic attitudes and actions over the centuries. Hearing Lamentations as a text by Jews and for Jews in which Gentile Christ-believers have often shamefully played out the role of the destructive nations would actually be one very constructive, chastening reading strategy.

---

9. See Soulen, *The God of Israel and Christian Theology*.

# GREAT IS THY FAITHFULNESS?

The text of Lamentations strikes a very different sound in the context of the church when heard in such ways. Consider the different ways in which the nations are related to Israel in the book:

- Some of the nations are those who were supposed allies, bound by treaties to support Israel if she was attacked. Yet, when the moment of truth arrived, they abandoned her to her enemies without a word of protest (1:2, 7; 4:17).
- The attacking nation uses lethal violence against Jerusalem and her people (1:15; 2:4, 21; 4:1–10).
- They enrich themselves on her wealth, stealing goods and property, and desecrating places and items of religious value (1:10; 2:6–7).
- They expel her people (1:3, 5, 18).
- They mock Jerusalem's suffering and rejoice in her downfall at their hands (1:7, 21; 2:15–17).
- They fail to offer comfort to the suffering city (1:2, 9, 16, 17, 21).[/BL]

It does not take much knowledge of Jewish-Christian relations throughout history to see how Lamentations might serve to expose past Christian acts for what they are.[10] As such Christians would be wise to pay careful attention to the traditional Jewish reading of the text on the 9th of Av as a prism for understanding a wide range of Israel's sufferings. We need to hear that and acknowledge the legitimacy of that interpretation—a legitimacy retained within a Christian theological frame of reference.[11] If we who are Christians are not prepared to face our history and to allow Scripture to expose our infidelity then what claims do we have to honor and tremble before God's word? I think that it would be perfectly appropriate for such unnerving use of the text to take place in the context of public Christian worship.

However, the Christian conviction is that while this text is truly Israel's scripture, Gentiles—through union with Israel's Messiah—can stand alongside an eschatologically renewed Israel as the new covenant people of Yhwh (cf. Eph 2:11–22). As such Lamentations is part of Christian Scriptures too and can thus be read by Gentiles, as by Jews, from the inside out.

### *Lamentations "Inside Out"—In the Worship of the Church*

The use of Lamentations in the Christian churches has been a far more ambiguous affair. It was not a text that generated a lot of comment in the New Testament,[12] nor in

---

10. See Cohn-Sherbok, *The Crucified Jew*; Keith, *Hated Without a Cause?*

11. The recent revival of a Messianic Jewish movement in the zone between Christianity and Judaism serves as a challenge to the way in which both faiths have defined themselves over against each other (see Rudolph, "Messianic Jews and Christian Theology"). This challenge seems to require that Christians rethink their ecclesiologies (on which see Kinzer, *Postmissionary Messianic Judaism*) and, if they do so, creates the theological space for the unconventional of use of Lamentations that I am proposing here.

12. Arguably Lam 4:13 is alluded to in Matt 23:35, and Lam 2:15 in Matt 27:39. There are also some other less certain allusions.

the patristic period,[13] although, as we shall see, both can provide fruitful resources for Christian recovery of Lamentations.

The most conspicuous use of Lamentations in Christian worship was in the Western church from the Middle Ages onwards in the Divine Office of Matins on Maundy Thursday, Good Friday, and Holy Saturday (otherwise known as Tenebrae).[14] Matins took place before dawn[15] and one can imagine the effect, in the days before electric lighting, of extinguishing fourteen of the fifteen candles illuminating the building one by one as the sacred texts were read out.[16] The Office was treated, for these three days, as a kind of funeral service.

The choice, number, and order of the readings from Lamentations varied from region to region (as did the number of candles to be extinguished) until the Council of Trent (1545–63). Trent standardized the readings and laid down rules for the musical and poetic structure of the Lamentations, though not so much as to remove all local discretion.

It is very interesting to observe the way that Lamentations was used in communal Christian worship. As Andrew Cameron-Mowat shows in his chapter, they were used in the fist nocturne of each day as follows:

### Thursday (Wednesday)

| | | | | | | |
|---|---|---|---|---|---|---|
| Nocturne 1 | Ps 68 | Ps 69 | Ps 70 | Lam 1:1–5 | Lam 1:6–9 | Lam 1:10–14 |
| Nocturne 2 | Ps 71 | Ps 72 | Ps 73 | Augustine on Ps 54:1 | Augustine on Ps 54:1 | Augustine on Ps 54:1 |
| Nocturne 3 | Ps 74 | Ps 75 | Ps 76 | 1 Cor 11:17–22 | 1 Cor 11:23–26 | 1 Cor 11:27–34 |

### Friday (Thursday)

| | | | | | | |
|---|---|---|---|---|---|---|
| Nocturne 1 Matins | Ps 2 | Ps 21 | Ps 26 | Lam 2:8–11 | Lam 2:12–15 | Lam 3:1–9 |
| Nocturne 2 Lauds | Ps 37 | Ps 39 | Ps 53 | Augustine on Ps 63:2 | Augustine on Ps 63:2 | Augustine on Ps 63:2 |
| Nocturne 3 | Ps 58 | Ps 87 | Ps 93 | Heb 4:11–15 | Heb 4:16—5:3 | Heb 5:4–10 |

---

13. See the chapter by Thomas, "Lamentations in the Patristic Period."

14. Tenebrae is Latin for "shadows." The number three looms large in Tenebrae: three services, with three nocturnes each, each containing three psalms (and their antiphons) and three readings (each followed by its response—extracts from the Bible or Augustine). The associations with Christ's three days and three nights in the tomb as well as with the Trinity are obvious.

15. The service was brought forward to the early evening of the previous day (i.e., Wednesday, Thursday, and Friday) from possibly as early as the thirteenth century, because it was more convenient.

16. There were fifteen candles. One candle was extinguished after each Psalm reading (nine in all) leaving six alight. Tenebrae was immediately followed by Lauds during which a further five candles were extinguished after readings leaving one alight. The extinguishing of the candles might date back to the fifth century.

## GREAT IS THY FAITHFULNESS?

**Saturday (Friday)**

| | | | | | | |
|---|---|---|---|---|---|---|
| Nocturne 1 Matins | Ps 4 | Ps 14 | Ps 15 | Lam 3:22–30 | Lam 4:1–6 | Lam 5:1–11 |
| Nocturne 2 Lauds | Ps 23 | Ps 26 | Ps 29 | Augustine on Ps 63:7 | Augustine on Ps 63:7 | Augustine on Ps 63:7 |
| Nocturne 3 | Ps 53 | Ps 75 | Ps 87 | Heb 9:11–14 | Heb 9:15–18 | Heb 9:19–22 |

So it was that texts from all five chapters of Lamentations were brought, in the context of Christian worship, into association with the darkness of Gethsemane, Golgotha, and the tomb of Christ.

The setting of the lessons from Lamentations to music was practiced from at least the twelfth century but it was the Renaissance that saw a veritable explosion of such musical settings for use in Tenebrae. Schopf's chapter very helpfully illuminates the work of Tomas Luis de Victoria but it could just as easily have considered the haunting settings of Thomas Tallis, Palestrina, Robert White, William Byrd, or a host of others.[17] These very carefully crafted polyphonic compositions were intended to create a solemn, lamenting frame of mind. Singers were careful to avoid any vocal ornamentation that might make the tone more joyful. They functioned as interpretations of the biblical text which, in turn, shaped the way in which congregations would hear it afresh (at least, those few that could understand Latin).

It strikes me that two of the features of Jewish reception to which I earlier drew attention are analogous to features that can be found in this particular Christian doxological tradition. First, the text of Lamentations is allowed to be a filter through which other catastrophes—in this case the death of the Messiah—are interpreted. And those other events, in turn, affect the way in which Lamentations in interpreted. Second, Tenebrae, as the 9th of Av, is overtly located in a wider liturgical context that culminates in redemption. On Easter Sunday the remaining lit candle is brought out and the building is once again illuminated. So Lamentations finds its home in a luminal liturgical zone that both gives it space to be itself and yet will not allow it to be the last word.

The planting of these Lamentations readings in the midst of a forest of readings from the book of Psalms also, as Cameron-Mowat shows, plays a role in influencing the way in which they are heard. The rationale behind the selection is sometimes clear enough, although it is not always perspicuous and the effect that it might have on the Latin-speakers present is, of course, underdetermined by the texts themselves. Once such a range of texts are set alongside each others it is not possible to tightly control the interpretative resonances that might be created. The following reflections are simply my own response to the way in which the selected Psalm readings affected my engagement with the Lamentations passages. Some of the resonances may not have been in the minds of those who selected the texts, but nonetheless they cohere within the liturgical context in which they exist.

---

17. Not to mention the musical settings for Lamentations that are not linked to Tenebrae (e.g., Leonard Bernstein's Jeremiah Symphony).

One theme that is prominent in a number of the selected Psalms is that of the righteous individual who is suffering at the hands of his enemies and cries out to God for salvation (in Tenebrae order: Ps 69, 70, 71, 73?, 26). In the Christian tradition, and clearly in this liturgical context, such Psalms were often read as Christ's prayers to the Father as well as models for the prayer of the faithful (the final reading from Hebrews on day 2 reinforces this interpretation). The reading from Augustine for the third day speaks of the importance of coming to God when we are in the "desert," driven by thirst, so that God can appear to us. This idea seems to be one of the keys behind the selection of Psalms. That this is so is evident also from our second theme.

A second recurring theme is the hope that God will indeed save the suffering one who seeks him, and will punish his enemies (in Tenebrae order: Ps 71, 73, 75, 37, 4, 23. cf., Tenebrae Psalms which promise blessing and salvation for those who walk in God's ways: Ps 37, 15, 26, 75). In the context of this service it is the resurrection of Christ that serves as his salvation. This would perhaps have been seen in the words from Ps 71:20, "You [i.e., God] who have made me [i.e., Jesus] see many troubles and calamities will revive me again; from the depths of the earth you will bring me up again." Related to this is the theme that God will cause his Davidic king to triumph (in Tenebrae order: Ps 72, 2, 21).

The third theme concerns the grounds for such hope—that in all things God is in control (in Tenebrae order: Ps 68, 93, 29). The reading from Augustine on day 1 (commenting on Ps 54:1) brings this out. Augustine reads King David as a type of his descendant, King Jesus. The Ziphites betrayed David to Saul but it was not in Saul's power to capture him. Similarly Christ's enemies betray and attack him but to destroy him is not in their power. Their attempt merely exposes their wickedness. This is the theological context within which Christ's death is situated.

The fourth Psalmic theme is one more obviously related to Lamentations. It concerns the suffering of Zion at the hands of its enemies, the prayer for salvation, and the promise that deliverance will come (in Tenebrae order: Ps 74, 76, 53, 87?, 14, 53, 87).

What are the theological connections that might be made here and how might they set up ways of interpreting Lamentations? Clearly this is Holy Week and the narrative of Jesus is central as the interpretative key. I suggest that it is the representative role of the Davidic king that brings all of the above themes together. The king represents his people and so his story of suffering, supplication, and salvation serves as a participation in and the pattern for the suffering, supplication, and salvation of Zion.[18]

Psalm 69, the second Psalm reading in Tenebrae, serves as a hermeneutical doorway through which the rest of the readings are approached. It is a Psalm of David, the righteous Messiah. He cries out to the God of Israel from the midst of his desperate situation and looks with hope to Yhwh to punish his enemies and redeem him, but not to redeem only him. The Psalm ends with the words, "For God will save Zion and build up the cities of Judah." The redemption of the king of Israel has implications for the suffering community of Zion. In this way the subsequent Psalms—which address the themes of

---

18. On the paradigmatic role of Jesus as Zion/man in Lamentations as well as Zion/church see Thomas "*Until He Looks Down and Sees.*"

the lament of the righteous individual, the vindication of the Davidic king, and the suffering and salvation of Israel—are intimately linked. And in Christian context this link is understood to be realized in Jesus.

In is within this biblical-theological framework that the Lamentations texts in Tenebrae are to be understood. Psalm 69 serves as a doorway yet again. There David says, "I looked for pity, but there was none, and for comforters, but I found none" (Ps 69:20). In the very same nocturne we get our first three Lamentations texts in which we read that Zion, like David, had none to comfort her in her suffering (Lam 1:2, 9). The difference is that Zion, unlike David, is not a righteous sufferer but an unrighteous one (Lam 1:5, 8, 14).

It is more than likely, given the replacement theology operative in most of Christian history, that Zion was seen as a type of the church. So the worshippers are invited to see themselves as Zion, the city of God, beloved of the Lord yet sinful, afflicted, looking for a coming deliverance akin to that experienced by her Messiah, Jesus.[19] Each Lamentations reading is followed by an exhortation based on Hos 14:1, *Jerusalem convertere ad Dominum Deum tuum* (Jerusalem, return to the Lord your God). Thus the readings serve to call the congregants to repentance.

## THE CANONICAL FORM AND CANONICAL CONTEXT OF LAMENTATIONS

These Jewish and Christian liturgical practices are a faithful response to the canonical status of the book of Lamentations. The text is preserved in both Jewish and Christian Bibles in such a way that it demands to be heard both in its final form and in its canonical context. Lamentations ends without resolution. By the end of the book God has neither spoken the longed for word of comfort nor acted to redeem. The book was canonized in this open and "incomplete" form, and, as such, any hearing of the text as Scripture demands that this fact is respected. Jewish and Christian Bibles give the text space to be itself and do not seek to tag on a happy ending in order to prematurely close down the pain or to tame the grief.

But the Jewish and Christian Bibles also locate Lamentations in a wider canonical context and as such they will not allow the book only to be heard apart from that wider story. In this volume Lena-Sofia Tiemeyer has very helpfully explored the ways in which parts of the book of Isaiah explicitly respond to the book of Lamentations. The Jewish interpretative tradition has long recognized this fact and the Jewish liturgy reflects it. To read the "no comfort" of Lamentations as part of the Bible, is to read it alongside the "comfort, comfort my people" of Isaiah. The "no comfort" of Lamentations is part of the story. The canonical context calls on the worshipping community to refuse it the last word, but at the same time the canonical form warns the community against prematurely collapsing the "no comfort" into the "comfort."

The balance, inherent in the canonical status of Lamentations, of allowing space for mourning and darkness (thereby acknowledging the final form) but locating that dark-

---

19. In this connection note the use of Lamentations in the current Church of England liturgy for Maundy Thursday: (http://www.cofe.anglican.org/worship/downloads/pdf/tspashw.pdf, 303).

ness in a wider, redemptive narrative (thereby acknowledging the canonical context) is mirrored in the way that Jews and, to a lesser extent, Christians have used Lamentations in their worship. The 9th of Av is dark in tone but is followed by the word of salvation. It uses canonically inspired liturgical time to hold the sorrow of Lamentations away from the joy of subsequent deliverance and yet at the same time refuses to allow them to be separated. It allows a time for mourning and a time for joy and it does so in such a way to resist the bleeding back of coming joy into the pain. Christian liturgical use of Lamentations goes some way towards this. Tenebrae certainly places the readings in a wider liturgical context of darkness followed by light, death followed by resurrection. It also keeps a temporal gap between the growing darkness and the return of the light. Furthermore the musical settings of Lamentations have been consistently mournful and somber. Yet the selection of Psalms read during Tenebrae very clearly and confidently anticipate the happy ending—more clearly and confidently than Lamentations itself. To some extent, therefore, this does dampen one aspect of the canonical form of the text.

## HEARING LAMENTATIONS AS CHRISTIAN SCRIPTURE

So the use of the text of Lamentations in the worship of Jews and some Christians provides helpful pointers for contemporary Christian use. In this section I wish to explore a little further the insightful association made in the Western church between Lamentations and the sorrow, death, and burial of Jesus. While the *Tenebrae* service offers no commentary at all on the readings of Lamentations, the very fact that the texts were associated with certain Psalms and particular events in the life of Jesus is deeply suggestive. I want to suggest that perceiving the sufferings of the Messiah in the sufferings of Lamentations is not arbitrary but is informed by the deep canonical logic of the Christian Bible.

### *Lamentations and the Rule of Faith*

While, as Ricoeur says, texts mean all that they can mean,[20] not all such interpretations would count as legitimate *Christian* interpretations. Christian communities have long read their Scriptures in the light of "the rule of faith." The rule of faith, a term first used by Irenaeus, was simply a narrative summary of the apostolic faith of the church. It did not exist in a single, fixed form but all the diverse versions we have express a common core: the story of the creator God revealed in Christ. It speaks of God the Father who sent his Son as a man in order to redeem the world. Jesus—God the Son made flesh—was crucified, buried, was raised and ascended to the right hand of the Father from where he sent the Spirit and from where he will one day return.[21] What might it mean to appreciate Lamentations in the light of the story of God-in-Christ?

20. Ricoeur, *Time and Narrative*.
21. The rule of faith was a somewhat elastic distillation of the theological tradition passed down in the churches established by the apostles. We find versions of it in Irenaeus, Tertullian, Hippolytus, Origen, Cyprian, Novatian, Dionysius of Alexandria, and the *Didascalia apostolorum*. It served to represent the heart of that tradition and probably developed for catechetical purposes. The later creeds evolved from it and effectively standardized its form. The rule served both as a summary of key aspects of the theology of the sacred texts (which later became the NT) and as a normative guide for interpreting those texts in

# GREAT IS THY FAITHFULNESS?

## *Lamentations and Christ*

I understand the Bible to suggest that Jesus, the Messiah of Israel, stood before God as the representative of the whole people of Israel. He was, one might say, one-man-Israel.[22] I must emphasize that Jesus does not thereby *replace* the Jewish people (the Jewish people are irreplaceable in God's purposes), but rather *represents* them and, in his person, embodies their story with the purpose of redeeming them. This idea seems implicit, as we have seen, in the readings used during Tenebrae.

Suppose that one reads Lamentations with this theological belief. How might we connect Jesus' story to this poetry? I have developed the following brief suggestions at more length elsewhere.[23] Here I simply indicate links that provide a basis for further reflection.

*Christ and Lady Zion* (Lam 1 and 2). If Jesus takes the covenant curses experienced by Israel to their climax then we can draw connections between Jesus' suffering and Judah's exilic suffering personified in the person of Lady Zion in Lam 1–2. Like Jerusalem, tears were upon his cheeks as he prayed alone in the garden. Like Jerusalem, he knew betrayal by his "friends" who left him to suffer alone. Like Jerusalem, Jesus was beaten, stripped naked, publicly humiliated, and afflicted. Like Jerusalem, he was reduced from a high and noble status to dust. Like Jerusalem, he bore the divine curse for covenant disobedience. Like Jerusalem, he was violently attacked by a pagan occupying force. Like Jerusalem, he felt abandoned by Yhwh in the face of these pagan military oppressors. Like Jerusalem, he was mocked and despised by those who looked on at his destruction.

*Christ and the destroyed temple* (Lam 2). In the New Testament, Jesus was seen as embodying the Jerusalem temple in his body. His death and resurrection were seen in terms of the destruction and rebuilding of the temple (cf. John 2:19–22). As such the destruction of the temple spoken of in Lamentations can be seen in the light of Christ. Given the cosmic symbolism of the temple (it symbolized the created order) the destruction of the temple represents cosmic, ecological devastation. Bringing such themes into contemplation of the temple and the death of Christ has considerable potential.

*Christ and the valiant man* (Lam 3). The story of the solitary sufferer in Lam 3 seems to me to be structurally similar to the story of Jesus. This can be brought out in the following chart.

---

*Christian* ways. For Irenaeus, it was living by the rule of faith (not merely having the right Scriptures) that separated Christians from heretics. Both the proto-orthodox and the Gnostics read the same sacred texts but they interpreted them in very different ways. Irenaeus' point is that *Christians read according to the rule of faith*.

22. I borrowed this phrase from Mark Kinzer's book, *Postmissionary Messianic Judaism*. The biblical-theological case for this claim is spelled out in Parry, *Lamentations*.

23. Parry, *Lamentations*, 168–73, 180–93.

| | | | | | | |
|---|---|---|---|---|---|---|
| Valiant Man | Embodies the suffering of Jerusalem | In the pit (metaphorical death) | Redeemed from the pit | His redemption is a sign of hope for the Israel | His enemies still plot against him | Final defeat of his enemies is future |
| Christ | Embodies the suffering of Jerusalem (and humanity) | In the grave (real death) | Raised from the dead | His redemption is a sign of hope for Israel (and the world) | His enemies still fight against him | Final defeat of his enemies is future |

*Christ and the righteous victims* (Lam 4:13). Matthew 23:35 alludes to Lam 4:13. In essence the Lamentations text sets out a general principle about divine judgment on those leaders who shed innocent blood. Matthew sees Jesus as the righteous victim par excellence whose innocent blood is shed by wicked leaders in Jerusalem. Therefore judgment will come upon them too.

*Christ and the captured Messiah* (Lam 4:20). Christians have long seen Lam 4:20 in the light of Christ. The text reads

> [The] breath of our nostrils, Yhwh's anointed,
>     was captured in their pits:
> [He of] whom we said, "In his shade,
>     we will live amongst the nations."

Lamentations is almost certainly referring to the capture of Zedekiah by the Babylonians. However, Christians have often seen a prefigurement of the death of Jesus at the hands of a pagan empire in these words. What is suggestive about the Christian interpretation is that this verse immediately precedes the most positive verses in the whole book (4:21–22). Lamentations 4:21–22 is akin to a prophetic oracle of salvation for Israel and judgment on its enemies. The promise comes from left of field and there is no obvious explanation for why it should occur here. But on a Christian reading, the very moment of despair—the defeat of Israel's king by the pagans—becomes the very basis for salvation. So the flow of chapter 4 appears in a new light.

## Lamentations and the Spirit

What of the Spirit of Yhwh? How does the Spirit stand in relation to the pain of Lamentations? The first thing that we must say is that Lamentations says absolutely nothing about the Spirit and so, at one level, it has nothing to contribute to our pneumatology. Any study on the theology of God's Spirit in Lamentations will rightly be composed of blank pages.[24] But suppose that our Christian reader is coming to the text with a pneumatology that already has some grasp of the relationship of the Spirit and the

---

24. Although, as Richard Harvey points out in his chapter, Alfred Edersheim saw a reference to the Spirit inspiring repentance in Lam 2:19.

grief of the world—how might that affect their theological engagement with the text of Lamentations? I shall offer a few thoughts on this possibility.[25]

Romans 8:18–30 helps us to get some insight into the Spirit and a certain mode of lament. Paul draws a parallel between Jesus' suffering, the suffering of Christians, and the suffering of the whole created order (8:17–25). Indeed, Paul's underlying theology is one that sees an intimate relationship between humanity, Israel, Christ, and the church. Israel represents all humanity before God (it is a microcosm of humanity). Jesus, as the Messiah of Israel, represents the whole people of Israel (he is Israel writ small).[26]

First of all, notice that the story of Christ, the church, and creation run in parallel: suffering then glory; death then life. Jesus was crucified, died, was buried, and then was raised from the dead by God through the Spirit (Rom 8:11). Paul is saying that the story of believers will be like Christ's. Currently we are in our mortal bodies and we suffer with Jesus. We shall die. But then we shall be raised by God (through the same Spirit he raised Christ by). Paul speaks of this future as one in which the very glory of God himself is revealed in us. It is a resurrection to immortality, it is our adoption as sons—that is, children and heirs of God.

In the same way, the story of the whole created order is one of frustration and slavery to death and decay followed by liberation and participating in the freedom of the children of God.[27] In other words, when God resurrects his people he will then resurrect the whole creation. And Paul pictures both the creation and the church—and, by implication, Jesus himself when he was on the cross—as currently "groaning." We'll come back to that.

So the story of the church and of creation is darkness now but light to come—a story already played out in the life of Jesus. Thus Paul can write that "our present sufferings are not worth comparing with the glory that will be revealed in us" (8:18). And Paul knew some serious sufferings and times of real despair (2 Cor 1:8–9; 11). But we need to see that for Paul this eager expectation of God's new day existed alongside the present experience of grief and sorrow. This is where the groaning comes in. Dunn notes that the groaning of Christ-believers is intended "to emphasize believers' involvement in the eschatological travail of creation . . . The point needs to be emphasized that the Spirit does not free from such tension, but actually creates or at least heightens that tension and brings it to more anguished expression."[28] The groaning is three things at once.

First, it is an expression of sorrow, pain, and frustration at the current state of affairs. In this respect it is something like a lament. It is like moan from the depths of our being—a painful awareness that all is not as it should be.

25. The following section draws heavily on my article "The Trinity and Lament."

26. This theological theme of Christ as Israel is integrated well into the systematic theological work of Thomas F. Torrance and the biblical exposition of N. T. Wright. In Romans 8, Paul's focus in on Christ, church and creation. I only mention humanity as a whole and Israel in particular because it helps us begin to imagine how Paul's teaching might begin to have wider implications than those he brings out in this context.

27. For contemporary theological reflections on this theme in the light of Darwinism and ecological concerns see Southgate, *The Groaning of Creation*.

28. Dunn, *Romans 1–8*, 417.

Second, it is simultaneously a groan of expectation for a better future. Paul describes it as "groaning as in the pains of childbirth"—notice how that image blends pain with an expectation of, and longing for, new life. He speaks of us "groaning eagerly as we wait eagerly for our adoption as sons" (cf. 2 Cor 5:2–4).

The idea of lament as an expression of grief and expectation is well put by Nicholas Wolterstorff in his comments on Matt 5:4, "Blessed are those who mourn, for they will be comforted." The mourners, he writes, "are aching visionaries."[29] Aching visionaries who simply refuse to accept the current state of affairs. Here we also glimpse something of the way in which the Spirit moves the people of God into action, even rage, against injustice and for love in his gathering up of the people of God into the responsive and creative action of lament. It is what John Swinton refers to as "raging with compassion."[30]

Third, it is intercession. Old Testament laments often serve as expressions of sorrow *and also* as prayers for salvation. In the same way, this deep primal moaning that Paul speaks of is also an expression of grief and simultaneously a prayer to God for new creation. It is at this point that Paul introduces the Holy Spirit. The Spirit himself groans. In sorrow for the present darkness? Yes. In hope for a better future? Yes. But most critically, in intercession for that new future. The Holy Spirit is praying for the church. The Holy Spirit knows the Father's will and purposes fully. We do not. So when the Spirit prays for us he is praying in perfect accord with God's cosmic purposes—his ultimate purposes for the whole created order.

I would like to reflect on the sufferings of Lamentations 1 pneumatologically. In the light of Romans 8, I suggest that the Spirit of God participates in Jerusalem's sorrows. The Spirit groans with all those who groan as they yearn for liberation.[31] Jerusalem groans at her humiliation and turns away her face from onlookers (1:8c), just as her priests groan at the cessation of temple festivals (1:4b) and her people groan as they search for food (1:11a). This groaning in Lam 1 looks back (mourning what is lost), looks around (expressing despair at the current situation), and looks forward (yearning for a reversal of the calamity). So also the Spirit, participating in the groaning of creation, groans as he looks back and looks around seeing a shattered world but he also groans like a woman in childbirth looking forward, bringing to birth a new creation (Isa 13:8; 21:3; 26:17–18; 66:7–8; Jer 4:31; 22:23; Hos 13:13; Mic 4:9–10). The Spirit's groaning, while a participation in creation's groaning, also transforms it. It is a hope-infused groaning which looks to the future with confidence. The Spirit can enable our groaning to become a participation in his groaning and in Christ's groaning.[32] That is to say, Spirit-transformed groaning is still an expression of pain at the current situation but it is not an expression of hopelessness. Indeed it is the foundation of the efficacy of our own intercessions

---

29. Wolterstorff, *Lament for a Son*, 85–86.

30. Swinton, *Raging with Compassion*. My thanks to Jason Goroncy for this observation on the active role of Spirit-inspired lament against injustice.

31. Liberation understood in various ways, e.g., liberation from oppression, injustice, or even deserved afflictions and sin.

32. We groan *because* we have the firstfruits of the Spirit (Rom 8:23, taking *echontes* as causal).

> We wait: but, because we wait upon God, our waiting is not in vain. We look out: but, because we have first been observed, we do not look out into the void. We speak: but, because there emerges in our speech that which cannot be uttered, we do not idly prattle. And so also we pray: but, because the Spirit makes intercession for us with groanings which—since his groanings must be songs of praise[33]—are beyond our competence, our prayers and groanings are distinct from that groaning which is weakness—and nothing else. The justification of prayer is not that we have attained some higher eminence on the ladder of prayer; for all ladders of prayer are erected within the sphere of the "No-God" of this world. The justification of our prayer and the reality of our communion with God are grounded upon the truth that Another, the Eternal, the Second Man from Heaven (1 Cor 15:47), stands before God pre-eminent in power and—in our place.[34]

So the Spirit is groaning with and for us as he seeks to bring us through to resurrection. The Spirit is praying creation into glory. And here is the amazing thing—the Spirit does not simply pray for us: he prays for us *through us*. He makes our own groanings a vehicle for his groanings.[35] And that is good because so often we do not know what we should pray for or how we should pray for it. But the Spirit does and he helps us in our weakness. This opens up new ways of appreciating the significance and possibilities of lament in general and Lamentations in particular Christian worship. The prayerful use of this ancient text can become a vehicle for the Spirit of God to groan with us and with creation.[36]

## LAMENTATIONS AND THE NARRATIVE DIMENSION OF CHRISTIAN WORSHIP

Traditional Christian worship has always had a narrative shape to it. The Christian Year itself was woven around the story of Jesus so that year by year the faithful would worship their way through the plot and hopefully develop a narrative shape and roundedness to their spirituality. It was in this story-shaped liturgical world that Lamentations found a home and made its contribution. As we have seen there is a good theo-logic behind this traditional use.

Now it is easy to idealize such modes of worship and to forget how they can degenerate into an empty ritual (a danger Israel's prophets were alert to: cf. Isa 1:11–17) or a form of musical entertainment.[37] Nevertheless, the context from which I write is very dif-

---

33. I would wish to add that such "praise" must not be understood to exclude lament.

34. Barth, *Romans*, 317.

35. New Testament scholars disagree about whether the Spirit's groanings are "groans not formulated in words" (so, e.g., Dunn, *Romans 1–8*, 478) or glossolalia (so Fee, *God's Empowering Presence*, 580–85). I see no reason why the Spirit's activity of "groaning" might not manifest in various forms, including glossolalia but not restricted to it (see Parry, *Lamentations*, 190–91, 205–6). This opens up the possibility to develop an unusual approach to speaking in tongues (see Macchia, "Sighs too Deep")

36. Heath Thomas suggests, in the light of my reading of Rom 8, that perhaps one way in which the Spirit leads the church into all truth (Jn 16:13)—not simply assent to rational truths, but the truth of the reality of God-in-Christ—is through such prayer, which leads one more deeply into the realm of Jesus' victory now/not yet.

37. Historically the musical settings for Lamentations degenerated in some places into a form of entertainment rather than a means of spiritual formation. Catherine Cessac writes, "During the reign of Louis

ferent and the dangers that many churches I know face are not this danger. I belong to an evangelical, charismatic, Free Church strand of the Christian tradition. In such contexts the last forty years have witnessed major changes in the way in which we worship, some of which are good and some of which are bad. One of the bad changes has been the rapid and widespread move towards worship-as-singing-one-song-after-another-without-much-thought-given-to-the-theological-shape-of-the-whole. A new ministry of worship leader has arisen in place of the priest or pastor leading the congregational worship. Now, in my view, this is not, in and of itself, a problem. The problem is rather that these worship leaders are rarely trained in leading worship in a theologically informed way. Their ability is in playing an instrument (normally a guitar) and singing, and worship is often understood too narrowly as an immanent encounter with God mediated through song. So the focus becomes one of encountering-God-now-as-I-sing with little sense of past or future. Where we have come from and were we are going are secondary—feeling God's presence now is the goal.

One result of this is that worship in such settings is usually detached from the rhythms of the traditional Christian Year. Last week is forgotten and next week is not on the horizon—all that counts is the present moment. But this means that you can take any worship encounter and swap it for any other in the year without significant loss because each becomes a stand-alone event. A consequence of that is that it is easy to lose any sense of the grand narrative of Scripture within which the community lives and moves and has its being. This narrative, which we should inhabit in our worship, tends to be pushed to the margins. A second result of the changes in contemporary evangelical worship culture is that the terrain covered in liturgically structured worship—confession of sin, adoration, intercession, supplication, listening to the word, receiving the Eucharist, etc.—is greatly reduced. One will often find only praise, thanksgiving, perhaps space for prophetic words, and a sermon. The Eucharist is too often missing, intercession is very often absent, confession is exceptionally rare, and lament is almost non-existent. Any sense of a shape or directionality to worship is often minimalist at best. In such a context it is hard to find a place for the book of Lamentations because, as we have seen, it really needs a way of being narratively located (both within a liturgical narrative and a biblical-theological narrative). So within my own tradition there is a great need to recover the narrative shape both of individual worship gatherings and of "seasons" of gatherings. Apart from that Lamentations, along with the practice of lament more generally, will struggle to find a foothold.

---

XIV, great crowds gathered for the *Tenebrae* lessons, which were celebrated in the capital's convents and churches. It is true that the lessons of Lambert, Charpentier, Couperin and Lalande offer a much more attractive style of music than the more generally practiced plainsong. The convent services were therefore gradually transformed into veritable society concerts. In his *Comparaison de la Musique française et italienne* published in 1705, Le Cerf de La Viéville could not hide his offence: 'They hire actresses who, behind the curtain that they lift up from time to time to smile at their friends in the audience, sing a lesson on Good Friday or a solo motet on Easter Sunday. One could hear them at a convent, where it was remarked: to their honour, the price you would have paid at the Opera is what you pay for the pew in the church.'" http://www.goldbergweb.com/en/magazine/essays/2004/02/20216_print.php.

## GREAT IS THY FAITHFULNESS?

But there are a few bricks of hope within this kind of Christianity from which it might be possible to build some new homes for Lamentations, albeit modest ones. For even within these Christian traditions fragments of the Christian Year still hold their ground against the assaults of "spontaneity." Those fragments are the fundamental, gospel-shaped "moments" of Christmas, Good Friday, and Easter Sunday. And, as we have seen, it is Passion Week that has been the natural home for Lamentations within the Christian tradition. The fact that this liturgical space has not yet been abandoned by those of us who have forsaken so much else within the liturgical history of Christianity is a basis for hope. Of course, more traditional Christians will find things that much less awkward in attempts to recover a use of Lamentations.

The discussion above proposing that we recover the traditional link between Passion Week and Lamentations suggests a pre-planned use of the text within worship. Now some will have a natural concern about this. The problem is that the chances are that on any particular Good Friday service in which worshippers were invited to participate in some way in the laments of the book many, indeed most of those present, may very well not feel like lamenting. The text will simply not reflect where many people are at—indeed, at the level of detail, it will not reflect where any of the worshippers are at. Within the worship culture of many modern evangelical churches this is enough to preclude its use. After all, who wants to have disengaged congregants speaking words that they do not mean? Is such worship not inauthentic at best?

What are we to say about this concern? Well, one is tempted to reply that this problem is simply the reverse of the "problem" that one finds week after week in such churches already. Modern evangelical worship is uncompromisingly happy and those present engage weekly in declaring how thankful and joyful they feel about God. If the concern is not to have people sing songs that do not reflect where they are at then what are we to say about the culture of unremitting joy? Is this inauthentic? It certainly can be. The songs that Christians sing, however, are not always used in a declarative mode (I am currently rejoicing in God) but are often appropriated in aspirational mode (I desire to rejoice in God). The singing of the song can cultivate Christian desires and aspirations. In a very similar way one can use laments as part of a process of aspirational spiritual formation even if one is not currently sad.

Now the most obvious objection to this proposal is that while we might understandably aspire to rejoice in the Lord who on earth would want to encourage people to lament? Is an aspiration to misery a Christian aspiration? To deal with this objection I will need to outline some of the reason why we do need to learn to engage with lament literature in worship.

### A TIME TO WEEP?

Is there "a time to weep" (cf. Rom 12:15) in Christian worship or have we moved into an era of unrelenting rejoicing since the resurrection? I have dealt with the issue of the general place of lament in Christian worship at length elsewhere,[38] but I would like to speak about the role that Lamentations in particular can play in spiritual formation, if used well within public worship. In opening that discussion it will be helpful to consider Stanley Hauerwas' discussion on the importance of engaging in Christian practices as a way of learning the habits essential to become a skilled practitioner in a trade. Hauerwas considers the way in which one learns to become as master bricklayer or a master stonemason.[39] To become such one must learn from the acquired wisdom of those who have practiced the trade before by inhabiting the history and traditions of the trade and by being apprenticed to a master. Part of this learning is learning the language of the trade and one must practice, practice, practice, and practice again the basic skills until they become second nature. Only then is one able to innovate with any skill. This is not cerebral learning but an engaged *learning by doing*. Now Hauerwas insists that a life of Christian virtue is acquired in the same way. Not by the impartation of information but by a participation of the prayerful and worshipful life of a Christian community. We learn to pray, "Our Father, in heaven," we partake in the Eucharist, we hear the Scriptures, and we intercede for others. We are inducted into the language of the Christian life through engaging in the prayers of the community even before we understand exactly what they mean and we practice, practice, practice, and practice again until the language and habits are part of the warp and weft of who we are. Engaging in the stories of the community in communal worship and Christian practice shapes us into a certain kind of people—people of Christian character. Clearly on this understanding of being formed into a Christian disciple there is an important place for engaging communally in practices that we might not fully understand and which might not express how we currently feel. But the ongoing participation in such practices is essential for rounded spiritual formation. So liturgical engagement with Lamentations can, in principle, play a role in the training of Christian emotions—not simply expressing how we currently feel but training us to see and to feel in certain kinds of ways.

Take Lamentations 1 and 2. The poetry presents the wretched figure of Lady Zion in her broken state—beaten, raped, and deprived of her beloved children. The narrator presents her tragic plight to the audience and we also hear her own impassioned voice. The poetry is unrelenting and refuses to allow the audience to glance away for relief but forces them to keep looking. The constant focus on the theme of Zion's lack of a comforter serves to invite the readers themselves to take on such a role—to weep with those who weep. To inhabit this poetry is to learn to become sensitized to pain, to pay attention to the suffering of others, to eschew the option to walk by on the other side. And as we proceed into chapter 2 we see that the narrator himself moves from his sympathetic but somewhat distant engagement with Zion's grief to a deep, gut wrenching sorrow. Readers are invited to make the same journey. To engage such literature in worship can play a role in the emotional formation of a community of disciples.

---

38. See Parry, *Lamentations*, 206–21.

39. See Hauerwas, "How We Lay Bricks"; and Hauerwas, "Carving Stone." See also Smith, *Desiring the Kingdom*.

What public use of Lamentations and other laments will also do is to provide a language of lament. If the only prayer language into which believers are inducted through communal worship is that of thanksgiving, praise, and adoration then we are depriving believers of a language for dealing with the dark periods of life. We are also communicating the message that to speak to God with words of complaint and lament is somehow inappropriate, irreverent, and unfaithful (in spite of the fact that Jesus himself took the words of a complaint Psalm upon his lips while on the cross). In this way we are in danger of failing to train disciples to walk with God through the valley of the shadow of death. It is important that the Christian community acknowledges and affirms the legitimacy of articulating honestly both the awkward and the uncomfortable—the fact that "things are not as they should be." Learning how to speak to and of God in such situations is important and it can only be done through inhabiting the narratives and worship practices reflected in the biblical story and in the Jewish and Christian traditions.

Beyond the potential for fruitful use of Lamentations at Easter through a retrieval of aspects of the Tenebrae tradition, I would also suggest that this very habit-forming practice will enable the more spontaneous use of the text as a communal response to actual crises within the life of the community—the local community or a wider community. So, for instance, a community that has indwelled a book like Lamentations in habit-forming ways can make use of the text in a spontaneous and heartfelt manner in response to an event such as 9/11—an event that other believers might find themselves conflicted to know how to respond to.

## CHRISTIAN USE OF LAMENTATIONS IN WORSHIP: A FEW IDEAS

The link between the death and burial of Christ and the "death" and "burial" of Judah in Lamentations will be the theological foundation upon which specifically Christian usage can creatively and innovatively build, but that building might be done in various ways. One way is that the connection between Christ and Jerusalem draws the attention of Christians to the very earthy, social, and political aspects of Christ's death. It is easy for believers to see the death of Jesus is purely "spiritual" terms and not to perceive its socio-political dimensions. But even a moment's thought would remind us that Jesus was "crucified under Pontius Pilate"; that he died the death of a political enemy of the Rome; that he was an innocent victim of lethal imperial violence—publically humiliated and executed. His fate embodied Jerusalem's fate which also was not simply "spiritual" but actually a complete and utter social and political collapse along with all the human suffering that accompanies such things.[40]

Lamentations thrusts such suffering in our face and helps us see the cross afresh. And by opening our eyes to the way in which the cross engages real embodied human suffering it opens up new ways of seeing the social and political suffering of various communities today. For instance, when considering the situation of the persecuted church in various places today. If we view certain current events through binoculars that contain the lenses of both Lamentations and Golgotha then we may be equipped to see those

---

40. On reading Lamentations politically, see Parry, "Lamentations and the Poetic Politics of Prayer."

events in fresh ways and to appreciate where God-in-Christ stands in relation to them and, further, how we should stand in relation to them. This is not about the application of simple hermeneutical rules whose outcome is easy to predict but about the learning of new ways of understanding, emotionally perceiving, and responding to the world.

There are many ways in which the text of Lamentations might find a space within worship. Most obviously in set readings, in sermons, or in music. The Tenebrae tradition offers a model for the use of set readings. I am not suggesting that communities take it off the peg, but I do think that there is scope for a range of various modified versions of Tenebrae. My own feeling is that some explanatory comments would be helpful to enable worshippers understand how the texts are being used. Similarly with music. There is a rich treasure trove of Christian music based on Lamentations but most of it is very old and only able to be performed by a trained choir. It still has a place but there is a need for new songs that reflect the neglected text of Lamentations. One can also envisage intercessory prayers that weave texts from Lamentations with prayers for contemporary events. One can even imagine a creative use of Lamentations in the celebration of the Eucharist once the link between the cross and the exile is appreciated. This would need to be done with skill but there is no reason why it could not be done in such a way as to refresh the theological imagination and open us up in new ways to God and his world.

Lamentations can be read from inside-out as worshippers are asked to identify with Zion in her grief. It can also read from outside-in as worshippers are asked to identify with the narrator observing Zion, or those on the road passing by, or even as the oppressing nations who cause the pain. As such it has the potential to teach us to express our pain before God, to call us to comfort others (Rom 12:15; 2 Cor 1), or as a sharp exposé of our communal sin by causing affliction to others, bringing conviction of sin and offering a call to confession and repentance. Using this book well in worship is not about becoming self-obsessed, miserable people but about becoming people who can respond to the pain of others in more appropriate ways (an outward-looking and missional practice if ever there was one) and who can respond to our own pain (either individual or communal) more honestly and faithfully.

## BIBLIOGRAPHY

Barth, Karl. *The Epistle to the Romans*. Translated by Edwin C. Hoskyns. London: Oxford University Press, 1933.
Cohn-Sherbok, Dan. *The Crucified Jew: 20 centuries of Christian Anti-Semitism*. Grand Rapids: Eerdmans, 1992.
Dobbs-Allsopp, F. W. *Weep, O Daughter of Zion: A Study of the City-Lament Genre in the Hebrew Bible*. Rome: Pontifical Biblical Institute Press, 1993.
Dunn, James D. G. *Romans 1–8*. Word Biblical Commentary 38A. Dallas: Word, 1988.
Eissfeldt, Otto. *The Old Testament: An Introduction*. Translated by Peter R. Ackroyd. New York: Harper & Row, 1965.
Fee, Gordon. *God's Empowering Presence: The Holy Spirit in the Letters of Paul*. Peabody, MA: Hendrickson, 1994.
Gunkel, Hermann. "Klagelieder Jeremiae." In *Die Religion in Geschichte und Gegenwart*, 2nd ed., 1049–52. Tübingen: Mohr Siebek, 1929.
Hauerwas, Stanley. "Carving Stone or Learning to Speak Christian." In *Living Out Loud: Conversations about Virtue, Ethics, and Evangelicalism*, edited by Luke Bretherton and Russ Rook, 60–79. Milton Keynes, UK: Paternoster, 2010.
———. "How We Lay Bricks and Make Disciples." In *Living Out Loud: Conversations About Virtue, Ethics, and Evangelicalism*, edited by Luke Bretherton and Russ Rook, 39–59. Milton Keynes, UK: Paternoster, 2010.
Jahnow, Hedwig. *Das hebräische Leichenlied im Rahmen der Völkerdichtung*. BZAW 36. Giessen: Töpelmann, 1923.
Keith, Graham. *Hated Without a Cause? A Survey of Anti-Semitism*. Carlisle, UK: Paternoster, 1997.
Kramer, Samuel N. *Lamentation over the Destruction of Ur*. Assyriological Studies 12. Chicago: University of Chicago Press, 1940.
Kinzer, Mark. *Postmissionary Messianic Judaism: Redefining Christian Engagement with the Jewish People*. Grand Rapids: Brazos, 2005.
Linafelt, Todd. *Surviving Lamentations: Catastrophe, Lament, and Protest in the Afterlife of a Biblical Book*. Chicago: University of Chicago Press, 2000.
Macchia, Frank. "Sighs Too Deep for Words: Toward a Theology of Glossolalia." *Journal of Pentecostal Theology* 1 (1992) 47–73.
Michalowski, Piotr. *The Lamentation over the Destruction of Sumer and Ur*. Winnona Lake, IN: Eisenbrauns, 1989.
Middlemas, Jill. *The Troubles of Templeless Judah*. Oxford Theological Monographs. Oxford: Oxford University Press, 2005.
Parris, David Paul. *Reception Theory and Biblical Hermeneutics*. Princeton Theological Monograph Series 107. Eugene, OR: Pickwick, 2009.
Parry, Robin A. *Lamentations*. Two Horizons. Grand Rapids: Eerdmans, 2010.
———. "Lamentations and the Poetic Politics of Prayer." *Tyndale Bulletin* 62 (2011) 65–88.
———. "The Trinity and Lament." In *In Praise of Worship: An Exploration of Text and Practice*, edited by David J. Cohen and Michael Parsons, 143–61. Eugene, OR: Pickwick, 2010.
Provan, Iain. "Reading Texts against a Historical Background: The Case of Lamentations." *Scandinavian Journal of the Old Testament* 1 (1990) 130–43.
Re'emi, S. Paul. "The Theology of Hope: A Commentary on the Book of Lamentations." In *God's People in Crisis*, by R. Martin-Achard and S. Paul Re'emi, 73–134. Grand Rapids: Eerdmans, 1984.
Renkema, Johan. *Lamentations*. HCOT. Leuven: Peeters, 1998.
Ricoeur, Paul. *Time and Narrative*. Vol. 1. Translated by Kathleen Blamey and David Pellauer. Chicago: Chicago University Press, 1984.
Rudolph, David J. "Messianic Jews and Christian Theology." *Pro Ecclesia* 14 (2005) 58–84.
Smith, James K. A. *Desiring the Kingdom: Worship Worldview and Cultural Formation*. Cultural Liturgies 1. Grand Rapids: Baker, 2009.
Soulen, R. Kendall. *The God of Israel and Christian Theology*. Minneapolis: Fortress, 1996.
Southgate, Christopher. *The Groaning of Creation: God, Evolution and the Problem of Evil*. Louisville: Westminster John Knox, 2008.

Swinton, John. *Raging with Compassion: Pastoral Responses to the Problem of Evil.* Grand Rapids: Eerdmans, 2007.
Thomas, Heath. *"Until He Looks Down and Sees": The Message and Meaning of the Book of Lamentations.* Grove Biblical Series 53. Cambridge, UK: Grove, 2009.
Westermann, Claus. *Lamentations: Issues and Interpretation.* Translated by Charles Muenchow. Minneapolis: Fortress, 1994.
Wolterstorff, Nicholas. *Lament for a Son.* Grand Rapids: Eerdmans, 1987.

# 4

## Confession and Complaint
### Christian Pastoral Reflections on Lamentations

IAN STACKHOUSE

### CONFESSION

GIVEN THE SPEED OF change in the last few decades, some things have disappeared from our culture leaving barely a trace. So pervasive has the technological revolution been that certain things that we grew up with, took for granted, have become cultural artifacts. For instance, at the risk of sounding banal, whatever became of muddy soccer pitches? Without getting too nostalgic about these things, in my day mud was part of the game and could actually determine a score line. These days, however, footballers enjoy almost pristine conditions—as do spectators.

About the same time as the disappearance of muddy soccer pitches, psychologist Karl Menninger pointed out a much more important cultural loss, but one that in a strange kind of way was the spiritual equivalent of sanitized sporting arenas. Caught as he was at the intersection of psychology and theology, and noting the rise of a therapeutic culture, he raised a question that is very much to the fore of my initial reflections here on the book of Lamentations: "Whatever became of sin?"[1]

What indeed? Sin has fallen upon hard times. It has been trivialized. Whereas our Christian forebears spoke quite freely of the deceitfulness of the human heart, these days sin might mean nothing more than an indulgence in chocolate sin cake. Amidst the plethora of self-help books that are on the market, one would be hard-pressed to find anything equivalent to Augustine's *Confessions*. Likewise, pastoral appointments these days mostly end up as *counseling* rather than *confessing*.[2] As Eugene Peterson demurs, in his own pastoral reflections on the *Megillot*: "Instead of attributing the suffering to the 'sins of the fathers,' it has assigned them to the neuroses of the mothers, and has put a

---

1. Menninger, *Whatever Became of Sin?*
2. See Kirkpatrick, *Psychological Seduction* for a restatement of the classical doctrine of sin over against the language of the therapeutic.

whole generation of pastors to work in eliminating suffering from the soul."[3] "Pastors can be so reluctant to use the word 'sin,'" notes Kathleen Norris, "that in church we end up confessing nothing except our highly developed capacity for denial."[4] Even the Anglican liturgy, replete with Cranmer's penitentiary language, attenuates in many contemporary services to something far more palatable.

Of course, anyone who has read the tortuous religious upbringing of Stephen Dedalus in *A Portrait of the Artist as a Young Man* will regard such a situation as progress: a welcome reprieve from the maudlin and often hypocritical moralizing that has characterized many periods of the church's history. In fact, the relativization of the language of sin and repentance is now regarded by many Christians as critical if the church is to seriously engage in mission in the postmodern context. It is deemed by some as the one sticking point for a culture that is otherwise wide open to things spiritual. Yet, as G. K. Chesterton pointed out, it is the one Christian doctrine that does not need proving, since empirical evidence of it is everywhere.[5] To ignore or to sideline the doctrine of sin, much as it is an attractive proposition, is to seriously misread the true state of our humanity, as well as to distort the true contours of the gospel, which, of course, assumes sin everywhere—*felix culpa*. Indeed, as far as pastor-theologian P. T. Forsyth was concerned, whose reflections I shall draw upon throughout this chapter, the lack of apostolic vigor in his own day was attributable, he argued, to the loss of this sin/grace dialectic: "We have churches of the nicest, kindest people," he noted, but "who have nothing apostolic or missionary, who never knew the soul's despair or its breathless gratitude."[6] What he means is this: our refusal to face up to the very real depravity, if not total depravity, of the human heart, means that we are robbed of the astonishment that comes with the announcement of grace. Instead, we end up with civic religion: positive, happy, and affirming, but in no way commensurate with the grand epics that play themselves out in the lives of even the most ordinary people. Without the injection of some kind of existential angst into the worship of our churches we are left with a "suburban piety," as Forsyth terms it, that fails to reach the hearty rebel in each one of us.

For this reason, therefore, I welcome the attempts in this book to retrieve Lamentations for the Christian church, whether by lection, worship, or pastoral resource. I welcome it not because there is any virtue in melancholy *per se*, less so any merit in self-flagellation. This is not what I mean. I too am on a spiritual journey to be rid of many of those self-destructive, self-loathing tendencies at the extreme end of our holiness tradition. (What are psalms of lament, to which Lamentations bears some comparisons, but testament to the belief that not everything that is wrong in our lives is attributable to sin?)[7] Nevertheless, without some measure of godly sorrow, without some deep lament over the condition of our soul, even our nationhood, such as we find in Lamentations, it is likely that the gospel in our own day will collapse into nothing more than Christian

3. Peterson, *Five Smooth Stones for Pastoral Work*, 138.
4. Norris, *Amazing Grace*, 165.
5. Chesterton, *Orthodoxy*, 10.
6. Forsyth, *Positive Preaching and the Modern Mind*, 244.
7. Psalm 44:17: "All this happened though we had not forgotten you or been false to your covenant."

nominality. In other words, before we can understand the good news, we must understand the bad news; those who celebrate with laughter must first experience the mourning of tears over sin; the road to *Paradisio*, as Dante was at pains to instruct us, is by way of the *Inferno*.

How this is achieved in the text—in terms of literary theory, redaction criticism, and historical context—is for others in this collection of essays to descry. But given that form and text are not irrelevant to the pastoral impact of the book, as we shall see later on, I want to argue first of all that the structure of Lamentations as a whole seems to support what we are proposing here. The hope that emerges in chapter 3, the quotidian mercy and compassion of God which, for various reasons, may be understood as the organizing centre of the book, can only emerge as the gracious surprise that it is, and the theme of so much Christian piety, *precisely because* it comes off the back of two and a half chapters of unmitigated despair. And in order for repentance to fully take root and to be the vital and necessary prelude to the good news, we will want to feel the full force of those chapters, as well as those that follow, lest grace ends up simply as a synonym for the niceness of God.[8] As William Kirk Kirkpatrick puts it in his critique of modern psychology and its almost uncritical appropriation by the church—what Philip Rieff calls "the triumph of the therapeutic"[9]—"Christianity wants you to feel good about yourself, but not until there is something to feel good about. It would like to get us on the road to recovery before it congratulates us on our good health."[10]

In short, grace can only be grace if it is set against the backcloth of judgment. A congregation can only fully celebrate the "new every morning" covenant faithfulness of God (3:22–23) and the dazzling revelation of a God who does not gleefully execute his punishment (3:32–33), if it has first remembered its own sense of plight; otherwise *ḥesed* love ends up as a dead metaphor, nothing more than a nice sentiment, and our gospel nothing more than a nice feeling of love. In words that mirror the structure of these first few chapters in Lamentations, Forsyth puts it this way: "If we spoke less about God's love and more about His holiness, more about his judgement, we should say much more when we did speak of His love."[11] Forsyth would characterize this love as "holy love": that special conjunction of judgment and mercy that we see reflected in chapter 3 of Lamentations: grace thrashed out on the anvil of sin and repentance.[12]

In my opinion, the sooner that this dialectic is re-appropriated by the Christian church the better, because it is for want of that tragic element that our worship has become bland. In striking similarity to the prophets of Jeremiah's day, whose cheery "Peace,

---

8. On the theme of the sin of Jerusalem and the grace of forgiveness see that chapter in this volume by Paul House, "Outrageous Demonstrations of Grace." On the early Christian reading of Lamentations that used the book for penitence and spiritual formation see the essay in this volume by Heath Thomas, "Lamentations in the Patristic Period."

9. Rieff, *The Triumph of the Therapeutic*.

10. Kirkpatrick, *Psychological Seduction*, 38.

11. Forsyth, *The Cruciality of the Cross*, 39.

12. For an exploration of the theme of holy love in the writings of P. T. Forsyth see McCurdy, *Attributes and Atonement*.

peace, when there is no peace" messages are alluded to in 2:13–14,[13] modern worship similarly "heals the wounds of my people lightly," mainly because it has become queasy about suffering and presumptuous about grace. If the people of Jeremiah's day were guilty of a presumption about the temple's inviolability,[14] there are traces of a similar false security in the way we talk about unconditional grace. Indeed, so fearful are we of judgment and of the accompanying language of judgment that large swathes of contemporary Christianity are practically Marcionite, as far as I can tell. The pitting of the God of the Old Testament against the God of the New, as a contest between a God of wrath and a God of mercy, is now commonplace, even among evangelicals, with the result that our understanding of grace is meaningless. Without the context of judgment, grace ends up as a saccharine word; without repentance it ends up as nothing more than "cheap grace," as Bonhoeffer so memorably described it.[15]

Speaking from the vantage point of the pastorate, from where, I believe, a lot more theology should be written, what a Christian retrieval of Lamentations achieves is an essential confessional for the grace notes. Announce the word of grace too early; avoid, for example, the prayers of examen, like those we see in 3:40–42; abandon altogether words like sin, repentance, and forgiveness, and, ironically, we do people a disservice. We strip them of their human freedom and responsibility, patronizing them in the process with a potpourri of self-help techniques and new age positivism. Have the courage, on the other hand, to embrace the pain of repentance and there is a chance we will come out the other side as more human. Lamentations reminds us that the reason the Bible takes sin seriously is because it takes people seriously. The point at which the God of Israel is most vehement with Israel over her disobedience is the point at which the Bible most dignifies us. As C. S. Lewis put it, "It appears, from all the records, that though He has often rebuked us and condemned us, He has never regarded us with contempt. He has paid us the intolerable compliment of loving us, in the deepest, most tragic, most inexorable sense."[16]

Without wanting to enter into the current debate about penal substitution and the antipathy in present day evangelicalism towards notions of wrath and propitiation, which is a complex debate to say the least, my sense is that there is a lot to prevent the emergence of this primitive kind of spirituality. After all, wrath seems so arbitrary, so brutal. To take the Marcionite thing one step further, it could well be that the general neglect of the Old Testament, Lamentations in particular, among Bible believing Christians is attributable to precisely this factor: an aversion to the dark side of biblical revelation. As Kathleen Norris points out with reference to the Presbyterian tradition she reconnected with after many years away: our prayers of confession "seem less prayer than a memo from one professional to another. At such times I picture God as a wily writing teacher who leans

---

13. Jeremiah 6:14; 8:11; 14:13–22; 23:9–40.

14. See Jeremiah's temple sermon in Jer 7:1–29 for an example of prophetic vehemence against the temple ideology.

15. Bonhoeffer, *The Cost of Discipleship*, 44–45.

16. Lewis, *The Problem of Pain*, 29 and quoted in Peterson, *Five Smooth Stones for Pastoral Work*, 140–41.

across the table and says, not at all gently, 'Could you possibly be troubled to say what you mean?'" To which question Norris replies: "It would be refreshing to answer, simply, 'I have sinned.'"[17]

Again, it is important to stress that the drive behind the recovery of this kind of churchy language is not pathological cruelty, but rather theological intent. Sin is such an integral part of the revelation as it has been given to us, that take this away, and we have no gospel.[18] And it occurred to me a number of years ago that one of the places we might begin to address this situation is in our Easter celebration. Notwithstanding Kathleen O'Connor's point that we need to be careful not to restrict Lamentations to funerals and services on Holy Thursday and Good Friday,[19] even so, I am most intrigued by Robin Parry's engagement with the ancient service of Tenebrae: Gathering Darkness.

I came across Tenebrae myself a number of years ago via a Baptist colleague who had been using it for the past ten years as a way of preparing his congregation for the Easter celebration. I am not aware that he adopted the Lamentations readings alongside the Psalms in the way that Cameron-Mowat and Parry describe;[20] nor did we when we ourselves performed a Tenebrae service one Maundy Thursday. All ten readings, in fact, were taken from the Gospels (with the final reading undertaken in almost total darkness, as the name of the service suggests). Nevertheless, the intention was the same: namely, to introduce a somber element right at the beginning of the Easter weekend, so that the surprise of Easter morning when it came truly was a surprise, and not an inevitability.

From the background I come from, which might best be described for our purposes here as radical iconoclasm, such a deliberate scheduling of the Easter weekend would have been frowned upon as a piece of spiritual chicanery: a sinister manipulation of the congregation, in order to induce an Easter experience. And for a long time I would have concurred with this. After all, every Sunday is Easter Sunday isn't it? Indeed, some charismatic churches I knew made something of a virtue of their non-observance. But these days I can only see benefits from adopting a more liturgical approach. At a time when there is every danger that contemporary Christianity will end up flat, clichéd, and predictable it is worth taking the risk with some spiritual dramaturgy, if only to make the point, as Bonhoeffer did with his congregation of German expatriates in Barcelona on Easter Sunday 1928, that there is nothing inevitable about Easter, just as there is nothing natural about death. "Good Friday is not, like winter, a transitional stage. No, it really is the end, the end of guilty humankind and the final judgment humankind pronounces on itself."[21] Tenebrae achieves this, all the more so when it is combined with the readings from Lamentations, by prefacing the Easter light with utter darkness.

---

17. Norris, *Amazing Grace*, 165.

18. See Calvin's point that sin leads towards forgiveness in Lamentations in Pete Wilcox's contribution in this volume, "John Calvin's Interpretation of Lamentations."

19. O'Connor, *Lamentations and the Tears of the World*, 134–35.

20. See Cameron-Mowat, "Lamentations and Christian Worship" and Parry, "Wrestling with Lamentations in Christian Worship" in this volume

21. Bonhoeffer, *Meditations on the Cross*, 71.

## COMPLAINT

It is at this point, however, that we need to recognize another strand in Lamentations. Lest we end up making a simple equation of sin and suffering—as many Christian traditions are prone to do, with all the disastrous pastoral ramifications that kind of simple causality creates—we need to recognize that alongside this necessary theodic element in Lamentations is a critical anti-theodic element: a protest, if you will, against the scale of the suffering inflicted by God.[22] As we move from chapter 1 to chapter 2, we sense that the narrator forgets Zion's guilt and turns instead on the divine aggressor, accusing God of actions that are tantamount to abuse and betrayal. Why else does he urge Daughter Zion to pour out her tears in the face of God, (2:19), if not to force YHWH to pay attention, to wake up and recognize that even he has gone too far—that she is more sinned against than sinning?

I am aware, of course, that such a reading of Lamentations flies in the face of a good deal of conservative scholarship, which sees the matter clearly in terms of sin and judgment. [Although, it ought to be clear by now that I myself have been keen to stress this strand of theology and spirituality within Lamentations, however unpalatable this might be.][23] But for one who has chosen to work out his theology from below, so to speak, from the context of the ecclesia rather than the academy, it seems entirely possible to me—source critical questions aside—that within the tears of confession one may also discern an equally real, dissonant cry of *protest* at the same time. We are, after all, a mystery, even to ourselves: our prayers fragmentary at best. It may be difficult for scholastic theology to hold together seemingly contradictory voices, but pastoral theology has no such problem. Confession spills into complaint, just as complaint may end up as confession. And what I would like to celebrate in the remainder of the chapter is the way Lamentations permits this voice of complaint alongside the more overtly pious voice of contrition.

It is not entirely clear, of course, how we might encourage this voice of protest, for just as it has proved unusual for me as a pastor to have someone come wanting to blurt out their confession, so it has been unusual for someone to come and bring their complaint or lament before God. The complaint is there, to be sure. My own experience of this is that there is a great deal of suppressed anger towards God under the surface of most congregations, but given the predilection towards a more quietist response and, furthermore, the association of real piety with a sense of spiritual resignation, then it is no surprise that such anger or complaint as there is barely makes the surface.

Why this should be the case is cause for some enquiry. My own sense is that it derives from a combination of historic pietism, with its emphasis on brokenness and submission, coupled to a suburban politeness that just cannot bring itself to admit feelings beyond those that can be controlled. But what Lamentations offers us, just as the Psalms offer us, is language to give voice to this complaint. Just as Lamentations counters the widespread presumption in our day—the trivialization of sin and the familiarity with

---

22. See Braiterman, "Lamentations in Modern Jewish Thought" and Thomas, "Holy Scripture and Hermeneutics" in this volume.

23. For an example of this see Longman, *Jeremiah/Lamentations*.

grace that we noted earlier—so too Lamentations works in another, to some degree opposite direction, in the way it counters our resignation: more specifically, the way we equate our piety not with presumption this time but with *passivity*. As Lytta Basset puts it: "To rebel against God does not seem at first glance to be a life choice. Religious education has a lot to do with this, given its propensity to confuse submission to authorities and submission to God. The biblical God, however, is always in search of a human face, be it smiling or frowning in anger."[24]

Clearly, this protest language is not the same as we find in Job. There is too much deserved punishment, too much Deuteronomistic theology in Lamentations for it to be that kind of thing. In Lamentations the people are most definitely guilty, whereas Job, despite the view of his so-called comforters, is innocent. But in so far as the punishment for guilt seems to have gone too far in Lamentations, then the prayers of complaint offer us an anti-theodicy:[25] language not only to confess but *also* to protest: language that helps us to do what so often we feel timid to do, which is to get straight into the face of God.[26] As F. W. Dobbs-Allsopp puts it: "In antiquity, the cultural assumption that sin triggers divine anger and punishment was matched by an equally strong assumption that repentance should bring about divine compassion and forgiveness . . . Thus, it is in the poet's interest to point out, as compellingly as possible, God's lack of care, in this case as manifested in the excessive and dire nature of God's human subject's suffering, as a means of winning the deity's attention."[27] Contrary to how some might view this, such praying is not impious or irreverent; nor must it be construed as presumptuous. Rather, it is a posture and a mood that lies right at the heart of biblical spirituality. Israel, after all, means one who has struggled with God.

Once again, it is P. T. Forsyth who serves as an ally to us in this matter. Averse as he was to what he saw as an unhealthy quietism in pietistic circles, in *The Soul of Prayer* he offers the image of *wrestling*, rather than acquiescence, as the dominant movement of prayer: "Does Christ not set more value upon importunity than upon submission?" he asks.[28] In much the same way as Lamentations surreptitiously warns us against a spirituality of victimization, Forsyth warns against "a pietist fatalism which thins the spiritual life, saps the vigour of character, makes humility mere acquiescence, and piety only feminine, by banishing the will from prayer as much as the thought has been banished from it." He goes on: "the popularity of much acquiescence is not because it is holier, but because it is easier. And an easy gospel is the consumption that attacks Christianity."[29] Prayer, Forsyth urges us, is protest.

---

24. Bassett, *Holy Anger: Jacob, Job, Jesus*, 80–81.

25. Dobbs-Allsopp, *Lamentations*, 27–33.

26. For an interesting comparison between Brueggemann and Kübler-Ross on the stages of grief and the unique place of petition within biblical lament as opposed to resignation within Kübler-Ross's model, see Capps, "Nervous Laughter," 71–72.

27. Dobbs-Allsopp, *Lamentations*, 61.

28. Forsyth, *The Soul of Prayer*, 101

29. Ibid., 107. Contemporary readers of Lamentations might be none too pleased with the synonymy of femininity and passivity in this quote from Forsyth. As Heath Thomas points out in his chapter on feminist

The protest element in Lamentations, it must be said, is not occasional but sustained: "Is there any suffering like my suffering, that was inflicted on me?" (1:12); "Look, O Lord, and consider: / Whom have you ever treated like this? / Should women eat their offspring, / the children they have cared for?" (2:20); "See Yahweh and observe/who it is that you have dealt with severely here?" (3:20). "Why do you continually forget us / [and] forsake us for so many days?" (5:20).

These complaints are, to use a title of one of Stanley Hauerwas' books, *Prayers Plainly Spoken*, and they are meant to elicit a response from God. Indeed, as Hauerwas notes in his memoirs, "When I write prayers, which may be as close as I get to prayer itself, my fundamental rule is never to think that it is my job to protect either God or us from the truth."[30] But, given the starkness of the language, it is likely that our congregations will not give themselves permission to pray these prayers. As with the so-called imprecatory psalms, they seem decidedly less than Christian. Indeed, my own experience as a pastor is that such praying with the congregation, or with an individual in the congregation, only really becomes possible when tragedy strikes. Until that point, there is every danger that we simply trade in safe clichés and platitudes. Our world of orientation, to use Brueggemann's designation, in which everything is going well, elicits from us unadventurous language.[31] To those who are used to managing things and are unfamiliar with the messiness of life, the world of Lamentations seems overdone, if not distasteful, to our modern suburban sensibilities.

Once tragedy strikes, however, which it does with merciless regularity, even in the suburbs, then suddenly the world of Lamentations makes a lot of sense. Not withstanding the particular and extreme context of exile, which we know is not our context, even so, the experience of personal tragedy makes Lamentations our world. As O'Connor puts it, "because it is an imagined symbolic world, it can, like all good poetry, intermingle with our real worlds to reveal, mirror, and challenge them. In this conversation between worlds, it can help us see our pain, and, by reflecting it back to us, however indirectly, it has the potential to affirm our human dignity in a first step towards healing."[32]

To be honest, in terms of using Lamentations in a pastoral setting, I can't say I have had much experience of this. The Psalms, yes. Every pastor without fail will have firsthand data of how the Psalms have tutored members of their congregation through times of bereavement, sickness, divorce, and the like. But the time is right, it seems to me, to reinstate this book also within the consciousness of Christian congregations: to appropriate it not simply at the personal level but also within our liturgies as a repository of deep repentance and honest faith.

Again, we are none too familiar with this. We live in a death-denying culture. Suffering is something we try to avoid at all costs. That these laments have been largely purged from the liturgy of the church says a great deal about the disjuncture that exists

---

readings of Lamentations, the Daughter of Zion in Lamentations is far from passive; feisty might be a better description of her spirituality.

30. Hauerwas, *Hannah's Child: A Theologians Memoir*, 256.
31. Brueggemann, *The Psalms in the Life of Faith*, 10–11.
32. O'Connor, *Lamentations and the Tears of the World*, 4.

between the Bible and the church. For all the gains of happy-clappy worship in recent decades, breathing life and celebration into our hymnody, it has been at the expense of legitimate expressions of protest, to the point that many have felt excluded. As Barbara Brown Taylor confesses, in her memoir of leaving church: "One thing that had always troubled me was the way people disappeared from the church when their lives were breaking down. Separation and divorce were the most common explanations for long absences, but so were depression, alcoholism, job loss, and mortal illness . . . I was sorry that the church did not strike these wounded souls as the place where they could bring the dark fruits of their equally dark nights."[33]

I have my own examples of this. One Easter Sunday I made a remark in a sermon that Jesus wept at the grave of Lazarus. To be honest, it was an incidental remark, and certainly not the main point of the sermon. In fact, it is doubtful whether the text supported my point, since the weeping of Jesus was probably as much in anger as in grief—something I would now bring out more clearly, especially in the light of our present discussion.[34] But whatever the exegetical issues, my point clearly left its mark on a number of people. One woman shared with me afterwards—in tears, of course—that she had never actually grieved her Father's death. The minister at the time had urged her not to cry at her Father's funeral, since he was now in heaven with Jesus. And consequently she had buried her sadness as well as her anger in a multitude of Christian activities.

It is difficult to know where to begin in addressing such a pastoral abuse. I'd like to say that these situations are rare, but alas I have encountered them all too often, and dare say I have been guilty myself at times of suppressing legitimate and necessary expressions of complaint. Sadly, platitudinous Christianity, of a kind that refuses to shout in the face of God, is sustained by a veritable cottage industry of Scripture text calendars and soft devotionals. And I guess one of the main reasons for it is simply our unfamiliarity with suffering. Unlike some cultures I have been too, like Pakistan and Colombia, where stories of violence and suffering abound, here we seem to do a good job in putting the lid on our tears. The amount of times I have heard Monty Python's "Always Look on the Bright Side of Life" played at the funeral just ahead of me in the crematorium would indeed be laughable if it wasn't so awful. It is as if our culture is engaged in one massive denial, often more so among those who call themselves believers.

John Swinton makes this very same observation about his own congregation following a bomb explosion in Omagh, Northern Ireland, August 15 1998, killing twenty-eight people. Actually, given the speed with which tragedies or natural disasters around the world now appear on our televisions or on the internet, I am one of those who think pastors should be more discerning in how many tragedies they expose their congregations too. Media saturation is a very real danger, even for the church. But given the closeness of the situation and the scale of the atrocity, it was clearly important that the liturgy that Sunday morning gave voice to the grief that many felt. But come the point at which something needed to be said, or prayed, Swinton became aware of a real problem:

---

33. Brown Taylor, *Leaving Church: A Memoir of Faith*, 147–48.
34. See Winkett, *Our Sound is our Wound* for an exploration of this theme.

"It strikes me, looking back, that my church community was stuck in a position of psychic numbing and stunned silence in the face of evil. It was not that people did not care about what happened in Northern Ireland on that dreadful day. We simply lacked the confidence to ask legitimate questions of God and had no language that might express the reality and pain of such evil and suffering."[35] Some kind of recognition of the place of Lamentations within the canon of Scripture, some acknowledgement that lament and protest are part of the whole counsel of God, arguably would have prevented such an embarrassing silence.

The way Lamentations gives voice to this language of protest is by acrostic: one of the oldest literary devices we know. Each of the first four poems, corresponding to the first four chapters, is a complete acrostic: each verse (or collection of verses in the case of chapter 3) linked to successive letters in the Hebrew alphabet—what we call an abecediary, with the fifth and concluding poem, although not technically an acrostic, also echoing the A–Z (or, more precisely, the א to ת) of the alphabet. What this suggests, pastorally, is an attentiveness to the particularities of what has happened, a slowing down if you like to the actualities of the situation: names, places, events. This is not easy. Typically, we are trained to skirt over, abstract, and dehistoricize. In a culture that has forgotten how to grieve, it is far easier to come up with the solution or engage in pious clichés, rather than listen to the problem. Furthermore, there just isn't time. Sheila Cassidy notes how powerful it is to listen to a fellow human being's story of suffering, but "the problem in the hospital, of course, is lack of time: everyone is so busy that they are mostly unable to give the people the time they need."[36]

Pastorally the acrostic intimates that pain and suffering are not endless—that as much as there is an alpha there is also, in hope, an omega point. But more importantly, it is a structure for taking suffering seriously, preventing us "from sliding prematurely over suffering towards happy endings."[37] As Peterson notes: "The endless patience for listening to and paying attention to suffering is emphasized in the fact that not only is Lamentations an acrostic—it *repeats* the acrostic form. It goes over the story again and again and again and again and again—five times."[38] The listener, of course, must be comfortable with the person's tears and be able to preserve a loving silence as the patient wrestles with his emotions. And this is not always easy. I have been a pastor for nearly two decades now, and for all my experience with suffering, and my own self-awareness, even I have felt uneasy at times with someone's tears, not to mention their anger. But what Lamentations offers us is permission to bring this anger and complaint as a legitimate part of our spiritual journey.

The other day I visited with a woman who recently lost her husband and was struggling to put her grief into words. Aware of this woman's difficulties, a friend of hers, she told me, had related a story of a young girl who was found sitting on a wall reciting the alphabet.

35. Swinton, *Raging with Compassion*, 103.
36. Cassidy, *Made for Laughter*, 162.
37. O'Connor, *Lamentations*, 86.
38. Peterson, *Five Smooth Stones*, 119.

"What are you doing?" asked the passer-by.

"I'm praying," said the little girl.

"But all you are doing is saying the alphabet."

"I know," she said, "but I don't know what to pray, so I am giving God the letters."

Lamentations is not so much giving God the letters, but Scripture giving us the letters with which to pray through our grief, giving us permission to voice our complaint, as well as our confession, and providing us with a more primitive language in order that we might overcome our suburban reticence to deal with these matters. To borrow the words of Jill Truman in her commendation for *Lament for a Son*—the disarmingly honest journal that philosopher Nicholas Wolterstorff kept in the first year after his son Eric's fatal mountain accident—"It is honest and analytical and loving in its attempts to understand the incomprehensible, to bear the unbearable . . . Refreshingly, Wolterstorff does not give God an easy ride."[39]

---

39. See Wolterstorff, *Lament for a Son*.

# BIBLIOGRAPHY

Basset, Lytta. *Holy Anger: Jacob, Job, Jesus*. London: Continuum, 2007.
Bonhoeffer, Dietrich. *Meditations on the Cross*. Louisville: Westminster/John Knox, 1999.
———. *The Cost of Discipleship*, New York: Touchstone, 1995.
Brown Taylor, Barbara. *Leaving Church: A Memoir of Faith*. San Francisco: Harper, 2006.
Brown, Sally A., and Patrick D. Miller, eds. *Lament: Reclaiming Practices in Pulpit, Pew and Public Square*. Louisville: Westminster/John Knox, 2007.
Brueggemann, Walter. *The Psalms in the Life of Faith*. Minneapolis: Fortress, 1995.
Capps, Donald. "Nervous Laughter: Lament, Death Anxiety, and Humor." In *Lament: Reclaiming Practices in Pulpit, Pew and Public Square*, edited by Sally A. Brown and Patrick D. Miller, 70–79. Louisville: Westminster/John Knox, 2007.
Cassidy, Sheila. *Made for Laughter*. London: DLT, 2006.
Chesterton, G. K. *Orthodoxy*. London; Hodder and Stoughton, 1996.
Dobbs-Allsopp, F. W. *Interpretation: Lamentations*. Louisville: Westminster/John Knox, 2002.
Forsyth, P. T. *The Cruciality of the Cross*. Rochester: Stanhope, 1948.
———. *Positive Preaching and the Modern Mind*. London: Independent, 1964.
———. *The Soul of Prayer*. Vancouver: Regent, 2002.
Hauerwas, Stanley. *Hannah's Child: A Theologian's Memoir*. London: SCM, 2010.
———. *Prayers Plainly Spoken*. London: Triangle, 1999.
Kirkpatrick, William Kirk. *Psychological Seduction: The Failure of Modern Psychology*. London: James, 1983.
Lewis, C. S. *The Problem of Pain*. New York: Macmillan, 1953.
Longman, Tremper. *Jeremiah/Lamentations*. New International Biblical Commentary. Milton Keynes, UK: Paternoster, 2008.
McCurdy, Leslie. *Attributes and Atonement: The Holy Love of God in the Theology of P. T. Forsyth*. Carlisle, UK: Paternoster, 1999.
Menninger, Karl. *Whatever Became of Sin?* New York: Hawthorn, 1978.
Norris, Kathleen. *Amazing Grace: The Vocabulary of Faith*. New York: Riverhead, 1998.
O'Connor, Kathleen M. *Lamentations and the Tears of the World*. Maryknoll, NY: Orbis, 2002.
Parry, Robin A. *Lamentations*. The Two Horizons Old Testament Commentary. Grand Rapids: Eerdmans, 2010.
Petersen, Eugene H. *Five Smooth Stones for Pastoral Work*. Grand Rapids: Eerdmans, 1980.
Rieff, Philip. *The Triumph of the Therapeutic*. New York: Harper Row, 1966.
Swinton, John. *Raging with Compassion: Pastoral Responses to the Problem of Evil*. Grand Rapids: Eerdmans, 2007.
van Deusen Hunsinger, Deborah. *Pray without Ceasing: Revitalizing Pastoral Care*. Grand Rapids: Eerdmans, 2006.
Winkett, Lucy. *Our Sound is Our Wound: Contemplative Listening to a Noisy World*. London: Continuum, 2010.
Wolterstorff, Nicholas. *Lament for a Son*. London: Spire, 1989.

# Appendix 1

## A Translation of LXX Lamentations

Kevin J. Youngblood

| LXX Lamentations 1 | Translation LXX Lam 1 |
|---|---|
| καὶ ἐγένετο μετὰ τὸ αἰχμαλωτισθῆναι τὸν Ισραηλ καὶ Ιερουσαλημ ἐρημωθῆναι ἐκάθισεν Ιερεμιας κλαίων καὶ ἐθρήνησεν τὸν θρῆνον τοῦ τον ἐπὶ Ιερουσαλημ καὶ εἶπεν | And it happened after Israel was exiled and Jerusalem was desolated that Jeremiah sat weeping and he voiced this lament over Jerusalem and said ... |
| *Αλφ* <br> ¹πῶς ἐκάθισεν μόνη ἡ πόλις ἡ πεπληθυμμένη λαῶν ἐγενήθη ὡς χήρα πεπληθυμμένη ἐν ἔθνεσιν ἄρχουσα ἐν χώραις ἐγενήθη εἰς φόρον | *Alph* <br> ¹How the city that once was full of people sat alone! <br> She became like a widow who once was full among the nations! <br> A princess among the countries has become levy! |
| *Βηθ* <br> ²κλαίουσα ἔκλαυσεν ἐν νυκτὶ καὶ τὰ δάκρυα αὐτῆς ἐπὶ τῶν σιαγόνων αὐτῆς καὶ οὐχ ὑπάρχει ὁ παρακαλῶν αὐτὴν ἀπὸ πάντων τῶν ἀγαπώντων αὐτήν πάντες οἱ φιλοῦντες αὐτὴν ἠθέτησαν ἐν αὐτῇ ἐγένοντο αὐτῇ εἰς ἐχθρούς | *Beth* <br> ²Weeping, she wept at night with her tears upon her cheeks. <br> And there is no one who consoles her from all her paramours. <br> All of her allies betrayed her. They have become her enemies. |
| *Γιμλ* <br> ³μετῳκίσθη ἡ Ιουδαία ἀπὸ ταπεινώσεως αὐτῆς καὶ ἀπὸ πλήθους δουλείας αὐτή ἐκάθισεν ἐν ἔθνεσιν οὐχ εὗρεν ἀνάπαυσιν πάντες οἱ καταδιώκοντες αὐτὴν κατέλαβον αὐτὴν ἀνὰ μέσον τῶν θλιβόντων | *Giml* <br> ³Judea was deported because of her humiliation and because of the abundance of servitude. <br> She sat among the nations; she found no rest. <br> All who were pursuing her; apprehended her among her oppressors. |
| *Δαλεθ* <br> ⁴ὁδοὶ Σιων πενθοῦσιν παρὰ τὸ μὴ εἶναι ἐρχομένους ἐν ἑορτῇ πᾶσαι αἱ πύλαι αὐτῆς ἠφανισμέναι οἱ ἱερεῖς αὐτῆς ἀναστενάζουσιν αἱ παρθένοι αὐτῆς ἀγόμεναι καὶ αὐτὴ πικραινομένη ἐν ἑαυτῇ | *Daleth* <br> ⁴The roads of Zion mourn because no one comes at feast time. <br> All her gates are destroyed; her priests groan. <br> Her virgins are led away, and she is embittered within herself. |

# APPENDIX 1

| LXX Lamentations 1 | Translation LXX Lam 1 |
|---|---|
| Η<br>⁵ἐγένοντο οἱ θλίβοντες αὐτὴν εἰς κεφαλήν καὶ οἱ ἐχθροὶ αὐτῆς εὐθηνοῦσαν ὅτι κύριος ἐταπείνωσεν αὐτὴν ἐπὶ τὸ πλῆθος τῶν ἀσεβειῶν αὐτῆς τὰ νήπια αὐτῆς ἐπορεύθησαν ἐν αἰχμαλωσίᾳ κατὰ πρόσωπον θλίβοντος | *He*<br>⁵Those who oppress her have come into authority; her enemies flourish.<br>For the Lord humiliated her due to the abundance of her transgressions.<br>Her infants went into exile before an oppressor. |
| Ουαυ<br>⁶καὶ ἐξῆλθεν ἐκ θυγατρὸς Σιων πᾶσα ἡ εὐπρέπεια αὐτῆς ἐγένοντο οἱ ἄρχοντες αὐτῆς ὡς κριοὶ οὐχ εὑρίσκοντες νομὴν καὶ ἐπορεύοντο ἐν οὐκ ἰσχύι κατὰ πρόσωπον διώκοντος | *Ouau*<br>⁶And removed from Daughter Zion is all her beauty.<br>Her rulers are like rams who cannot find pasture, And they were going away without strength before a pursuer. |
| Ζαι<br>⁷ἐμνήσθη Ιερουσαλημ ἡμερῶν ταπεινώσεως αὐτῆς καὶ ἀπωσμῶν αὐτῆς πάντα τὰ ἐπιθυμήματα αὐτῆς ὅσα ἦν ἐξ ἡμερῶν ἀρχαίων ἐν τῷ πεσεῖν τὸν λαὸν αὐτῆς εἰς χεῖρας θλίβοντος καὶ οὐκ ἦν ὁ βοηθῶν αὐτῇ ἰδόντες οἱ ἐχθροὶ αὐτῆς ἐγέλασαν ἐπὶ μετοικεσίᾳ αὐτῆς | *Zai*<br>⁷Jerusalem remembered the days of her humiliation and her expulsion,<br>All her treasures which were from days of old, When her people fell into the hands of the oppressor and she had no helper. |
| Ηθ<br>⁸ἁμαρτίαν ἥμαρτεν Ιερουσαλημ διὰ τοῦτο εἰς σάλον ἐγένετο πάντες οἱ δοξάζοντες αὐτὴν ἐταπείνωσαν αὐτήν εἶδον γὰρ τὴν ἀσχημοσύνην αὐτῆς καί γε αὐτὴ στενάζουσα καὶ ἀπεστράφη ὀπίσω | *Eth*<br>⁸Jerusalem committed a grave sin; therefore she entered into tribulation.<br>All who used to honor her humiliated her because they saw her shame.<br>Indeed, she was groaning and turned away. |
| Τηθ<br>⁹ἀκαθαρσία αὐτῆς πρὸς ποδῶν αὐτῆς οὐκ ἐμνήσθη ἔσχατα αὐτῆς καὶ κατεβίβασεν ὑπέρογκα οὐκ ἔστιν ὁ παρακαλῶν αὐτήν ἰδέ κύριε τὴν ταπείνωσίν μου ὅτι ἐμεγαλύνθη ἐχθρός | *Teth*<br>⁹Her impurity was at her feet; she did not remember her destiny,<br>and she brought down ghastly things; there is no one who consoles her.<br>See, O Lord, my humiliation, that an enemy has become powerful! |
| Ιωθ<br>¹⁰χεῖρα αὐτοῦ ἐξεπέτασεν θλίβων ἐπὶ πάντα τὰ ἐπιθυμήματα αὐτῆς εἶδεν γὰρ ἔθνη εἰσελθόντα εἰς τὸ ἁγίασμα αὐτῆς ἃ ἐνετείλω μὴ εἰσελθεῖν αὐτὰ εἰς ἐκκλησίαν σου | *Ioth*<br>¹⁰An oppressor has extended his hand over all of her treasures.<br>For she saw nations entering her sanctuary, the very ones you commanded not to enter your assembly. |
| Χαφ<br>¹¹πᾶς ὁ λαὸς αὐτῆς καταστενάζοντες ζητοῦντες ἄρτον ἔδωκαν τὰ ἐπιθυμήματα αὐτῆς ἐν βρώσει τοῦ ἐπιστρέψαι ψυχήν ἰδέ κύριε καὶ ἐπίβλεψον ὅτι ἐγενήθην ἠτιμωμένη | *Chaph*<br>¹¹All of her people, groaning, seeking nourishment,<br>gave away her treasures for food in order to revive life.<br>Look, O Lord and notice that I am disgraced! |

| LXX Lamentations 1 | Translation LXX Lam 1 |
|---|---|
| *Λαβδ* <br> ¹² οὐ πρὸς ὑμᾶς πάντες οἱ παραπορευόμενοι ὁδόν ἐπιστρέψατε καὶ ἴδετε εἰ ἔστιν ἄλγος κατὰ τὸ ἄλγος μου ὃ ἐγενήθη φθεγξάμενος ἐν ἐμοὶ ἐταπείνωσέν με κύριος ἐν ἡμέρᾳ ὀργῆς θυμοῦ αὐτοῦ | *Labd* <br> ¹² Not to you, all you who pass along the way. Turn and see if there is pain like my pain which has occurred. <br> The Lord humbled me on the day of his fierce wrath. |
| *Μημ* <br> ¹³ ἐξ ὕψους αὐτοῦ ἀπέστειλεν πῦρ ἐν τοῖς ὀστέοις μου κατήγαγεν αὐτό διεπέτασεν δίκτυον τοῖς ποσίν μου ἀπέστρεψέν με εἰς τὰ ὀπίσω ἔδωκέν με ἠφανισμένην ὅλην τὴν ἡμέραν ὀδυνωμένην | *Mem* <br> ¹³From his height, he sent fire in my bones; he brought it down. <br> He spread a net for my feet; he turned me to the things behind me. <br> He gave me up as one removed from his sight, enduring pain all day long. |
| *Νουν* <br> ¹⁴ ἐγρηγορήθη ἐπὶ τὰ ἀσεβήματά μου ἐν χερσίν μου συνεπλάκησαν ἀνέβησαν ἐπὶ τὸν τράχηλόν μου ἠσθένησεν ἡ ἰσχύς μου ὅτι ἔδωκεν κύριος ἐν χερσίν μου ὀδύνας οὐ δυνήσομαι στῆναι | *Noun* <br> ¹⁴He was kept awake because of my transgressions. By my own hand were they woven together. They came up upon my neck; my strength failed. Because the Lord placed it in my hand, I am unable to stand. |
| *Σαμκ* <br> ¹⁵ ἐξῆρεν πάντας τοὺς ἰσχυρούς μου ὁ κύριος ἐκ μέσου μου ἐκάλεσεν ἐπ᾽ ἐμὲ καιρὸν τοῦ συντρῖψαι ἐκλεκτούς μου ληνὸν ἐπάτησεν κύριος παρθένῳ θυγατρὶ Ιουδα ἐπὶ τούτοις ἐγὼ κλαίω | *Samk* <br> ¹⁵The Lord removed from my midst all of my strong men. <br> He summoned against me a time to crush all of my choice men. <br> The Lord trampled the winepress for Virgin Daughter Judah. For these I weep. |
| *Αιν* <br> ¹⁶ ὁ ὀφθαλμός μου κατήγαγεν ὕδωρ ὅτι ἐμακρύνθη ἀπ᾽ ἐμοῦ ὁ παρακαλῶν με ὁ ἐπιστρέφων ψυχήν μου ἐγένοντο οἱ υἱοί μου ἠφανισμένοι ὅτι ἐκραταιώθη ὁ ἐχθρός | *Ain* <br> ¹⁶My eyes gush water because the one who comforts me is far from me—the one who restores my life. <br> My sons are removed from my sight because an enemy was empowered. |
| *Φη* <br> ¹⁷ διεπέτασεν Σιων χεῖρας αὐτῆς οὐκ ἔστιν ὁ παρακαλῶν αὐτήν ἐνετείλατο κύριος τῷ Ιακωβ κύκλῳ αὐτοῦ οἱ θλίβοντες αὐτόν ἐγενήθη Ιερουσαλημ εἰς ἀποκαθημένην ἀνὰ μέσον αὐτῶν | *Phe* <br> ¹⁷Zion extended her hands; there is no one who comforts her. <br> The Lord commanded concerning Jacob that his oppressors encircle him. <br> Jerusalem has become one who sits away from their midst. |
| *Σαδη* <br> ¹⁸ δίκαιός ἐστιν κύριος ὅτι τὸ στόμα αὐτοῦ παρεπίκρανα ἀκούσατε δή πάντες οἱ λαοί καὶ ἴδετε τὸ ἄλγος μου παρθένοι μου καὶ νεανίσκοι μου ἐπορεύθησαν ἐν αἰχμαλωσίᾳ | *Sade* <br> ¹⁸The Lord is justified because I embittered his mouth. <br> Do listen, all peoples, and see my pain. <br> My virgins and my young men went away in exile. |

# APPENDIX 1

| LXX Lamentations 1 | Translation LXX Lam 1 |
|---|---|
| Κωφ<br>¹⁹ἐκάλεσα τοὺς ἐραστάς μου αὐτοὶ δὲ παρελογίσαντό με οἱ ἱερεῖς μου καὶ οἱ πρεσβύτεροί μου ἐν τῇ πόλει ἐξέλιπον ὅτι ἐζήτησαν βρῶσιν αὐτοῖς ἵνα ἐπιστρέψωσιν ψυχὰς αὐτῶν καὶ οὐχ εὗρον | *Koph*<br>¹⁹I summoned my lovers, but they defrauded me. My priests and my elders fainted in the city because they sought food for themselves that they might revive themselves and they found none. |
| Ρης<br>²⁰ἰδέ κύριε ὅτι θλίβομαι ἡ κοιλία μου ἐταράχθη καὶ ἡ καρδία μου ἐστράφη ἐν ἐμοί ὅτι παραπικραίνουσα παρεπίκρανα ἔξωθεν ἠτέκνωσέν με μάχαιρα ὥσπερ θάνατος ἐν οἴκῳ | *Res*<br>²⁰See, Lord, that I am afflicted! My stomach was in turmoil!<br>My heart turns within me because I am profoundly embittered.<br>Outside the sword bereaves, just like death does in the house. |
| Σεν<br>²¹ἀκούσατε δὴ ὅτι στενάζω ἐγώ οὐκ ἔστιν ὁ παρακαλῶν με πάντες οἱ ἐχθροί μου ἤκουσαν τὰ κακά μου καὶ ἐχάρησαν ὅτι σὺ ἐποίησας ἐπήγαγες ἡμέραν ἐκάλεσας καιρόν καὶ ἐγένοντο ὅμοιοι ἐμοί | *Sen*<br>²¹Do listen, because I am groaning! There is no one who comforts me!<br>All my enemies heard about my misfortunes and they rejoiced that you did it.<br>You brought a day, you summoned a time, and they became like me. |
| Θαυ<br>²²εἰσέλθοι πᾶσα ἡ κακία αὐτῶν κατὰ πρόσωπόν σου καὶ ἐπιφύλλισον αὐτοῖς ὃν τρόπον ἐποίησαν ἐπιφυλλίδα περὶ πάντων τῶν ἁμαρτημάτων μου ὅτι πολλοὶ οἱ στεναγμοί μου καὶ ἡ καρδία μου λυπεῖται | *Thau*<br>²²May all of their evil come before you, and you glean them,<br>just like you made a gleaning because of all of my sins!<br>Because my groans are many and my heart is grieved. |

| LXX Lamentations 2 | Translation LXX Lam 2 |
|---|---|
| *Αλφ* <br> ¹πῶς ἐγνόφωσεν ἐν ὀργῇ αὐτοῦ κύριος τὴν θυγατέρα Σιων κατέρριψεν ἐξ οὐρανοῦ εἰς γῆν δόξασμα Ισραηλ καὶ οὐκ ἐμνήσθη ὑποποδίου ποδῶν αὐτοῦ ἐν ἡμέρᾳ ὀργῆς αὐτοῦ | *Alph* <br> ¹ How the Lord darkened with his wrath Daughter Zion <br> He threw down from heaven to earth Israel's glory, <br> and he did not remember the footstool of his feet. |
| *Βηθ* <br> ²κατεπόντισεν κύριος οὐ φεισάμενος πάντα τὰ ὡραῖα Ιακωβ καθεῖλεν ἐν θυμῷ αὐτοῦ τὰ ὀχυρώματα τῆς θυγατρὸς Ιουδα ἐκόλλησεν εἰς τὴν γῆν ἐβεβήλωσεν βασιλέα αὐτῆς καὶ ἄρχοντας αὐτῆς | *Beth* <br> ²On the day of his wrath, the Lord engulfed unsparingly all of Jacob's beauties. <br> He razed in his fury the fortresses of Daughter Judah. <br> He joined to the ground, he desecrated her king and her officials. |
| *Γιμλ* <br> ³συνέκλασεν ἐν ὀργῇ θυμοῦ αὐτοῦ πᾶν κέρας Ισραηλ ἀπέστρεψεν ὀπίσω δεξιὰν αὐτοῦ ἀπὸ προσώπου ἐχθροῦ καὶ ἀνῆψεν ἐν Ιακωβ ὡς πῦρ φλόγα καὶ κατέφαγεν πάντα τὰ κύκλῳ | *Giml* <br> ³He broke in his furious wrath every horn of Israel. <br> He removed his right hand from the presence of an enemy, <br> and he ignited in Jacob like a fire, a flame and consumed all the environs. |
| *Δαλεθ* <br> ⁴ἐνέτεινεν τόξον αὐτοῦ ὡς ἐχθρός ἐστερέωσεν δεξιὰν αὐτοῦ ὡς ὑπεναντίος καὶ ἀπέκτεινεν πάντα τὰ ἐπιθυμήματα ὀφθαλμῶν μου ἐν σκηνῇ θυγατρὸς Σιων ἐξέχεεν ὡς πῦρ τὸν θυμὸν αὐτοῦ | *Daleth* <br> ⁴He bent his bow like an enemy; he fixed his right arm like an attacker, <br> and he killed all of the treasures of my eyes in the tent of Daughter Zion. <br> He poured out like fire his wrath. |
| *Η* <br> ⁵ἐγενήθη κύριος ὡς ἐχθρός κατεπόντισεν Ισραηλ κατεπόντισεν πάσας τὰς βάρεις αὐτῆς διέφθειρεν τὰ ὀχυρώματα αὐτοῦ καὶ ἐπλήθυνεν τῇ θυγατρὶ Ιουδα ταπεινουμένην καὶ τεταπεινωμένην | *He* <br> ⁵The Lord became like an enemy; he engulfed Israel. <br> He engulfed her fortifications; he annihilated its strongholds, <br> and he multiplied in Daughter Judah she who is humiliated and she who has been humiliated. |
| *Ουαυ* <br> ⁶καὶ διεπέτασεν ὡς ἄμπελον τὸ σκήνωμα αὐτοῦ διέφθειρεν ἑορτὴν αὐτοῦ ἐπελάθετο κύριος ὃ ἐποίησεν ἐν Σιων ἑορτῆς καὶ σαββάτου καὶ παρώξυνεν ἐμβριμήματι ὀργῆς αὐτοῦ βασιλέα καὶ ἱερέα καὶ ἄρχοντα | *Ouau* <br> ⁶And he tore down like a vine his tent; he annihilated his feast. <br> The Lord removed from memory in Zion feast and Sabbath, <br> and he provoked with the indignity of his wrath king and priest and official. |
| *Ζαι* <br> ⁷ἀπώσατο κύριος θυσιαστήριον αὐτοῦ ἀπετίναξεν ἁγίασμα αὐτοῦ συνέτριψεν ἐν χειρὶ ἐχθροῦ τεῖχος βάρεων αὐτῆς φωνὴν ἔδωκαν ἐν οἴκῳ κυρίου ὡς ἐν ἡμέρᾳ ἑορτῆς | *Zai* <br> ⁷The Lord reputed his altar; he cast off his sanctuary. <br> He crushed by the hand of an enemy the wall of her fortification. <br> They raised a shout in the house of the Lord as on a feast day. |

# APPENDIX 1

| LXX Lamentations 2 | Translation LXX Lam 2 |
|---|---|
| Ηθ | *Eth* |
| ⁸καὶ ἐπέστρεψεν κύριος τοῦ διαφθεῖραι τεῖχος θυγατρὸς Σιων ἐξέτεινεν μέτρον οὐκ ἀπέστρεψεν χεῖρα αὐτοῦ ἀπὸ καταπατήματος καὶ ἐπένθησεν τὸ προτείχισμα καὶ τεῖχος ὁμοθυμαδὸν ἠσθένησεν | ⁸The Lord returned to destroy the wall of Daughter Zion. He stretched out a measuring line; he did not withdraw his hand from destruction, and rampart and wall grieve; together they faint. |
| Τηθ | *Teth* |
| ⁹ἐνεπάγησαν εἰς γῆν πύλαι αὐτῆς ἀπώλεσεν καὶ συνέτριψεν μοχλοὺς αὐτῆς βασιλέα αὐτῆς καὶ ἄρχοντας αὐτῆς ἐν τοῖς ἔθνεσιν οὐκ ἔστιν νόμος καί γε προφῆται αὐτῆς οὐκ εἶδον ὅρασιν παρὰ κυρίῳ | ⁹Her gates were sunk in the ground. He destroyed and crushed her barriers, her king, and her officials among the nations. There is no law. Even her prophets see no vision from the Lord. |
| Ιωθ | *Ioth* |
| ¹⁰ἐκάθισαν εἰς τὴν γῆν ἐσιώπησαν πρεσβύτεροι θυγατρὸς Σιων ἀνεβίβασαν χοῦν ἐπὶ τὴν κεφαλὴν αὐτῶν περιεζώσαντο σάκκους κατήγαγον εἰς γῆν ἀρχηγοὺς παρθένους ἐν Ιερουσαλημ | ¹⁰They sat on the ground; the elders of Daughter Zion were silent. They threw dust on their heads; they girded themselves with sackcloth. They forced to the ground leaders, virgins of Jerusalem. |
| Χαφ | *Chaph* |
| ¹¹ἐξέλιπον ἐν δάκρυσιν οἱ ὀφθαλμοί μου ἐταράχθη ἡ καρδία μου ἐξεχύθη εἰς γῆν ἡ δόξα μου ἐπὶ τὸ σύντριμμα τῆς θυγατρὸς τοῦ λαοῦ μου ἐν τῷ ἐκλιπεῖν νήπιον καὶ θηλάζοντα ἐν πλατείαις πόλεως | ¹¹My eyes were spent with tears; my stomach was in turmoil. My glory was poured out on to the ground over the ruin of the Daughter of my people while infant and nursing babes expired in the city squares. |
| Λαβδ | *Labd* |
| ¹²ταῖς μητράσιν αὐτῶν εἶπαν ποῦ σῖτος καὶ οἶνος ἐν τῷ ἐκλύεσθαι αὐτοὺς ὡς τραυματίας ἐν πλατείαις πόλεως ἐν τῷ ἐκχεῖσθαι ψυχὰς αὐτῶν εἰς κόλπον μητέρων αὐτῶν | ¹²To their mothers they said, "Where are grain and wine?" as they collapsed like a fatally wounded man in the city squares, as their lives were poured out at their mothers' breast. |
| Μημ | *Mem* |
| ¹³τί μαρτυρήσω σοι ἢ τί ὁμοιώσω σοι θύγατερ Ιερουσαλημ τίς σώσει σε καὶ παρακαλέσει σε παρθένος θύγατερ Σιων ὅτι ἐμεγαλύνθη ποτήριον συντριβῆς σου τίς ἰάσεταί σε | ¹³What shall I testify concerning you, or what shall I compare to you, Daughter Jerusalem? What shall I equate with you and I will comfort you, Virgin Daughter Zion? For enlarged is the cup of your destruction. Who will heal you? |
| Νουν | *Noun* |
| ¹⁴προφῆταί σου εἴδοσάν σοι μάταια καὶ ἀφροσύνην καὶ οὐκ ἀπεκάλυψαν ἐπὶ τὴν ἀδικίαν σου τοῦ ἐπιστρέψαι αἰχμαλωσίαν σου καὶ εἴδοσάν σοι λήμματα μάταια καὶ ἐξώσματα | ¹⁴Your prophets saw for you worthless things and foolishness, and they did not reveal concerning your injustice so as to turn away your exile. And they saw for you worthless commissions and expulsions. |

| LXX Lamentations 2 | Translation LXX Lam 2 |
|---|---|
| Σαμκ | Samk |
| ¹⁵ἐκρότησαν ἐπὶ σὲ χεῖρας πάντες οἱ παραπορευόμενοι ὁδόν ἐσύρισαν καὶ ἐκίνησαν τὴν κεφαλὴν αὐτῶν ἐπὶ τὴν θυγατέρα Ιερουσαλημ ἦ αὕτη ἡ πόλις ἥν ἐροῦσιν στέφανος δόξης εὐφροσύνη πάσης τῆς γῆς | ¹⁵All those who passed along the way clapped their hands at you. They hissed and shook their heads over Daughter Jerusalem. Is this the city concerning which they will say, "The crown of glory; the joy of all the earth"? |
| Φη | Phe |
| ¹⁶διήνοιξαν ἐπὶ σὲ στόμα αὐτῶν πάντες οἱ ἐχθροί σου ἐσύρισαν καὶ ἔβρυξαν ὀδόντας εἶπαν κατεπίομεν αὐτήν πλὴν αὕτη ἡ ἡμέρα ἣν προσεδοκῶμεν εὕρομεν αὐτήν εἴδομεν | ¹⁶All your enemies opened wide their mouths against you. They hissed and gnashed their teeth; they said, "We gulped her down. Surely this is the day for which we were waiting; we found it; we saw!" |
| Αιν | Ain |
| ¹⁷ἐποίησεν κύριος ἃ ἐνεθυμήθη συνετέλεσεν ῥήματα αὐτοῦ ἃ ἐνετείλατο ἐξ ἡμερῶν ἀρχαίων καθεῖλεν καὶ οὐκ ἐφείσατο καὶ ηὔφρανεν ἐπὶ σὲ ἐχθρόν ὕψωσεν κέρας θλίβοντός σε | ¹⁷The Lord did what he plotted; he accomplished his oracles, what he decreed from days of old. He destroyed and he did not restrain himself, and an enemy rejoiced over you. He exalted the horn of the one who oppresses you. |
| Σαδε | Sade |
| ¹⁸ἐβόησεν καρδία αὐτῶν πρὸς κύριον τείχη Σιων καταγάγετε ὡς χειμάρρους δάκρυα ἡμέρας καὶ νυκτός μὴ δῷς ἔκνηψιν σεαυτῇ μὴ σιωπήσαιτο θύγατερ ὁ ὀφθαλμός σου | ¹⁸Their heart cried out to the Lord. Rampart of Zion, gush tears like a torrent day and night! Give yourself no respite! May your eyes, Daughter, not be silenced! |
| Κωφ | Koph |
| ¹⁹ἀνάστα ἀγαλλίασαι ἐν νυκτὶ εἰς ἀρχὰς φυλακῆς σου ἔκχεον ὡς ὕδωρ καρδίαν σου ἀπέναντι προσώπου κυρίου ἆρον πρὸς αὐτὸν χεῖράς σου περὶ ψυχῆς νηπίων σου τῶν ἐκλυομένων λιμῷ ἐπ' ἀρχῆς πασῶν ἐξόδων | ¹⁹Rise! Shout for joy in the night at the beginning of your watch! Pour your heart out like water before the presence of the Lord. Lift your hands to him for the life of your infants who faint with hunger at the start of every exit. |
| Ρης | Res |
| ²⁰ἰδέ κύριε καὶ ἐπίβλεψον τίνι ἐπεφύλλισας οὕτως εἰ φάγονται γυναῖκες καρπὸν κοιλίας αὐτῶν ἐπιφυλλίδα ἐποίησεν μάγειρος φονευθήσονται νήπια θηλάζοντα μαστούς ἀποκτενεῖς ἐν ἁγιάσματι κυρίου ἱερέα καὶ προφήτην | ²⁰Look, Lord, and observe whom you gleaned in this manner! Will women eat the fruit of their womb? A butcher made a gleaning. Will you kill in the Lord's sanctuary priest and prophet? |
| Σεν | Sen |
| ²¹ἐκοιμήθησαν εἰς τὴν ἔξοδον παιδάριον καὶ πρεσβύτης παρθένοι μου καὶ νεανίσκοι μου ἐπορεύθησαν ἐν αἰχμαλωσίᾳ ἐν ῥομφαίᾳ καὶ ἐν λιμῷ ἀπέκτεινας ἐν ἡμέρᾳ ὀργῆς σου ἐμαγείρευσας οὐκ ἐφείσω | ²¹Young and old fell asleep on the ground by the exits. My virgins and my young men fell by the sword. You killed on the day of your wrath; you butchered; you did not restrain yourself. |

# APPENDIX 1

| LXX Lamentations 2 | Translation LXX Lam 2 |
|---|---|
| Θαυ<br>²²ἐκάλεσας ὡς εἰς ἡμέραν ἑορτῆς παροικίας μου κυκλόθεν καὶ οὐκ ἐγένοντο ἐν ἡμέρᾳ ὀργῆς κυρίου ἀνασῳζόμενος καὶ καταλελειμμένος ὡς ἐπεκράτησα καὶ ἐπλήθυνα ἐχθρούς μου πάντας | *Thau*<br>²²You summoned as to a feast day my sojourns from all around,<br>and there was no survivor or remnant on the day of the Lord's wrath<br>as I overpowered and increased all my enemies. |

| LXX Lamentations 3 | Translation of LXX Lam 3 |
|---|---|
| Αλφ | Alph |
| ¹ἐγὼ ἀνὴρ ὁ βλέπων πτωχείαν ἐν ῥάβδῳ θυμοῦ αὐτοῦ ἐπ᾽ ἐμέ | ¹I am the man who sees affliction by the rod of his anger. |
| ²παρέλαβέν με καὶ ἀπήγαγεν εἰς σκότος καὶ οὐ φῶς | ²Me he took and led into darkness and not light. |
| ³πλὴν ἐν ἐμοὶ ἐπέστρεψεν χεῖρα αὐτοῦ ὅλην τὴν ἡμέραν | ³Indeed against me he turned his hand all day long. |
| Βηθ | Beth |
| ⁴ἐπαλαίωσεν σάρκας μου καὶ δέρμα μου ὀστέα μου συνέτριψεν | ⁴He wore out my body and skin; my bones he crushed. |
| ⁵ἀνῳκοδόμησεν κατ᾽ ἐμοῦ καὶ ἐκύκλωσεν κεφαλήν μου καὶ ἐμόχθησεν | ⁵He besieged me and encircled my head and it grew weary. |
| ⁶ἐν σκοτεινοῖς ἐκάθισέν με ὡς νεκροὺς αἰῶνος | ⁶In darkness he sat me like those long dead. |
| Γιμλ | Giml |
| ⁷ἀνῳκοδόμησεν κατ᾽ ἐμοῦ καὶ οὐκ ἐξελεύσομαι ἐβάρυνεν χαλκόν μου | ⁷He besieged me, and I will not escape; he weighed down my brass. |
| ⁸καί γε κεκράξομαι καὶ βοήσω ἀπέφραξεν προσευχήν μου | ⁸Indeed, because I shall cry out, I will call, he blocked out my prayer. |
| ⁹ἀνῳκοδόμησεν ὁδούς μου ἐνέφραξεν τρίβους μου ἐτάραξεν | ⁹He barricaded my paths; he blocked my roads; he thwarted. |
| Δαλεθ | Daleth |
| ¹⁰ἄρκος ἐνεδρεύουσα αὐτός μοι λέων ἐν κρυφαίοις | ¹⁰A bear waiting to ambush he is to me, a lion in hidden places. |
| ¹¹κατεδίωξεν ἀφεστηκότα καὶ κατέπαυσέν με ἔθετό με ἠφανισμένην | ¹¹He hunted down a fugitive, he pulled me down, he made me like a woman banished from sight. |
| ¹²ἐνέτεινεν τόξον αὐτοῦ καὶ ἐστήλωσέν με ὡς σκοπὸν εἰς βέλος | ¹²He stretched his bow and set me up as a target for an arrow. |
| Η | He |
| ¹³εἰσήγαγεν τοῖς νεφροῖς μου ἰοὺς φαρέτρας αὐτοῦ | ¹³He drove into my kidneys the sons of his quiver. |
| ¹⁴ἐγενήθην γέλως παντὶ λαῷ μου ψαλμὸς αὐτῶν ὅλην τὴν ἡμέραν | ¹⁴I became a laughingstock to all my people, their song all day long. |
| ¹⁵ἐχόρτασέν με πικρίας ἐμέθυσέν με χολῆς | ¹⁵He gorged me with bitterness; he made me drunk on gall. |
| Ουαυ | Ouau |
| ¹⁶καὶ ἐξέβαλεν ψήφῳ ὀδόντας μου ἐψώμισέν με σποδόν | ¹⁶He knocked out my teeth with gravel; he made me eat ash. |
| ¹⁷καὶ ἀπώσατο ἐξ εἰρήνης ψυχήν μου ἐπελαθόμην ἀγαθὰ | ¹⁷He banished my soul from peace; I forgot good things. |
| ¹⁸καὶ εἶπα ἀπώλετο νεῖκός μου καὶ ἡ ἐλπίς μου ἀπὸ κυρίου | ¹⁸And I said, "My victory perished along with my hope from the Lord." |
| Ζαι | Zai |
| ¹⁹ἐμνήσθην ἀπὸ πτωχείας μου καὶ ἐκ διωγμοῦ μου πικρίας καὶ χολῆς μου | ¹⁹I did remember, because of my poverty and persecution, bitterness and gall. |
| ²⁰μνησθήσεται καὶ καταδολεσχήσει ἐπ᾽ ἐμὲ ἡ ψυχή μου | ²⁰My soul will remember and mutter complaints against me. |
| ²¹ταύτην τάξω εἰς τὴν καρδίαν μου διὰ τοῦτο ὑπομενῶ | ²¹This I will fix inside my heart; therefore I will endure. |

# APPENDIX 1

| LXX Lamentations 3 | Translation of LXX Lam 3 |
|---|---|
| | *Eth* |
| ²²τὰ ἐλέη κυρίου ὅτι οὐκ ἐξελίπομεν ὅτι οὐ συνετελέσθησαν οἱ οἰκτιρμοὶ αὐτοῦ ²³καινὰ Εἰς τὰς πρωΐας πολλὴ ἡ πίστις σου ²⁴μερίς μου κύριος εἶπεν ἡ ψυχή μου διὰ τοῦτο ὑπομενῶ αὐτόν | ²²These are the mercies of the Lord, that we did not expire, ²³that his compassionate feelings did not cease. ²⁴New things emerge every morning. Great is your fidelity. |
| | *Teth* |
| ²⁵ἀγαθὸς κύριος τοῖς ὑπομένουσιν αὐτόν ψυχῇ ἣ ζητήσει αὐτὸν ἀγαθὸν ²⁶καὶ ὑπομενεῖ καὶ ἡσυχάσει εἰς τὸ σωτήριον κυρίου ²⁷ἀγαθὸν ἀνδρὶ ὅταν ἄρῃ ζυγὸν ἐν νεότητι αὐτοῦ | ²⁵The Lord is good to those who wait for him, to the soul that seeks him. ²⁶It is good, and he will wait and remain still for the Lord's salvation. ²⁷It is good for a man when he bears a yoke in his youth. |
| | *Ioth* |
| ²⁸καθήσεται κατὰ μόνας καὶ σιωπήσεται ὅτι ἦρεν ἐφ' ἑαυτῷ ²⁹δώσει ἐν χώματι στόμα αὐτοῦ εἰ ἄρα ἐστιν ἐλπίς ³⁰δώσει τῷ παίοντι αὐτὸν σιαγόνα χορτασθήσεται ὀνειδισμῶν | ²⁸He will sit alone and keep silence because he takes it upon himself. ²⁹He will place his mouth in dirt ramparts if perchance there is hope. ³⁰He will offer to the striker his cheek; he will be sated with insults. |
| | *Chaph* |
| ³¹ὅτι οὐκ εἰς τὸν αἰῶνα ἀπώσεται κύριος ³²ὅτι ὁ ταπεινώσας οἰκτιρήσει κατὰ τὸ πλῆθος τοῦ ἐλέους αὐτοῦ ³³ὅτι οὐκ ἀπεκρίθη ἀπὸ καρδίας αὐτοῦ καὶ ἐταπείνωσεν υἱοὺς ἀνδρός | ³¹For the Lord will not banish forever. ³²For the one who humbles will show compassion according to his abundant mercy. ³³For he did not respond from his heart though he humbled a man's sons. |
| | *Labd* |
| ³⁴τοῦ ταπεινῶσαι ὑπὸ τοὺς πόδας αὐτοῦ πάντας δεσμίους γῆς ³⁵τοῦ ἐκκλῖναι κρίσιν ἀνδρὸς κατέναντι προσώπου ὑψίστου ³⁶καταδικάσαι ἄνθρωπον ἐν τῷ κρίνεσθαι αὐτὸν κύριος οὐκ εἶπεν | ³⁴To humiliate under his foot all the prisoners of earth, ³⁵To reject a man's legal case before the presence of the Most High, ³⁶To condemn someone while still deciding his case; did the Lord not see? |
| | *Mem* |
| ³⁷τίς οὕτως εἶπεν καὶ ἐγενήθη κύριος οὐκ ἐνετείλατο ³⁸ἐκ στόματος ὑψίστου οὐκ ἐξελεύσεται τὰ κακὰ καὶ τὸ ἀγαθόν ³⁹τί γογγύσει ἄνθρωπος ζῶν ἀνὴρ περὶ τῆς ἁμαρτίας αὐτοῦ | ³⁷Who is this? He spoke, and it happened. Did the Lord not command? ³⁸Will not the bad things as well as the good thing proceed from the mouth of the Most High? ³⁹Will a living person dare complain, a man concerning his sin? |
| | *Noun* |
| ⁴⁰ἐξηρευνήθη ἡ ὁδὸς ἡμῶν καὶ ἠτάσθη καὶ ἐπιστρέψωμεν ἕως κυρίου ⁴¹ἀναλάβωμεν καρδίας ἡμῶν ἐπὶ χειρῶν πρὸς ὑψηλὸν ἐν οὐρανῷ ⁴²Ἡμεῖς ἡμαρτήσαμεν ἠσεβήσαμεν καὶ οὐχ ἱλάσθης | ⁴⁰Our path was examined and tested; so let us return to the Lord ⁴¹Let us take up our hearts on our hands toward the high place in heaven. ⁴²We ourselves transgressed and provoked, and you did not reconcile us to yourself. |

| LXX Lamentations 3 | Translation of LXX Lam 3 |
|---|---|
| | *Samk* |
| ⁴³ἐπεσκέπασας ἐν θυμῷ καὶ ἀπεδίωξας ἡμᾶς ἀπέκτεινας οὐκ ἐφείσω | ⁴³You covered in wrath and chased us away; you killed, you did not spare. |
| ⁴⁴ἐπεσκέπασας νεφέλην σεαυτῷ εἵνεκεν προσευχῆς | ⁴⁴You covered yourself in a cloud with respect to prayer. |
| ⁴⁵καμμύσαι με καὶ ἀπωσθῆναι ἔθηκας ἡμᾶς ἐν μέσῳ τῶν λαῶν | ⁴⁵To cow me and to banish you placed us in the midst of the peoples. |
| | *Phe* |
| ⁴⁶διήνοιξαν ἐφ' ἡμᾶς τὸ στόμα αὐτῶν πάντες οἱ ἐχθροὶ ἡμῶν | ⁴⁶All of our enemies open against us their mouths. |
| ⁴⁷φόβος καὶ θυμὸς ἐγενήθη ἡμῖν ἔπαρσις καὶ συντριβή | ⁴⁷Fear and pit were ours, a pile of rubble and ruin. |
| ⁴⁸ἀφέσεις ὑδάτων κατάξει ὁ ὀφθαλμός μου ἐπὶ τὸ σύντριμμα τῆς θυγατρὸς τοῦ λαοῦ μου | ⁴⁸My eyes will gush a waterfall over the ruin of the Daughter of my people. |
| | *Ain* |
| ⁴⁹ὁ ὀφθαλμός μου κατεπόθη καὶ οὐ σιγήσομαι τοῦ μὴ εἶναι ἔκνηψιν | ⁴⁹My eye is spent, yet I will not be silenced so as not to be sobered |
| ⁵⁰ἕως οὗ διακύψῃ καὶ ἴδῃ κύριος ἐξ οὐρανοῦ | ⁵⁰until the Lord bends and sees from heaven. |
| ⁵¹ὁ ὀφθαλμός μου ἐπιφυλλιεῖ ἐπὶ τὴν ψυχήν μου παρὰ πάσας θυγατέρας πόλεως | ⁵¹My eye will glean my soul more than all the daughters of the city. |
| | *Sade* |
| ⁵²θηρεύοντες ἐθήρευσάν με ὡς στρουθίον οἱ ἐχθροί μου δωρεάν | ⁵²My enemies, while hunting, hunted me like a sparrow for sport. |
| ⁵³ἐθανάτωσαν ἐν λάκκῳ ζωήν μου καὶ ἐπέθηκαν λίθον ἐπ' ἐμοί | ⁵³They ended my life in a well and placed a stone over me. |
| ⁵⁴ὑπερεχύθη ὕδωρ ἐπὶ κεφαλήν μου εἶπα ἀπῶσμαι | ⁵⁴Water was poured over my head; I said, "I am banished." |
| | *Koph* |
| ⁵⁵ἐπεκαλεσάμην τὸ ὄνομά σου κύριε ἐκ λάκκου κατωτάτου | ⁵⁵I summoned your name, Lord, from the deepest well. |
| ⁵⁶φωνήν μου ἤκουσας μὴ κρύψῃς τὰ ὦτά σου εἰς τὴν δέησίν μου | ⁵⁶You heard my voice. Don't cover your ears to my petition. |
| ⁵⁷εἰς τὴν βοήθειάν μου ἤγγισας ἐν ᾗ σε ἡμέρᾳ ἐπεκαλεσάμην εἶπάς μοι μὴ φοβοῦ | ⁵⁷You came to my rescue; on the day when I summoned you, you said, "Don't fear." |
| | *Res* |
| ⁵⁸ἐδίκασας κύριε τὰς δίκας τῆς ψυχῆς μου ἐλυτρώσω τὴν ζωήν μου | ⁵⁸You vindicated, O Lord, my soul's cause; you redeemed my life. |
| ⁵⁹εἶδες κύριε τὰς ταραχάς μου ἔκρινας τὴν κρίσιν μου | ⁵⁹You saw, O Lord, my troubles; you adjudicated my case. |
| ⁶⁰εἶδες πᾶσαν τὴν ἐκδίκησιν αὐτῶν εἰς πάντας διαλογισμοὺς αὐτῶν ἐν ἐμοί | ⁶⁰You saw all of their vengeance, all of their plots against me. |
| | *Sen* |
| ⁶¹ἤκουσας τὸν ὀνειδισμὸν αὐτῶν πάντας τοὺς διαλογισμοὺς αὐτῶν κατ' ἐμοῦ | ⁶¹You heard their insult, all of their plots against me, |
| ⁶²χείλη ἐπανιστανομένων μοι καὶ μελέτας αὐτῶν κατ' ἐμοῦ ὅλην τὴν ἡμέραν | ⁶²lips which opposed me and their schemes against me all day long. |
| ⁶³καθέδραν αὐτῶν καὶ ἀνάστασιν αὐτῶν ἐπίβλεψον ἐπὶ τοὺς ὀφθαλμοὺς αὐτῶν | ⁶³Note carefully their sitting and rising. I am their music. |

# APPENDIX 1

| LXX Lamentations 3 | Translation of LXX Lam 3 |
|---|---|
|  | *Thau* |
| ⁶⁴ἀποδώσεις αὐτοῖς ἀνταπόδομα κύριε κατὰ τὰ ἔργα τῶν χειρῶν αὐτῶν | ⁶⁴You will repay them a reward, O Lord, appropriate to the deeds of their hands. |
| ⁶⁵ἀποδώσεις αὐτοῖς ὑπερασπισμὸν καρδίας μόχθον σου αὐτοῖς | ⁶⁵You will repay them a hardness of heart; your hardship will be theirs |
| ⁶⁶καταδιώξεις ἐν ὀργῇ καὶ ἐξαναλώσεις αὐτοὺς ὑποκάτω τοῦ οὐρανοῦ κύριε | ⁶⁶You will hunt down in anger and you will annihilate them under heaven, O Lord. |

| LXX Lamentations 4 | Translation of LXX Lam 4 |
|---|---|
| | *Alph* |
| ¹πῶς ἀμαυρωθήσεται χρυσίον ἀλλοιωθήσεται τὸ ἀργύριον τὸ ἀγαθόν ἐξεχύθησαν λίθοι ἅγιοι ἐπ' ἀρχῆς πασῶν ἐξόδων | ¹How the gold will be tarnished; the fine silver will be tinged. The sacred stones were poured out at the opening of all the exits |
| | *Beth* |
| ²υἱοὶ Σιων οἱ τίμιοι οἱ ἐπηρμένοι ἐν χρυσίῳ πῶς ἐλογίσθησαν εἰς ἀγγεῖα ὀστράκινα ἔργα χειρῶν κεραμέως | ²The noble sons of Zion, who were exalted with gold, how they were considered for clay jars, the work of a potter's hands! |
| | *Giml* |
| ³καί γε δράκοντες ἐξέδυσαν μαστούς ἐθήλασαν σκύμνοι αὐτῶν θυγατέρες λαοῦ μου εἰς ἀνίατον ὡς στρουθίον ἐν ἐρήμῳ | ³Even dragons offered breasts, they nursed their young. The daughters of my people became intractable like an ostrich in a desert. |
| | *Daleth* |
| ⁴ἐκολλήθη ἡ γλῶσσα θηλάζοντος πρὸς τὸν φάρυγγα αὐτοῦ ἐν δίψει νήπια ᾔτησαν ἄρτον ὁ διακλῶν οὐκ ἔστιν αὐτοῖς | ⁴The tongue of a nursing babe clung to his palate in thirst. Infants requested food; there was no one to apportion it to them. |
| | *He* |
| ⁵οἱ ἔσθοντες τὰς τρυφὰς ἠφανίσθησαν ἐν ταῖς ἐξόδοις οἱ τιθηνούμενοι ἐπὶ κόκκων περιεβάλοντο κοπρίας | ⁵Those accustomed to eating delicacies perished in the exits. Those raised in scarlet were covered with dung. |
| | *Ouau* |
| ⁶καὶ ἐμεγαλύνθη ἀνομία θυγατρὸς λαοῦ μου ὑπὲρ ἀνομίας Σοδομων τῆς κατεστραμμένης ὥσπερ σπουδῇ καὶ οὐκ ἐπόνεσαν ἐν αὐτῇ χεῖρας | ⁶The crimes of the daughter of my people were greater than the crime of Sodom which was overthrown as in an instant though they did not labor against it with hands. |
| | *Zai* |
| ⁷ἐκαθαριώθησαν ναζιραῖοι αὐτῆς ὑπὲρ χιόνα ἔλαμψαν ὑπὲρ γάλα ἐπυρρώθησαν ὑπὲρ λίθους σαπφείρου τὸ ἀπόσπασμα αὐτῶν | ⁷Her nazirites were purified more than snow, they were whiter than milk. They were reddened more than stones. Their cut was lapis lazuli. |
| | *Eth* |
| ⁸ἐσκότασεν ὑπὲρ ἀσβόλην τὸ εἶδος αὐτῶν οὐκ ἐπεγνώσθησαν ἐν ταῖς ἐξόδοις ἐπάγη δέρμα αὐτῶν ἐπὶ τὰ ὀστέα αὐτῶν ἐξηράνθησαν ἐγενήθησαν ὥσπερ ξύλον | ⁸Their appearance became darker than soot; they were not recognized in the exits. Their skin clung to their bones; they were dried up; they were like wood. |
| | *Teth* |
| ⁹καλοὶ ἦσαν οἱ τραυματίαι ῥομφαίας ἢ οἱ τραυματίαι λιμοῦ ἐπορεύθησαν ἐκκεκεντημένοι ἀπὸ γενημάτων ἀγρῶν | ⁹Better off were those wounded by the sword than those wounded by hunger. They wandered stabbed with pain from the lack of the produce of the fields. |

# APPENDIX 1

| LXX Lamentations 4 | Translation of LXX Lam 4 |
|---|---|
| | *Ioth* |
| ¹⁰χεῖρες γυναικῶν οἰκτιρμόνων ἥψησαν τὰ παιδία αὐτῶν ἐγενήθησαν εἰς βρῶσιν αὐταῖς ἐν τῷ συντρίμματι τῆς θυγατρὸς λαοῦ μου | ¹⁰The hands of gentle women gripped their children; they became their food in the destruction of the Daughter of my people. |
| | *Chaph* |
| ¹¹συνετέλεσεν κύριος θυμὸν αὐτοῦ ἐξέχεεν θυμὸν ὀργῆς αὐτοῦ καὶ ἀνῆψεν πῦρ ἐν Σιων καὶ κατέφαγεν τὰ θεμέλια αὐτῆς | ¹¹The Lord exhausted his wrath; he emptied out his furious wrath, and a fire burned in Zion and consumed her foundations. |
| | *Labd* |
| ¹²οὐκ ἐπίστευσαν βασιλεῖς γῆς πάντες οἱ κατοικοῦντες τὴν οἰκουμένην ὅτι εἰσελεύσεται ἐχθρὸς καὶ ἐκθλίβων διὰ τῶν πυλῶν Ιερουσαλημ | ¹²The kings of the earth could not believe, nor all the inhabitants of the world, that an enemy entered, even an oppressor, through Jerusalem's gates. |
| | *Mem* |
| ¹³ἐξ ἁμαρτιῶν προφητῶν αὐτῆς ἀδικιῶν ἱερέων αὐτῆς τῶν ἐκχεόντων αἷμα δίκαιον ἐν μέσῳ αὐτῆς | ¹³Because of the sins of her prophets, the injustices of her priests who poured out the blood of the righteous in her midst. |
| | *Noun* |
| ¹⁴ἐσαλεύθησαν ἐγρήγοροι αὐτῆς ἐν ταῖς ἐξόδοις ἐμολύνθησαν ἐν αἵματι ἐν τῷ μὴ δύνασθαι αὐτοὺς ἥψαντο ἐνδυμάτων αὐτῶν | ¹⁴Her sentries were shaken in the exits; they were stained with blood. Because they could not help it, they touched their clothes. |
| | *Samk* |
| ¹⁵ἀπόστητε ἀκαθάρτων καλέσατε αὐτούς ἀπόστητε ἀπόστητε μὴ ἅπτεσθε ὅτι ἀνήφθησαν καί γε ἐσαλεύθησαν εἴπατε ἐν τοῖς ἔθνεσιν οὐ μὴ προσθῶσιν τοῦ παροικεῖν | ¹⁵Move away from the unclean ones! Call them. Move away! Move away! Do not touch! They were inflamed; indeed they were shaken. Say among the nations, "They will never sojourn again." |
| | *Phe* |
| ¹⁶πρόσωπον κυρίου μερὶς αὐτῶν οὐ προσθήσει ἐπιβλέψαι αὐτοῖς πρόσωπον ἱερέων οὐκ ἔλαβον πρεσβύτας οὐκ ἠλέησαν | ¹⁶The presence of the Lord is their portion. He will not again have regard for them. They did not favor the priests; they did not pity the old ones. |
| | *Ain* |
| ¹⁷ἔτι ὄντων ἡμῶν ἐξέλιπον οἱ ὀφθαλμοὶ ἡμῶν εἰς τὴν βοήθειαν ἡμῶν μάταια ἀποσκοπευόντων ἡμῶν ἀπεσκοπεύσαμεν εἰς ἔθνος οὐ σῷζον | ¹⁷While we still existed, our eyes failed looking for our help in vain even as we watched intently. |
| | *Sade* |
| ¹⁸ἐθηρεύσαμεν μικροὺς ἡμῶν τοῦ μὴ πορεύεσθαι ἐν ταῖς πλατείαις ἡμῶν ἤγγικεν ὁ καιρὸς ἡμῶν ἐπληρώθησαν αἱ ἡμέραι ἡμῶν πάρεστιν ὁ καιρὸς ἡμῶν | ¹⁸We watched intently for a nation that could not save. We hunted our little ones so that they would not venture out into our public squares. |

| LXX Lamentations 4 | Translation of LXX Lam 4 |
|---|---|
| | *Koph* |
| ¹⁹κοῦφοι ἐγένοντο οἱ διώκοντες ἡμᾶς ὑπὲρ ἀετοὺς οὐρανοῦ ἐπὶ τῶν ὀρέων ἐξήφθησαν ἐν ἐρήμῳ ἐνήδρευσαν ἡμᾶς | ¹⁹Our time has arrived; our days are complete; our time is here.<br>Those who chased us were swifter than the eagles of the sky.<br>On the mountains they were on our heels; in the desert they waited to ambush us. |
| | *Res* |
| ²⁰πνεῦμα προσώπου ἡμῶν χριστὸς κυρίου συνελήμφθη ἐν ταῖς διαφθοραῖς αὐτῶν οὗ εἴπαμεν ἐν τῇ σκιᾷ αὐτοῦ ζησόμεθα ἐν τοῖς ἔθνεσιν | ²⁰The breath of our face, the Lord's anointed one was taken by their corrupt ones.<br>Concerning him we said, "In his shade we will live among the nations." |
| | *Sen* |
| ²¹χαῖρε καὶ εὐφραίνου θύγατερ Ιδουμαίας ἡ κατοικοῦσα ἐπὶ γῆς καί γε ἐπὶ σὲ διελεύσεται τὸ ποτήριον κυρίου καὶ μεθυσθήσῃ καὶ ἀποχεεῖς | ²¹Rejoice and celebrate, Daughter of Idumea who inhabits the land.<br>Also upon you will come the Lord's cup; you will get drunk and vomit. |
| | *Thau* |
| ²²ἐξέλιπεν ἡ ἀνομία σου θύγατερ Σιων οὐ προσθήσει ἔτι ἀποικίσαι σε ἐπεσκέψατο ἀνομίας σου θύγατερ Εδωμ ἀπεκάλυψεν ἐπὶ τὰ ἀσεβήματά σου | ²²Your punishment is over, Daughter Zion, he will no longer exile you.<br>He noticed your crimes, Daughter Edom. He revealed your transgressions. |

# APPENDIX 1

| LXX Lamentations 5 | Translation of LXX Lam 5 |
|---|---|
| ¹μνήσθητι κύριε ὅ τι ἐγενήθη ἡμῖν ἐπίβλεψον καὶ ἰδὲ τὸν ὀνειδισμὸν ἡμῶν | ¹Remember, O Lord, what has happened to us. Look and see our disgrace. |
| ²κληρονομία ἡμῶν μετεστράφη ἀλλοτρίοις οἱ οἶκοι ἡμῶν ξένοις | ²Our heritage was turned over to strangers; our houses to foreigners. |
| ³ὀρφανοὶ ἐγενήθημεν οὐχ ὑπάρχει πατήρ μητέρες ἡμῶν ὡς αἱ χῆραι | ³We became orphans, there is no father. Our mothers are like widows. |
| ⁴ἐξ ἡμερῶν ἡμῶν ξύλα ἡμῶν ἐν ἀλλάγματι ἦλθεν | ⁴Since our days, our wood came at a price. |
| ⁵ἐπὶ τὸν τράχηλον ἡμῶν ἐδιώχθημεν ἐκοπιάσαμεν οὐκ ἀνεπαύθημεν | ⁵Upon our throats we were pursued. We toiled, we found no rest. |
| ⁶Αἴγυπτος ἔδωκεν χεῖρα Ασσουρ εἰς πλησμονὴν αὐτῶν | ⁶Egypt gave a hand; Assyria for an abundance of food. |
| ⁷οἱ πατέρες ἡμῶν ἥμαρτον οὐχ ὑπάρχουσιν ἡμεῖς τὰ ἀνομήματα αὐτῶν ὑπέσχομεν | ⁷Our fathers sinned, they are no more. We bore their wickedness. |
| ⁸δοῦλοι ἐκυρίευσαν ἡμῶν λυτρούμενος οὐκ ἔστιν ἐκ τῆς χειρὸς αὐτῶν | ⁸Servants ruled over us. One is not ransomed by their hand. |
| ⁹ἐν ταῖς ψυχαῖς ἡμῶν εἰσοίσομεν ἄρτον ἡμῶν ἀπὸ προσώπου ῥομφαίας τῆς ἐρήμου | ⁹At the cost of our lives we will bring home our food away from the presence of the desert sword. |
| ¹⁰τὸ δέρμα ἡμῶν ὡς κλίβανος ἐπελειώθη συνεσπάσθησαν ἀπὸ προσώπου καταιγίδων λιμοῦ | ¹⁰Our skin like an oven was blackened because of the tempest of famine. |
| ¹¹γυναῖκας ἐν Σιων ἐταπείνωσαν παρθένους ἐν πόλεσιν Ιουδα | ¹¹They humiliated women in Zion, virgins in the cities of Judah. |
| ¹²ἄρχοντες ἐν χερσὶν αὐτῶν ἐκρεμάσθησαν πρεσβύτεροι οὐκ ἐδοξάσθησαν | ¹²Rulers were hung up by their hands; elders were not honored. |
| ¹³ἐκλεκτοὶ κλαυθμὸν ἀνέλαβον καὶ νεανίσκοι ἐν ξύλῳ ἠσθένησαν | ¹³Choice men took up the millstone, and young men stumbled with wood. |
| ¹⁴καὶ πρεσβῦται ἀπὸ πύλης κατέπαυσαν ἐκλεκτοὶ ἐκ ψαλμῶν αὐτῶν κατέπαυσαν | ¹⁴Even elders ceased from the gate, choice men from their pieces of music. |
| ¹⁵κατέλυσεν χαρὰ καρδίας ἡμῶν ἐστράφη εἰς πένθος ὁ χορὸς ἡμῶν | ¹⁵The joy of our hearts ceased; Our dance turned into mourning. |
| ¹⁶ἔπεσεν ὁ στέφανος τῆς κεφαλῆς ἡμῶν οὐαὶ δὴ ἡμῖν ὅτι ἡμάρτομεν | ¹⁶The victor's wreath fell from our heads. Woe to us, for we sinned! |
| ¹⁷περὶ τούτου ἐγενήθη ὀδυνηρὰ ἡ καρδία ἡμῶν περὶ τούτου ἐσκότασαν οἱ ὀφθαλμοὶ ἡμῶν | ¹⁷Over this our heart was grief-stricken. Over this our eyes grew dark. |
| ¹⁸ἐπ' ὄρος Σιων ὅτι ἠφανίσθη ἀλώπεκες διῆλθον ἐν αὐτῇ | ¹⁸Over mount Zion because it is gone; foxes traverse in it. |
| ¹⁹σὺ δέ κύριε εἰς τὸν αἰῶνα κατοικήσεις ὁ θρόνος σου εἰς γενεὰν καὶ γενεάν | ¹⁹But you, O Lord, live on forever; your throne continues from one generation to the next. |

| LXX Lamentations 5 | Translation of LXX Lam 5 |
|---|---|
| ²⁰ἵνα τί εἰς νῖκος ἐπιλήσῃ ἡμῶν καταλείψεις ἡμᾶς εἰς μακρότητα ἡμερῶν | ²⁰Will you forget us until the final victory? Will you abandon us days without end? |
| ²¹ἐπίστρεψον ἡμᾶς κύριε πρὸς σέ καὶ ἐπιστραφησόμεθα καὶ ἀνακαίνισον ἡμέρας ἡμῶν καθὼς ἔμπροσθεν | ²¹Restore us, O Lord, and we will be restored, and renew our days just as before. |
| ²²ὅτι ἀπωθούμενος ἀπώσω ἡμᾶς ὠργίσθης ἐφ' ἡμᾶς ἕως σφόδρα | ²²For by rejecting, you rejected us. You were angry over us to an extreme. |

# Appendix 2

## A Translation of Targum Lamentations[1]

CHRISTIAN M. M. BRADY

### TRANSLATOR'S INTRODUCTION

THE FOLLOWING TRANSLATION ITALICIZES text that represents the expansions of the Targumist. CODEX VATICANUS URBINAS HEBR. 1 (Urb. 1) is the basis of our transcription and translation. Urb. 1 was copied in 1294 CE by Yitzak ben Shimeon ha-Levi. See the facsimile introduced and translated by Étan Levine (Étan Levine, *The Targum of the Five Megillot: Codex Vatican Urbanati 1*. Jerusalem: Makor, 1977) for further details about the physical condition of the manuscript. Urb. 1 is the second oldest manuscript, regardless of tradition, and is preceded only by the Codex Solger MS 1-7.2° (Solger) manuscript of Nürnberg, which is also a WT. Solger is only three years older than Urb. 1, dated to 1291, and is likely to be the basis for the Rabbinic Bible, prepared by Felix Pratensis and printed in 1517 by Daniel Bomberg and reprinted without Tiberian pointing (and other minor alterations) by Lagarde in 1872. See Alberdina Houtman, "Targum Isaiah According to Felix Pratensis." *JAB* 1 (1999) 191–202. See especially the references to other recent scholarship on the relationship between Solger and the Rabbinic Bible (ibid., 192–93). Unfortunately a double-leaf of the Solger manuscript with TgLam 1–9a has been lost and since the first four verses of TgLam contain an extensive amount of material the loss makes Solger unsuitable as the basis for our translation and study. Where Solger is extant the differences between the two manuscripts are slight. In those cases extant where they do differ it is because Urb. 1 has omitted a portion of the text that offers a (apparently) literal rendering of MT. I have cautiously emended our text, as noted, only when Urb. 1 fails to represent the Hebrew text and Solger offers such a reading. In the one instance where Solger is not available (TgLam 1.3) I have followed Lagarde (Paulus Anton de Lagarde, *Prophetae Chaldaice e fide codicis reuchliniani*. Leipzig: Teubner, 1872). This is the only situation where I have emended the text and I have done so on the assumption that the Targumist would have fulfilled the initial and basic task of a Targum, providing a rendering of the Hebrew text, and that the omission of such a rendering is most likely the result of a copyist's error. Since there is clear evidence from Solger that an Aramaic rendering of these few omissions existed, such emendation seems reasonable.

## Targum Lamentations 1 (פרק א) | Translation Targum Lam 1

| | |
|---|---|
| 1 אמר ירמיהו נביא וכהנא רבא איכדין אתגזר על ירושלם ועל עמהא לאתדנא בתירוכין ולמספד עליהון איכה היכמה דאתדנן אדם וחוה דאתתרכו מגנתא דעדן ואספד עליהון מרי עלמא איכה ענת מדת דינא וכן אמרת על סגיאות חובהא אשתדר ומה דבגוהא בגין תהא יתבא בלחודהא כגבר דמכתש סגירו על בסריה דבלחודוהי יתיב וקרתא דהוה מליא אוכלוסין ועממין סגיאין אתרוקנת מנהון והות דמיא כארמלא ודמתרברבא בעמיא ושליטא באפרכיא והוון מסקין לה מסין הדרת למהוי מכיכא ולמתן לה כרגא בתר דנא: | 1. *Jeremiah the Prophet and High Priest told* how *it was decreed that Jerusalem and her people should be punished with banishment and that they should be mourned with 'ekah. Just as when Adam and Eve were punished and expelled from the Garden of Eden and the Master of the Universe mourned them with 'ekah. The Attribute of Justice spoke and said, "Because of the greatness of her rebellious sin that was within her, thus she will* dwell alone *as a man plagued with leprosy upon his skin who sits alone." And* the city which was full *of crowds and many* peoples *has been emptied of them and* she has become like a widow. She who was great among the nations and a ruler over provinces *which had* brought her tribute *has become lowly again and gives head tax to them from thereafter.* |
| 2 כד שלח משה נביא עזגדין לאללא ית ארעא תבו עזגדיא ואסיקו טיב ביש על ארעא דישראל וההוא לילא תשעא ביומין באב הוה וכד שמעו עמא בית ישראל ית בשורתא בישתא הדא דאתבשרו על ארע. דישראל בטלו עמא ית קלהון ובכו עמא בית ישראל בליליא ההוא מן יד תקיף רוגזא דיי עליהון וגזר למהוי בכן בליליא הדא לבריהון על חורבן בית מוקדשא וכדו אתאמר בנבואה לירמיהו כהנא רבא למהוי חריבא בית ישראל וסריבו לקבלא בכן עאל נבוכד נצר רשיעא וצדא ית ירושלם ובית מקדשא אוקיד בנורא בתשעא יומין בירחא דאב וביה בליליא בכי.ת כנשתא דישראל בכותא ודמעא זליג על לסתהא לית די ימלל תנחומין על לבהא מן כל טע- וותא די רחימת למיזל בתריהון ובגין כן כל חברהא ארשיעו בהא אתהפכו לה למהוי לה לבעיל דבבין: | 2. *When Moses the Prophet sent messengers to spy out the land, the messengers returned and gave forth a bad report concerning the land of Israel. This was the night of the ninth of Ab. When the people of the House of Israel heard this bad report which they had received concerning the land of Israel, the people lifted up their voice and* the people *of the House of Israel* wept during that night. *Immediately the anger of the LORD was kindled against them and he decreed that it should be thus in that night throughout their generations over the destruction of the Temple. When it was told through prophecy to Jeremiah the High Priest that Jerusalem would be destroyed at the hand of the wicked Nebuchadnezzar unless they repented, he immediately entered and rebuked the people of the House of Israel, but they refused to accept it. Therefore the wicked Nebuchadnezzar entered and razed Jerusalem and set fire to the Temple on the ninth day in the month of Ab. On that night, the Congregation of Israel* wept bitterly and her tears flowed down her cheeks. There was no one to speak comfortingly to her *heart* from among all *her idols* which she loved *to follow after. As a result,* all her friends *were wicked to her; they* turned against her and became her enemies. |

# APPENDIX 2

| Targum Lamentations 1 (פרק א) | Translation Targum Lam 1 |
|---|---|

3 אזלו בית יהודה בגלותא על דהוו בענן יתמין וארמלן ועל סגיאות פולחנא דהוו מפלחין באחיהון בני ישראל דאזדבנו להון ולא קרו חירותא לעבדיהון ולאמהתהון דהוו מזרעית ישראל ובגין כן אף אנון אתמסרו ביד עממיא וכנשתא דבית יהודה יתבא בגו עממיא ולא אשכחת נייח מפולחנא קשיא דשעבידו יתה [וכל דהוה רדיף יתה אדביקו יתה]² כד היא מתחבאה בין תחומיא ואעיקו לה:

3. *The House of* Judah went into exile because they were oppressing *the orphans and the widows and because of* the great servitude *to which they were subjecting their brothers, the sons of Israel, who had been sold to them. And they did not declare freedom to their servants and handmaids who were of the seed of Israel. As a result they themselves were delivered into the hand of the nations. And the Congregation of the House of Judah* dwells among the nations and finds no rest *from the hard labor to which they subject her.* [All who pursued her overtook her]² *as she was hiding* in the border regions *and they persecuted her.*

4 כל זמן דהות ירושלם מתבניא סריבו בני ישראל למסק לאתחזאה קדם יי תלת זמנין בשתא ועל חוביהון דישראל אתצדיאת ירושלם ואתעבידו שבילי ציון אבילין מדלית עאיל בה בזמן מועדיא כל תרעהא צדיין וכהנתא אנחין על דבטילו קורבניא בתולתא ספדן על דפסקו למפק בחמשא עשר יום בו וביומא דכפור דהוא בעשרא יומין בתשרי לחנגא בחנגין אף איהיא מריר לבא לחדא:

4. *All the while that Jerusalem was built, the sons of Israel refused to go up to be seen before the LORD three times a year. Because of Israel's sins Jerusalem was destroyed and* the roads to Zion are made mournful, for there is no one entering her at the time of the festivals. All the gates are desolate and her priests groan *because the sacrifices have ceased.* Her virgins mourn *because they have stopped going out on the fifteenth of Ab and on the Day of Atonement (which is on the tenth day of Tishri) to dance the dances.* Therefore she too is very bitter in her heart.

5 הוו מעיקהא מתמנן עלהא לרישין ובעלי דבבהא הוו יתבין בשלוה ארום יי תבר יתה על סגי[אות]³ מרודהא רביהא אזלו בשבייתא קדם מעיקא:

5. Those who oppress her were appointed over her as leaders and her enemies *were dwelling in* security since the LORD has broken her due to her great rebelliousness. Her children go before the oppressor into captivity.

6 ונפק מן כנשתא דציון כל זיוהא הוו רבנהא מסת־חרן על מיכלא היכמא דמסחרן איילא במדברא ולא אשכחו אתר כשר למרעיהון ואזלו בתשות כוחא ולא להום חילא למערק לאשתיזבא קדם רדיף:

6. All the glory of the Congregation of Zion has gone out from her. Her nobles *were wandering for food,* like stags who *wander in the desert* and find no *suitable place for their pasture.* They went out *in great weakness* and they had no strength *to flee to safety (from)* before the pursuer.

---

2. Found in Lagarde and necessary in order to match MT.
3. End of line, but no abbreviation.

| Targum Lamentations 1 (פרק א) | Translation Targum Lam 1 |
|---|---|
| 7 הות דכירא ירושלם יומין קדמאין דהות מדורה בכרכיא ובפצחין תקיפין ומרדא ושלטה בכל עלמא וכל רגוגא דהוו לה מלקדמין ועל חובהא נפלו עמהא בידוי דנבוכד נצר רשיעא ואעיק להון ולית די סייע לה חזונהא מעיקיא דאזלא בשביתא חייכו על טובהא דפסק מבינהא: | 7. Jerusalem remembered the days of old, *when she was surrounded by walled cities and strong open towns*, rebelling *and reigning over all the earth, and* all her lovely things which she had in earlier times. *But because of her sins,* her people fell into the hands *of the wicked Nebuchadnezz*ar *and he oppressed them and there was no one to save her.* The persecutors watched *her go into captivity* and they laughed because *her good fortune had* ceased from her. |
| 8 חובא רבא חבת ירושלם בגין כן לטלטיל הות כל עממיא דהוו מיקרין לה מלקדמין נהגו בה זילתא ארום חזו בדקהא ברם היא מתאנחא ורעתת לאחורא: | 8. Jerusalem sinned a great sin, therefore she has become a wanderer. All *the nations which* had honored her *in earlier times* treat her with contempt for they have seen her nakedness. But she groans and shrinks back. |
| 9 סואבות דם ריחוקהא בשיפולהא לא אדכיאת מניה ולא תהת על חובהא ולא דכירת מה דעתיד למיתי עלהא בסיף יומיא ונחתת ונפלת והות פרישן ולית די ימליל תנחומין לה חזי יי ותהא מסתכל ארום אתרברבו עלי בעלי דבבא: | 9. The impurity *of the menstrual blood* in her skirts *has not been cleansed from her. And she did not regret her sins, nor* did she think of *what would befall her in* the end *of days.* And she went down *and fell and* was set aside. *And* there was no one to speak comfortingly to her. Look, O LORD *and see* for my enemies have exalted themselves over me. |
| 10 ידיה אושיט נבוכד נצר רשיעא ושלף סייפא וקטע כל רגוגהא אף כנשתא דישראל שריאת ליללא ארום חזת עממין נוכראין עלו לבית מוקדשהא די פקדתה על ידוי דמשה נביא על עמון ומואב דלא ידכון למיעל בקהלא די לך: | 10. The wicked Nebuchadnezzar stretched out his hand and drew forth his sword and cut off all her lovely things. Indeed, the Congregation of Israel began to howl for she saw foreign nations go into her Temple; those about whom you commanded by Moses the prophet concerning Ammon and Moab, that they were not worthy to enter your assembly. |
| 11 כל עמא דירושלם אנין מכפנא ותבען לחמא למיכול יהבו רגוגיהום בסעיד לחמא לקיימא נפש חזי יי ותהי מסתכל ארום הויתי גרגרניתא: | 11. All the people *of Jerusalem* groan *from hunger* and search for bread *to eat.* They gave their precious things for sustenance in order to stay alive. Look O LORD and see for I have become voracious. |
| 12 אשביעית לכון כל דעברין באורחא זורו הכא איס-תכלו וחזו אין אית כיבא ככיבי דאסתקף לי דיתבר יי יתי ביום תקוף רוגזיה: | 12. I adjure you, all who pass by on the road, *turn around here.* Look and see. Is there any pain like my pain, that which has been visited upon me because the LORD shattered me in the day of his great anger? |

# APPENDIX 2

| Targum Lamentations 1 (פרק א) | Translation Targum Lam 1 |
|---|---|
| 13 מן שמיא שלח אשתא בכרכי תקיפין וכבש יתהון פרש מצדתא לרגלי ארתעני קדל קדם בעלי דבבי יהבני למהוי צדיא כל יומא מרחקא וחלישא: | 13. From heaven he sent fire into my strong cities and conquered them. He spread a net for my feet. He caused me to shrink back *before my enemies*. He caused me to be desolate all day, *abominable and* weak. |
| 14 אתיקר ניר מרודי בידיה אשתבשו בשובשין דגופנא סלקו על צורי אתקל חילי מסר יי יתי בידא מאן דלית אנא יכיל למקם: | 14. The yoke of my rebellion *was heavy* in his hand. Intertwined *like the tendrils of a vine*, they climbed upon my neck. My strength is weakened. The LORD has given me into the hands of one whom I cannot withstand. |
| 15 כבש כל תקיפי יי ביני אראע עלי זמן לתברא חיל עולימי ועלו עממי על גזירת מימרא דיי וסאיבו בתולתא דבית יהודה על די הוה דמהון דבתולתהן מתשד היך כחמר מן מעצרתא בעדן דגבר מבעט ית ענבין חמר ענבוהי שדיין: | 15. The LORD has crushed all my mighty ones within me; he has established a time against me to shatter *the strength of* my young men. *The nations entered by the decree of the Memra of* the LORD *and defiled* the virgins of the House of Judah *until their blood of their virginity was caused to flow like wine from a wine* press *when a man is* treading *grapes and grape-wine flows*. |
| 16 על טפליא דאתרעישו ועל נשיא מעבריאתא דאתבקעו כריסיהום אמרת כנשתא דישר אנא בכיא ועל עיניי זלגן דמעא מבועא דמיא ארום יתרחק מני מנחם מקים יתי וממלל תנחומין על נפשי הוו בניי צדיין ארום יתגבר עליהון בעיל דבבא: | 16. Because *of the babies who were smashed and the pregnant mothers whose wombs were ripped open*, the Congregation of Israel said, "I weep *and* my eyes flow with *tears, a spring of* water, for far from me is any comforter to revive *me and speak words of comfort for* my soul. My sons are desolate for the enemy has become master *over them*." |
| 17 פרשת ציון ידהא מן עקתא היכמה דמפרשא אתתא על מתברא פגנת ולית די ימלל תנחומין על לבבהא פקד יי לבית יעקב פקודיא ואוריתא למנטר והנון עברו על גזירת מימריה בגין כן אסתחרו חזור חזור ליעקב מעיקוהי הות ירושלם דמיא לאתתא מרחקא ביניהון: | 17. Zion spreads out her hands *from anguish like a woman spread upon the birth stool. She screams but* there is no one to speak comfortingly to her *heart*. The LORD commanded *the House of* Jacob *to keep the commandments and Torah, but they transgressed the decree of his Memra. Therefore* his oppressors *completely* encircle *Jacob*. Jerusalem is *like an* unclean *woman* amongst them. |

| Targum Lamentations 1 (פרק א) | Translation Targum Lam 1 |
|---|---|
| 18 אמר יי לעמא בית ישראל דלא יעבר קטלין בחרבא בארעהון אזל יאשיהו מלכא שלף סייפא על פרעה חגירא בבקעת מגדו מה דלא אתפקד ולא תבע אולפן מן קדם יי בגין כן רגימו רגומיא גירין למלכא יאשיהו ומית תמן ועד דלא נפקת נשמתיה הוה רחי בשפוותוי וכן אמר זכאי הוא יי ארום על מימריה עברית שמעו כען כל עממיא הספדין דאספיד ירמיהו על יאשיהו וחזו כיבי דערעני בתר מותוה בתולותיי וריביי אזלו בשבייתא: | 18. *The LORD told the people of the House of Israel that they should not allow those who kill by the sword to pass through their land. Josiah the king went forth and drew his sword against Pharaoh the Lame on the plain of Megiddo, which he had not been commanded [to do] and he had not sought instruction from before the LORD. Therefore archers shot arrows at King Josiah and he died there. Before his spirit left him he moved his lips and said, "The LORD is blameless for I have transgressed against his Memra."* Hear now all peoples, *the lamentations which Jeremiah made over Josiah* and see my affliction *which has come upon me after his death.* My maidens and young men have gone into exile. |
| 19 אמרת ירושלם כד אתמסרית בידוי דנבוכד נצר קריתי למרחמיי בני עממיא דקיימית עמהון קיים יסייעוני ואנון חכימו מני ואתהפכו לחבלא יתי הנון רומאי דעלו עם טיטוס ואספסינוס רשיעא ובנו כרכומין על ירושלם וכהניי וסביי בגו קרתא מן כפנא אתנגידו ארום תבעו סעיד לחמא הוה למיכל ויקימון ית נפשהון: | 19. *"When I was delivered into the hand of Nebuchadnezzar,"* Jerusalem said, *"I called to my friends, sons of the nations, with whom I had made treaties, to come to my aid. But they deceived me and turned to destroy me.* (These are the Romans who entered with Titus and the wicked Vespasian and they built siege works against Jerusalem.) My priests and my elders within the city *perish from hunger,* because they searched for sustenance *for themselves to eat, in order to* preserve their lives." |
| 20 חזי יי ארום אעיק לי בגין כן מעי אדגרו אתהפך לבי בגווי ארום מעבר עברית על גזירת מימרא דיי ומן בגלל הכי מן ברא תכלת חרבא ומלגיו תרגת כפנא כמלאכא מחבלא דממני על מותא: | 20. *"Look, O LORD, for I am in anguish.* Therefore my bowels are piled up and my heart turns within me, for I have surely transgressed *the decree of the Memra of the LORD. Consequently,* outside the sword bereaves and inside *the agony of starvation,* like *the Destroying Angel who is appointed over* death." |
| 21 שמעו אומיא ארום מתאנחה אנא ולית די ינחם לי כל בעלי דבבי שמעו בישתא דמטת עלי בדחו ארום את הוא יי דעבדתא איתיתהון עלי יום־פורענותא ערעתא עלי מערע לצדאותני כדין תערע עליהון ויהון צדיין כוותי: | 21. "Hear *O nations!* For *I am groaning and there is no one to comfort me. All my enemies heard of the evil* which overcame me *and were glad. For you LORD are the one who* has done *it.* You have *caused them to* bring upon me a day of retribution. *You have summoned against me a coalition to destroy me.* May you summon against them that *they may be made desolate* like me." |

# APPENDIX 2

| Targum Lamentations 1 (פרק א) | Translation Targum Lam 1 |
|---|---|
| 22 תיעול ליום דינא רבא כל בשותהום דאבישו לי קדמך ותסתקף להום היכמה דאסתקפתא עלי על סגיאות מרודי ארום סגיאו אנחתיי ולבי חלש: | 22. "May there enter before you *on the great judgment day* all their evil deeds *which they have done to me*. May you turn against them as you have turned against me because of my great rebellion. For my groaning are great and my heart is weak." |

| Targum Lamentations 2 (פרק ב) | Translation Targum Lam 2 |
|---|---|
| 1 איכדין יקוץ יי בתקוף רוגזיה ית כנשתא דציון טלק מן שמיא לארעא תושבחת דישראל ולא דכר בית מקדשיה דהוה גלוגדקא דרגלוהי ולא חס עלוהי ביום תקוף רוגזיה: | 1. How the LORD has detested the Congregation of Zion in his *fierce* anger. He threw down from the heavens to the earth the glory of Israel and he did not remember *the Temple which was* his footstool *nor did he spare it* in the day of his *fierce* anger. |
| 2 שיצי יי ולא חס ית כל עידית בית יעקב פגר ברוגזיה כנשתא דבית יהודא אמטי לארעא אפיס מלכותא דהם רברבנהא: | 2. The LORD destroyed and did not spare any of the choice dwellings of *the House of* Jacob. In his anger he destroyed the Congregation of the House of Judah and brought them to the ground. He broke the kingdom, crushed her leaders. |
| 3 קצץ בתקוף רגז ית כל יקרא דיעקב ארתע לאחורא [יד][4] ימיניה ולא סייע לעמיה מן קדם בעיל דבבא ואדלק בבית יעקב כאשתא דמלהבא אכלת חזור חזור: | 3. In his fierce anger he cut off all the glory of Israel.[4] He drew back his right [hand][3] *and did not help his people* from before the enemy and he burned in the House of Jacob like a searing fire which consumes on all sides. |
| 4 מתח קשתיה וגרם עלי גירין כבעיל דבבא אתעתד על ימיניה דנבוכד נצר וסייעיה כאילו הוה מעיק לעממיה בית ישראל וקטל כל עולם וכל דמרגגין לחיזו עינא במשכן כנשתא דציון שדא כבעור אשתא רוגזא: | 4. He drew his bow *and shot arrows at me* like an enemy. He stood ready at the right *of Nebuchadnezzar and aided him* as if *he himself were* oppressing *his people, the House of Israel*. And he killed *every young man and* everything which was beautiful to see. In the tent of the Congregation of Zion he poured out *his anger* like a burning fire. |
| 5 הוה יי לבעיל דבבא שיצי ישראל שיצי כל בירניתיה [תרגום אחר] מטורחא חביל כל קרוי פצחהא ואסגי בכנשתא דישר דבית יהודא אבילותא ואנינותא: | 5. The LORD has become like an enemy. He destroyed Israel. He destroyed all her forts and razed all her open cities. He has increased in *the Congregation of* the House of Judah mourning and grief. |
| 6 ושרש כגנתא בית מקדשיה חביל אתר מזומן לכפרא על עמיה אנשי יי בציון חדות יומא טבא ושבתא ושנא בתקוף רוגזיה מלכא וכהנא רבא: | 6. He uprooted his Temple like a garden. He razed the place appointed *for the atonement of his people*. The LORD has caused *the joy of* the festival and the Sabbath to be forgotten and in his fierce anger he hates the king and *high* priest. |
| 7 אשלי יי בית מדבחיה בעט מקדשיה מסר ביד בעיל דבבא שורי בירנייתהא קלא יהבו בבית מוקדשא דיי כקל עמא בית ישראל דמצלין בגויה ביומא דפסחא: | 7. The LORD has abandoned his altar. He has trampled his Temple. He has handed over the walls of the forts to the enemy. They raised a shout in the Temple of the LORD like *the shout of the people of the House of Israel praying in it on* the day of Passover. |

4. Omitted by Urb. 1, but found in most MSS, including Solger.

# APPENDIX 2

| Targum Lamentations 2 (פרק ב) | Translation Targum Lam 2 |
|---|---|
| 8 חשיב יי לחבלא שור כנשתא דציון סאט משקליתיא ולא אתיב ידיה מלשיצאה ואביל מקפנא ושורא כחדא אתפרו: | 8. The LORD resolved to destroy the wall of the Congregation of Zion. He swung the plummet and did not turn back his hand from destroying it. He caused the rampart and the wall to mourn; they were destroyed together. |
| 9 טמעו בארע תרעהא על די מן נכסו חזירא ואובילו דמיה עלויהון הובד ותבר מזוזתהא מלכה ורברבנהא גלו ביני עממיא על דלא נטרו פתגמי אוריתא כאילו לא קבילו יתה בטורא דסיני אף נבייהא אתמנע מנהון רוח נבואת קודשא ולא אתאמר להום פתגם נבואה מן קדם יי: | 9. Her gates have sunk into the earth *because they slaughtered a pig and brought its blood over them*. He has destroyed and shattered her doorposts. Her king and rulers were exiled among the nations *because they did* not *keep the decrees of Torah, as if they had not received it on Mount Sinai*. Even her prophets *had the holy spirit of prophecy withheld from them and they* were not told a word *of prophecy* from *before the* LORD. |
| 10 יתבין לארעא וישתקין סבי כנשתא דציון אסיקו אפר מקלה על רישיהון קמארו סקן על בשריהון אחיתו לעפרא דארעא רישיהון בתולתא דירושלם: | 10. The Elders of the Congregation of Zion sit on the ground in silence. They throw *wood* ashes upon their heads. They gird sackcloth *upon their bodies*. The virgins of Jerusalem bow their heads to *the dust of* the earth. |
| 11 ספק בדמעין עיני אדגראן מעיי אתשד לארעא כבדי על תבר כנשתא דעמי כד צווחו עולימא וינקא בפתאוות קרייאתא: | 11. My eyes are spent with tears, my bowels are piled up, my liver is spilt onto the ground because of the destruction of the Congregation of my people as youths and infants cried out in the open places of the cities. |
| 12 לאמיהון אמרין רוביא דישראל אן עיבור וחמר כד הוו צחיין בקטיל חרבא מן צחותא בפתאוות קרייאתא כד אתשד נפשהון מן כפנא לגו עטיף אמהון: | 12. *The youth of Israel* ask their mother, "Where is the bread and wine?" as they thirst *in the same way* as one wounded *by the sword [suffers] from thirst* in the open places of the cities, as their life is poured out *from hunger* into their mother's bosom. |
| 13 מה אסהד בך ומה אהי מדמי לך כנשתא דירושלם מה אחבר לך ואיהי מנחם לך בתולתא דכנשתא דציון ארום סגא תבריך כסגיאות תבר גללי ימא רבא בעדן נחשוליהון ומאן הוא אסא די יסי יתיך מן מרעיתך: | 13. What can I bring to bear witness to you? Or to what can I compare you, O Congregation of Jerusalem? How shall I befriend you that I may console you, O Virgin of the Congregation of Zion? For *great is* your breaking, as great as the *breaking of the waves of the Great* Sea *during the season of their gales*. And who is the doctor who can heal you *of your affliction*? |

| Targum Lamentations 2 (פרק ב) | Translation Targum Lam 2 |
|---|---|
| 14 נביאי שקר דבביניך הינון חזו ליך שקראולית מששלנבואתהון ולא פרסימו ית פורענותא דעתיד למיתי עלך בגלל חובך לאהדרותיך בתיובתא אלהן נביאו לך נבואת מגן ומלי טעותא: | 14. *The false* prophets *within you, they* have seen falsehood for you *and there is* no substance *to their prophecies*. Nor did they make known *the punishment which would overtake you* as a result of your sin, in order to make you turn back in repentance. *Rather,* they prophesied to you vain prophecies and erring words. |
| 15 שפקו עלך ידיהון כל עברי אורחא שרקו בשפוותהום וטלטילו ברישיהון על כנשת דירושלם אמרן בפומהון הדא היא קרתא דהוו אמרין אבהתן וסביא דמלקדמין דהיא גמירת נוי ושופרא חדות כל יתבי ארעא: | 15. All those who passed by the way clapped their hands at you. They hissed *with their lips* and wagged their heads at the Congregation of Jerusalem. *They said with their mouths,* "Is this the city *which* our fathers and elders of old called the perfection of beauy *and loveliness;* the joy of all the earth's *inhabitants?*" |
| 16 פתחו עליך פומהון כל בעלי דבביך שרקו בשפוותהום ועסיאו שניאון אמרו שיצינא ברם דין יומא דהוינא מתיאנן אשכחנא חזינא: | 16. All your enemies open their mouths at you. They hissed *with their lips* and gnashed their teeth and say, "We have destroyed! Surely this is the day we have waited for. We have found it; we have seen it." |
| 17 עבד יי מה דחשיב גמר מימר פומיה די פקיד למשה נביא מן יומין קדמאין דאי לא נטרין בני ישראל ית פקודיא דיי עתיד לאתפרעא מנהון פגר ולא חס ואחדי עלך בעיל דבבא ארום יקר מעיקיך: | 17. The LORD has done what he planned. He completed the *Memra* of his *mouth* which he commanded *to Moses the prophet* long ago: *that if the children of Israel did not keep the commandments of the LORD he was going to punish them.* He destroyed and had no mercy. He has caused the enemy to rejoice over you for he has exalted your oppressors. |
| 18 צווח לבהון דישראל קדם יי די ירחם עליהון שורא דקרתא דציון זלוגי כנחלא דמעין יומא וליליא לא תתני תנחומא לצעריך לפייגא צלותא דיליך ולא תשתוק בבת עיניך מלדמע: | 18. The heart of Israel cried out before the LORD, *to have mercy on them.* O wall of the city of Zion, weep tears like a torrent day and night. Give no *comfort to your sorrows, to* slacken *in the prayer that is* yours. May your eyes not cease *from weeping.* |
| 19 קומי כנשתא דישר דשריא בגלותא עסוקי במשנה בליליא ארום שכנתא דיי שריא לקביליך ובפתגמי אוריתא בשירוי מטרת שפרפרא שדיאי הי כמיא עקמומית לביך והדרי בתיובתא וצליאי בית כנשתא קביל אפי יי טולי לותיה בצלו ידיך על נפשת עולימיך דצחיין בכפנא בריש כל מחוזין: | 19. Arise, *O Congregation of Israel dwelling in exile.* Busy yourself *with Mishnah* in the night, *for the Shekinah of the LORD is dwelling before you, and with the words of Torah* at the beginning *of the morning* watch. Pour out like water *the crookedness of* your heart *and turn in repentance. And pray in the synagogue* before the face of the LORD. Raise your hands to him in prayer for the life of your children *who thirst* with hunger at the head of every open market. |

# APPENDIX 2

| Targum Lamentations 2 (פרק ב) | Translation Targum Lam 2 |
|---|---|
| 20 חזי יי ותהי מסתכל מן שמיא למן אסתקפתא כדנן אם חזי לבנאתא דישר למיכל בכפנא פירי בטניהון עולימיא רגיגתא דהוו מתלפפין בסדיניא דמילתין ענת מדת דינא וכן אמרת אם חזי למקטל בבית מקדשא דיי כהנא ונבייא כמה דקטלתון לזכריה בר עדוא כהנא רבא ונביא מהימן בבית מקדא דיי ביומא דכפוריא על דאוכח יתכון דלא תעבדון דביש קדם יי: | 20. See, O LORD, and observe *from heaven* against whom you have turned. Thus is it *right for the* daughters *of Israel* to eat the fruit *of their wombs due to starvation, lovely* children wrapped *in fine linen? The Attribute of Justice replied, and said,* "Is it right to kill priest and prophet in the Temple of the LORD, *as when you killed Zechariah son of Iddo, the High Priest and faithful prophet in the Temple of the LORD on the Day of Atonement because he told you not to do evil before the LORD?"* |
| 21 דמכו על ארעא דמחוזין עולימא וסבא דהוו רגילין למשכוב על כרין דמילא ועל ערסין דשן דפיל בתולתיי וריביי נפלו קטלין בחרבא קטלתא ביום רוגזך נכסתא ולא חסתא: | 21. The young and the old *who were accustomed to recline on pillows of fine wool and upon ivory couches* were prostrate on the earth of the open markets. My virgins and youths have fallen, *killed* by the sword. You have killed in the day of your anger; you have slaughtered and shown no pity. |
| 22 תהי קרי חירותא לעמך בית ישראל על יד מלכא משיחא היכמא דעבדתא על יד משה ואהרן ביומא דאפיקת ית ישראל ממצרים ואתכנשון עולימיי חזור חזור מן כל אתר דאתבדרו תמן בים תקוף רוגז יי ולא הוה בהום שיזבא ושארא דלפיפית בסדינין ודרביתי בתפנוקי מלכין בעלי דבבי שיציאונן: | 22. You will declare *freedom to your people, the House of Israel, by the King Messiah just* as *you did by Moses and Aaron* on the day when you brought Israel up from Egypt. *My children will gather* all around, *from every place to which they had scattered* in the day of your *fierce* anger, O LORD, and there was no escape for them nor any survivors *of those whom I had* wrapped *in fine linen.* And my enemies destroyed those whom I had raised *in royal comfort.* |

חצי הספר (Middle of the Book)

| Targum Lamentations 3 (פרק ג) | Translation of LXX Lam 3 |
|---|---|
| 1 אנא הוא גברא דחזא ענוייא בחוטרא דרדי ברוגזיה: | 1. I am *that* man who has seen affliction by the rod *which chastises in* his anger. |
| 2 יתי דבר ואוביל לחשוכא ולא לנהורא: | 2. He has led and brought me to darkness, and not to light. |
| 3 ברם בי יתוב יגלגל עלי מחתיה כל יומא: | 3. To me only does he turn, heaping *upon* me his blows all day. |
| 4 עתק בשרי ממכתשין ומשכי מן מחתא תבר גרמי: | 4. My flesh is worn out *from beatings,* my skin *from the blow.* He has shattered my bones. |
| 5 בנה כרכומין ואקף קרתא ועקר רישי עמא ושלהיאונון: | 5. He has built *siegeworks* and surrounded *the city. He has uprooted* the heads *of the people* and wearied *them.* |
| 6 בבית אסורין דחשוכא אותבני כמיתין דאזלו לעמא אוחרן: | 6. He has caused me to dwell in a dark *prison* like the dead *who have gone to the other* world. |
| 7 סגר בתריי בגין דלא אפוק מן טריקא יקר על רגליי כבלין דנחשא: | 7. He has locked me in *so that* I cannot go out *from the prison.* He has put heavy brass *fetters on my feet.* |
| 8 אף ארום אצוח ואצלי אסתתם בית צלותי: | 8. Even when I cry out and pray *the house of* my prayer is blocked. |
| 9 סגר אורחי במרמרין פסילן שבילוי סראו: | 9. He has closed my paths with hewn *marble* stones. He has confounded my paths. |
| 10 דיבא מכמן הוא לי אריה דמטמר בכיבשא: | 10. He is a bear, lying in wait for me; a lion *hiding* in a hallow. |
| 11 אורחי סראב ושסעיני שויאני צדו: | 11. He has confounded my path and rent me. He has made me desolate. |
| 12 מתח קשתיה ועתדני היכפל גליסא לגירא: | 12. He draws his bow and has set me as a target for the arrow. |
| 13 אעיל בכיליתאיי בירית תיקיה: | 13. He made the arrows of his quiver enter my vitals. |
| 14 הויתי חוכא לכל פריצי עמי ומזמרן עלי כל יומא: | 14. I have become a laughing stock to all *the* bold of my people; they mock me in song all day. |
| 15 אשבעני מרירות חיוון ארווי נגיריא: | 15. He has sated me with gall *of snakes* and made me drunk with wormwood. |
| 16 ורצץ בפרירן שניי בניעיתני קטמא: | 16. And he crushed my teeth with gravel; he has pressed me into ashes. |
| 17 וקצת מלמשאל בשלם נפשי אנשיתי טיבותא: | 17. And my soul shrinks from greeting; I have forgotten goodness. |
| 18 ואמרית הובד תוקפי וטובא דהויתי אוריך מן קדם יי: | 18. And I said, "My strength is destroyed and *the goodness which* I had waited for from *before* the LORD." |

# APPENDIX 2

| Targum Lamentations 3 (פרק ג) | Translation of LXX Lam 3 |
|---|---|
| 19 אדכר ענוי נפשי ומה דאמרירו בישנאי ואשקיאו יתי גדין ורישי חיון: <br> 20 מדכר תדכר ותצלי עלי נפשי על סגופא: <br> 21 דא נחמתא אתיב על לבי בגין כן אוריך: | 19. "Remember the affliction *of my soul and how my foes* embittered *me and caused me to drink* wormwood *and the poison of snakes.*" <br> 20. My soul surely will remember and bow down within me *due to affliction.* <br> 21. This *consolation* I call to mind, therefore I have hope: |
| 22 טיבותא דיי ארום לא פסקו ארום לא אתמנעו רחמוהי: <br> 23 נסין חדתין מרחישבצפריא סגיאה היא הימנותך: <br> 24 חולקי יי אמרת נפשי בגין כן אוריך ליה: | 22. The goodness of the LORD, for his mercies do not end nor have they ceased. <br> 23. *He brings forth* new *wonders* in the mornings; great is your faithfulness. <br> 24. "The LORD is my portion," says my soul; therefore I will hope in him. |
| 25 טב הוא יי לסברין לפורקניה לנפשא דתבע אולפניה: <br> 26 טב לאורכא ולמשתק עד כדו דתמטי פורקנא דיי: <br> 27 טב הוא לגברא ארום יאלף נפשיה לסוברא ניר פקודיא בטליותיה: | 25. The LORD is good to those who hope *for his salvation;* to the soul who seeks his *instruction.* <br> 26. It is good to wait and be silent until the salvation of the LORD *comes.* <br> 27. It is good for a man *to train himself* to bear the yoke *of the commandments* in his youth. |
| 28 יתיב בלחודוהי וישתיק ויסבול אסורין דאתין עלוהי בגין יחודא דשמא דיי דמשתלחין לאתפרעא מניה על חובא קלילא דחב בעלמא הדין עד כדו די יחוס עלוהי ויטלענון מניה ויקבל אפי שלים לעלמא דאתי: <br> 29 יתן בעפרא פומיה וישתטח קדם ריבוניה מאים אית סבר: <br> 30 יושיט למחי ליה ליסתא בגין דחלתא דיי יסבע דקלנא: | 28. Let him sit alone and be silent, bearing *the corrections which have come* upon him, *for the sake of the unity of the name of the LORD, which have been sent to punish him for the minor sins which he has committed in this world, until he have mercy upon him and lift them from him so that he may receive him perfected in the world to come.* <br> 29. Let him put his mouth to the dust *and prostrate himself before his master,* perhaps there is hope. <br> 30. Let him turn his cheek to the one that smites; *for the sake of the fear of the LORD,* let him be filled with insult. |
| 31 ארום לא ישלי יי לעובדוהי לעלם לממסרנון בידא דסנאיהון: <br> 32 ארום אלהן ברישא יתבר ובתר כן יתוב וירחם לצדיקיא בסגיאות טיבותיה: <br> 33 ארום מן בגלל דלא עני גבר ית נפשיה ואעדי זחוחא מלביה בגין כן גרם לאסתקפא תברא בבני אנשא: | 31. For the LORD will not neglect *his servants* forever, *giving them over into the hand of their enemy.* <br> 32. But *first he breaks and afterwards he repents and* has mercy *on the righteous* in the abundance of his goodness. <br> 33. For *since man did not* afflict *himself nor removed arrogance* from his heart, *therefore* he *caused* destruction *to come* among humanity. |

| Targum Lamentations 3 (פרק ג) | Translation of LXX Lam 3 |
|---|---|
| 14 למככה ולכבשא תחות רגלוי כל אסירי ארעא: <br> 14 ולמצלי דין גבר מסכן כל קבל אפי עלאה: <br> 14 לסבבא אנשמסכן במצותיה אפשר דמן קדם יי לא אתגלי: | 34. Humbling *and subduing* all the prisoners of the earth under his feet, <br> 35. Perverting the justice of a *poor* man in the presence of the Most High, <br> 36. Confounding a *poor* man in his quarrels; *is it possible that this will not* be revealed before the LORD? |
| 37 מן הוא אנש דאמר והות בשתא מתעבדא בעלמא אלהן מן בגלל דעבדו מה דלא אתפקדו מן פומא דיי: <br> 38 מפום אלהא עלאה לא תפוק בשתא אלהן על ברת קלא רמיחא בגין חטופין דאתמליאת ארעא ועדן דבעי למגזר טובא בעלמא מן פום קודשיה נפקא: <br> 39 מה ממון ושכח אנשדי יחוב כל יומי חיוהי גברא רשיעא על חובוהי: | 37. Who is the man who has spoken *and an evil thing* was done *in the world, unless because they did that which they* were not commanded by *the mouth of* the LORD? <br> 38. From the mouth of *God* Most High there does not issue evil, *rather by the hint of a whisper, because of the violence with which the land is filled. But when he desires to decree* good *in the world it issues from the holy mouth.* <br> 39. What profit shall a man *find who sins all the days of* his life; *a wicked* man for his sins? |
| 40 נבלוש אורחנא ונבקר ונתוב בתיובתא קדם יי: <br> 41 נטול לבבנא בריר ונרמי חטוף וגזילן מן ידנא ונתוב קדם אלהא דמדור שכנתיה בשמי מרומא: <br> 42 נחנא מרדנא סראבנא ומן בגלל דלא הדרנא לוותך אנת לא שבקתא: | 40. Let us search and examine our ways; and turn *in repentance* before the LORD. <br> 41. Let us lift our *cleansed* hearts *and cast away theft and robbery from* our hands. *And let us repent* before God *the dwelling of whose Shekinah is* in heaven *above.* <br> 42. We have rebelled and been disobedient *and since we did not return to you,* you have not forgiven. |
| 43 טללתא עלנא ברגוז ורדפתנא בגלותא קטלתא ולא חסתא: <br> 44 טללתא שמיא בעננין יקרא דילך מן בגלל דלא תעבר לותך צלותנא: <br> 45 טלטולין ורטישין שויתא יתנא בגו עממיא: | 43. You have covered *us* in anger and pursued us *in exile.* You have killed and have not pitied. <br> 44. You have covered *the heavens* with your clouds *of glory* so that *our* prayers cannot cross to you. <br> 45. You have made us like wanderers and vagabonds among the nations. |
| 46 פתחו עלנא פומהון כל בעלי דבבנא למגזר עלנא גזירן בישין: <br> 47 אימתא וזיעא הות לנא מנהון אחדת יתנא רתיתא ותברא: <br> 48 היכיבלין דמיא זלגת עיני דמען על תבירא דכנשת עמי: | 46. All our enemies have opened their mouths against us, *to announce evil decrees against us.* <br> 47. Panic and fear have come upon us *because of them,* trembling and destruction *have seized us.* <br> 48. *Like* streams of water my eye weeps tears because of the destruction of the Congregation of my people. |

# APPENDIX 2

| Targum Lamentations 3 (פרק ג) | Translation of LXX Lam 3 |
|---|---|
| 49 עיני זלגת דמעין ולא תשתיק מלמבכי מדלית פאיג עקתי וממלל תנחומין לי: <br> 50 עד כדו דסיתכי ויחזו עולבני יי מן שמיא: <br> 51 בכותא דעייני אסתקפת למרע נפשי על חורבן פילכי עמי וניוול בנתא דירושלם קרתי: | 49. My eye weeps *tears* and does not cease *from crying*. There is no respite *from my anguish or anyone to comfort me;* <br> 50. Until the LORD looks out and sees *my humiliation* from heaven. <br> 51. *The weeping of* my eyes is the cause *of the affliction of* my soul *over the destruction of the districts of my people and the humiliation of* the daughters *of Jerusalem, my city.* |
| 52 כמנא כמנו לי הי כצפורא בעלי דבבי על מגן: <br> 53 עברו בגובא חיי ורגמא אבנא בי: <br> 54 שאטו מיא על רישי אמרית במימרי אתגזרית מן עלמא: | 52. My enemies, without cause, laid a trap for me like a bird. <br> 53. They have caused my life to pass in the pit and cast stones at me. <br> 54. Waters flowed over my head. I said *in my word,* "I am cut off *from the world."* |
| 55 צליתי לשמך יי מן גוב ארעיתא: <br> 56 צלותי קבילתא בזמנא ההיא וכען לא תכסי אודנך מלקבלא צלותי לארווחותני בגין בעותי: <br> 57 קריבתא מלאכא לשיזבותני ביומא דצליתי לך אמרת במימרך לא תדחל: | 55. I prayed to your name, O LORD, from the depths of the pit. <br> 56. You received my prayer *at that time, and now* do not cover your ears *from receiving my prayer* to give me relief *because of* my plea. <br> 57. You brought *the angel* near *to save me,* in the day that I prayed to you. You said *by your Memra,* "Do not fear." |
| 58 נציתא יי לעבדי מצותא לנפשי פרקתא מן ידיהון חוי: <br> 59 חזית יי סרוך דסריכו לי דון דינייי: <br> 60 גלי קדמך כל נקמתהון כל מזמתהון עלי: | 58. You have fought, O LORD, *against those who made* a quarrel with my soul. You delivered my life *from their hands.* <br> 59. You have seen, O LORD, *the wrong by which* they wronged me. Judge my case. <br> 60. All their vengeance has been revealed *before you,* all their evil plans against me. |
| 61 שמיע קדמך כסופיהון יי כל מזימתהון עלי: <br> 62 שפוות קיימין עלי ולהיגיונהום עלי כל יומא: <br> 63 מותבנהון וזקיפתהון אסתכל אנא זמריהון: | 61. Their taunts were heard *before you,* O LORD, all their evil plans against me. <br> 62. The lips of the enemies *are against me* and their mutterings are against me all day. <br> 63. Look at their sitting and rising! I am [the object of] their taunt-songs. |
| 64 תתיב להון גמולא בישא יי כעובדי ידיהון: <br> 65 תתן להון תבירות לבא ושלהאותך ישלהי להון: <br> 66 תדלוקנן ברוגזא ותשיצנון מתחות שמי מרומא דיי: | 64. May you return to them *evil* recompense, O LORD, according to the works of their hands. <br> 65. May you give them brokenness of heart and may your *weariness* wear them out. <br> 66. Pursue them in anger and destroy them from under the *high* heaven of the LORD. |

| Targum Lamentations 4 (פרק ד) | Translation of Targum Lam 4 |
|---|---|
| 1 היכדין עמא דהב בית מוקדשא אשתני פידלון בחיר משתדיין מרגלאוון קדישין בריש כל מחוזין: | 1. How the gold *of the Temple* has dimmed, the choice gold leaf has changed! The sacred jewels are scattered at the head of every street. |
| 2 בני ציון יקרין דמתילין איקוניהון לדהב טב היכדין הוו עממין מסאבין מחתן יתהום כל קביל ערסיהון ומסתכלין בהון בגין דילדון נשיהון בנין שפיריא כשופריהון ואתחשיבו ללגינין [דחסף]⁵ עובדי ידי פחרא: | 2. The precious *Sons of Zion* which were comparable *in their appearance to that of fine* gold, *how the unclean people brought them down near to their beds and stare at them, so that their wives might bear sons as beautiful as they and* they are considered as [clay]⁵ vessels which were made by the hands of the potter. |
| 3 אף בנאתא דישראל מפנקאתא לבני עממיא דדמין לחורמנא טלען תדיהון וריבי כנשתא דעמי מסירן לאכזוראין ואמהון ספדן עליהון כנעמיא במדברא: | 3. Even *the pampered daughters of Israel* untie their breasts *to the nations who are like* the basilisk. And the young men of the Congregation of my people *are handed over to cruel men and their mothers mourn over them* like ostriches in the desert. |
| 4 אדבק לישן עולימא למוריגיה בצחותא טליא תבעו לחמא מושיט לית להום: | 4. The infant's tongue clings to its palate from thirst. Youngsters ask for bread, but there is no one who offers it to them. |
| 5 דהוו רגילין למיכל תפנוקין אשתוממו במחוזין דאתרביאו על צבע זהורין גפיפו קיקלאתן: | 5. Those who *used to* eat delicacies were desolate in the markets. Those who were reared in *the color* crimson embrace dunghills. |
| 6 וסגי חובת כנשתא דעמי מן חובת סדום דאתהפכת כשעתא ולא שריאו בה נביאיא לאתנבאה לאהדרותא בתיובתא: | 6. The sin of the Congregation of my people is greater than the sin of Sodom which was overthrown in a moment. And no *prophets* were left in her *to prophesy, to turn her back in* repentance. |
| 7 הוו בריריו נזירהא מתלגא שעעו יתיר מן חלבא סמיקו חיזו יתיר מזהורין ושבזיזא פרציפיהוון: | 7. Her Nazarites were purer than snow, smoother than milk. Their appearance was ruddier than crimson and their faces like sapphires. |
| 8 חשך מן אוכמתא דגלותא ריויהון לא אשתמודעו במחוזין אדק משכיהון על גרמיהון פריך הוה בקיסא: | 8. Their appearance was darker than the blackness *of the exile*; they were not recognized in the markets. Their skin clung to their bones; brittle as a twig. |
| 9 מעלי הוו קטילי סייפא יתיר מקטילי כפן דקטילי סייפא דייבו כד אנון מבזעין בכריסיהון מן מה דאכלו מעלל חקלא ונפיחי כפנא פריק כריסיהון מן מיכלא: | 9. Better were those who were slain by the sword than those who were slain by hunger, *for those slain by the sword* perished⁶ when pierced *in their bellies because they ate of* the gleanings of the field; *and those who were bloated from hunger; their bellies burst from food.* |

---

5. Found in Solger and necessary in order represent all of MT.
6. Literally, "flowed."

# APPENDIX 2

| Targum Lamentations 4 (פרק ד) | Translation of Targum Lam 4 |
|---|---|
| 10 ידי נשיא דהואן מרחמן על מסכינין בשילו עולי־מיהון הוו למסעד להום ביום תבר כפנא דאתברת כנשתא דעמי: | 10. The hands of women *who were* merciful *towards the poor* boiled their young, they became sustenance for them when *the day of famine* broke, *when* the Congregation of my people *was destroyed*. |
| 11 סף יי חמתיה שדא על ירושלם ית תקוף רוגזיה ואסיק בעור אשתא בציון ואכלת אושוותהא: | 11. The LORD has finished his anger; he has poured out his *fierce* wrath *upon Jerusalem* and he has brought up a *raging* fire in Zion, and it consumed her foundations. |
| 12 לא הוו מהומנין מלכות ארעא וכל דיירי תבל ארום יעול נבוכד נצר רשיעא ונבוזר אדן בעיל דבבא לנכסא עמא בית ישראל בתרעיא דירושלם: | 12. The kingdoms of the earth did not believe, nor did those who dwell in the world, that *the wicked* Nebuchadnezzar *and Nebuzaradan* the enemy would enter *to slaughter the people of the House of Israel* in the gates of Jerusalem. |
| 13 ענת מדת דינא וכן אמרת לא הוות כל דא אלהן מחובת נביאהא דמנבאן לה נבואת שקרא ומעווית כהנתא דאסיקו קטורת בוסמין לטעוותא ואנן גרמו לאתשד בגווה דם זכאין: | 13. *The Attribute of Justice* spoke up and said, "All this would not have happened but for the sins of her prophets *who prophesied to her false prophesies* and the iniquity of her priests *who offered up burning incense to idols*. They themselves caused the blood of the innocent to be shed in her midst." |
| 14 אטלטלו עוירן במחוזין אטנפו בדם קטילין דחרבא ועל דלא הוו יכילין למחמי קריבו בלבושיהון: | 14. The blind wandered about in the markets, defiled with the blood *of those slain by the sword and since* they could not *see* they touched their clothes. |
| 15 זורו ממסאבא קרו עממיא זורו לא תקרבון בהום ארום אתקוטטו אף אטלטלו אמרו במהויהון בשלוותהום דביני עממיא לא יסופון למדר: | 15. "Turn away from the unclean!" cried *the peoples*, "Turn away, turn away! Do not touch them!" For they quarreled, indeed they wandered. They said, *when they were peacefully established* among the nations, "They shall not continue to dwell [here]." |
| 16 מן קדם אפי יי אתפליגו לא יוסיף לאסתכלא בהום בגין כן אומיא רשיעיא אפי כהניא לא סברו ועלוי סביא לא חסו: | 16. They were dispersed *from before* the face of the LORD, he no longer regarded them. *Therefore the wicked nations* did not respect the priests nor did they spare the elders. |
| 17 עוד ספאן עיינא לאסתכלא לסיוענא דהוינא מתינן לרומאי דאתהפיך לנא להבלו בסכיתנא דאסתכיתנא לאדומאי דאנון עמא דלא יפרוק: | 17. Our eyes still fail to see our help *which we expected to come from the Romans, but which turned* to naught *for us*. In hope we watched for the *Edomites who were a* nation which could not save. |

244

| Targum Lamentations 4 (פרק ד) | Translation of Targum Lam 4 |
|---|---|
| 18 הנון צדאן שבילנא מלמיהך לרוחצן בפלטייתנא אמרנא קריב סופנא אתמליאו יומנא ארום מטא סופנא: | 18. They prowled our paths so that we could not walk *safely* in our open places. *We said,* "Our end is near; our days are fulfilled," for our end had come. |
| 19 קלילן הוו רדיפנא יתיר מנשרי שמיא על טווריא אדלקו יתנא במדברא כמאנו לנא: | 19. Our pursuers were swifter *than* the eagles of the heavens; unto the mountains they chased us, in the desert they lay in wait for us. |
| 20 מלכא יאשיהו די הוה חביב לנא כנשמת רוח חיים דבאפנא והוה מתרבי במשח רבותא דיי אתחד במצד חבולהון דמצראי דהוינא אמרין עלוהי בטלל זכותיה ניחי ביני עממיא: | 20. *King Josiah, who was as dear to us as the breath of* the spirit *of life in* our nostrils *and was anointed with* the anointing *oil of the* LORD, was locked *up in Egypt's* snare *of corruption.* It was he of whom we said, "In the shadow *of his merit* we will live among the nations." |
| 21 חדאי ובדו.י. קושטנטינא קרתא דאדום רשיעא דמתבניאה בארע ארמניאה בסביאן אוכלוסין דמן עמא דאדום אף עלייך עתיד למיתי פורענותא ויצדון יתך פרכוואי ותיעבר עלייך כס דלווט תרווי ותתרוקני: | 21. Rejoice and be of good cheer *Constantinople,* city of *wicked* Edom, *which is* built in the land of Armenia *with crowds from the people of Edom. Retribution is about to come upon* even you, *and the Parkevi will destroy you and* the accursed cup shall pass *to you and* you shall become drunk and exposed. |
| 22 ובתר כן ישלים עוויתיך כנשתא דציון ותתפרקון על ידוי דמלכא משיחא דאליהו כהנא רבא ולא יוסיף יי תוב לאגלותיך ובי הוא זמנא אסער עוותיך רומי רשעא דמתבניאה באיטליאה ומליאה אוכלוסין מבני אדום וייתון פרסאי ויעיקון עלך וליצדון יתך ארום אתפרסם קדם יי על חובתיך: | 22. *And after this* your iniquity will be finished, O Congregation of Zion. *But you will be freed by the hands of the King Messiah and Elijah*[7] *the High Priest and* the LORD will no longer exile you. *And at that time* I will punish your iniquities, *wicked Rome, built in Italy and filled with crowds* of Edomites. *And the Persians will come and oppress you and destroy you for* your sins have been made known *before the LORD*. |

---

7. Following Solger which reads ואליהו.

# APPENDIX 2

| Targum Lamentations 5 (פרק ה) | Translation of Targum Lam 5 |
|---|---|
| 1 הוי דכיר [יי] מה דאתגזר למהוי לנא אסתכל מן שמיא וחזי ית כסופנא: | 1. Remember, [O LORD], what *was decreed* to befall us; look *from heaven* and see our disgrace. |
| 2 אחסנתנא אתהפכת לחלונאין ביתנא לעמין נוכראין: | 2. Our inheritance has been turned over to strangers; our house to foreign peoples. |
| 3 הוינא מתילן ליתמין דלית להון אבא אמהתנא כארמלן דאזלו גבריהון בקרוי ימא ומספקא להון אין נון קיימין: | 3. We have become *like* orphans who have no father, our mothers like widows *whose husbands have gone into the cities of the sea and it is uncertain if they are alive.* |
| 4 מימנא בכספא שתינא וקיסנא בדמין יתון: | 4. We drink our water for money and our wood comes at a price. |
| 5 על פריקת צוורנא אטעננא כד הוינא אזלן בשביתא חמא נבוכד נצר רשיעא סרכיא דבני ישראל דאזלין ריקנין פקיד לחייטא ספרי אוריתא ולמעבד מנהון גואלקן ומליאו יתהון מן פרידא דעל ספר פרת וטען יתהון על צווריהון בההיא זמנא לעינא ולא הוות נייחא לנא: | 5. Upon *the bone of* our necks we were laden *when we went into exile. The wicked Nebuchadnezzar saw that the commanders of the Israelites were going without any load [and] he ordered that they sew Torah scrolls and make sacks out of them. And they filled them with pebbles from the edge of the Euphrates and they loaded them upon their necks. At that time* we were tired and there was no rest for us. |
| 6 מצרים יהבנא סעד לאתפרנסא תמן ולאתור למסבע לחמא: | 6. We gave support to Egypt *so that we might be sustained there* and to Assyria *so that we might have enough bread.* |
| 7 אבהתנא חבו וליתיהום בעלמא ונחנא בתריהון עוויתהום סוברנא: | 7. Our fathers sinned and are no longer *in the world, but* we have borne their sins *after them.* |
| 8 בנוי דחם דאתיהיבו עבדין לבנוי דשם אנון שליטו בנא פריק לית מידהום: | 8. *The sons of Ham, who were given as* slaves *to the sons of Shem,* ruled over us and there was no one to deliver us from their hands. |
| 9 בסכנת נפשנא נייתי לחם פרנסותנא מן קדם קטול דחרבא דאתי מן סטר מדברא: | 9. At *the risk* of our lives we gather bread *to sustain us* from before the *slaying* sword *which comes from across* the wilderness. |
| 10 משכנא הי כתנורא אתקדרו מן קדם מפח כפנא: | 10. Our skin has become black like an oven from before the despair of starvation. |
| 11 נשיא דהוו נסיבן לגבר בציון אתעניאו מן רומאי ובתולתא בקרוי יהודה מן כסדאי: | 11. Women *who were married to men* in Zion were raped *by Romans*. And virgins in the cities of Judah *by Chaldeans.* |
| 12 רברבנין בידיהון אצטליבו אפי סביא לא סברו: | 12. Princes were hung up by their hands and they did not show respect to the elders. |

| Targum Lamentations 5 (פרק ה) | Translation of Targum Lam 5 |
|---|---|
| 13 רובין ריחיא נטלו וטליא בצליבת קיסא תקלו: | 13. The young men carried millstones; and the boys staggered under crosses. |
| 14 סביא מתרע סנהדרי אתבטלו ורובין מן בית זמרהון: | 14. The elders ceased from the gates *of the Sanhedrin*; and the young men from their *houses of* music. |
| 15 בטל חדות לבבנא אתהפך לאבלא חינוגנא: | 15. The joy of our hearts has ceased; our dancing has turned into mourning. |
| 16 נפלת כליליא דרישנא ווי לנא ארום חבנא: | 16. The crown of our head has fallen; Woe to us! for we have sinned. |
| 17 על דין בית מקדשנא דאתצדי הוה חליש לבבנשו על אלין עמא בית ישראל דאזל בגלותא מתמן הוו חשכן עיננא: | 17. Because of *our Temple which is desolate*, our heart was weak. And because of these *people of the House of Israel who went into exile from there* our eyes have become dim. |
| 18 על טורא דציון דהוא צדי תעלין הליכו ביה: | 18. Because of Mount Zion which is desolate; foxes prowled on it. |
| 19 את הוא יי לעלם בית מותבך בשמי מרומא כורסי יקרך לדרי דריא: | 19. You, O LORD, are eternal. Your dwelling *place is in the heavenly heights.* Your *glorious* throne is from generation to generation. |
| 20 למה לעלמין תשלינא תשבקננא לאורכות יומין: | 20. Will you forget us forever and forsake us for a long time? |
| 21 אתיב יתנא יי לותך וניתוב בתיובתא שלמתא תחדת יומנא לטב כזמן יומיא טביא דהוו מלקדמין: | 21. Restore us, O LORD, to yourself and we will return *in complete repentance.* May you renew our days *for good as the festival days* of old. |
| 22 ארום אילהן מיקץ תיקוץ בנא רגזתא עלוונא עד לחדא: | 22. For you have utterly loathed us; you have been extremely angry with us. |

השיבנו יהוה אליך ונשובה
חדש ימינו כקדם

*Restore us to yourself, O LORD, that we may be restored;*
*Renew our days as of old*

# Appendix 3

## Lamentations Rabbati on Lamentations 3:1–21

---

Translation and comments by Jacob Neusner

---

EDITORS' NOTE

THE FOLLOWING TEXT IS reproduced with kind permission from Professor Jacob Neusner. It was originally published in *Lamentations Rabbah: An Analytical Translation*. Brown Judaic Studies, 193. Atlanta: Scholars, 1989.

A few explanatory comments are in order. Neusner followed the standard printed text in the translation of A. Cohen.[1] He also consulted the 1899 scholarly edition of Salomon Buber.[2] Neusner's basic practice is to follow the standard Hebrew text in accord with Cohen's translation of it, but on occasion he chooses to follow Buber's formulations of a passage (such deviations are noted in the text).

The most distinctive and helpful aspect of Neusner's "analytic translation" is his reference system that isolates the smallest units of thought and brings out the way in which they are connected into larger units. So the text is presented in such a way as to highlight the patterns of rhetoric and logic that characterize the text. Neusner also inserts summary comments (here presented in boxes) following each principal component of a chapter to guide readers towards an appreciation of the logic of each section and how it functions in its context.

Neusner's reference system works as follows:

- Letters = smallest units of thought.

- Arabic numerals = paragraphs (completed propositions of thought).

- Roman numeral = chapters (entire cogent statements or arguments). These can be either short chapters (*petihta*) or very long chapters (*parashah*). Each chapter from the start of *Lamentations Rabbah* to the end is numbered. Our sample extends

---

1. A. Cohen. *Lamentations*. In *Midrash Rabbah, vol. VII*, edited by H. Freedman and M. Simon. London: Soncino, 1939.

2. S. Buber. *Midrash Echa Rabbati*.

from chapters 79–85 out of a total of 144. The upper case Roman numeral indicates chapter number, and the lower case Roman numeral indicates the principal components of a chapter.

Full references would look like the following: *Lam Rab* LXXIX.i.1.D (which means Lamentations Rabbah, chapter 79, first principal component, paragraph 1, unit D).

## 79. PARASHAH THREE: LAMENTATIONS 3:1–3

*I am the man who has seen affliction under the rod of his wrath; he has driven and brought me into darkness without any light; surely against me he turns his hand again and again the whole day long.*
LXXIX.i.

1. A. "I am the man [who has seen affliction under the rod of his wrath; he has driven and brought me into darkness without any light; surely against me he turns his hand again and again the whole day long]:"

    B. R. Hama b. Hanina commenced by citing this text: "'Then Jeremiah took another scroll and gave it to Baruch the scribe, the son of Neriah, who wrote on it at the dictation of Jeremiah all the words of the scroll which Jehoiakim, king of Judah, had burned in the fire; and many *similar* words were added to them' (Jer 36:32).

    C. "There was no need for the word 'similar' ['and many similar words were added to them']. What is the purpose of that clause?"

    D. R. Kahana said, "'and many similar words were added to them'—this refers to the first, second, and fourth chapters of Lamentations; 'many' to the fifth chapter of Lamentations; 'similar' to the third, which consists of a series of three verses, each starting with the same letter of the alphabet. That is in line with this verse: 'Have I not written to you *excellent* things' (Prov 22:20). The word for 'excellent,' *shalishim*, may be read, 'thrice,' hence, words thrice repeated. [XXVIII.i.1.D, H give references to Lam 2:1, which commences:] 'How the Lord in his anger has set the daughter of Zion under a cloud! He has cast down from heaven to earth the splendor of Israel. He has not remembered his footstool in the day of his anger.' 'Words': this refers to [Lam 4:1, which commences:] 'How the gold has grown dim, how the pure gold is changed! The Holy Stones lie scattered at the head of every street.' 'Many': this refers to [Lam 3:1, which commences:] 'I am the man who has seen affliction under the rod of his wrath; he has driven and brought me into darkness without any light; surely against me he turns his hand again and again the whole day long.' 'Similar': this refers to [Lam 5:1, which commences:] 'Remember, O Lord, what has befallen us; behold and see our disgrace! Our inheritance has been turned over to strangers, our homes to aliens. We have become orphans, fatherless; our mothers are like widows.'"

# APPENDIX 3

2. A. ["Have I not written to you *excellent* things" (Prov 22:20):] R. Samuel b. Nahmani said, "What is the meaning of *shalishim*?"

   B. "It means 'mighty warriors,' in line with this verse: 'And captains [*shalishim*] over them' (Exod 14:7)."

3. A. Another interpretation of "Have I not written to you *excellent* things" (Prov 22:20):

   B. [The word *shalishim*] refers to the third chapter of Lamentations, which consists of a series of three verses [each starting with the same letter of the alphabet].

> The opening intersecting verse leads to this chapter and its use of the Hebrew alphabet for its structure in a manner different from the other four chapters of the book. The point is made twice, once with Jer 36:32, the other time with Prov 22:20; Nos. 1 and 2–3 can and should stand apart from one another.

## LXXIX:ii.

1. A. "I am the man [who has seen affliction under the rod of his wrath; he has driven and brought me into darkness without any light; surely against me he turns his hand again and again the whole day long]:"

   B. Said R. Joshua of Sikhnin in the name of R. Levi, "The community of Israel says before the Holy One, blessed be He, 'Lord of the ages, I am he, and I am experienced in whatever you bring upon me' [following Buber; Cohen: 'I am indeed experienced in sufferings; what pleaseth thee is beneficial to me.']

   C. "The matter may be compared to the case of a noble lady, against whom the king grew angry. He drove her out of the palace. What did she do? She went and pressed her face against the pillar.

   D. "The king passed by and saw her and said to her, 'You have gall [to cling to the palace after you were driven out]!'

   E. "She said to him, 'My lord, king, this is proper for me, this is good for me, this is right for me, for no other woman took you but for me.'

   F. "The king said to her, 'No, but I am the one who rejected all other women on account of you.'

   G. "She said to him, 'No, but they are the ones who did not accept you.'

   H. "So the Holy One, blessed be He, said to the community of Israel, 'You have gall [Cohen, *Lamentations*, 189, n. 2: by praying to me after being driven into exile].'

   I. "The community of Israel replied, 'Lord of the world, this is proper for me, this is good for me, this is right for me, for no other nation accepted the Torah except for us.'

   J. "He said to her, 'No, but I am the one who rejected all other nations on account of you.'

K. "She said to him, 'How come you went with your Torah around to all the other nations for them to reject it?'

L. "And he said, The Lord came from Sinai and rose from Seir to them' (Deut 33:2), but they rejected it.

M. "Then he offered it to the sons of Ishmael: 'He shined forth from Mount Paran' (Deut 33:2), but they rejected it.

N. "Finally he offered it to Israel, who accepted it: 'And he came forth from the myriads holy, at his right hand was a fiery Torah for them' (Deut 33:2), 'All that the Lord has spoken we will do and obey' (Exod 24:7)."

2. A. "I am the man [who has seen affliction under the rod of his wrath; he has driven and brought me into darkness without any light; surely against me he turns his hand again and again the whole day long]:"

B. R. Joshua b. Levi said, "'I am the man:' I am Job:

C. "'What man is like Job, who drinks up scorning like water' (Job 34:7)."

3. A. "... who has seen affliction:"

B. R. Samuel b. Nahman said, "The community of Israel said, 'Since he has seen me impoverished [the word for poor and for affliction is the same] as to the performance of religious duties and good deeds, therefore he brought upon me the rod of his wrath.'"

4. A. "[I am the man] who has seen affliction [under the rod of his wrath; he has driven and brought me into darkness without any light; surely against me he turns his hand again and again the whole day long]:"

B. R. Berekiah said, "I strengthened me [reading the letters for the word 'man' as though they had vowels to yield 'strong men'] to withstand all [affliction].

C. "You may know that that is the case, for after the ninety-eight reproofs that are catalogued in Deuteronomy [chapter 28], what is written?

D. "'You are standing this day all of you' (Deut 29:9),

E. "which we translate into Aramaic in this way: 'You endure this day, all of you.'

F. "You are strong enough to withstand all these [afflictions]."

We turn now to the base verse itself, beginning at Nos. 1, 2 with the opening clause, "I am the man." This yields at No. 1 the powerful parable of Israel after rejection. No. 2 does not develop its point; but in Buber's version there is a substantial and compelling use of the analogy of Israel to Job. No. 3 provides the connection between clauses, producing the anticipated theodicy. No. 4 turns matters around, with God now strengthening Israel to accept its fate.

# APPENDIX 3

LXXIX:iii.

1. A. "he has driven [and brought me into darkness without any light]:"
   B. in this world, which is "darkness without any light."

2. A. "surely against me he turns his hand again and again the whole day long:"
   B. Said R. Simeon b. Laqish, "Even though the Holy One, blessed be He, grows angry with his servants, the righteous, in this world, he goes and has mercy upon them:
   C. "'he turns his hand again' [from anger to mercy].'"

The exposition of the concluding two verses of the triplet is routine and makes familiar points.

## 80. PARASHAH THREE: LAMENTATIONS 3:4–6

*He has made my flesh and my skin waste away, and broken my bones; he has besieged and enveloped me with bitterness and tribulation; he has made me dwell in darkness like the dead of long ago.*

LXXX.i.

1. A. "He has made my flesh and my skin waste away:"
   B. "my flesh" is the community.
   C. "my skin:" the sanhedrin.
   D. Just as the skin covers the flesh, so the sanhedrin covers Israel.

2. A. "and broken my *bones*:"
   B. [The word for bones can be read 'strength,' hence:] he has broken my *strength*, the ones who were mightiest [following Cohen's reading, *Lamentations*, 190].

3. A. "he has besieged and enveloped me with bitterness and tribulation:"
   B. [Because the word for "bitterness" can be read as "head," the verse] refers to Nebuchadnezzar: "You are the head of gold" (Dan 2:38).
   C. "tribulation:" this speaks of Nebuzaradan.

4. A. "he has besieged and enveloped me with bitterness and tribulation:"
   B. "bitterness" is Vespasian.
   C. "tribulation" is Trajan.

5. A. "he has made me dwell in darkness like the dead of long ago:"
   B. R. Samuel said, "Four classes of persons are as though they were dead:

C. "the blind: 'he has made me dwell in darkness like the dead of long ago.'

D. "the leper: 'Let her not, I pray you, be as one dead' (Num 12:12).

E. "the childless: 'Give me children or else I die' (Gen 30:1).

F. "the impoverished: 'For all the men are dead that sought your life' (Ex 4:19). [But there were Dathan and Abiram, who were still alive] so were they dead? But it means that they had become impoverished."

The word-by-word exegesis is carried forward, without any further interest in developing an intersecting-verse/base-verse composition. The result is mildly interesting. Nos. 3-4 make the point that the two calamities are congruent, and that again yields the reassurance that just as the first was followed by a restoration, so would the second be followed by the same. No. 5 comes at the end, because the base verse plays no definitive role but merely supplies proof for a subordinated proposition.

## PARASHAH THREE: LAMENTATIONS 3:7-9

*He has walled me about so that I cannot escape; he has put heavy chains on me; though I call and cry for help, he shuts out my prayer; he has blocked my ways with hewn stones, he has made my paths crooked.*

### LXXXI.i.

1. A. "He has walled me about so that I cannot escape:"

   B. R. Aibu said, "This refers to the Persian [better: Roman] camp."

   C. R. Berekhiah said, "This refers to the Arab camp."

   D. And rabbis say, "This refers to the Samaritan mines."

2. A. "he has put heavy chains on me:"

   B. "He has imposed on me taxes on land, the head taxes, and the corvée."

3. A. "though I call and cry for help, he shuts out my prayer:"

   B. R. Aha and Rabbis:

   C. R. Aha said, "Whoever says his prayers with the congregation finds that his prayer is heard.

   D. "To what may the matter be compared? To the case of ten men who made a crown for the king, and a poor man came along and helped out.

   E. "What did the king say? 'Shall I not put on this crown [merely] on account of that poor man?'

   F. "The king forthwith accepts the crown and puts it on his head.

## APPENDIX 3

G. "So if there are ten righteous persons standing in the synagogue and saying their prayers, and a wicked man is standing with them, what does the Holy One, blessed be He, say?

H. "'On account of that wicked man shall I not accept the prayer? I shall accept it as is.'"

I. And rabbis say, "Whoever says his prayers after the congregation says theirs finds that his actions are spelled out [and scrutinized in detail].

J. "To what may the matter be compared? To the case of a king, whose sharecroppers and staff came before his presence to honor him. One person came late. Said the king, 'Let the wine bottle be stopped up for him.'

K. "What made this [insult] come about? That the man came late.

L. "So too, whoever says his prayers after the congregation says theirs finds that his actions are spelled out [and scrutinized in detail].

M. "That is in line with this verse of Scripture: 'though I call and cry for help, he shuts out my prayer.'

N. "The word 'shuts out' is written as though it read 'for it has finished,' [meaning, because the congregation had *finished* their prayer]."

4. A. "He has blocked my ways with hewn stones, he has made my paths crooked:"

B. [The journey to Jerusalem used to be so easy that] the women of Lud would knead their dough, go up to Jerusalem and say their prayers, [and return] before the dough had leavened.

C. [The journey to Jerusalem used to be so easy that] the women of Sepphoris would spend the Sabbath in Jerusalem, [and return so promptly that they could pick their figs early Sunday morning], and yet no one came in the morning earlier than they did to gather figs.

D. The school teacher in Magdala would arrange the candles Fridays [in the synagogue], go up to Jerusalem and say his prayers, come back and light the candles [prior to sunset on Friday evening].

E. [Cohen, p. 192:] Some say he would go up and expound the scriptural reading in the Temple and return home to keep the Sabbath there.

5. A. A man was ploughing and his cow ran off.

B. [Cohen's version, *Lamentations*, 193:] He went and told people what had happened, and they asked, "Which way did it go?"

C. He started to indicate it but could not find it, and to him they applied the verse, "he has blocked my ways with hewn stones, he has made my paths crooked."

6. A. ["he has blocked my ways with hewn stones, he has made my paths crooked:"]

B. The word for crooked means, "He has made desolate," as the same letters bear that meaning in this verse: "A ruin, a ruin, a ruin will I make it" (Ezek. 21:32).

The verse is amplified in some units, simply utilized in others. No. 1 means to find concrete illustrations of the statement that "I" am imprisoned. No. 2 contributes the same type of amplification. No. 3 does not deal with the verse, but only appeals to it for evidence in behalf of an autonomous proposition. No. 4 sets forth four illustrations of how easy it was to go to Jerusalem before the destruction, by contrast to the situation prevailing now. No. 5 treats the verse in the same way in which No. 3 has treated it, and No. 6 clarifies a word choice. All of this is routine and in no way opens fresh perspectives.

## 82. PARASHAH THREE: LAMENTATIONS 3:10-12

*He is to me like a bear lying in wait, like a lion in hiding; he led me off my way and tore me to pieces; he has made me desolate; he bent his bow and set me as a mark for his arrow.*

LXXXII.i

1. A. "He is to me like a bear lying in wait"
   B. This speaks of Nebuchadnezzar.
   C. "Like a lion in hiding:"
   D. This speaks of Nebuzaradan.

2. A. Another interpretation: "He is to me like a bear lying in wait:"
   B. This speaks of Vespasian.
   C. "Like a lion in hiding:"
   D. This speaks of Trajan.

3. A. "He led me off my way and tore me to pieces; he has made me desolate:"
   B. "Tore me to pieces" means, split in pieces,
   C. in line with the use of the word in the following passage of the Mishnah:
   D. A tree that is split—they tie it up in the sabbatical year [M. Shebi. 4:6].

4. A. "He bent his bow and set me as a mark for his arrow:"
   B. Two rabbis:
   C. One said, "[Cohen, p. 193:] As a wedge for the log."
   D. The other said, "Like the post for arrows at which all shoot, while the post remains standing."

APPENDIX 3

5. A. ["he bent his bow and set me as a mark for his arrow:"]

   B. Said R. Judah, "[The letters for *set me* may be read to mean,] 'He made me stand firm against [all afflictions].'

   C. "You find that after the ninety-eight rebukes in the book of Deuteronomy, what is written?

   D. "'You are standing this day all of you' (Deut 29:9), which we translate into Aramaic as, 'you endure, this day, all of you,' meaning, you are strong enough to take it all."

> Nos. 1–2 repeat the familiar point that the two destructions are comparable, bearing the unstated implication that as redemption followed the first, so the same will happen after the second. No. 3 contributes the clarification of a word choice, and the same is given by Nos. 4, 5.

### 83. PARASHAH THREE: LAMENTATIONS 3:13–15

*He drove into my heart the arrows of his quiver; I have become the laughingstock of all peoples, the burden of their songs all day long. He has filled me with bitterness, he has sated me with wormwood.*

### LXXXIII.i

1. A. "He drove into my heart the arrows of his quiver:"

   B. Rab and Samuel:

   C. Rab said, "'The arrows of his quiver' [expressed as 'the sons of his quiver'] are the children of those he has laid in ruins [following Cohen, *Lamentations*, 194]."

   D. Samuel said, "They are the men who eat a lot of food and produce a lot of shit. These he brought against me [following Cohen, *Lamentations*, 194]."

2. A. "I have become the laughingstock of all peoples, the burden of their songs all day long:"

   B. "They who sit in the gate gossip about me [and I am the song of drunkards]" (Ps 69:13): this refers to the nations of the world, who take their seats in theaters and circuses.

   C. "and I am the song of drunkards:"

   D. After they take their seats and eat and drink and get drunk, they sit and gossip about me and make fun of me,

   E. saying, "We don't have to eat cheap food such as carobs, like the Jews."

   F. And they say to one another, "How long do you want to live?"

   G. And one replies, "Like the shirt of a Jew that he keeps for the Sabbath."

H. And they bring a camel into their theaters, and put their shirts on it, and ask, "Why is the camel in mourning?"

I. And one replies, "These Jews are observing the Seventh Year, so they don't have greens, and they are eating the thorns that belong to such as this, so he is in mourning on their account."

J. And they bring a clown [following Cohen, *Lamentations*, 23] into the theater, with his head shaved, and they say to one another, "How come this one's head is shaved?"

K. And one replies, "These Jews keep the Sabbath, so whatever they earn all week long, they eat upon on the Sabbath. They don't have wood to cook with, so they break up their beds and use the wood for cooking and then they sleep on the dirt and get covered with the dust, and therefore they have to cover themselves with oil, which gets very costly on that account." [Cohen, *Lamentations*, 23, n. 3: "Therefore, after a time they cannot afford it at all, and so shave their heads so as not to need it."]

3. A. Another interpretation of the verse: "They who sit in the gate gossip about me:" this refers to Israel, who take seats in synagogues and school houses.

   B. "and I am the song of drunkards:" after they have sat and eaten and drunk and gotten drunk at the banquet prior to the ninth of Ab,

   C. they sit down and recite lamentations and dirges:

   D. "Alas! Lonely sits the city once great with people!"

4. A. "He has filled me with bitterness:"

   B. On the first night of Passover: "They shall eat it with unleavened bread and bitter herbs" (Num 9:11).

5. A. "He has sated me with wormwood:"

   B. With what he filled me on the first night of Passover, which is wormwood, he has sated me on the night of the ninth of Ab.

   C. The night of the week on which the first day of Passover falls is always the same as that on which the ninth of Ab occurs.

No. 1 clarifies a word choice and imputes a meaning on that basis. Nos. 2-3 serve *Petihta* 17 and recur verbatim, without the attribution found above. Nos. 4-5 serve *Petihta* 18 and recur verbatim as well. Clearly, the framers of the whole have no new ideas in store for us.

## 84. PARASHAH THREE: LAMENTATIONS 3:16-18

*He has made my teeth grind on gravel and made me cower in ashes; my soul is bereft of peace, I have forgotten what happiness is; so I say, "Gone is my glory, and my expectation from the Lord."*

# APPENDIX 3

LXXXIV.i

1. A. "He has made my teeth grind on gravel and made me cower in ashes:"

    B. There is the case of the son of R. Hanina b. Teradion, who joined up with guerillas. He snitched on them and they killed him.

    C. His father went and found him in the wilderness, with his mouth full of dirt and gravel.

    D. A few days later they put him in a coffin and out of respect for his father, they wanted to have a eulogy said for him. The father would not permit it. He said to them, "Let me speak concerning my son."

    E. He commenced by citing this verse: "Neither have I hearkened to the voice of my teachers, nor inclined my ear to those who taught me. I was well nigh in all evil in the midst of the congregation and assembly" (Prov 5:13–14).

    F. His mother commenced by citing this verse over him: "A foolish son is a vexation to his father, and bitterness to her that bore him" (Prov 17:25).

    G. His sister cited this verse: "Bread of falsehood is sweet to a man, but afterwards his mouth will be filled with gravel" (Prov 20:17).

2. A. "He has made my teeth grind on gravel and made me cower in ashes:"

    B. We have learned: On the eve of the ninth of Ab, one may not eat meat, nor drink wine, nor may one cook two cooked dishes, nor may one bathe and anoint the body. But at a meal not prior to the fast of the ninth of Ab [on the eighth of Ab, that is] one may eat meat, drink wine, and enjoy two cooked dishes.

    C. When Rab would eat the meal prior to the ninth of Ab, he took a piece of bread, sprinkled some ashes on it, and said, "This is the meal prior to the ninth of Ab, meant to fulfill this verse: 'He has made my teeth grind on gravel and made me cower in ashes.'"

3. A. "my soul is bereft of peace, I have forgotten what happiness is:"

    B. Said R. Eleazar b. R. Yose in the name of R. Hananiah b. R. Abbahu, "There is the case of a woman in Caesarea, who took her son to a baker and said to him, 'Teach my son the trade.'

    C. "He said to her, 'Leave him with me for five years, and I shall teach him how to make five hundred kinds of wheat bread.'"

    D. R. Aha and Rabbis:

    E. R. Aha said, "With wheat of *minnit* [Ezek 27:17] there is no limit to the kinds of bread one can make."

    F. Rabbis said, "There are five hundred kinds of bread that one can make with wheat, according to the numerical value of the letters of the word *minnit*."

G. R. Hinena and R. Jonathan were in session and counted up to sixty before concluding.

4. A. [A further illustration of the verse, "my soul is bereft of peace, I have forgotten what happiness is:"]

B. Said R. Eleazar b. R. Yose, "There was the case of a woman who brought her son to a cook and said to him, 'Teach my son the trade.'

C. "He said to her, 'Leave him with me for five years, and I shall teach him how to make five hundred kinds of omelet.'"

D. Rabbi [Judah the Patriarch] heard and said, "That kind of luxury we have never seen" [after the destruction of the Temple, thus "my soul is bereft of peace, I have forgotten what happiness is"].

E. R. Simeon b. Halafta heard and said, "Of such luxury we have never even heard."

5. A. [A further illustration of the verse, "my soul is bereft of peace, I have forgotten what happiness is:"] R. Judah b. Betera came to Nisibis on the eve of the great fast [the Day of Atonement].

B. He ate and finished [eating prior to the fast].

C. The head of the community came to him to invite him. He said to him, "I have already eaten and completed eating [prior to the fast]."

D. He said to him, "Pay attention to me, [Cohen: 'Let my master favor me by coming to my house for the meal'], so that people should not say that master paid no attention to me."

E. Since he insisted, the other went with him.

F. The head of the community [Cohen, *Lamentations*, 197:] thereupon instructed his young servant, saying, "Any course which you serve us once must not be repeated."

G. They brought before them eighty courses, and he took a small taste of each, and drank a cup of each jar of wine.

H. The host said to him, "My lord, did you not say to me, 'I have already eaten and finished [the final meal prior to the Day of Atonement]'? Now you were served with eighty courses, and you took a small taste of each, and drank a cup of each jar of wine. [Cohen, *Lamentations*, 197, n. 3: He made this remark to boast of his lavish hospitality and insinuate that his guest had previously had an insufficient meal.]

I. He said to him, "Why is it that the appetite is called capacious [*nefesh*]? The more you give it, the more it expands [*nefishah*]."

6. A. [A further illustration of the verse, "my soul is bereft of peace, I have forgotten what happiness is:"] R. Abbahu went to Bosrah and was received by Yose, nicknamed "the head."

B. They brought before him eighty kinds of birds' brains.

C. He said to him, "Let my lord not be angry with me, for the yield [of birds today] has not been enough."

D. People called him "the head" because all his food was only birds' brains.

7. A. [A further illustration of the verse, "my soul is bereft of peace, I have forgotten what happiness is:"] R. Hiyya the Elder went to the South and was received by R. Joshua b. Levi.

B. Twenty-four cooked dishes were set before him.

C. He said to him, "What do you do then on the Sabbath [which is marked by more substantial meals than the weekday]?"

D. He said to him, "We have double that number."

E. Later on R. Joshua b. Levi went to Tiberias and was received by R. Hiyya the Elder.

F. The host gave the disciples of R. Joshua some funds and said to them, "Go, buy for your master what he is used to eating."

8. A. [A further illustration of the verse, "my soul is bereft of peace, I have forgotten what happiness is:"] R. Isaac b. R. Eliezer knew the proper sequence of meals in accord with the days of the year [so that on each day he would serve a different menu].

B. That is when he could afford it.

C. But when he could not afford it, he would take fruit pits and count them in order not to forget them.

9. A. "I have forgotten what happiness is:"

B. Taught R. Simeon b. Gamaliel, "This refers to washing the hands and feet after a bath."

10. A. "so I say, 'Gone is my glory, and my expectation from the Lord.'"

B. Said R. Simeon b. Laqish, "Even though the Holy One, blessed be He, grows angry with his servants, the righteous, in this world, he goes and has mercy upon them:

C. "That is in line with this verse: 'so I say, "Gone is my glory, and my expectation from the Lord."'" [Cohen, *Lamentations*, 198, n. 7, interprets the sense as follows: "so I say, 'Gone is my glory'"—in this world, but "and my expectation from the Lord"—in the world to come.]

> No. 1 has no bearing upon the interpretation of our document. The pertinence clearly derives from the reference to "making teeth grind on gravel," but even the texts cited by the members of the deceased's family do not allude to our base verse. No. 2 is relevant in a general way; at least the base verse serves as a proof text. Nos. 3–7 are parachuted down with little reason; they are supposed to illustrate the level

of luxury that prevailed. But since our context requires that luxury be followed, after the destruction, by penury, only No. 8 is remotely pertinent. No. 9 continues the line of essentially irrelevant materials. Only No. 10 serves, and that is shared with LXXIX:iii.2. Why it is more at home in one passage rather than in the other I cannot say; Cohen's amplification seems to me right on target, but that explains only why the passage is at least pertinent here.

## 85. PARASHAH THREE: LAMENTATIONS 3:19-21

*Remember my affliction and my bitterness, the wormwood and the gall! My soul continually thinks of it and is bowed down within me. But this I call to mind and therefore I have hope.*

LXXXV.i.

1. A. "Remember my affliction and my bitterness, the wormwood and the gall!"
   B. Said the Community of Israel before the Holy One, blessed be He, "Lord of the world, I remember my affliction and the rebellion that I waged against you."
   C. "the wormwood and the gall:"
   D. "Let the one expiate the other."

2. A. "My soul continually thinks of it and is bowed down within me:"
   B. R. Hiyya taught, "The matter may be compared to the case of a king who went to battle and took his sons with him. One time they angered him, and he took an oath not to take them along again.
   C. "Then he remembered them and wept, saying, 'Would that my sons were with me, even though they anger me!'
   D. "[Cohen's text, not in Buber:] The king is the Holy One, blessed be He, and the sons are Israel. When the Israelites went forth to battle, the Holy One, blessed be He, would go with them. But when they angered him, he did not accompany them [Cohen, *Lamentations*, 199, n. 2: which caused their overthrow and exile]. When Israel was no longer in the land, he said, 'Would that Israel were with me, even though they anger me.'
   E. "That is in line with the following: 'Oh that I were in the wilderness, in a lodging place of wayfaring men' (Jer 9:1): 'would that my people were with me as in the past when they were in the wilderness.'
   F. "'Son of man, when the house of Israel dwelled in their own land, they defiled it' (Ezek 36:17). [Cohen, *Lamentations*, 199, n. 3: 'Would that Israel dwelt in their own land though they defiled it.']

# APPENDIX 3

G. "And the present passage: 'My soul continually thinks of it and is bowed down within me.'"

**3.** A. R. Yudan said, "'My soul continually thinks of it and is bowed down within me:'

B. "Said the Community of Israel before the Holy One, blessed be He, 'Lord of all ages, I know that you remember the nations of the world and so will exact from them all that they have done to me.

C. "'But what shall I do, for "my soul is bowed down within me"?'

D. "So goes the proverb: While the fat one gets thinner, the thin one dies."

**4.** A. "But this I call to mind and therefore I have hope:"

B. R. Abba bar Kahana said in the name of R. Yohanan, "The matter may be compared to the case of a king who took a wife and wrote out for her a document specifying a very large marriage-settlement: 'So many [Cohen:] state-apartments I am making ready for you, so many purple garments I am giving you.'

C. "Then he left her for many years and went overseas, and her neighbors aggravated her, saying, 'The king has abandoned you, gone overseas and will never return.'

D. "She wept and sighed, but she would go into her room and open and read her marriage-settlement. When she saw in the document, 'So many state-apartments I am making ready for you, so many purple garments I am giving you,' she took comfort.

E. "After days and years had gone by, the king came home. He said to her, 'My daughter, I am surprised that you were able to wait for me all these years.'

F. "She said to him, 'My lord, king, were it not for the marriage-settlement that you wrote out for me, with its generous settlement, my neighbors would have misled me.'

G. "So the nations of the world aggravate Israel, saying to them, 'Your God does not want you any more, he has hidden his face from you, he has removed his Presence from your midst and will return to you no more. [Buber's text: Come to us and we shall appoint you dukes, lords, and generals.]'

H. "And when the Israelites go into their synagogues and study houses and recite in the Torah: 'And I shall have respect for you and make you fruitful and multiply you ... and I will set my tabernacle among you ... and I will walk among you' (Lev 26:9-11), they take comfort.

I. "Tomorrow, when the redemption comes, the Holy One, blessed be He, will say to the Israelites, 'My children, I am surprised that you were able to wait for me all these years.'

J. "And they will reply to him, 'Lord of all the ages, were it not for your Torah, which you have given to us, the nations of the world would long ago have led us astray from you.'

K. "That is in line with this verse: 'But this I call to mind and therefore I have hope.'

L. "Now the word 'this' refers only to the Torah: 'And this is the Torah' (Deut 4:44).

M. "So David says, 'Unless your Torah had been my delight, I should then have perished in my affliction' (Ps 119:92)."

5. A. "therefore I have hope:"

B. So I proclaim the unity of his name twice every day: "Hear O Israel, the Lord our God, the Lord is one" (Deut 6:4).

The message of No. 1 is at 1.D, and that is a familiar proposition; there is no pretense at an intersecting verse. No. 2 presents a parable, and No. 4 another. The point of No. 2 is that God suffers along with Israel, and the point of No. 3 is that Israel's loyalty will be recognized and appreciated by God, and, in the meantime, the Israelites will find in the Torah the comfort that they require. No. 3 underlines that the nations will be repaid for their actions toward Israel in the interval. No. 5 provides what seems to me an appropriate conclusion to No. 4, though rhetorically it is an autonomous item.

# Appendix 4

## Rashi on Lamentations 3:1–21

*Translated by Rabbi A. J. Rosenberg*[1]

*1. I am the man who has seen affliction by the rod of his wrath.*

**I am the man who has seen affliction:** Jeremiah lamented, saying, "I am the man who has seen affliction," for the Temple was not destroyed in their days, but it was in my days.

**by the rod of his wrath:** of the One who chastises and smites, i.e., the Holy One, blessed be He.

*2. He has led me and made me walk [in] darkness and not [in] light.*

*3. Only against me would He repeatedly turned His hand to all day long.*

**Only against me would He repeatedly:** I alone am constantly smitten, for the entire repetition of his blows is upon me.

*4. He has made my flesh and my skin waste away [and] has broken my bones.*

**He has made my flesh and my skin waste away:** Heb. בלה, like (Isa 44:19): 'to rotten wood (לבול עץ).' Another explanation: He has made my flesh and my skin waste away, like (ibid. 51:6): "And the earth shall rot away (תבלה) like a garment," i.e., both young and old lay on the ground with neither pillow nor cushion, and their flesh wore out when they were going into exile.

*5. He has built up [camps of the siege] against me, and encompassed [me with] gall and travail.*

**and encompassed:** He encompassed me.

**gall:** Heb. ראש like Deut 29: "gall (ראש) and wormwood." The Midrash Aggadah (Lam. Rabbah), states: ראש refers to Nebuchadnezzar in the exile of Jehoiachin.

---

1. From *Five Megilloth: The Books of Lamentations, Ecclesiastes. A New English Translation of the Text, Rashi, and a Commentary Digest*. Judaica Books of the Hagiographa, vol. 2. Translated by Rabbi A. J. Rosenberg. New York: Judaica, 1992.

**travail:** Nebuzaradan, who completed the blow in the days of Zedekiah, and he wearied me.

*6. He has made me dwell in darkness like those are forever dead.*

*7. He has fenced me in, so that I cannot get out; He has made my chains heavy.*

**He has fenced me in:** He has made a wall opposite me so that I should be imprisoned.

**so that I cannot get out:** He stationed camps and troops of soldiers lying-in-wait around me.

**He has made my chains heavy:** He made heavy fetters for my feet so that I would be able to walk, *f(i)eryes* in Old French, chains.

*8. Though I cry out and plead, He shut out my prayer.*

**He shut out my prayer:** he shut the windows of the sky before it.

*9. He has walled up my roads with hewn stones, He has made my paths crooked.*

**He has made my paths crooked:** if I wish to go out, I do not go out on roads paved in a straight way, because of the enemies, but I go out on a crooked road.

*10. He is to me a bear lying in wait, a lion in hiding.*

**He is to me a bear lying in wait:** the Holy One, blessed be He, turned into a bear lying in wait for me.

*11. He scattered thorns on my ways, He caused me to spread my legs apart, and made me desolate.*

**He scattered thorns on my ways:** Heb. סורר, and expression of סירים, thorns. סורר means that He "thorned" them, He scattered thorns on my ways.

**He caused me to spread my legs:** Heb. ויפשחני, an expression of spreading the legs. One who passes on roads that are not cleared must widen his stride, and there is an example of this in the language of the Gemara (M.K. 10b): "The one who pruned (דפשח) a date palm" [meaning that he separated the branches from the trunk].

*12. He bent His bow and set me up as a target for the arrow.*

**and set me up as a target:** He set me up opposite his arrows to shoot at me like a target, *asenayl* in Old French, target.

*13. He has caused the arrows of His quiver to enter into enter my reins.*

**The arrow of His quiver:** arrows that are placed within the quiver, called *cuyvre*, quiver.

*14. I have become the laughing stock of all my people, their song [of derision] all day long.*

*15. He has filled me with bitterness; He has sated me with wormwood.*

# APPENDIX 4

*16. Indeed, He has made my teeth grind on gravel and caused me to wallow in ashes.*

**He has made me ... grind:** Heb. ויגרס, and He broke, and an example is (Ps 119:20): "My soul is crushed (גרסה)"; and similarly (Lev 2:14): "ground (גרש) when still fresh."

**on gravel:** Heb. בחצץ, fine pebbles that are in the midst of the dust, for the exiles knead their dough in the pits that they would dig in the ground, and the gravel would enter it, as the Holy One, blessed be He, said to Ezekiel (12:3), "Make yourself implements the exile," in which to drink and in which to knead a small cake, so that they should learn to do likewise, as it is stated (ibid., 24:24): "And Ezekiel will be to you for a sign," but they ridiculed him and did not do so; [so] their teeth were ultimately broken.

**And caused me to wallow:** He turned me over in ashes like a vessel inverted on its mouth, *adenter* in Old French, to throw flat on one's face. There is a similar word in the Mishnah (sic) (Yev. 107b): Pishon the camel driver measured with an inverted (כפושה) measure.

*17. And my soul is hope removed from peace, I have forgotten [what] goodness [is].*

*18. So I said, "Gone is my life, and my expectation from the Lord."*

**so I said, Gone is my life:** Heb. נצחי. I said to myself in the midst of my many troubles, "My world and my hope are gone."

*19. Remember my affliction and my misery, wormwood and gall.*

**and my misery:** Heb. ומרודי, complaint, wailing.

*20. My soul well remembers and is bowed down within me.*

**well remembers:** my soul [well remembers] my affliction and my misery and is bowed down within me. This is the simple meaning according to the context of the verse. The Midrash Aggadah (Lam. Rabbah), however, [explains it as follows:] I know that You will ultimately remember what was done to me, but my soul is bound down within me waiting for the time of remember. All this the liturgical poet based [his poem]: "With this I know that You have to remember, but my soul is bound down within me until You remember."

*21. This I reply to my heart; therefore I have the hope.*

**This I reply to my heart:** After my heart said to me that my hope from the Lord was gone, I will reply this to my heart, and I will continue to hope. Now what is it that I will reply to my heart?

# Appendix 5

## Calvin on Lamentations 3:1–23

JOHN CALVIN

*Translated by John King*

### EIGHTH LECTURE

1. I *am* the man *that* has seen affliction by the rod of his wrath.

The word, עברה properly means assault, passing over limits; but what is peculiar to man is often in Scripture ascribed to God. Here also he changes the person, for he spoke before of the people under the person of a woman, as it is often done; but now the Prophet himself comes before us. At the same time there is no doubt but that by his own example he exhorted all others to lamentation, which was to be connected with true repentance. And this chapter, as we shall see, is full of rich instruction, for it contains remarkable sentiments which we shall consider in their proper places.

Some think that this Lamentation was written by Jeremiah when he was cast into prison; but this opinion seems not probable to me; and the contents of the chapter sufficiently show that this ode was composed to set forth the common calamity of the whole people. Jeremiah, then, does not here plead his own private cause, but shows to his own nation what remedy there was for them in such a state of despair, even to have an immediate recourse to God, and on the one hand to consider their sins, and on the other to look to the mercy of God, so that they might entertain hope, and exercise themselves in prayer. All these things we shall see in their due order.

The Prophet then says that he was an *afflicted man*, or a man who saw affliction. This mode of speaking, we know, is common in Scripture—to see affliction—to see good and evil—to see life and death. He then says that he had *experienced* many afflictions, and not only so, but that he had been given up as it were to miseries. How? *By the rod of his fury*. He does not mention the name of God, but Jeremiah speaks of him as of one well known, using only a pronoun. Now, then, at the very beginning, he acknowledges that whatever he suffered had been inflicted by God's hand. And as all the godly ought to be convinced of this, that God is never angry without just reasons, there is included in the word *wrath*

# APPENDIX 5

a brief confession, especially when it is added, *by the rod*, or *staff*. In short, the Prophet says that he was very miserable, and he also expresses the cause, for he had been severely chastised by an angry God.

2. He has led me, and brought *me into* darkness, but not *into* light.

The letters of the alphabet are tripled in this chapter, which I had omitted to mention. In the first two chapters each verse begins with the successive letters of the alphabet, except that in the last chapter there is one instance of inversion, for Jeremiah has put פ before ע; or it may be that the order has been changed by the scribes; but this is uncertain. Here then, as I have said, each letter is thrice repeated. Then the first, the second, and the third verse begin with א and the fourth begins with ב and so he goes on to the end.

He confirms here the last verse, for he shows the cause or the manner of his afflictions, for he had been led into darkness and not into light. This kind of contrast has not the same force in other languages as it has in Hebrew. But when the Hebrews said that they were in darkness and not in the light, they amplified that obscurity, as though they had said that there was not even a spark of light in that darkness, it being so thick and obscure. This is what the Prophet now means. And we know what is everywhere understood in Scripture by darkness, even every kind of Lamentation: for the appearance of light exhilarates us, yea, the serenity of heaven cheers and revives the minds of men. Then darkness signifies all sorts of adversities and the sorrow which proceeds from them. He afterwards adds,

3. Surely against me is he turned; he turns his hand *against me* all the day.

Now he says that *God was an adversary to him;* for this is what the verb ישׁב means "he is turned" against me. As an enemy, when intending to fight, comes to meet one from the opposite side, so the Prophet says of God, who had become an enemy to him; and he teaches the same thing in another way when he says that he perceived that the hand of God was against him: *He turns,* he says, *against me his hand daily,* or all the day, כל-היום. But the Prophet simply means constancy, as though he had said that there was no truce, no cessation, because God manifested the rigor of his vengeance without limit or end. He afterwards adds,

4. My flesh and my skin has he made old; he has broken my bones.

These, as it evidently appears, are metaphorical words. Illness often makes people to look old, for from pain proceeds leanness: thus the skin is contracted, and the wrinkles of old age appear even in youths. As, then, sorrows exhaust moisture and strength, hence he is said to grow old who pines away in mourning. This is what the Prophet now means. *God,* he says, *has made my flesh and my skin, to grow old,* that is, he hath worn me out, within and without, so that I am almost wasted away.

He then adds, *He hath broken my bones.* This seems to be hyperbolical; but we have said elsewhere that this simile does not in every instance express the greatness of the sorrow which the faithful feel under a sense of God's wrath. Both David and Hezekiah spoke in this way; nay, Hezekiah compares God to a lion, "As a lion," he says, "has he broken my bones" (Isa 38:13). And David says at one time that his bones wasted away, at another that they were broken, and at another that they were reduced to ashes; for there is nothing more dreadful than to feel that God is angry with us. The Prophet, then, did not only regard outward calamities, but the evidence of God's vengeance; for the people could see nothing else in their distresses except that God was their enemy—and this was true; for God had often exhorted them to repentance; but upon those whom he had found incurable, he at length, as it was just, poured forth his vengeance to the uttermost. This, then, was the reason why the Prophet said, that God had broken his bones. He then adds,

5. He has built against me, and encompassed *me* with gall and travail.

The words, as translated, may seem harsh, yet they have no common beauty in Hebrew. The Prophet says he was blocked up and straitened as it were by walls; and as we shall see, he repeats this comparison three times; in other words, indeed, but for the same purpose.

God, he says, *has built against me,* as, when we wish to besiege any one, we build mounds, so that there may be no escape. This, then, is the sort of building of which the Prophet now speaks: God, he says, holds me confined all around, so that there is no way of escape open to me.

He then gives a clearer explanation, that he was surrounded by gall or poison and trouble. He mentions poison first, and then, without a figure, he shows what that poison was, even that he was afflicted with many troubles. He afterwards adds,

6. He has set me in dark places, as *they that be* dead of old.

Here he amplifies what he had before said of poison and trouble; he says that he was placed in darkness, not that he might be there for a little while, but remain there for a long time; he hath made me, he says, to dwell in darkness. But the comparison which follows more clearly explains the Prophet's meaning, as the dead of ages. The word עולם may refer to future or past time. Some say, as *the dead for ever,* who are perpetually dead. But the Scripture elsewhere calls those *the dead of ages* who have been long buried, and have decayed, and whose memory has become nearly extinct. For as long as the dead body retains its form, it seems more like a living being; but when it is reduced to ashes, when no bone appears, when the whole skin and nerves and blood have perished, and no likeness to man remains, there can then be no hope of life. The Scripture then calls those the dead of ages, who have wholly decayed. So also in this place the Prophet says, that he dwelt in darkness, into which he had been cast by God's hand, and that he dwelt there as though he had been long dead, and his body had become now putrid.

This way of speaking appears indeed hyperbolical; but we must always remember what I have reminded you of, that it is not possible sufficiently to set forth the greatness of that sorrow which the faithful feel when terrified by the wrath of God. He then adds,

# APPENDIX 5

7. He has hedged me about, that I cannot get out: he has made my chain heavy.

Here he says, first, that he was held *shut up;* for גדר is to enclose, and גדרה means a fence or a mound, or an enclosure of any kind. He then says, that he was shut up as it were by a fence, so that he could not go forth; literally, it is, and *I shall not go forth;* but the conjunction here is to be taken as denoting the end. He has *shut me up,* he says, or he has enclosed me, that I might not get out.

It then follows, *He has made heavy my fetter.* His meaning is, that he was not only bound with fetters, but so bound that he could not raise up his feet, as though he had said, that he not only had fetters, but that they were so heavy that he could not even move his feet.

8. Also when I cry and shout, he shuts out my prayer.

The Prophet describes here the extremity of all evils—that it availed him nothing to cry and to pray. And yet we know that we are called to do this in all our miseries. "The strongest tower is the name of the Lord, to it will the righteous flee and shall be safe." (Prov 18:10). Again, "Whosoever shall call on the name of the Lord shall be saved." (Joel 2:32). And Scripture is full of testimonies of this kind; that is, that God graciously invites all the faithful to himself: "He shall call upon me, and I will hear him." (Ps 91:15); "In the day when I call, answer me speedily." (Ps 102:2); "Before they call, I will answer." (Isa 65:24). In short, there is no need to collect all the passages; but we may be content with this one thing, that when God claims to himself this prerogative—that he answers prayers—he intimates that it is what cannot be separated from his eternal essence and godhead; that is, that he is ready to hear prayer. And hence the Psalmist concludes, "To you shall all flesh come" (Ps 65:3).

When, therefore, Jeremiah complains that his prayers were in vain, and without any fruit or effect, it seems strange and inconsistent. But we know that God holds the faithful in suspense, and so hears as to prove and try their patience, sometimes for a long time. This is the reason why he defers and delays his aid.

It is no wonder, then, that God did not hear the prayers of his servant, that is, according to the judgment of the flesh. For God never rejects his own, nor is he deaf to their prayers and their sighs; but the faithful often speak according to what the flesh judges. As, then, the Prophet found that he obtained nothing by prayer, he says that his prayer was shut out, or that the door was closed against him, so that his prayer did not come to God.

Now, this passage is worthy of special notice; for except God immediately meets us, we become languid, and not only our ardor in prayer is cooled but almost extinguished. Let us, then, bear in mind, theft though God may not help us soon, yet our prayers are never repudiated by him; and since we see that the holy fathers experienced the same thing, let us not wonder, if the Lord at this day were to try our faith in the same manner. Let us, therefore, persevere in calling on Him; and should there be a longer delay, and our complaint be that we are not heard, yet let us proceed in the same course, as we shall see the Prophet did. It follows,

9. He has enclosed my ways with hewn stone, he has made my paths crooked.

Other metaphors are used. Some think that the Prophet refers to the siege of Jerusalem, but such a view is not suitable. The metaphors correspond with one another, though they are somewhat different. He had said before, that he was enclosed by God, or surrounded as with a mound; and now he transfers this idea to his ways. When the life of man is spoken of, it is, we know, compared to a way. Then the Prophet includes under this word all the doings of his life, as though he had said that all his plans were brought into straits, as though his way was shut up, so that he could not proceed: "Were I to proceed ill any direction, an obstacle is set before me; I am compelled to remain as it were fixed." So the Prophet now says, his *ways were enclosed,* because God allowed none of His counsels or His purposes to be carried into effect. And to the same purpose he adds, that God had perverted his ways; that is, that he had confounded all his doings, and all his counsels.

But these words are added, *with a squared stone.* The verb גזז means "to cut"; hence the word גזית signifies a polished stone, or one trimmed by the hammer. And we know that such stones are more durable and firmer than other stones. For when unpolished stones are used, the building is not so strong as when the stones are squared, as they fit together better. Then the Prophet intimates that the enclosures were such that he could by no means break through them, as they could not be broken. He, in short, means that he was so oppressed by God's hand, that whatever he purposed God immediately reversed it. We now, then, perceive what he means by saying, that all his ways were subverted or overturned by God. This is not to be understood generally, for it is God who directs our ways. But he is said to pervert our ways, when he disconcerts our counsels, when all our purposes and efforts are rendered void; in a word, when God as it were meets us as an adversary, and impedes our course; it is then that he is said to pervert our ways. But this ought not to be understood as though God blinded men unjustly, or as though he led them astray. The Prophet only means that he could find no success in all his counsels, in all his efforts and doings, because he had God opposed to him. Here I stop.

## PRAYER

Grant, Almighty God, that as you did in former times so severely chastise your people, we may in the present day patiently submit to all your scourges, and in a humble and meek spirit suffer ourselves to be chastised as we deserve; and that we may not, in the meantime, cease to call on you, and that however slowly you may seem to hear our prayers, we may yet persevere continually to the end, until at length we shall really find that salvation is not in vain promised to all those who in sincerity of heart call on you, through Christ our Lord. Amen.

# APPENDIX 5

## NINTH LECTURE

10. He *was* to me *as* a bear lying in wait, *and as* a lion in secret places.

Harsh is the complaint when Jeremiah compares God to a. bear and a lion. But we have said that the apprehension of God's wrath so terrified the faithful, that they could not sufficiently express the atrocity of their calamity; and then borne in mind must also be what we have stated, that they spoke according to the judgment of the flesh; for they did not always so moderate their feelings, but that something fell from them worthy of blame. We ought not, then, to make as a rule in religion all the complaints of holy men, when they were pressed down by the hand of God; for when their minds were in a state of confusion, they uttered much that was intemperate. But we ought, on the other hand, to acknowledge how great must be our weakness, since we see that even the strongest; have thus fallen, when God exercised severity towards them.

Though, then, it does not seem that it was said in due honor, that God did *lie in wait* as *bears* for travelers, or as lions in their dens; yet, if we consider how much the faithful dreaded the tokens of God's wrath, we shall not wonder at this excess. It is then certain that the Prophet brings before us here not only evidences of the fear of God, of religion and humility, but also of the corrupt feelings of the flesh; for it cannot be, but that the infirmity of men will betray itself ill extreme evils. He adds, what is of the same import,

11. He has turned aside my ways, and pulled me in pieces: he has made me desolate.

In this verse also the Prophet shows how grievously the faithful are disturbed when they feel that God is adverse to them. But he uses the same figure as yesterday, though the word סורר is different: what he used yesterday was עוה but in the same sense.

He then says that his ways had been perverted; and for this reason, because he had been disappointed in his purpose; whatever he did was made void, because God by force prevented him. When we undertake to do anything, a way is open to us; but when there is no success, our way is said to be perverted. And this is done by God, who has all events, prosperous as well as adverse, in his own hand. As, then, God directs our ways when he blesses our counsels and our actions; so, on the other hand, he perverts them, when all things turn out unsuccessfully, when our purpose is not done and events do not answer our expectations.

He afterwards adds, *He has torn me* or broken me. The verb פשח means properly "to cut," but here "to tear" or "scatter." It follows lastly, *he has made me a waste* In this expression he includes the other two things; for he who is reduced to desolation, does not hold on his way, nor find any exit; he is also drawn here and there, as though he was torn into several parts. We hence see that the Prophet here complains of extreme evils, for there was no hope of deliverance left. He adds,

12. He hath bent his bow, and set me as a mark for the arrow.

Here the Prophet introduces another metaphor—that God had shot him with arrows, as he was made a mark to them. Jeremiah has elsewhere often used the word מתרא for a prison; but here it means a mark at which arrows are leveled, and such is its meaning in Job 16:12, where there is a similar complaint made. The meaning is that the people, in whose name Jeremiah speaks, had been like marks, because God had directed against them all his arrows. It is, indeed, a fearful thing when God aims at us, that he may discharge his darts and arrows in order to hit and wound us. But as God had so grievously afflicted his people, that he seemed to have poured forth all his vengeance, the Prophet justly complains that the people had been like marks for arrows.

13. He has caused the arrows of his quiver to enter into my reins.

He goes on with the same metaphor; he said in the last verse that God had leveled his bow; he now adds that his arrows had penetrated into his reins, that is, into his inward parts. But we must bear in mind what the Prophet meant, that God had dealt so severely with the people, that no part, even the innermost, was sound or untouched, for his arrows had perforated their very reins. He afterwards adds,

14. I was a derision to all my people; *and* their song all the day.

The Prophet again complains of the reproaches to which God had exposed the Jews. We have said that of all evils the most grievous is reproach, and experience teaches us that sorrow is greatly embittered when scoffs and taunts are added to it; for he who silently bears the most grievous sorrows, becomes broken in heart when he finds himself contumeliously treated. This, then, is the reason why the Prophet again amplifies the miseries of the people, because they were exposed to the scoffs of all men. But it may seem a strange thing that the Jews were derided by their own people. This is the reason why some think that the Prophet complains of his own private evils, and that he does not represent the whole people or the public condition of the Church. But it may also be said in reply, that the Prophet does not mean that the people were derided by themselves, which could not be; but it is the same as though he had said, that their state was so disgraceful, that while they looked on one another, they had a reason for taunting, if this their condition was allowed to continue.

In short, the Prophet does not mean what was actually done, but he simply complains that their calamity was liable to all kinds of reproaches, so that any one looking on Jerusalem might justly deride such a disgraceful spectacle. And it was, as we have said, a most equitable reward, for they had not ceased to reproach God. Then rendered to them was what they had deserved, when God loaded them in turn with dishonor.

He afterwards adds that he was *their song,* that is, of derision; for it is a confirmation of the former clause, and the same complaint is also formal in Job. He says that he was their song *daily* or all the day. This constancy, as it has been said, proved more clearly the grievousness of the evil.

15. He has filled me with bitterness, he has made me drunken with wormwood.

Some render the last word "wormwood," but this word seems not to me to suit the passage, for though wormwood is bitter, yet it is a wholesome herb. I therefore take it in this and like places for poison or gall; and ראש, as we shall see, is joined with it. To satiate, is also a very common metaphor. Then the Prophet means that he was full of bitterness and gall; and he thus had regard to those calamities from which so much sorrow had proceeded.

We hence also gather that the faithful were not free from sorrow in their evils, for bitterness and gall sufficiently show that their minds were so disturbed that they did not bear their troubles with sufficient patience. But they struggled with their own infirmity, and the example is set before us that we may not despond when bitterness and gall lay hold on our minds; for since the same thing happened to the best servants of God, let us bear in mind our own infirmity, and at the same time flee to God. The unbelieving nourish their bitterness, for they do not unburden their souls into the bosom of God. But the best way of comfort is when we do not flatter ourselves in our bitterness and grief, but seek the purifying of our souls, and in a manner lay them open, so that whatever bitter thing may be there, God may take it away and so feed us, as it is said elsewhere, with the sweetness of his goodness. He adds,

16. He has also broken my teeth with gravel stones, he has covered me with ashes.

Many renderings are given of these words; there is, however, no over-statement here; for, as it has been often said, the grief of the people under such a mass of evils could not be sufficiently expressed. The Prophet, no doubt, extended here his hand to the weak who would have otherwise lain down as dead; for under such evils the ruin of the whole nation, the fall of the city, and the destruction of the temple, it could not be but such thoughts as these must have occurred. Now, as to any one unacquainted with such a trial, he would soon succumb, had no remedy been presented to him. The Prophet then dictates for all the godly such complaints as they might, so to speak, pour forth confidently and freely into the bosom of God.

We hence see that here is even expressed whatever might occur to the minds of God's children, so that they might not hesitate in their straits to direct their prayers to God, and freely confess whatever they suffered in their souls. For shame closes up the door of access; and thus it happens; that we make a clamour as though God were far away from us; hence impatience breaks out almost to a rage. But when an access to God is opened to us, and we dare to confess what burdens our minds, this, as I have said, is the best way for obtaining relief and comfort. We must then understand the design of the Prophet, that he suggests words to the faithful, that they might freely cast their cares and sorrows on God, and thus find some alleviation.

For this reason, he says that his teeth had been broken by a little stone or pebble. The same expression, if I mistake not, is found in Job. It is a metaphor taken from those who press stones instead of bread under their teeth; for when grit lies hid in bread, it hurts the teeth. Then inward and hidden griefs are said to be like small stones, which break or shatter the teeth. For the Prophet does not speak here of large stones, but on the contrary he speaks of pebbles or small stones, which deceive men, for they lie hid either in bread or in meat, or in any other kind of food. As, then, the teeth are hurt by pressing them, so the Prophet says that his sorrows were most bitter, as that part, as it is well known, is very tender; and when any injury is done to the teeth, the pain spreads instantly almost through the whole body. This is the reason why he says that his teeth were broken.

Then he adds, that he was *covered with dust,* or that he was lying down or dragged along in the dust. The expression is taken from those who are drawn by way of reproach along the ground, as a carcass is, or some filthy thing which we abhor. Thus the Prophet complains that there was nothing short of extreme evils. He adds,

17. And you have removed my soul far off from peace: I forgot prosperity.

By saying that his *soul was remote from peace,* he means that no good remained; for by peace, as it is well known, the Hebrews understood every kind of prosperity. And he explains himself by another clause, that, he had *forgotten every good;* and this forgetfulness ought to be understood, so to speak, as real or entire; for if there had been any reason for rejoicing, it would not have been forgotten; for all are naturally pleased with what is pleasant, nay, they with avidity seek what delights them. It would then be contrary to nature to forget things good and pleasant, to us. But the Prophet means here a privation. Hence the forgetfulness of which he speaks is nothing else but alienation from everything good, as though he had said (as the previous clause shows) that he was removed from every hope of peace.

But the expression is much more emphatic, when he says, that his soul was far removed from peace. By soul he does not mean himself only, (for that would be frigid,) but he understands by it all things connected with him, as though he had said, "Wherever I look around me, I find no peace, and no hope appears to me." Hence it was, that all the faculties of his soul were far removed from all experience of good things. It follows,

18. And I said, "My strength and my hope are perished from the LORD":

This verse shows what I have before reminded you of, that the Prophet does not here speak as though he was divested of every sin, and prescribed a perfect rule for prayer. But, on the contrary, in order to animate the faithful to seek God, he sets before them here an instance of infirmity which every one finds true as to himself. It was yet a most grievous trial, because the Prophet almost despaired; for since faith is the mother of hope, it follows that when any one is overwhelmed with despair, faith is extinct. Nevertheless the Prophet makes this declaration, *Perished,* he says, *has my strength and my hope from God.*

He does not speak through some inconsiderate impulse, as though he was suddenly carried away, as many things happen to us which we have had no thought of; but he speaks what was, as it were, fixed in his mind. As he said, "Perished has my hope and strength from Jehovah," it is evident that his faith was not slightly shaken, but had wholly failed; but the expression, *I said,* renders the thing still stronger; for it means, as it is well known, a settled conviction. The Prophet was then fully persuaded that he was forsaken by God; but what does this mean? We ought indeed to maintain this: that faith sometimes is so stifled, that even the children of God think that they are lost, and that it is

# APPENDIX 5

all over with their salvation. Even David confesses the same thing; for it was an evidence of despair, when he declared, "I said in my haste, Vanity is every man" (Ps 116:11). He had almost failed, and he was not master of himself when he was thus agitated. There is no doubt but that the Prophet also expressly reminded the faithful that they ought not to despair, though despair laid hold on their minds, or though the devil tempted them to despair, but that they ought then especially to struggle against it. This is indeed, I allow, a hard and perilous contest, but the faithful ought not to faint, even when such a thing happens to them, that is, when it seems to be all over with them and no hope remains; but, on the contrary, they ought nevertheless to go on hoping, and that, indeed, as the Scripture says elsewhere, against hope, or above hope (Rom 4:18).

Let us then learn from this passage, that the faithful are not free from despair, for it enters into their souls; but that there is yet no reason why they should indulge despair; on the contrary, they ought courageously and firmly to resist it; for when the Prophet said this, he did not mean that he succumbed to this trial, as though he had embraced what had come to his mind; but he meant, that he was, as it were, overwhelmed for a short time. Were any one to ask, How can it be that hope and despair should reside in the same man? the answer is, that when faith is weak, that part of the soul is empty, which admits despair. Now, faith is sometimes not only enfeebled, but is also nearly stifled. This, indeed, does not happen daily, but there is no one whom God deeply exercises with temptations, who does not feel that his faith is almost extinguished. It is often no wonder, that despair then prevails; but it is for a moment. In the meantime, the remedy is, immediately to flee to God and to complain of this misery, so that he may succor and raise up those who are thus fallen. He then adds,

19. Remembering my affliction and my misery, the wormwood and the gall.

The verb may be considered as an imperative; it is an infinitive mood, but it is often taken in Hebrew as an imperative. Thus, many deem it a prayer, *Remember my affliction and my trouble, the gall and the poison*. This might be admitted; but what others teach I prefer: that this verse depends on the last. For the Prophet seems here to express how he had almost fallen away from hope, so that he no longer found strength from God, even because he was overwhelmed with evils; for it is very unreasonable to think, that those who have once experienced the mercy of God should cast away hope, so as not to believe that they are to flee to God any more. What seems then by no means congruous the Prophet here in a manner excuses, and shows that it was not strange that he succumbed under extreme evils, for he had been so pressed down by afflictions and troubles, that his soul became as it were filled with poison and gall.

But in the meantime, he shows by the word *remember*, how such a trial as this, when it comes, lays hold on our minds, that is, when we think too much of our evils. For the faithful ought to hold a middle course in their afflictions, lest they contract a torpor; for as hence indifference and stupidity arise, they ought to rouse themselves to a due consideration of their evils; but moderation ought to be observed, lest sorrow should swallow us up, as Paul also warns us (2 Cor 2:7). They then who fix their minds too much on the remembrance of their evils, by degrees open the door to Satan, who may fill their hearts and all their thoughts with despair. The Prophet then describes here the fountain of evils, when he says, that he remembered his affliction and trouble; and suitable to this is what immediately follows,

20. My soul has *them* still in remembrance, and is humbled in me.

The Prophet seems in other words to confirm what he had said, even that the memory of afflictions overwhelmed his soul. For the soul is said to be humbled in or upon man, when he lies down under the burden of despair. It is the soul that raises man up, and as it were revives him; but when the soul is cast as it were on man, it is a most grievous thing; for it is better to lie down a dead body than to have this additional burden, which makes the case still worse. A dead body might indeed lie on the ground without strength and motion, but it may still retain its own place; but when the soul is thus cast down, it is said to press down man, though lifeless, more and more. This then is what the Prophet means. And yet he says that he was so occupied with this remembrance, that he could not thence withdraw his mind.

There is no doubt but that he also intended here to confess his own infirmity, and that of all the faithful; and the reason of this we have already explained. Then relying on this doctrine, even when all our thoughts press us down, and not only lead us to despair, but also hurry us on and cast us headlong into it, let us learn to flee even then to God and to lay before him all our complaints, and let us not be ashamed, because we see that this mode of proceeding is suggested to us by the Holy Spirit. It follows,

21. This I recall to my mind, therefore have I hope.

We see here what I have already stated, that if we struggle against temptations, it will be a sure remedy to us, because our faith will at length emerge again, and gather strength, yea, it will in a manner be raised up from the lowest depths. This is what the Prophet now shows. *I will recall this,* he says, *to my heart, and therefore will I hope.* How can despair produce hope from itself? This would be contrary to nature. What then does the Prophet mean here, and what does he understand by the pronoun *this,* זאת? Even that being oppressed with evils, he was almost lost, and was also nearly persuaded that no hope of good anymore remained. As then he would recall this to mind, he says that he would then have new ground of hope, that is, when he had recourse to God; for all who devour their own sorrows, and do not look to God, kindle more and more the hidden fire, which at length suddenly turns to fury. Hence it comes that they clamor against God, as though they were doubly insane. But he who is conscious of his own infirmity, and directs his prayer to God, will at length find a ground of hope. When therefore we recall to mind our evils, and also consider how ready we are to despair, and how apt we are to succumb under it, some hope will then arise and aid us, as the Prophet here says.

It must still be observed, that we ought to take heed lest we grow torpid in our evils; for hence it happens that our minds become wholly overwhelmed. Whosoever then would profit by his evils, should consider what the Prophet says here came to his mind, for he at length came to himself, and surmounted all obstacles. We see then that God brings light out of darkness, when he restores his faithful people from despair to a good hope; yea, he makes infirmity itself to be the cause of hope. For whence is it that the unbelieving cast away hope? Even because security draws them away from God; but a sense of our own infirmity draws us even close to him; thus hope, contrary to nature, and through the incomprehensible and wonderful kindness of God, arises from despair. It follows,

22. *It is of* the LORD's mercies that we are not consumed, because his compassions fail not.

The first clause may be explained in two ways: The view commonly taken is that it ought to be ascribed to God's mercy that the faithful have not been often consumed. Hence a very useful doctrine is elicited—that God succors his own people, lest they should wholly perish. But if we attend to the context, we shall see that another sense is more suitable, even that the *mercies of God were not consumed, and that his compassion's had not failed* The particle כִּי is inserted, but ought to be taken as an affirmative only, *surely the mercies of God are not consumed;* and then,—surely his compassion's have not failed. And he afterwards adds,

23. *They are* new every morning: great *is* thy faithfulness.

This verse confirms what I have said, that the same truth is here repeated by the Prophet, that God's mercies were not consumed, nor had his compassion's failed. How so? Because they were new, or renewed, every day; but he puts *morning*, and that in the plural number. I am surprised at the hour striking so soon; I hardly think that I have lectured a whole hour.

### PRAYER

Grant, Almighty God, that as there are none of us who have not continually to contend with many temptations, and as such is our infirmity, that we are ready to succumb under them, except you help us,—O grant, that we may be sustained by your invincible power, and that also, when you would humble us, we may loathe ourselves on account of our sins, and thus perseveringly contend, until, having gained the victory, we shall give you the glory for your perpetual aid in Christ Jesus our Lord. Amen.

# Index of Scripture

## OLD TESTAMENT

### Genesis
| | |
|---|---|
| 1:1—6:8 | 90 |
| 1–2 | 19 |
| 1–3 | 48, 49 |
| 3:1–15 | 49 |
| 3:8 | 84 |
| 30:1 | 253 |

### Exodus
| | |
|---|---|
| 4:19 | 253 |
| 14:7 | 250 |
| 21–24 | 84 |
| 24:7 | 251 |
| 34:6–7 | 39, 46, 48, 49 |

### Leviticus
| | |
|---|---|
| 2:14 | 266 |
| 16 | 50 |
| 26 | 39 |
| 26:9–11 | 262 |
| 26:44–45 | 40, 45, 47 |

### Numbers
| | |
|---|---|
| 5:11–31 | 39 |
| 9:11 | 257 |
| 11:2 | 44 |
| 12:12 | 253 |
| 13–14 | 84 |
| 14 | 72 |

### Deuteronomy
| | |
|---|---|
| 1 | 84 |
| 22:13–21 | 39 |
| 27–28 | 39 |
| 28 | 29, 30, 66, 72, 251 |
| 28:15–68 | 29, 30 |
| 28:53 | 66 |
| 29 | 251, 256, 264 |
| 29:9 | 251, 256 |
| 30:1–10 | 30, 40, 41, 45, 47, 50 |
| 30:2 | 30 |
| 33:2 | 251 |
| 4:44 | 263 |
| 6:4 | 263 |

### Judges
| | |
|---|---|
| 1–2 | 39 |

### 1 Kings
| | |
|---|---|
| 7:15–22 | 155 |
| 8:30 | 67 |

### 2 Kings
| | |
|---|---|
| 17 | 39, 45 |
| 23:28–30 | 39 |
| 25 | 157 |

### 2 Chronicles
| | |
|---|---|
| 35:25 | 85, 86, 154 |
| 36 | 40 |
| 36:11–21 | 157 |

### Ezra
| | |
|---|---|
| 4:7 | 70 |

### Nehemiah
| | |
|---|---|
| 1:2–8 | 48 |
| 9:1–37 | 39 |

### Job
| | |
|---|---|
| 16:1–22 | 41 |
| 16:12 | 273 |
| 34:7 | 251 |

### Psalms
| | |
|---|---|
| 1:1 | 85 |

## Index of Scripture

**Psalms** (*cont.*)

| | |
|---|---|
| 2 | 140, 183 |
| 2:1 | 84, 86 |
| 2:6 | 86 |
| 3–5 | 44 |
| 4 | 141, 183 |
| 4:17 | 86 |
| 6 | 44 |
| 6:7 | 118 |
| 7 | 44 |
| 9–10 | 42 |
| 14 | 141, 183 |
| 15 | 141, 183 |
| 18:50 | 102 |
| 20 | 183, 184 |
| 21 | 140, 141, 183 |
| 21:18 | 141 |
| 21:27 | 141 |
| 22:1 | 105 |
| 23 | 183 |
| 25 | 42 |
| 26 | 141, 183 |
| 29 | 183 |
| 32 | 44 |
| 33 | 42 |
| 34 | 42 |
| 37 | 42, 183 |
| 37:1–11 | 46 |
| 38 | 42 |
| 44:17 | 199 |
| 50 | 131, 139 |
| 51 | 44, 131 |
| 53 | 183 |
| 54:1 | 183 |
| 65:3 | 270 |
| 68 | 140, 183 |
| 69 | 81, 140, 183, 184, 256 |
| 69:13 | 81, 256 |
| 70 | 140, 183 |
| 71 | 181, 183 |
| 72 | 183 |
| 73 | 183 |
| 73:1–26 | 47 |
| 74 | 183 |
| 75 | 183 |
| 76 | 183 |
| 87 | 183 |
| 89 | 39 |
| 91:15 | 270 |
| 93 | 183 |
| 94 | 42 |
| 102:2 | 270 |
| 104–6 | 40 |
| 106:40–48 | 30 |
| 107 | 50 |
| 107:1–3 | 40 |
| 111 | 42 |
| 112 | 42 |
| 116:11 | 276 |
| 119 | 42 |
| 119:20 | 266 |
| 119:92 | 263 |
| 140 | 131 |
| 141 | 131 |
| 145 | 42 |

**Proverbs**

| | |
|---|---|
| 5:13–14 | 258 |
| 17:25 | 258 |
| 18:10 | 270 |
| 20:17 | 258 |
| 22:20 | 249, 250 |

**Isaiah**

| | |
|---|---|
| 1–12 | 40 |
| 1–6 | 39 |
| 1:1–27 | 90 |
| 1:11–17 | 190 |
| 4:2–6 | 30 |
| 6–12 | 47 |
| 9:6 | 102 |
| 13:8 | 189 |
| 17:5–6 | 68 |
| 21:3 | 189 |
| 22:1–8 | 39 |
| 24:13 | 68 |
| 26:17–18 | 189 |
| 27:12 | 68 |
| 38:13 | 269 |
| 40—55:13 | 58 |
| 40–66 | 57, 62, 172 |
| 40–63 | 90 |
| 40–55 | vii, x, 34, 55–62 |
| 40–48 | 59 |
| 40:1 | 57, 60, 90 |
| 42:5—43:10 | 90 |
| 44:19 | 264 |
| 44:26 | 60 |
| 47 | 57, 61 |
| 47:1 | 57 |

## Isaiah (cont.)

| | |
|---|---|
| 48:2 | 60 |
| 48:20 | 60 |
| 49–55 | 59, 60 |
| 49:1—54:17 | 57 |
| 49:1–12 | 58 |
| 49:13—50:3 | 58 |
| 49:13a | 57 |
| 49:14 | 57, 61, 90 |
| 49:15–23 | 61 |
| 49:16 | 60 |
| 49:19 | 60 |
| 50:4–11 | 58 |
| 51:12—52:12 | 58 |
| 51:12 | 57, 90 |
| 51:17–23 | 58 |
| 51:17–22 | 57 |
| 51:20–23 | 58 |
| 51:3 | 60 |
| 52:1 | 58 |
| 52:11 | 58 |
| 52:13—53:12 | 58, 59 |
| 52:9 | 60 |
| 53 | 140 |
| 54 | 58, 60, 62 |
| 54:1–17 | 58 |
| 54:1 | 90 |
| 54:7–8 | 61 |
| 54:11–12 | 60 |
| 54:11 | 90 |
| 60:1 | 90 |
| 61:10 | 90 |
| 65:24 | 270 |
| 66:7–8 | 189 |

## Jeremiah

| | |
|---|---|
| 1–20 | 36, 39 |
| 1:1 | 46, 90 |
| 2–3 | 36 |
| 2:13–14 | 201 |
| 4:10 | 40 |
| 4:31 | 189 |
| 5:10–11 | 68 |
| 6:9 | 68 |
| 6:14 | 201 |
| 7 | 30 |
| 7:1–29 | 201 |
| 7:16 | 67 |
| 8:8–10 | 46 |
| 8:11 | 201 |
| 8:14–20 | 40 |
| 8:18—9:3 | 46 |
| 9:1 | 261 |
| 9:19–21 | 79 |
| 11:14 | 40, 67 |
| 11:18–23 | 46 |
| 12:1–6 | 46 |
| 13:20–27 | 36 |
| 14:11 | 40, 67 |
| 14:13–22 | 201 |
| 14:13–14 | 40 |
| 15:1–2 | 40 |
| 15:15–18 | 40 |
| 16:10–13 | 40 |
| 20:7–18 | 41, 46 |
| 20:9 | 67 |
| 21:1–10 | 157 |
| 22:23 | 189 |
| 23:9–40 | 46, 201 |
| 26 | vii, 6, 30, 32, 60, 61, 105, 118, 140, 151, 173, 188, 204 |
| 30–33 | 40 |
| 31:18 | 104 |
| 31:33–34 | 104 |
| 36 | 85, 86, 249, 250 |
| 36:21–25 | 85 |
| 36:32 | 85, 86, 249, 250 |
| 39–40 | 46 |
| 39 | 45 |
| 41:5 | 45 |
| 49:9 | 68 |

## Lamenatations

| | |
|---|---|
| 1–4 | 32, 57 |
| 1–2 | 6, 33, 35, 36, 37, 40, 41, 43, 46, 50, 58, 92, 172, 186, 203 |
| 1 | xi, 1, 4, 5, 7, 16, 19, 23, 31, 32–41, 43, 45–47, 50, 57, 58, 61, 67, 68, 72, 73, 76, 84, 85, 89, 102, 114, 121–23, 140, 148, 157, 158, 162, 163, 169, 171, 172, 176, 184, 186, 189, 193, 203 |
| 1:1–14 | 123 |
| 1:1–9a | 41 |
| 1:1–5 | 140 |
| 1:1 | 1, 16, 32, 34, 38, 39, 41, 45, 46, 50, 72, 73, 84, 102, 114, 123, 140, 158, 163, 169, 176 |

## Index of Scripture

**Lamenatations** (*cont.*)

| | |
|---|---|
| 1:2 | 16, 19, 32, 41, 45–47, 49, 57, 61, 68, 84, 163, 176, 180, 184 |
| 1:2a | 176 |
| 1:3 | 121, 122, 148 |
| 1:4b | 189 |
| 1:4c | 176 |
| 1:5 | 73, 89, 158, 169, 184 |
| 1:6–9 | 140 |
| 1:6 | 176 |
| 1:7c | 41 |
| 1:8–9 | 45 |
| 1:8–9a | 41 |
| 1:8 | 73, 89, 169, 184 |
| 1:8c | 189 |
| 1:9 | 16, 45, 57, 84, 158, 163, 184 |
| 1:9a | 41 |
| 1:9c | 16, 44, 176 |
| 1:10–14 | 140 |
| 1:10 | 1, 114, 163, 169 |
| 1:11 | 45, 158, 163 |
| 1:11a | 189 |
| 1:11c | 16, 44, 176 |
| 1:12 | 45, 46 |
| 1:12c–15 | 176 |
| 1:13–15 | 34 |
| 1:14–16 | 45 |
| 1:14 | 73, 86, 169, 176, 184 |
| 1:14a | 176 |
| 1:15 | 1, 73 |
| 1:16–17 | 163 |
| 1:16 | 41, 45, 57, 102 |
| 1:17 | 41, 45, 57, 86, 158 |
| 1:18–19 | 45 |
| 1:18 | 41, 176 |
| 1:18a | 176 |
| 1:19 | 38, 39, 45 |
| 1:19a | 39 |
| 1:20–22 | 16, 19, 34, 41, 44, 47, 158 |
| 1:20–21 | 46 |
| 1:20 | 45, 86, 158, 163 |
| 1:20a | 16, 176 |
| 1:21–22 | 176 |
| 1:21 | 32, 41, 45, 176 |
| 1:21 | 32, 41, 45, 46, 57, 163, 176 |
| 1:22 | 32, 41, 45, 61, 68 |
| 1:22b | 176 |
| 1:32 | 148 |
| 2 | 1, 4, 5, 7, 15, 16, 23, 29, 31, 41–43, 46, 47, 57, 58, 66, 71, 73, 85, 89, 118, 123, 139, 140, 141, 157, 162, 163, 169–72, 176, 180, 186, 187, 193, 249 |
| 2:1–22 | 41 |
| 2:1–10 | 1, 41, 46 |
| 2:1–2 | 41, 118 |
| 2:1 | 29, 32, 41–43, 46, 57, 58, 89, 118, 141, 163, 169, 180, 187, 249 |
| 2:2–3 | 89 |
| 2:2 | 1, 15, 16, 41, 46, 47, 58, 66, 71, 89, 139, 157, 170–72 |
| 2:3 | 157 |
| 2:4–5 | 73 |
| 2:8–19 | 139 |
| 2:8–11 | 140, 141 |
| 2:8–10 | 123 |
| 2:10 | 57 |
| 2:11–14 | 139 |
| 2:11–13 | 46 |
| 2:11–12 | 57, 163 |
| 2:11 | 41, 46, 57, 163 |
| 2:12–15 | 140, 141 |
| 2:12 | 163 |
| 2:13–19 | 57 |
| 2:13 | 41, 57, 89 |
| 2:14 | 46, 169 |
| 2:15–16 | 46 |
| 2:15 | 29, 46, 180 |
| 2:16–17 | 42, 43 |
| 2:17–19 | 46 |
| 2:17 | 41, 46 |
| 2:18 | 42, 118 |
| 2:19 | 46, 58, 187 |
| 2:20–22 | 15, 16, 19, 41, 44, 46, 47, 158 |
| 2:20 | 1, 15, 16, 41, 46, 47, 66, 68, 73, 170–72 |
| 2:20b | 66 |
| 2:21 | 163 |
| 2:22 | 46 |
| 3 | 2, 4–7, 16, 18–20, 22, 24, 26–34, 37, 39, 44, 46, 47, 49, 50, 52, 56, 58, 59, 64, 65, 67, 70, 71, 73, 74, 76, 77, 83, 85, 86, 89, 90, 93, 101, 102, 104, 107, 114, 116–18, 120, 122, 123, 125–28, 131, 134, 138, 140, 141, 147, 151, 155, 156, 162, 163, 166, 169, 171, 172, 175, 176, 180, 186, 199, 200, 201, 205, 207, 230, 248–53, 255–59, 261–64, 267, 268 |

Lamenatations (*cont.*)

| | |
|---|---|
| 3:1–66 | 49 |
| 3:1–23 | 267 |
| 3:1–21 | 248, 264 |
| 3:1–18 | 34, 44, 46, 49 |
| 3:1–17 | 1 |
| 3:1–9 | 123, 140, 141 |
| 3:1–3 | 249 |
| 3:1 | 4, 7, 18, 32, 34, 46, 47, 49, 116, 140, 141, 249 |
| 3:4–6 | 252 |
| 3:7–9 | 253 |
| 3:10–12 | 255 |
| 3:10 | 86 |
| 3:13–15 | 256 |
| 3:16–18 | 257 |
| 3:16 | 86 |
| 3:17 | 18 |
| 3:18–39 | 7 |
| 3:18 | 7, 46 |
| 3:19–39 | 7 |
| 3:19–24 | 34, 47, 49 |
| 3:19–22 | 46 |
| 3:19–21 | 261 |
| 3:21–39a | 163 |
| 3:22–30 | 123, 141 |
| 3:22–24 | 64 |
| 3:22a | 49 |
| 3:22b | 49 |
| 3:23–24 | 46 |
| 3:23 | 46, 49 |
| 3:25–30 | 46 |
| 3:25 | 46, 74 |
| 3:26–41 | 31 |
| 3:27 | 118 |
| 3:28 | 118 |
| 3:29 | 65 |
| 3:30 | 116 |
| 3:31–39 | 47 |
| 3:33 | 28, 29, 34, 47 |
| 3:38 | 30 |
| 3:39 | 4, 44, 169 |
| 3:40–51 | 47 |
| 3:40–42 | 30, 47, 201 |
| 3:40–41 | 117 |
| 3:40 | 30, 47, 93, 117 |
| 3:43 | 86 |
| 3:48 | 117, 118 |
| 3:50 | 18 |
| 3:51 | 68 |
| 3:52–66 | 47 |
| 3:53 | 116 |
| 3:55–66 | 19, 44, 158 |
| 3:56–66 | 7 |
| 3:59–66 | 16 |
| 3:59 | 16 |
| 4–5 | 6 |
| 4 | 2, 4, 5, 7, 16, 18, 22, 23, 28, 31, 37, 47, 48, 50, 56, 58, 65, 70, 71, 83–88, 93, 101, 103, 110, 113, 114, 116–18, 121, 123, 125, 128, 131, 141, 148, 155, 157, 162, 163, 165, 167, 169, 176, 180, 187, 189, 198, 199, 205, 235, 249, 251, 252, 254–57, 259, 262–64, 268 |
| 4:1–16 | 47 |
| 4:1–10 | 57 |
| 4:1–6 | 141 |
| 4:1 | 47, 58, 85, 141, 157, 169, 180, 187, 249 |
| 4:4–10 | 163 |
| 4:4 | 163 |
| 4:7 | 84, 87 |
| 4:8 | 86 |
| 4:9–10 | 163 |
| 4:10 | 1 |
| 4:11 | 47 |
| 4:12 | 29 |
| 4:13–16 | 58 |
| 4:13–15 | 169 |
| 4:13 | 58, 169, 180, 187 |
| 4:15 | 86 |
| 4:17–20 | 47 |
| 4:20 | 29, 47, 86, 113, 116–18, 187 |
| 4:21–22 | 47, 187 |
| 4:21 | 47, 84 |
| 4:22 | 18, 47 |
| 4:22a | 18 |
| 5 | 4, 32, 47, 57, 86, 92 |
| 5 | 2, 4, 5, 7, 16, 19, 22, 28, 31, 37, 39, 49, 50, 51, 56, 57, 62, 65, 68, 71, 84, 85, 89, 93, 97, 102, 104, 106, 108, 114, 121, 123, 125, 128, 130, 132, 138, 140, 141, 148, 151, 155, 158, 162, 163, 166, 167, 171, 172, 176, 180, 199, 205, 243, 249, 252–57, 259, 263, 264, 267–69, 278 |
| 5:1–22 | 44, 49, 50 |
| 5:1–11 | 123, 141 |

*Index of Scripture*

**Lamenatations** (*cont.*)
| | |
|---|---|
| 5:1 | 16, 19, 47, 49, 50, 84, 141, 249 |
| 5:2–18 | 47 |
| 5:11 | 163 |
| 5:13 | 84 |
| 5:16 | 47 |
| 5:19–22 | 47 |
| 5:19 | 29 |
| 5:20 | 57, 68 |
| 5:22 | 7, 89, 92, 93 |

**Ezekiel**
| | |
|---|---|
| 12:3 | 266 |
| 16 | 36, 40 |
| 21:32 | 255 |
| 23 | 5, 31, 36, 40, 52, 58, 60, 96, 105, 106, 118, 123, 124, 129, 137, 150, 158, 172, 186, 203, 257, 278 |
| 24:24 | 266 |
| 27:17 | 258 |
| 36:17 | 261 |
| 36:26–27 | 104 |

**Daniel**
| | |
|---|---|
| 2:38 | 252 |
| 9:1–20 | 39 |
| 9:1–19 | 30, 40 |

**Hosea**
| | |
|---|---|
| 11:1–19 | 40 |
| 13:13 | 189 |
| 14:1–9 | 40 |
| 14:1 | 184 |

**Joel**
| | |
|---|---|
| 2:12–17 | 39 |
| 2:32 | 270 |

**Amos**
| | |
|---|---|
| 7:1–6 | 39 |
| 9:1–15 | 30 |

**Obadiah**
| | |
|---|---|
| 1:5 | 68 |

**Micah**
| | |
|---|---|
| 4:9–10 | 189 |
| 7:1 | 68 |

**Habakkuk**
| | |
|---|---|
| 1:2—2:1 | 39 |

**Zephaniah**
| | |
|---|---|
| 3:1–20 | 46 |
| 3:6–20 | 40 |
| 3:8–20 | 30 |

**Zechariah**
| | |
|---|---|
| 7:3 | 56 |

**Malachi**
| | |
|---|---|
| 3:7 | 93 |

~

## NEW TESTAMENT

**Matthew**
| | |
|---|---|
| 5:4 | 189 |
| 6:10 | 19 |
| 8:5–17 | 139 |
| 11:20–30 | 50 |
| 11:29–30 | 121 |
| 20:1–16 | 49 |
| 23:35 | 180, 187 |
| 27:39 | 180 |

**Mark**
| | |
|---|---|
| 15:34 | 103 |

**Luke**
| | |
|---|---|
| 13:22–30 | 49 |
| 15:11–23 | 49 |

**John**
| | |
|---|---|
| 2:19–22 | 186 |
| 14:1–11 | 50 |
| 16:13 | 190 |

**Acts**
| | |
|---|---|
| 2:23 | 106 |

**Romans**
| | |
|---|---|
| 4:18 | 276 |
| 6:8 | 18 |
| 8 | 188–90 |
| 8:11 | 188 |
| 8:17–25 | 188 |

## Romans (*cont.*)

| | |
|---|---|
| 8:18–30 | 188 |
| 8:23 | 189 |
| 12:15 | 192, 195 |

## 1 Corinthians

| | |
|---|---|
| 9:10 | 179 |
| 15:47 | 190 |

## Ephesians

| | |
|---|---|
| 2:11–22 | 180 |

## 2 Corinthians

| | |
|---|---|
| 1 | 16, 188, 195 |
| 1:3–4 | 16 |
| 1:8–9 | 188 |
| 1:11 | 188 |
| 2:7 | 276 |
| 5:2–4 | 189 |

## 2 Timothy

| | |
|---|---|
| 3:17 | 179 |

## Hebrews

| | |
|---|---|
| 12:1 | 133 |

## 1 Peter

| | |
|---|---|
| 1 | 18 |

## Revelation

| | |
|---|---|
| 21 | 17, 19 |
| 22:20 | 19 |

# SEPTUAGINT

## Jeremiah

| | |
|---|---|
| 20:9 | 67 |

## Lamentations

| | |
|---|---|
| 1:13 | 67 |
| 2:8 | 66, 68 |
| 2:20 | 67 |
| 3 | 67 |
| 5:20 | 68 |

# TARGUM OF LAMENTATIONS

| | |
|---|---|
| 1–9a | 228 |
| 1:1 | 73 |
| 1:3 | 228 |
| 1:4 | 73 |
| 1:7–9 | 73 |
| 1:15 | 74 |
| 2:19 | 74, 75 |
| 3:25–30 | 75 |
| 3:25 | 74, 75 |
| 3:26 | 74 |
| 3:27 | 74 |
| 3:28 | 73, 74 |
| 3:30 | 74 |
| 3:31 | 74 |
| 3:32 | 74 |
| 3:39 | 73 |
| 3:40 | 74 |
| 3:41 | 74 |
| 4:22 | 75 |

# Index of Names

Adam, Michael, 49, 72, 81, 101
Aichele, George, 168, 172, 174
Albertz, Rainer, 43, 52, 56, 62
Albrektson, Bertil, 3, 5, 22, 27–30, 32, 40, 52, 76, 117, 119
Alexander, Philip S., 76, 117, 119, 124
Alexiou, Margaret, 136–38
Alter, Robert, 5, 22
Ambrose, 117
Aquila, 65–66, 69, 114, 119
Aquinas, Thomas, 4, 115
Archer, John, 163, 165
Assan-Dote, Isabelle, 66, 68–69
Auerbach, Erich, 5, 22

Bakhtin, Mikhail, 13, 35, 172
Barr, James, 10–12, 14, 22, 24
Barry, Peter, 166, 174
Barstad, Hans M., 59, 62
Barthelemey, Domininique, 114
Bartholomew, Craig, 2, 14, 22–24
Baruch, 23, 64, 66, 68–69, 85, 86, 249
Bass, Shabbetai, 84
Basset, Lytta, 204, 209
Ben Shimeon ha-Levi, Yitzak, 228
Berkovits, Eliezer, 94
Berkovitz, Eliezer, 105
Berlin, Adele, 15, 22, 32, 43, 52, 56, 62
Bernstein, A., 101, 106, 107, 110, 147, 182
Bernstein, Leonard, 101, 106–7, 110, 147, 182
Bialik, Hayyim, Nachman, 94, 97
Bloom, Harold, 8, 22
Blumenthal, David R., 15, 22
Boda, Mark, 44, 52
Bomberg, Daniel, 228
Bonhoeffer, Dietrich, 201–2, 209
Brady, Christian M. M., 3, 70, 72, 76, 89, 228
Braiterman, Zachary, 15–16, 22, 92, 94, 97, 178, 203
Brandscheidt, Renate, 4–5, 22

Brown, Sally A., 20, 22, 91, 206, 209, 248
Brueggemann, Walter, 3, 22, 204–5, 209
Buber, Salomon, 35, 248, 250–51, 261–62
Byrd, William, 147, 151, 182

Calvin, John, 4, 10, 125–29, 130, 202, 267
Calvini, Ioannis, 125, 130
Calvinus, Iohannes, 127, 130
Cameron-Mowat, Andrew, 132, 137, 139, 181–82, 202
Canterbury, Anselm of, 121
Cassian, John, 118
Cassidy, Sheila, 207, 209
Cessac, Catherine, 190
Chagall, Marc, 154
Chesterton, G. K., 199, 209
Childs, Brevard, 14, 17, 22
Cohen, A., 23, 196, 248, 250, 252, 254–57, 259, 260–62
Collodan, Nicholas, 126
Constantinou, Eugenia Scarvelis, 131
Cooke, Deryck, 148, 153
Craft, Robert, 151, 153
Cranmer, Thomas, 199
Cross, Saint John of, 18, 23, 105–6, 155, 200, 202, 209

Davies, Philip R., 2, 22
Dawkins, Richard, 12–14, 22
Dedalus, Stephen, 199
Deutz, Rupert of, 121
Dillard, Raymond B., 5–6, 24
Dobbs-Allsopp, F. W., 5, 7, 15–16, 22, 34, 35, 52, 175, 196, 204, 209
Dunn, James D. G., 188, 190, 196
Durham, John I., 155, 157, 160

Eco, Umberto, 16, 22, 24
Edersheim, Alfred, 102–3, 187
Eichrodt, Walter, 11, 22
Eikah, vii, 101

287

*Index of Names*

Eissfeldt, Otto, 176, 196
Ellison, Harry, 101–4, 106, 110
Eshel, Amir, 96–97
Evans, Mary, 2, 22–23, 76, 167, 172–74

Fackenheim, Emil, 94
Fiorenza, Schussler, 166–67, 174
Forsyth, P. T., 199–200, 204, 209
Frazer, James, 136, 138
Frei, Hans, 2, 23–24
Freud, Sigmund, 8, 23, 162, 165
Freytag, Gustav, 5–6, 23
Frye, Northrop, 8, 23

Gadamer, Hans-Georg, 11, 23
Gottwald, Norman K., 3, 5, 23, 27–30, 32, 34, 38, 52, 57, 59–60, 62, 72, 76
Greenberg, Clement, 92–94, 96, 97
Greenberg, Irving, 92–93, 94, 96–97
Greenstein, Ed, 93, 97
Gregory the Great, 22, 113, 115–16, 118–20, 137, 138
Gruber, Mayer I., 4, 15, 83, 87, 92
Gunkel, Hermann, 176, 196
Gwaltney Jr., W. C., 5, 23, 96–97

Harvey, Richard, 101, 110, 187
Hauer, Matthias, 149
Hauerwas, Stanley, 193, 196, 205, 209
Hillers, Delbert, 7, 23
Hogg, David, 120, 132
Houtman, Alberdina, 228
Hugh of St. Victor, 8, 23–24, 121–22, 165

Irenaeus, 113, 116, 117, 119, 185–86
Izhaqi, Rabbi Solomon (Isaac), 83, 259, 264

Jahnow, Hedwig, 176, 196
Jerome, 114–15, 117–19, 126, 128
Jocz, Jacob, 105
Josephus, 85, 114
Joyce, Paul M., 4, 8, 23, 161, 165

Kahana, R. Abba bar, 86, 249, 262
Kaiser, Barbara, 5
Kaiser, Walter, 6–7
Kaplan, Dana, 95, 97
King, John, 70, 85–86, 102, 107, 136, 155, 183, 267

Kinzer, Mark, 107, 108, 110, 180, 186, 196
Kirkpatrick, William Kirk, 198, 200, 209
Kramer, Lawrence, 148, 153, 175, 196
Krenek, Ernst, 147, 149–53
Kroeger, Catherine Clark, 167, 172–74
Kugel, James L., 1, 23

Labahn, Antje, 5, 23, 163, 165
Lagarde, Paulus Anton de, 76, 228, 230
Lee, Nancy C., 8, 23, 42–43, 46, 52, 169, 174
Levenson, Jon, 35
Levine, Etan, 76, 228
Lewis, Alan C., 18, 23
Lewis, C. S., 201, 209
Linafelt, Tod, 8, 15, 23, 27, 33–34, 37–38, 40, 52, 58, 60–62, 91, 93, 97, 105, 110, 162, 165, 177, 196
Lipton, Diana, 8
Longman, Tremper, 5–6, 17, 24, 203, 209
Loyola, Ignatius, 162

Mandolfo, Carleen, 8, 13, 15, 23–24, 35–40, 52, 61–62, 170–74
Menninger, Karl, 198, 209
Michelangelo, 158–159
Middlemas, Jill, 4, 5, 24, 58–59, 62, 176, 196
Miller, Patrick D., 18, 20, 22, 24, 209
Mintz, Alan, 94, 97
Mirkus, Johannes, 123–24
Moore, Michael S., 9, 12, 22, 162, 165, 174

Neusner, Jacob, 15, 77, 92, 97, 101, 110, 248
Newsom, Carol A., 24, 60, 62, 174
Newsome, Carol, 60
Nogent, Guibert de, 121
Norris, Kathleen, 199, 201, 202, 209

O'Donovan, Oliver, 17, 24
Origen, 114, 115, 119, 128, 185

Parry, Robin, 17, 22, 24, 118–19, 131, 132, 137, 175, 186, 190, 193–94, 196, 202, 209
Petersen, Eugene, 209
Pilitsis, George, 136, 138
Pratensis, Felix, 228
Provan, Iain, 4, 24, 27, 32, 52, 175, 196
Pyper, Hugh, 8–9, 13, 24, 162, 165

## Index of Names

Rabanus Maurus, 120
Radbertus, Paschasius, 115, 119–121
Rashi, 4, 10, 83–87, 92, 178, 264
Reimer, David J., 162, 165
Rembrandt, 154–60
Renkema, Johan, 5, 18, 24, 27, 31–32, 44–45, 52, 177, 196
Resnick, Russ, 107
Richter, David H., 167, 174
Ricoeur, Paul, 11, 14, 24, 177, 185, 196
Rieff, Philip, 200, 209
Rijn, Rembrandt van, 154–56, 160
Rosenberg, Rabbi A. J., 264
Roskies, David, 94, 97
Rubenstein, Richard, 94
Rufinus, 116–17

Sadan, Tsvi, 102–3, 110
Sakenfeld, Doob, 166, 174
Saruq, Menahem ben Jacob Ibn Saruq, 84, 86
Saruq, Menahem Ibn, 84, 86
Schoenberg, Arnold, 149, 151
Schopf, F. Jane, 147, 182
Schweid, Eliezer, 93–94, 96–97
Seidman, Naomi, 13, 14, 24, 95–97, 168, 174
Seitz, Christopher, 24, 58, 61–62
Seville, Isidore of, 122
Siedman, Naomi, 170–71, 173
Smith-Christopher, Daniel, 163, 165
Snow Flesher, Leanne, 170, 172–74
Sommer, Benjamin D., 55–57, 62
Sophia-Tiemeyer, Lena, 16
Spiegel, Yorick, 24, 97, 161–62, 165, 174
Stackhouse, Ian, 198
Stern, David, 15, 88, 91, 101, 110, 177–78
Stern, Elsie R., 19
Stravinsky, Igor, 147, 151–53
Swinton, John, 189, 197, 206–7, 209

Tallis, Thomas, 147, 151, 182
Taylor, Barbara Brown, 206, 209
Tertullian, 114, 117, 185
Theodotion, 65
Thiselton, Anthony, 2–3, 14, 24
Thomas, Heath A., 1, 4, 5, 15–16, 23–24, 52, 95, 113, 115, 119, 124, 147, 154, 163, 165–66, 181–83, 188, 190, 197, 200, 203–4
Tiemeyer, Lena-Sofia, 55, 62, 184
Trible, Phyllis, 167, 174
Truman, Jill, 208

Vermigli, Peter Martyr, 128
Victoria, Tomas Luis de, 147–48, 150, 152–53, 182

Waskow, Arthur, 95–97
Wertheim, Janie-Sue, 107–8, 110
Westermann, Claus, 4–5, 24, 27, 30–33, 52, 56, 59, 62, 72, 76, 176, 197
Wiesel, Elie, 105
Wieselthier, Samuel, 104
Wilcox, Pete, 4, 125, 130, 202
Wolterstorff, Nicholas, 189, 197, 208–9

Youngblood, Kevin J., 3, 16, 64, 66, 69, 114, 211

Ziegler, Joseph, 64–65, 69, 114

# Index of Subjects

Aaron, 24
abandon, 8, 13–14, 17, 57, 68, 79, 80, 89, 90, 105, 123, 140–41, 168, 179, 180, 186, 192, 201, 262
Abel, 39, 81
Abraham, 49, 78, 79
abuse, 13, 15, 22, 33, 41, 67, 168, 169–71, 173, 203, 206
acrostic, 7, 32, 42–43, 45, 64–65, 67, 69, 85–86, 115, 127, 128, 176, 207
Adam, 49, 72, 81, 101
Adonis, 136–38
adoption, 2, 10, 14, 38, 59, 66, 87, 150, 171, 188–89, 202
affliction, 17, 28, 34, 46, 58, 80, 121–22, 129, 140, 189, 195, 249, 250–51, 256, 261, 263–64, 266–68, 276, 277
afterlife, 8, 23, 33, 52, 62, 91, 97, 110, 165, 196
Aggadah, 264, 266
Aggadic, 71, 84, 85, 87
agony, 140–41
Augustine, 24, 117–18, 162, 181, 183, 198
alienation, 89–91, 275
allegorical, 2, 115–16, 121
allusion, 55–57, 62, 72, 81, 84, 119, 128
alphabet, 7, 64, 85–86, 115, 127–28, 207, 208, 249, 250, 268
Altar, 123–24, 139, 140, 157
analogy, 7, 17–19, 65, 114, 155, 167, 182, 251
ancestors, 81, 88, 108, 178
angels, 133–35
anger, 4, 8, 15, 19, 38, 48, 50, 79, 80–81, 89, 95, 150, 161, 203, 204, 206, 207, 209, 249, 252, 261
anti-Semitic, 103, 179, 196
anti-theodic, 203
antitheodic, 16, 34, 35
anti-theodicy, 95, 204
Apocalypse, 94, 97
Apokathelosis, 134

apostle, 116, 123, 134, 158, 185
apostolic, 116, 119, 185, 199
Aramaic, 3, 70, 71, 73, 76, 83, 84, 86, 87, 89, 119, 228, 251, 256
Armageddon, 95
art, 5, 17, 22, 23, 25, 92, 150, 154, 172
artist, 62, 149, 154, 199
artistic, 134, 143, 162
artistry, 48–49, 133
asceticism, 117, 119
atonement, 78, 80, 90, 103, 104, 200, 209, 259
Auschwitz, 15–16, 22, 94, 97, 105–6, 109
Authority, 10, 13, 22, 35, 36, 56, 77, 119, 149, 171, 172, 173, 204
authorship, 85, 96, 154

Babylon, 4, 38–39, 57, 59–60, 70, 114
Babylonia, 4, 28, 45, 59, 62, 73, 79, 80–81, 83–85, 87, 104, 114, 175, 177, 187
belief, 4, 10, 22, 26–32, 39, 41, 43, 48, 50–51, 71, 72, 74, 79, 94, 101, 105, 108, 164, 172, 186, 199, 201, 276
believer, 114, 177, 179, 188, 194, 206
bereave, 8, 23, 161, 205

canon, 15, 20, 21, 22, 24, 37, 38, 40–41, 50, 67, 120, 150, 151, 167, 207
canonical, 14, 22, 26, 30, 32, 35, 37, 38–40, 42, 45, 47, 66, 184–85
catastrophe, 6, 23, 26, 41, 52, 58, 62, 88–89, 91, 94, 96–97, 105–6, 110, 165, 177, 182, 196
chant, 88, 131, 133, 139, 140, 152
Christ, 2, 15–21, 86, 101, 103, 105, 106, 110, 114–18, 122, 123, 129, 132–37, 140–41, 150, 155, 179, 181–83, 185, 186–89, 194, 204, 271, 278
Christian tradition, 10, 101, 154, 191, 192
christological, 102–103, 108, 113, 117–18, 122, 132

*Index of Subjects*

Church, 4, 10, 12, 15, 21, 24–25, 31, 104, 113–19, 121–24, 126, 128–29, 131–38, 149, 150–52, 175, 177, 179–81, 183–85, 188–91, 194, 199–200, 202, 205–7, 209, 273
Codex Solger, 228, 235, 243, 245
community, 4, 10, 11–12, 16, 20, 33, 34, 44, 47, 58, 59–61, 67, 70, 74–75, 77, 80, 83, 89–91, 95, 106, 108, 171, 173, 175–79, 183–185, 191, 193–95, 207, 250–52, 259, 261–62
complain, 16, 33–34, 44, 118, 129, 169, 198, 203, 205, 270, 272–77
condemn, 74, 122, 139, 201
confess, 15–16, 20, 42, 47, 50, 169, 198, 199, 204, 206, 274, 276–77
congregation, 72, 74–75, 88, 89–90, 107–8, 110, 133, 134–35, 182, 184, 191–92, 200, 202–3, 205–6, 253, 254, 258
covenant, 28, 30, 39, 46, 48–49, 66, 77, 78, 82, 84, 89, 103, 122, 126–27, 157, 158, 159, 178, 180, 186, 199–200
creation, 17–19, 90, 123, 136, 170, 177, 188–90, 196
creation-fall-redemption, 17
Creed, 116, 139, 185
criticism, biblical, 161, 162, 166–68, 170, 172
Cross, 18, 23, 59, 103, 105–6, 123, 133–35, 155, 188, 194, 195, 200, 202, 209
crucified, 106, 133–34, 180, 185, 188, 194, 196
crucifixion, 34, 133, 140
cry, 18, 46–47, 89, 92, 94, 103, 105, 108, 140–41, 150, 173, 176, 203, 206, 253, 254, 265, 270
cult, 30, 43, 67, 136

David, 22–23, 47, 49, 62, 67, 91, 94, 97, 101–2, 105, 110, 120, 132, 155, 165, 174, 183–84, 196, 263, 268–69, 276
death, 17–19, 43, 50, 85, 92, 102, 106–7, 116–18, 123, 129, 135–37, 141, 161, 162, 165, 177, 182–83, 185–88, 194, 202, 205–6, 209, 267
Decalogue, 84
deconstruction, 9, 27
defiled, 73, 169, 261
deliverance, 42, 75, 183–85, 272
depression, 161, 163, 206

despair, 46, 75, 78, 89, 91, 102, 105, 126, 129, 147–48, 152, 178, 187–200, 267, 275, 276–78
destruction, 3–4, 13, 34, 38, 40, 46, 56, 61, 68, 71–72, 74, 78–80, 82, 84, 88–89, 92, 94, 96, 97, 102, 106–7, 114, 129, 141, 154–59, 163, 168–69, 173, 175, 177–79, 186, 196, 255–56, 259, 261, 274
Deutero-Isaiah, 57, 63
Deuteronomic, 3, 28, 29–30, 40, 72, 89, 204
discourse, 7, 13–14, 20, 24, 72, 95, 166, 168, 170, 172–73
doctrine, 14, 24, 104, 115, 129, 198–99, 277–78
dogmatics, 10–11
doxological, 175, 177, 182

Easter, 182, 191–92, 194, 202, 206
Eastern Orthodox, 132, 137, 175
ecclesiastical, 118, 133, 137, 147, 152, 173
ecclesiology, 179–80
ecology, 173, 186, 188
eschatology, 19, 68, 106, 180, 188
ethics, 24, 138, 173, 196
Eucharist, 121, 191, 193, 195
Eusebius, 117–18
Evangelicalism, 24, 52, 103, 131, 170, 191, 192, 196, 201
evil, 28, 80, 94, 97, 116, 196–97, 207, 209, 258, 267, 273
exile, 3–4, 18, 24, 43, 52, 56, 59, 60, 62, 66, 68, 74, 78–82, 84, 93, 94, 96, 102, 104, 107–8, 121, 126, 163, 165, 169, 195, 205, 250, 261, 264, 266
exiles, 4, 60–61, 84, 128, 266
exilic, 3–4, 44, 52, 56, 58–60, 62, 94, 186
expiate, 80, 261

fasting, 107, 117–18
feminism, iv, viii, xii, 9, 12–13, 67, 95, 166–74, 204
fidelity, 13, 167, 170–71, 173
figuration, 97, 158
form criticism, 38
Freud, 162
Freytag's Pyramid, 5–6, 23
funeral, 85–86, 103, 132, 134, 136–37, 176, 181, 202, 206

*Index of Subjects*

genocide, 50
genre, 3, 27, 37, 38, 42–45, 85, 127, 140, 176, 196
Glossa Ordinaria, 120, 121, 124
God-in-Christ, 185, 190, 195
Gospel, 133, 139, 192, 199, 200, 202, 204
Grace, 26, 48, 199–200, 202, 209
grave, 30, 39, 131, 135–36, 206
Greek Minor Prophets, 65
grief, 6, 23, 31–32, 34, 68, 71–72, 96, 105, 107–8, 128, 135, 140–41, 158, 159, 161–63, 165, 175, 184, 188–89, 193, 195, 204, 206–8, 272–75, 277
guilt, 32, 42, 48, 72, 94, 169, 176, 201–4, 206

Hades, 133, 135–36
haftarah, 90, 107
halakhic, 74, 85, 87
Hashivenu, 102, 106, 108–9
heavens, 18–19, 74, 80, 90, 93–94, 116–17, 133, 190, 193, 206, 249, 268
hermeneutics, 1–2, 14, 113–14, 117, 119, 121, 127, 162, 170–74, 177–78, 183, 195–96, 203
Hexapla, 114
historical-critical, 17, 27
historical-political, 38
history, 1–5, 8–11, 17–19, 22–30, 32, 39, 52–53, 62, 72–75, 81, 88, 94, 99, 106–8, 111, 113, 118–19, 121–23, 149, 152, 161–62, 165, 167, 168, 177, 180, 184, 192–93, 199
holiday, 88–91, 93, 97
Holocaust, 27, 50, 94–96, 101–2, 104–6
Holy Week, 1, 10, 12, 21, 58, 75, 83, 107, 133–46, 141, 200, 251, 270, 272
homily, 118, 123–24
hymn, 132–36

icon, 80, 133–34, 137
ideology, 36, 60, 62, 167–68, 201
idolatry, 79, 81
images, 1, 23, 29, 33, 48, 58, 60, 73, 92–93, 95, 97, 148, 167–69, 189, 204
imagery, 7, 43, 57, 58, 73, 95–96, 155, 171, 173
imagination, 17, 19, 22, 92, 167, 195
iniquity, 18, 48, 103, 118, 169
inner-biblical allusions, 55–56

intercession, 36, 46, 49, 67, 108, 189, 190–91, 193, 195
intertextual, 55, 62, 121, 159
Islam, 101

Jesus, 15–16, 18–19, 25, 34, 49–50, 86, 101–3, 105–8, 110, 113, 116–17, 121–22, 134, 136, 139, 155, 179, 183–88, 190, 194, 204, 206, 209, 278
Jewish tradition, 15, 108, 176–78
Judaism, 66, 68–69, 76, 83, 86–87, 92, 95–97, 101–2, 104, 108, 110, 179, 180, 186, 196
judgment, 15, 19, 20, 29–30, 40–42, 45, 47–48, 50, 67, 74, 89–91, 106, 122, 126, 187, 200–203, 270, 272
justification, 15, 49, 60, 89, 149, 162, 168–70, 176, 190

Kaige-Theodotion, 65–66
kingdom, 17–20, 24, 40, 116, 126, 133, 135, 157, 193, 196

Lady Jerusalem, 177, 186, 193
Lady Zion, 177, 186, 193
lament, 7, 15, 18, 20, 22–24, 26–27, 31–32, 36–37, 42–45, 47, 52, 55–57, 60–62, 66, 72, 85–86, 88–89, 91–92, 96–97, 109–10, 131–32, 135–38, 140, 154–57, 165, 168, 175–78, 182, 184, 188–94, 196, 197, 199, 203–5, 207–9, 264
lectionary, 71, 88, 90–91, 106–7, 123, 199
liberation, 167, 188–89
literary, 1, 5–7, 9, 14, 21, 26–27, 29, 32–33, 35, 37, 38, 42–43, 45, 55, 57–58, 62, 127–28, 148, 167, 169, 172, 174, 176, 200, 207
liturgy, 3,–5, 15–16, 20, 24, 27–28, 31, 43, 52, 56, 76, 88–91, 93, 95, 102, 106, 108, 119, 122–24, 131–33, 137, 139–41, 147, 151, 168, 175–78, 182–85, 190–93, 196, 199, 202, 205–6, 266
LXX Tradition, 65–66

Maundy Thursday, 123, 181, 184, 202
medieval interpretation, 113, 115, 120, 122
meditation, 103, 115, 118, 158–59, 202, 209
Megillot, 23, 76, 198, 228, 264
memory, 49, 58, 62, 76, 93–97, 128, 167, 174, 269, 277

293

*Index of Subjects*

mercy, 17–19, 46, 48–49, 51, 71, 74, 79–81, 89, 106, 126, 131, 136, 200–201, 205, 252, 260, 267, 276, 278
Messiah, 9, 75, 95, 99, 101–8, 110, 117, 123, 141, 179, 180, 182–88, 196
metaphor, 5, 8, 23, 36, 39, 68, 73, 149, 154, 167, 169, 172, 177, 200, 268, 271–74
metapsychology, 23, 165
midrash, 57, 74, 76–77, 84–87, 101–3, 178, 248, 264, 266
Mishnah, 70–72, 74–76, 83–84, 86, 88, 255–66
mission, 103, 195,199
modernist, 12, 94
Mosaic, 39
Moses, 42, 47, 49, 80, 81, 84, 117, 157
mourn, 43, 46, 48, 74–75, 78–80, 88, 94, 96, 106–7, 117, 118, 132, 134, 137, 141, 158, 161–63, 165, 176–77, 184–85, 189, 200, 257, 268
music, 8, 139, 147, 148–53, 181–82, 185, 190–91, 195
myth, 59, 62, 88

Narrative, 2, 5, 7, 19, 22–23, 46, 60, 66, 84–85, 107, 139–40, 177, 183, 185, 190–91, 194, 196
Nazis, 104, 106, 149

oppression, 2, 8–9, 12–13, 80, 122, 148, 166, 167–70, 172, 179, 186, 189, 195, 271
orthodoxy, 75, 93, 95, 131–38, 199, 209

parables, 49–50, 251, 263
parallelism, 5
pastoral, 72, 74, 118, 125, 128, 133, 161, 191, 197–201, 203, 205–7, 209
Patristics, 4, 113–15, 117, 135, 181, 200
Paul, 3, 8, 11, 18, 23–24, 26, 52, 76, 102, 104, 110, 138, 153, 159, 161, 165, 177–79, 188, 189, 196, 200, 276
Pentateuch, 79, 83–84
personification, 5, 8, 23, 45, 58–60, 62, 67, 73, 133, 136, 158, 162, 168–69, 171, 186
pesher exegesis, 68
piety, 97, 118, 137, 199–200, 203–4
poem, 6–7, 10, 19, 29, 31–33, 42–44, 64–66, 32, 41–43, 45, 47, 64, 88–89, 94–95, 107, 115–16, 127, 170, 175–77, 207, 266

poetics, 5, 43, 92, 97, 135, 176, 181, 194, 196
poetry, 3, 5, 7, 10, 15, 22, 43, 96–97, 128, 158–59, 162–63, 168–71, 175, 186, 193, 205
political, 1, 2, 38, 39, 45, 166, 167–68, 171, 194
pornoprophetics, 168, 174
Post-Holocaust, 8, 15, 22, 94–95, 97
Postmodern, 8–9, 12, 22, 24, 92, 127, 174, 199
prayer, 14–16, 18–20, 24, 31, 34–35, 40–41, 44–47, 49–52, 75, 89, 108, 126, 127–29, 132–33, 135, 139, 141, 158–59, 163, 165, 171, 183, 186, 189–90, 193–94, 196, 201, 204–6, 208–9, 250, 253–54, 265, 267, 270–71, 275, 276–78
preaching, 102, 116, 119, 125, 199, 209
prophecy, 78–80, 84, 90, 116–17, 121, 126
psychoanalysis, 23, 162, 164–65
psychological, 61, 159, 161–65, 198, 200, 209
psychology, 8, 161–65, 198, 200, 209

Qumran, 3, 106

rabbinic, 65, 70, 72–77, 84–86, 88, 228
reconciliation, 28, 43, 61, 81, 90–91, 93, 178
redaction criticism, 4, 59, 200
redemption, 31, 78–81, 90, 103, 108, 122, 182–83, 185, 256, 262
repentance, 40, 44, 50, 67, 72, 74, 80, 88, 93–95, 102, 104, 106, 117, 126, 127, 131, 173, 179, 184, 187, 195, 199, 200–201, 204–5, 267, 269
restoration, 19, 46, 48, 59–60, 96, 104, 107–8, 163, 253
Resurrection, 17–19, 23–24, 106–7, 123, 132, 135–37, 140–41, 183, 185–86, 188, 190, 192
retribution, 42–43, 57
revelation,
    Scripture as, 9–10, 14–15, 20, 24, 103–4, 122, 200–202
ritual, 89, 136–38, 190
Rosh Hashana, 83, 90–91, 107, 178
Rule of Faith, 118, 185

Sabbath, 81, 90, 107, 178, 254, 256–57, 260
sacrifice, 50, 105–6, 108
salvation, 19, 58, 74, 79, 122, 127, 183–85, 187, 189, 271, 276

sanctuary, 29, 67, 114, 133–34, 170
sin, 4, 8, 15–16, 18–20, 28, 40, 42, 45–49, 58, 61, 73, 78, 79–80, 89, 97, 102–3, 105–6, 108, 117–18, 121–22, 137, 169, 172, 178, 189, 191, 195, 198, 199, 200–204, 209, 275
Spirit, 14–15, 17, 80, 102–3, 141, 185, 187–90, 196, 271, 277
suffer, 30, 34, 37–39, 42, 44, 46–47, 50–51, 78, 80, 118, 184, 186, 188, 263, 271
suffering, 15–19, 27–31, 34–35, 37, 38, 40–41, 43, 45–46, 50–51, 58–59, 61, 74, 80–81, 89–90, 93–95, 103–7, 116–17, 121, 125, 140–41, 148, 150, 158, 162, 165, 171, 173, 176, 178–80, 183–86, 188–89, 193–94, 198–99, 201, 203–7, 250
Suffering Servant, 58, 62–63, 140, 141
synagogue, 12, 70, 75, 83, 88–90, 175, 177, 254, 257, 262

Tabernacle, 81, 157, 262
Talmud, 83–85, 87, 102
Targum, 3, 68, 70, 71, 72–76, 89, 115, 117, 119, 154, 178, 228
Targum Lamentations, 72–75, 228
temple, 29–30, 45, 64, 66, 67–69, 72, 74, 78–79, 81, 84–85, 88, 94–96, 102, 106–7, 127, 129, 141, 155, 157–58, 171, 175, 178, 186, 189, 201, 254, 259, 264, 274

theodicy, 4, 9, 16, 27–32, 34–35, 38, 42, 61, 51, 93–94, 168–70, 203, 251
Tisha b'Av, 72, 74–75, 88–90, 94–96, 106–8, 168, 178
Torah, 70–72, 74–75, 78–80, 84, 88, 90, 103, 108, 110, 154–55, 158–59, 250–51, 262–63
tragedy, 5, 7, 16, 71, 74–75, 84, 88, 106–8, 141, 205–6

violence, 1, 12–13, 15, 33–37, 89, 95, 162–63, 168–69, 172, 179–80, 194, 206
Vulgate, 85, 114–15, 117, 127

wisdom, 23–24, 47, 49, 50, 103, 115, 165, 193
worldview, 13, 89, 169, 196
worship, 8, 14, 16, 31, 44–45, 67, 72, 74–75, 84, 89–91, 107–8, 129, 131, 136–37, 139, 175–77, 179, 180–82, 184–85, 190, 191, 192–96, 199–202, 206

YHWH, 7, 18, 26–51, 89–90, 169, 175–76, 179–80, 183, 186–87, 203, 205

Zion, 3, 8, 13, 15, 18, 23–24, 29–30, 33–36, 40, 43, 47, 52, 57–62, 67, 68, 71, 73, 89–90, 92–93, 105, 107, 109, 154, 158–59, 162, 169–77, 183–84, 186, 193, 195–96, 203, 205, 249
Zionism, 93–94